DIGITAL NOMADS

Thriving in the AI Age

Geoffrey Zachary

CONTENTS

Infrastructure

DIGITAL NOMADS: THRIVING IN THE AI AGE

PART 1: INTRODUCTION TO THE DIGITAL NOMAD LIFESTYLE

CHAPTER 1 : THE RISE OF DIGITAL NOMADS

As the plane touched down in Bali, Sarah felt a mix of excitement and freedom. She had left behind the constraints of a 9-to-5 office job and embraced the life of a digital nomad. Armed with her laptop and AI-powered tools, Sarah was able to run her graphic design business from anywhere in the world, whether it was a beachside café in Thailand or a coworking space in Lisbon. This was the new reality for millions of professionals—an era where technology had untethered them from traditional workspaces and allowed them to build a career on their terms.

The Evolution of Remote Work into a Global Phenomenon

Remote work is not a new concept. For years, people have worked from home, telecommuting when needed. However, the digital nomad movement is a more recent phenomenon, driven by advances in technology, including the rapid development of artificial intelligence (AI). The concept of being location-independent, where workers can travel the world while earning an income, has only become viable in the past decade.

The COVID-19 pandemic further accelerated this shift. Companies across the globe were forced to adapt to remote work, discovering that many jobs could be done just as efficiently—if not more so—outside of a traditional office setting. But while the pandemic may have sparked the mass adoption of remote work, AI is the engine driving the digital nomad lifestyle to new heights.

AI as the Game-Changer

AI has become the secret weapon in the digital nomad's toolkit. Take Sarah's story: before discovering AI-powered design tools, her work was painstakingly manual. Each project took hours of her time, from brainstorming creative ideas to executing complex design tasks. But once she integrated AI into her workflow, 70% of her tasks were automated. Tools like Canva, which uses AI to generate design templates, and Jasper AI for content creation, helped her focus on the more creative aspects of her work. The mundane tasks were now handled by AI.

This combination of AI and digital nomadism opens up limitless possibilities. Freelancers, entrepreneurs, and remote workers can now scale their businesses, deliver faster results to clients, and create more time for travel and leisure. It's no longer just about working remotely; it's about working smarter with the help of AI.

Practical AI Applications for Digital Nomads

So, how can you apply AI to your career as a digital nomad? Whether you're a content creator, consultant, developer, or marketer, here are some AI-powered tools and strategies to integrate into your workflow:

1. Content Creation: Platforms like Jasper AI and Writesonic can help generate blog ideas, social media posts, and even long-form articles in a matter of minutes. Instead of spending hours brainstorming and drafting content, these tools can give you a head start by automating much of the writing process.

2. Editing and Proofreading: Tools like Grammarly or ProWritingAid use AI to enhance your writing, suggesting grammatical improvements, stylistic changes, and better clarity in real-time. This ensures your work is polished and professional, even when you're racing to meet deadlines.

3. Data Analysis and Research: Whether you're a digital marketing strategist or a financial consultant, AI-powered platforms like Tableau or Google Analytics use machine learning to help you analyse data and generate insights faster than ever before. This means less time crunching numbers and more time delivering actionable insights to your clients.

4. Customer Service Automation: If you're running an online business, chatbots like Intercom or Zendesk can handle customer inquiries while you sleep, providing 24/7 support without needing to be glued to your device.

By incorporating these AI tools into your workflow, you not only save time but also position yourself as a more competitive digital nomad in the global market.

Challenges and Opportunities

Of course, with every technological advancement, there are challenges to consider. For many digital nomads, the question looms: will AI eventually replace jobs? The reality is that AI will continue to automate repetitive tasks, which means some roles will be displaced. However, the good news is that AI also creates new opportunities. As some jobs fade, others emerge—such as AI consultants, automation specialists, or content optimization experts. The key is to remain adaptable and invest in continuous learning.

To thrive as a digital nomad in the AI age, it's essential to stay ahead of the curve by learning how to work alongside AI rather than fearing it. By acquiring new skills, such as prompt engineering or AI project management, you can future-proof your career and ensure that you remain relevant in a rapidly changing world.

A Vision for the Future

Now, let's look beyond the immediate applications of AI and digital nomadism and into the future. Imagine a world where AI assists with every mundane task in your business. You wake up in a new city, your AI assistant has already compiled your to-do list, responded to client emails, and drafted proposals. Your time is no longer spent managing the day-to-day operations; instead, you focus on the creative, strategic, and meaningful aspects of your work.

In this vision of the future, the digital nomad lifestyle becomes even more fluid. AI could one day predict the best locations for you to work based on your productivity patterns, weather preferences, and cost of living. It might even suggest networking events or local meetups that align with your industry and interests.

A Global and Cultural Impact

As AI continues to reshape the digital nomad landscape, its influence is being felt globally. In India, for example, small businesses are using AI to scale their operations and reach international clients. Meanwhile, in countries like Estonia, where e-residency programs cater to digital nomads, AI is integrated into government services, making it easier for nomads to work and pay taxes seamlessly, regardless of their physical location.

The digital nomad movement is no longer just a Western trend; it's becoming a global phenomenon, with AI enabling people from all walks of life to pursue careers that transcend borders and cultures.

Conclusion: AI and Purpose-Driven Nomadism

AI is not just a tool to make work easier; it's a way to reclaim time, pursue personal passions, and lead a more purpose-driven life. Digital nomads like Sarah aren't just chasing financial freedom—they're seeking fulfilment, adventure, and the ability to contribute to causes they care about. By leveraging AI, they can achieve these goals more efficiently, freeing up time to explore new cultures, build relationships, or focus on personal growth.

As you navigate the ever-evolving landscape of remote work and AI, remember: the future is full of possibilities. Embrace AI not just as a tool for productivity, but as a partner in building the life you truly want.

CHAPTER 2: THE AI REVOLUTION: A NEW FRONTIER

As Oliver sat in a café overlooking the Atlantic in Lisbon, he marvelled at how much his life had changed over the last few years. Once confined to a cubicle in San Francisco, he now worked as a digital marketing strategist, using AI to automate most of his workflow. With just a few clicks, AI tools would analyse data, predict customer behaviours, and craft personalized marketing strategies. What used to take a team of people, hours of meetings, and manual analysis now took him minutes. For Oliver, AI was more than just a tool— it was a gateway to freedom.

Understanding AI: The Technologies Powering the Revolution

Artificial Intelligence (AI) is not a monolithic concept. It's a collection of various technologies that have the power to mimic human intelligence. The AI that digital nomads like Oliver use is made possible by a range of interconnected technologies that work together to reshape the workplace. These technologies are transforming how digital nomads approach their careers, businesses, and lifestyles.

Here's a breakdown of the core technologies behind AI that are reshaping the work landscape:

1. Machine Learning (ML):

- At the heart of AI is machine learning, which allows systems to learn from data and improve their performance over time without being explicitly programmed. For digital nomads, this means that tools can analyse their past work, anticipate needs, and offer solutions tailored to their preferences.

- Example: A freelance photographer could use AI-powered image editing software that learns their editing style over time. With each project, the software gets better at automating repetitive tasks, allowing them to focus on creativity.

2. Natural Language Processing (NLP):

- NLP enables computers to understand, interpret, and respond to human language. It's the reason why tools like Jasper AI can generate blog content and why voice assistants like Siri or Alexa can have conversations with us.

- Example: A content writer on the go might use Grammarly, which uses NLP to suggest better ways to phrase sentences, making writing smoother and faster. The AI understands context, tone, and grammar, allowing for seamless editing.

3. Robotic Process Automation (RPA):

- RPA refers to software that can automate routine tasks typically performed by humans. For digital nomads, this means fewer hours spent on repetitive tasks, such as scheduling meetings or data entry.

- Example: A virtual assistant running an online business could use RPA to automatically generate invoices, update spreadsheets, and even manage email campaigns, freeing them up to focus on strategy.

4. Computer Vision:

- This branch of AI enables computers to interpret and

make decisions based on visual data. It's the technology behind image recognition in apps like Google Photos or autonomous driving in Tesla vehicles.

- Example: A digital nomad photographer could rely on AI-powered tools that categorize their photos based on content—whether it's nature, urban, or portrait shots—without manual tagging, allowing them to quickly organize and share their portfolio.

5. Predictive Analytics:

- By using algorithms to analyse large amounts of data, AI can predict trends, behaviours, and outcomes. For digital nomads, predictive analytics offers powerful insights into client needs, market shifts, and industry trends.

- Example: A freelance marketer could use AI-driven analytics tools to predict consumer behaviour, helping clients target the right audience and optimize marketing campaigns, all while sipping coffee in a Tokyo café.

Practical Applications of AI in the Workplace

For digital nomads, AI isn't just a distant technological concept; it's a set of practical tools that are making their day-to-day work easier and more efficient. Here are some actionable ways AI is transforming the nomadic lifestyle:

1. Streamlining Workflow:

- Whether you're a content creator or a developer, tools like Zapier automate workflows by connecting various apps and services. For example, you can set it up to automatically upload your finished designs from Canva to Dropbox and notify your clients via Slack—all without lifting a finger.

2. Enhancing Creativity:

- AI-powered platforms like Adobe Sensei are transforming creative industries. Designers, video editors, and content creators can use these tools to automate mundane tasks like photo retouching or video clipping, giving them more time to focus on innovation and creativity.

- Pro Tip: Use Lumen5 to convert your blog posts into engaging video content, leveraging AI to craft high-quality videos in minutes.

3. Customer Engagement:

- Digital nomads running online businesses or managing client services can use AI-driven chatbots like Intercom or Drift to provide customer support, answer inquiries, and manage interactions even when they're off exploring the streets of Barcelona.

- Pro Tip: Automate FAQs and basic customer support with AI, freeing up time for more complex client requests.

Visionary Perspectives: The Future of Work in an AI-Powered World

The possibilities AI opens up for digital nomads are exciting, but what does the future look like? As AI continues to evolve, the line between human and machine tasks will blur, allowing digital nomads to achieve a level of productivity and creativity previously unimaginable. Imagine:

- AI-Assisted Creativity: You might be working on a design project, and your AI assistant suggests innovative layout ideas based on the latest design trends—ideas you hadn't even thought of.
- Predictive Client Outreach: AI tools could analyse global trends and suggest the best regions or industries to target for freelance gigs, ensuring you stay ahead of the competition.
- Smart Contracts and Blockchain Integration: AI and blockchain technology could merge, enabling digital nomads to work seamlessly with clients worldwide. Smart contracts could automate payment processes and legal agreements, eliminating the need for lengthy negotiations or third-party intervention.

This future isn't as far off as it might seem. By continuously integrating AI into your work, you'll be able to adapt to whatever the future holds, allowing for even more freedom and flexibility in your nomadic journey.

Balancing Opportunity with Caution

While AI offers tremendous potential, it also comes with challenges. The rise of automation raises concerns about job displacement, privacy, and data security. As digital nomads, it's crucial to stay informed about how AI impacts not only your industry but also your personal privacy and data rights.

One way to ensure you're staying ahead is to acquire new skills regularly. AI will continue to evolve, and those who embrace learning will thrive in this new landscape. Consider enrolling in online courses to deepen your understanding of AI's role in your field, from machine learning basics to advanced AI applications.

A Global Perspective: AI's Impact Across Borders

AI is reshaping work around the world, but the impact varies by region. In the United States, companies are rapidly adopting AI to enhance productivity. In Southeast Asia, digital nomads are using AI to scale small businesses and reach global markets. Meanwhile, in Estonia, the government's embrace of digital transformation has made it a top destination for digital nomads, offering services like e-residency to enable entrepreneurs to manage businesses remotely with ease.

This global shift means that digital nomads can now leverage AI to build businesses that transcend borders. By embracing AI, you open doors to markets, clients, and opportunities that were previously out of reach.

Conclusion: Embracing AI for Purpose and Fulfilment

The AI revolution is about more than just technology; it's

about creating a lifestyle that aligns with your values, passions, and dreams. Digital nomads like Oliver aren't just using AI to work more efficiently—they're using it to unlock time, freedom, and purpose. Whether it's exploring new cultures, pursuing creative passions, or contributing to causes that matter, AI is a tool that enables you to live a more meaningful, purpose-driven life.

As you continue your journey, remember: AI is not the future —it's the present. Embrace it, and you'll find new ways to thrive in the AI-powered digital nomad age.

CHAPTER 3: WHO ARE DIGITAL NOMADS?

Samantha leaned back in her chair, the sound of waves crashing against the shore just beyond the café window in Bali. Her laptop screen displayed her latest client project, an AI-driven marketing campaign she had crafted while traveling across Southeast Asia. It wasn't long ago that she had been working in a traditional office environment, glued to a desk and dreaming of a life with more freedom. Today, she's part of a growing global community of digital nomads —individuals who've embraced technology, particularly AI, to live and work from anywhere in the world.

What Defines a Digital Nomad?

At its core, a digital nomad is someone who leverages technology to work remotely, untethered by a fixed location. For many, it's not just about having the freedom to travel but also about creating a lifestyle that blends work with adventure, personal growth, and, often, a deeper sense of purpose. Unlike remote workers who might still be tied to one location or time zone, digital nomads live a fully mobile lifestyle, constantly on the move—whether from country to country or even within their own region.

The term "digital nomad" first came into prominence around the early 2000s, but the movement has significantly evolved since then. Early nomads were typically freelancers, entrepreneurs, or tech workers who realized that their work was not location-bound. With the advent of faster internet, collaboration tools, and AI-powered technologies, the movement has gained traction, and the profile of a digital nomad has diversified.

The Evolution of Digital Nomads in Recent Years

Samantha's journey from corporate life to digital nomadism highlights how accessible this lifestyle has become in recent years, thanks to AI and remote work advancements. Several key factors have contributed to this shift:

1. AI and Automation: In the early days, digital nomads often worked in fields like writing, web development, and design—jobs that required creativity but also a heavy time commitment. Now, AI tools such as Jasper AI, Canva, and Grammarly have automated much of the routine work, allowing nomads to do more in less time. These tools can generate content, design graphics, analyse data, and even write code, freeing up time for nomads to focus on their passions or simply enjoy their surroundings.

Case in Point: Samantha, who runs an AI consulting business, manages multiple clients with ease. She uses Jasper AI to draft initial marketing content, and AI-powered analytics tools help her generate data-driven insights for her clients. What used to take her days, now takes mere hours, giving her more time to surf the waves in Bali or explore local markets.

2. Globalization and Accessibility: Another significant change is the widespread availability of high-speed internet and coworking spaces in even the most remote parts of the world. Countries like Thailand, Estonia, and Mexico have embraced digital nomads by offering affordable e-visas and setting up infrastructure that caters to this growing

demographic. Estonia's e-residency program, for example, allows digital nomads to set up and manage businesses remotely, creating a seamless global work environment.

3. Post-Pandemic Shift: The COVID-19 pandemic was a catalyst for remote work, demonstrating to companies worldwide that many jobs could be done from anywhere. As traditional companies adapted to a more remote-friendly mindset, more employees gained the freedom to explore the nomadic lifestyle. Many traditional workers, once bound to office life, have now joined the ranks of digital nomads, embracing a life that's less about "work-life balance" and more about "work-life integration."

Practical Applications: Becoming a Digital Nomad in the AI Age

For aspiring digital nomads, the AI revolution provides a golden opportunity to transition into a more mobile lifestyle. Here are some practical tips for leveraging AI to ease the transition:

1. Build a Portfolio of AI-Enhanced Skills: Whether you're a writer, designer, marketer, or developer, it's crucial to learn how to use AI tools in your industry. Tools like ChatGPT for customer support, Grammarly for editing, or Lumen5 for video creation can help you streamline your workflow and demonstrate your efficiency to clients. Consider taking online courses to deepen your AI knowledge, such as those on Coursera or Udemy.

2. Streamline Client Communication: AI tools can make client management a breeze, especially when you're working across different time zones. Slack integrated with AI chatbots can handle client queries, while Calendly can automate scheduling. Trello or Asana, enhanced with AI-driven task management, can help you stay on top of projects, no matter where you are.

3. AI-Assisted Marketing and Networking: Use AI to grow your digital nomad business. HubSpot's AI-powered CRM systems can help you manage leads and clients. For networking, platforms like LinkedIn have AI-driven tools that suggest connections based on your field of work, helping you stay engaged with potential clients and collaborators across the globe.

Inspiring Perspectives: The Future of Digital Nomads

What does the future hold for digital nomads as AI continues to advance? It's exciting to imagine a future where AI does much more than streamline tasks—it could enhance every aspect of the digital nomad experience. Picture this: your AI assistant not only automates your work but also provides real-time travel recommendations based on your preferences, books flights and accommodations, and even analyses your productivity trends to suggest optimal working hours.

In the future, AI may transform cities into "nomad hubs" where digital nomads from across the world gather, network, and collaborate in AI-powered coworking spaces that adapt to your needs. These spaces might have intelligent lighting systems, mood-adjusting AI algorithms, and virtual work assistants, creating environments where work and creativity seamlessly blend.

Balancing Opportunities and Challenges

While the digital nomad lifestyle offers unparalleled freedom, it's not without challenges. As AI automates more jobs, some digital nomads fear that the competition will increase, particularly in fields where creativity or human intuition has traditionally been a significant differentiator. However, by embracing AI as a partner rather than a competitor, nomads can maintain their edge. Developing complementary skills, like learning AI-enhanced project management or staying updated on the latest tech trends, is key to staying relevant in this fast-evolving landscape.

Moreover, nomads must be mindful of maintaining work-life balance. With AI making it easier to work from anywhere, it's essential to set boundaries and ensure that the "always-on" nature of remote work doesn't lead to burnout.

A Global Perspective: The Rise of the Global Nomad

In regions like Southeast Asia and Eastern Europe, the rise of digital nomads has led to a cultural shift, with cities like Chiang Mai and Tallinn becoming nomad-friendly hotspots. Meanwhile, developing countries are leveraging AI to offer new opportunities for freelancers, allowing them to compete in the global market.

In India, for instance, AI is transforming small businesses by allowing them to reach international clients. As AI continues to reshape industries, the digital nomad lifestyle becomes increasingly viable for individuals across different socioeconomic backgrounds, creating a more inclusive global workforce.

Conclusion: Purpose-Driven Nomadism in the AI Age

Ultimately, digital nomads are not just looking for freedom from a desk—they're searching for a purpose-driven life. By integrating AI into their work, nomads like Samantha are finding more time for exploration, personal growth, and meaningful contributions to the world around them. AI is not just a tool for efficiency; it's an enabler for a richer, more fulfilling lifestyle.

As the digital nomad movement grows, so too will the possibilities. Whether you're an aspiring nomad or already on your journey, remember that AI is your ally in crafting the life of your dreams. Embrace the technology, adapt, and thrive—because the future belongs to those who see the opportunities that AI brings.

CHAPTER 4: NOMADIC LIFE: BENEFITS AND CHALLENGES

Carlos had been living the digital nomad dream for the past three years. From the snowy streets of Prague to the sun-kissed beaches of Bali, he had worked on AI-powered marketing campaigns for clients all over the world, all while living a life of adventure. For him, the biggest advantage of being a digital nomad was the freedom to work wherever he wanted. But as exhilarating as it was, there were challenges—constant movement meant adjusting to different time zones, navigating visa restrictions, and dealing with spotty Wi-Fi in remote locations. Carlos's journey captures the reality of digital nomadism: full of rewards but not without its hurdles.

The Benefits of the Digital Nomad Lifestyle

1. Geographic Freedom:
   - The hallmark of the digital nomad lifestyle is the ability to work from virtually anywhere. Whether it's the vibrant streets of Tokyo, a serene café in Lisbon, or a coworking space in Medellín, digital nomads aren't tied to one location. This mobility allows individuals to explore the world while still pursuing meaningful work.

- Case Study: Carlos, as a freelance marketer, utilized AI-driven tools like HubSpot and Hootsuite to manage global marketing campaigns. By automating parts of his work, he was able to handle his clients' needs from wherever he travelled, whether it was Mexico City or Croatia.

2. Work-Life Integration:

- Unlike the traditional work-life balance, where people separate their jobs from their personal lives, digital nomads experience a more integrated approach. Work and life blend together, allowing for flexibility. Want to take a break and hike a mountain trail in the afternoon? No problem. Work can resume once you return, with AI tools optimizing efficiency so you never miss a deadline.

- Practical Tip: Tools like Trello and Asana make managing tasks across different time zones easier, allowing you to set priorities and collaborate with clients or teams, no matter where you are.

3. Increased Productivity Through AI:

- AI-powered tools have become a game-changer for digital nomads, enabling them to work smarter, not harder. From automating repetitive tasks to providing insights into customer behaviour, AI has allowed nomads to maximize productivity while enjoying the freedom of travel.

- Example: Carlos often used Jasper AI for generating copy and Grammarly to refine his writing, reducing the time spent on content creation by over 50%. The time saved allowed him to pursue other passions, like learning local languages or attending cultural events.

4. Financial Independence and Diversified Income Streams:

- Many digital nomads find financial freedom by diversifying their income streams. With AI helping automate and scale businesses, nomads can run online shops, offer consultancy services, or create digital products while maintaining multiple revenue sources.

- Pro Tip: Explore passive income opportunities through online platforms. AI tools can help automate e-commerce, run ads, or even handle customer support via chatbots, allowing you to focus on growing your brand.

The Challenges of the Digital Nomad Lifestyle

1. Loneliness and Isolation:
- While the idea of traveling the world may sound glamorous, many digital nomads face loneliness. Constant movement can make it difficult to form deep connections, especially when working in isolation. The nature of the lifestyle means constantly leaving behind new friends and communities.
- Solution: Many digital nomads combat isolation by joining coworking spaces or nomad communities, such as Remote Year or Outsite, where they can work alongside like-minded individuals and foster a sense of belonging.

2. Unpredictable Internet and Workspaces:
- Not every destination is ideal for remote work. Poor internet connections or unreliable infrastructure can hinder productivity. Imagine working on a critical client project only to lose internet access in the middle of a remote island or bustling café.
- Solution: To mitigate this, Carlos always made sure to research coworking spaces ahead of time or invested in portable Wi-Fi solutions. Platforms like NomadList offer insights into the best places for digital nomads based on factors like internet speed, cost of living, and overall quality of life.

3. Time Zone Juggling and Client Expectations:
- Navigating multiple time zones can be one of the most challenging aspects of nomadic life. While you may enjoy breakfast in Bangkok, your client in New York might be waiting for an urgent response.

- Practical Tip: AI scheduling tools like Calendly can help automate meeting setups, taking the hassle out of coordinating across different time zones. Additionally, setting clear boundaries and expectations with clients regarding response times can prevent burnout and ensure smooth communication.

4. Visa and Legal Issues:

- Visa regulations can be another significant challenge. Some countries only allow digital nomads to stay for a few months, while others require specific permits. Navigating these legal complexities can be time-consuming and expensive.

- Solution: Many countries, like Estonia and Barbados, now offer special digital nomad visas that allow remote workers to stay for extended periods. Keeping up-to-date with visa options and tax regulations is crucial to avoiding legal headaches.

Visionary Perspectives: AI and the Future of Digital Nomadism

Looking ahead, the digital nomad lifestyle will continue to evolve, particularly as AI technology advances. Imagine a future where your AI assistant not only helps automate your work but also manages your travel logistics. AI could book flights based on your productivity patterns, recommend coworking spaces that match your preferences, and even help you navigate visa requirements through automated legal assistance.

Moreover, as AI tools become more sophisticated, they will open up new opportunities for digital nomads to create hyper-efficient businesses with minimal human input. Entire businesses could run on AI, allowing nomads to focus solely on creative or strategic tasks while their AI systems manage the day-to-day operations.

Balancing Inspiration with Reality

While the digital nomad lifestyle offers unparalleled freedom, it's essential to strike a balance between inspiration and caution. AI might take care of many tasks, but human adaptability, creativity, and emotional intelligence remain irreplaceable. To thrive, digital nomads must stay adaptable and continue developing new skills, particularly those related to AI and automation.

It's also important to recognize that while AI can enhance productivity, it's crucial to avoid burnout. Without proper boundaries, work can spill into every part of life. Embrace tools that help manage your workload and invest time in activities that nourish your mental and physical well-being.

Global Impact: The Digital Nomad Movement Around the World

As the digital nomad movement continues to expand, it's having a significant cultural and economic impact on countries across the globe. In Thailand, Bali, and Portugal, digital nomad communities are helping boost local economies, driving innovation, and creating a melting pot of ideas and cultures.

Countries like Estonia have paved the way for nomads by offering digital-first policies and e-residency programs, while in countries like Brazil, the influx of nomads is sparking conversations about flexible work policies and the future of work. This global shift indicates that the nomadic lifestyle is not a passing trend, but a long-term shift in how work is approached across borders.

Conclusion: The Nomad Mindset

The digital nomad lifestyle is about more than just traveling the world. It's about freedom, flexibility, and using AI to maximize both personal fulfilment and professional growth. But it also comes with its challenges—unpredictability, loneliness, and legal hurdles. With the right tools, mindset, and strategies, however, the benefits far outweigh the challenges.

As you embark on or continue your nomadic journey, remember that AI isn't just a tool to help you work faster. It's a partner that enables you to design the life you want, one filled with adventure, purpose, and fulfilment. So, whether you're working from a mountain retreat in Patagonia or a coworking space in Tokyo, embrace the possibilities, adapt to the challenges, and keep moving forward—because the world is truly your office.

CHAPTER 5: THE INTERSECTION OF AI AND REMOTE WORK

As Lena sipped her coffee in a bustling café in Medellín, Colombia, she marvelled at how technology had transformed her career. Once confined to a corporate office in Berlin, she now managed her growing consulting business from anywhere in the world, thanks to AI. Lena had always dreamed of traveling, but the constraints of her previous job made that difficult. Everything changed when she discovered the power of AI. From automating administrative tasks to generating personalized marketing strategies for her clients, AI allowed her to scale her business while embracing the freedom of the digital nomad lifestyle. Lena's story is just one example of how AI and remote work are colliding in powerful ways to reshape careers.

How AI Is Influencing Digital Nomads' Work

1. Automation of Repetitive Tasks:
   - AI's ability to automate routine tasks is perhaps the most transformative aspect of its influence on remote work. Digital nomads, often juggling multiple clients and projects, use AI to offload administrative burdens, streamline workflows, and save time.
   - Case Study: Lena used AI-powered platforms like Zapier to connect her various apps and automate routine tasks such

as invoicing, email follow-ups, and report generation. By integrating AI into her operations, Lena cut down the time spent on repetitive administrative work by 60%. This meant more time to focus on client relationships and exploring new cities.

2. Enhanced Collaboration Tools:
 - AI is reshaping collaboration, particularly for remote teams spread across different time zones. Tools powered by machine learning help predict workflow bottlenecks, automate communication, and ensure that team members stay aligned, regardless of their location.
 - Practical Application: Tools like Slack now integrate AI to streamline team communication. Lena and her globally dispersed team use it to ensure seamless communication by summarizing key discussions, automating task reminders, and predicting who might be needed for specific tasks. AI tools like Zoom's transcription service also make it easy to catch up on meetings, even when working asynchronously.

3. AI-Powered Creativity:
 - For many digital nomads, creativity is the core of their work—whether they are content creators, designers, or marketers. AI tools are providing a new layer of creative assistance, allowing nomads to generate ideas, design visuals, and develop content with greater speed and precision.
 - Example: Lena, who specializes in marketing strategy, often leverages Canva's AI-powered design features to quickly create customized visuals for her clients' campaigns. AI-driven tools like Jasper AI also help her generate personalized content ideas, allowing her to craft targeted strategies more effectively.

4. Predictive Analytics for Better Decision-Making:
 - Digital nomads can now use AI-driven predictive analytics to make smarter, data-driven decisions. From

forecasting trends to optimizing marketing strategies, AI can analyse data at a speed and depth that's impossible for humans to replicate.

- Example: Lena uses HubSpot's AI-driven marketing tools to predict customer behaviour and optimize her clients' digital marketing strategies. These insights help her craft more effective campaigns, leading to higher client satisfaction and repeat business. The AI models analyse thousands of data points from customer interactions, allowing her to stay ahead of market trends and anticipate client needs.

Emerging AI Trends Shaping the Digital Nomad Landscape

1. AI-Assisted Freelance Platforms:
   - Freelance platforms like Upwork and Fiverr are increasingly leveraging AI to match freelancers with clients. By analysing skills, work history, and client reviews, AI can suggest the best job opportunities for freelancers, helping digital nomads land higher-quality gigs faster.
   - Practical Tip: If you're a digital nomad seeking freelance work, make sure your profile on these platforms is optimized with relevant keywords. AI-driven algorithms will boost your visibility based on how well your profile aligns with client needs.

2. AI-Enhanced E-Learning for Continuous Development:
   - The rapidly changing work landscape means that continuous learning is more important than ever. AI is enhancing e-learning platforms like Coursera and LinkedIn Learning, offering personalized learning paths and recommending courses based on your career goals and interests.
   - Pro Tip: As a digital nomad, staying competitive in your field requires ongoing skill development. AI-powered e-learning platforms can help you stay ahead by recommending the most relevant courses, whether you're

learning new coding skills, digital marketing tactics, or project management strategies.

3. AI for Remote Client Management:

- Managing client relationships remotely can be challenging, especially when time zones and cultural differences come into play. AI-driven CRM systems like Salesforce and Zoho are helping digital nomads keep track of client communications, predict client needs, and even automate follow-ups.

- Practical Application: Lena uses Zoho CRM to manage her client database. AI-driven insights remind her when clients might be ready for a service renewal or when a special follow-up is needed, making her client interactions feel seamless and personalized.

Visionary Perspectives: The Future of AI in Remote Work

Imagine a world where digital nomads can rely on AI to handle every mundane task. From managing client communications to automating content creation, AI will likely play an even greater role in the lives of digital nomads. Some futurists predict that AI could evolve to the point where it operates entire businesses autonomously, allowing nomads to focus solely on high-level creative or strategic work.

For instance, AI tools may soon develop the capability to fully automate client onboarding and service delivery. An AI-driven system could manage contracts, deliver personalized solutions to clients, and even handle disputes or customer service issues. Meanwhile, nomads would spend their time working on innovation, building relationships, or simply enjoying the freedom that AI provides.

AI may also play a pivotal role in shaping future nomadic hubs. Governments and cities might create AI-powered "smart cities" designed to cater to digital nomads, offering adaptive workspaces, AI-driven legal and tax services, and automated visa applications. This could transform the digital nomad movement from a niche lifestyle to a mainstream work model embraced by millions worldwide.

Balancing Inspiration with Caution

While AI is unlocking unprecedented opportunities for digital nomads, it's essential to be aware of the challenges that come with it. Job displacement due to AI automation is a growing concern, particularly in fields that rely heavily on repetitive tasks. For digital nomads, the key to thriving in an AI-dominated future is continuous learning. Acquiring new skills, particularly those focused on AI and automation, will help future-proof careers.

AI also raises privacy and ethical concerns. Digital nomads must be mindful of the data they're sharing, especially when using AI-driven platforms. Ensuring that the AI tools you use comply with privacy regulations, like GDPR, is essential for protecting both your own data and your clients' sensitive information.

Global and Cultural Dimensions of AI in Remote Work

AI's impact on remote work extends beyond individual digital nomads—it's reshaping industries and economies worldwide. In countries like India, AI is enabling small businesses to access global markets, while in Estonia, digital-first policies are attracting digital nomads with their seamless e-residency programs. These global developments highlight the power of AI to create more inclusive economic opportunities for digital nomads across different cultural contexts.

As AI continues to advance, its role in transforming global industries will only deepen, creating new opportunities for nomads to collaborate across borders and contribute to economic innovation.

Conclusion: Thriving at the Intersection of AI and Remote Work

The intersection of AI and remote work offers unparalleled possibilities for digital nomads. From automating mundane tasks to enhancing creativity and improving decision-making, AI is transforming how nomads live and work. While challenges like job displacement and privacy concerns must be addressed, the benefits far outweigh the risks —especially for those who continue to evolve with the technology.

As a digital nomad in the AI age, the key to success is embracing AI as a tool that empowers you to live a life of freedom, creativity, and purpose. By staying adaptable, continuously learning, and leveraging the full potential of AI, you can thrive in a rapidly changing world where the future is full of endless possibilities.

PART 2: CAREERS TRANSFORMED BY AI

CHAPTER 6: AUTOMATION AND AI: JOB DISRUPTION

Sitting in a sunlit coworking space in Lisbon, Andre reflected on his journey. A few years ago, he was a data entry specialist, diligently entering information into spreadsheets for a large corporation. But as AI automation became more prevalent, he started hearing whispers around the office—entire departments were being downsized, jobs were disappearing, and people were being replaced by algorithms. Faced with the possibility of redundancy, Andre took a proactive step: he reskilled, learning how to manage the very AI systems that were disrupting his career. Today, he thrives as a digital nomad, offering consulting services to businesses looking to integrate AI systems into their workflows. His adaptability and forward-thinking mindset allowed him to survive—and thrive—in the age of automation.

The Impact of AI on Jobs: Which Careers Are Most Affected?

AI is transforming industries at a rapid pace, automating tasks and altering the workforce landscape. Many professions that rely on repetitive, manual labour have seen the most significant disruption. But the impact isn't limited to blue-collar jobs—white-collar professions are also being reshaped by automation. Let's explore the areas where AI has had the most profound effects:

1. Administrative and Data-Entry Roles:

- As AI becomes more proficient at handling large volumes of data, routine administrative tasks like data entry, scheduling, and customer support are increasingly automated. AI-powered tools such as UiPath and Blue Prism can perform tasks once handled by entire departments.

- Example: Andre's initial career in data entry was one of the first casualties of AI automation. Repetitive tasks like inputting invoices, filing, and updating records were taken over by AI-powered software. But instead of letting automation push him out, Andre used the same technology to reinvent himself as a remote AI consultant, helping companies streamline their operations through automation.

2. Customer Service and Support:

- AI chatbots and virtual assistants like Intercom and Zendesk are replacing traditional customer service roles. These tools handle inquiries, provide technical support, and solve routine problems—often more efficiently than human agents.

- Pro Tip: If you're working in customer service and worried about automation, consider transitioning into AI support or chatbot development. AI systems still require human oversight for complex issues, and professionals who understand how to build and manage these systems are in high demand.

3. Accounting and Finance:

- AI's ability to analyse massive amounts of financial data in seconds has transformed accounting and finance. Tools like Xero and QuickBooks automate bookkeeping, while machine learning algorithms analyse financial trends and optimize investment strategies.

- Solution: Many digital nomads who previously worked in finance have adapted by offering consulting services around AI-driven financial analysis or learning how to use these tools to provide higher-level insights to clients, such as forensic accounting or financial strategy development.

4. Legal and Paralegal Work:
- Document review, contract analysis, and legal research—tasks once performed by paralegals and junior lawyers—are now being handled by AI tools like RAVN and Kira Systems. These tools can scan and process legal documents, flagging relevant information in a fraction of the time it would take a human.
- Pro Tip: Legal professionals can remain relevant by focusing on areas that require human judgment and expertise, such as client relationship management, litigation, or interpreting complex legal scenarios. Many are also transitioning into AI legal consulting, helping firms integrate AI systems effectively.

5. Marketing and Content Creation:
- While marketing once required significant human effort, AI is now capable of generating content, analysing customer behaviour, and optimizing marketing strategies. Tools like Jasper AI create written content, while HubSpot's AI optimizes campaigns and tracks performance metrics.
- Case Study: Sarah, a freelance content marketer, noticed the rise of AI tools in her field and quickly adopted them. Rather than resist automation, she now uses Jasper AI to generate blog posts and Grammarly to fine-tune the content. This allows her to take on more clients and spend more time on creative strategy rather than routine tasks.

How Digital Nomads Are Adapting to AI Disruption

For digital nomads, the rise of AI is both a challenge and an opportunity. Many nomads have faced the possibility of their work becoming obsolete, but those who have embraced AI as a tool rather than a threat are thriving. Here's how they're adapting:

1. Reskilling and Upskilling:

- One of the most effective ways digital nomads are adapting to AI-driven disruption is by learning new skills. Andre's journey from data entry specialist to AI consultant highlights the importance of staying ahead of technological trends. Online platforms like Coursera and Udemy offer courses on AI, machine learning, and automation, helping nomads upskill from anywhere in the world.

- Practical Tip: If you're in a career that's being disrupted by AI, consider learning how to manage or develop AI systems. Understanding how AI works gives you a competitive advantage, whether you're a freelancer, consultant, or entrepreneur.

2. Leveraging AI for Efficiency:

- Rather than fear job loss, digital nomads are using AI to work smarter. By automating mundane tasks, nomads can focus on high-level strategy, creative thinking, and problem-solving—areas where human input is still invaluable.

- Example: Freelancers in fields like content marketing or graphic design are using AI tools like Canva, Jasper AI, and Grammarly to streamline their workflows, allowing them to take on more clients and enhance their creativity.

3. Offering AI Integration Services:

- Digital nomads are also finding new opportunities by helping businesses adopt AI. Many companies are eager to integrate AI into their operations but lack the expertise to do so. Nomads like Andre, who specialize in AI consulting, are helping businesses streamline processes, reduce costs, and enhance efficiency through automation.

- Pro Tip: If you've mastered the use of AI tools, consider offering consulting services to businesses seeking to integrate AI. As more industries adopt these technologies, demand for AI-savvy professionals will continue to grow.

Visionary Perspectives: AI, Automation, and the Future of Work

Looking to the future, the intersection of AI and automation with digital nomadism will continue to evolve. Entire industries will likely be redefined by automation, but this doesn't mean the end of work. Instead, it's an opportunity for nomads to focus on work that requires human creativity, emotional intelligence, and adaptability.

Imagine a Future Where:
- AI handles all administrative tasks, allowing nomads to focus solely on strategy and innovation.
- Businesses rely on digital nomads for their AI expertise, tapping into a global pool of AI consultants to stay competitive.
- AI and blockchain technologies converge, automating contracts and payments for freelancers, reducing the need for human intermediaries.

Balancing Inspiration with Caution

While the future of AI holds tremendous promise, it's essential to approach it with a balanced mindset. AI will undoubtedly disrupt many careers, but the opportunities for those willing to adapt are vast. Continuous learning and embracing change are the keys to staying relevant in an AI-driven world.

Privacy and data security are also significant concerns in the age of AI. As nomads increasingly rely on AI tools, they must remain vigilant about how data is collected, used, and stored. Understanding the ethical implications of AI and staying informed about data privacy regulations, like GDPR, is critical to building trust with clients and maintaining ethical business practices.

Conclusion: Thriving in an AI-Driven World

Automation and AI are transforming the way we work, but rather than fear these changes, digital nomads are finding ways to adapt and thrive. By reskilling, leveraging AI tools, and offering valuable services in AI integration, nomads are turning disruption into opportunity.

As you navigate this rapidly changing landscape, remember that adaptability, creativity, and continuous learning are your most valuable assets. The future of work may be uncertain, but with AI as your ally, the possibilities are limitless. Stay curious, stay informed, and embrace the tools that will help you build a purpose-driven, flexible, and fulfilling career in the AI age.

CHAPTER 7: AI-POWERED FREELANCE MARKETPLACES

As Maya scrolled through her Upwork dashboard from a café in Bali, she smiled at the opportunities in front of her. Just a few years ago, finding freelance clients meant endless cold emails and networking, often with limited success. Today, platforms like Upwork and Fiverr, powered by advanced AI, not only bring clients to her but also help her manage projects, track earnings, and even suggest ways to grow her business. For Maya, and countless digital nomads like her, these AI-driven freelance marketplaces have transformed the way remote work operates, opening doors to new opportunities while streamlining the work process.

How AI Transforms Freelance Platforms

Freelance marketplaces such as Upwork, Fiverr, and Freelancer.com have integrated AI in ways that make finding and managing work more efficient for both freelancers and clients. By leveraging machine learning algorithms, natural language processing (NLP), and predictive analytics, these platforms have evolved from simple job boards into sophisticated ecosystems where AI helps bridge the gap between supply and demand.

1. Smart Job Matching and Recommendations

- AI plays a pivotal role in job matching on these platforms. Instead of manually searching through endless job listings, freelancers can rely on AI algorithms to surface the most relevant projects based on their skills, past performance, and client feedback.

- Case Study: Maya, a freelance web developer, noticed a significant shift when Upwork's AI system began recommending projects that matched her specific expertise in e-commerce platforms. The system took into account her recent projects, ratings, and even job descriptions she had interacted with, providing her with tailored suggestions that saved her hours of searching and maximized her chances of securing high-paying gigs.

2. Streamlined Communication

- Communication is essential in any freelance project, and AI is making it smoother and more efficient. With AI-powered chatbots, freelancers can automatically respond to client inquiries, and predictive text features help speed up message exchanges.

- Example: On Fiverr, Maya uses the platform's AI-enhanced messaging system that suggests pre-written responses to common client queries. This allows her to maintain clear, fast communication without needing to be available 24/7. Additionally, AI-assisted language translation tools ensure that freelancers and clients from different linguistic backgrounds can communicate effortlessly.

3. Skill Assessment and Credentialing

- AI-powered platforms also help freelancers build credibility. Many platforms offer skill tests or automated assessments that validate a freelancer's capabilities. These tests not only rank freelancers against industry benchmarks but also provide clients with confidence in their hiring decisions.

- Practical Application: By completing Fiverr's AI-driven skill tests in UX design and coding, Maya earned top ratings that were showcased on her profile. This boosted her visibility on the platform, helping her stand out among thousands of freelancers, leading to more client inquiries and better-paying projects.

4. AI-Powered Project Management

- From setting milestones to tracking progress, AI helps automate project management tasks, freeing freelancers from administrative burdens. AI-driven platforms can now generate contracts, handle invoices, and manage deadlines, allowing freelancers to focus more on their craft.

- Pro Tip: Maya uses Upwork's automated time tracker, which monitors her working hours for each project and generates detailed reports for her clients. This not only ensures transparency but also saves her the hassle of manual tracking.

5. Enhanced Payment and Financial Management

- AI is also changing how freelancers get paid. Platforms now automate complex financial transactions, from currency conversion to invoicing, ensuring freelancers are paid on time and in the right currency.

- Example: Maya, who works with clients in multiple countries, uses Upwork's AI-powered payment system to handle different currencies. The system also integrates with accounting tools to generate invoices and manage her income, giving her a clear view of her earnings without needing an external accountant.

Practical Tips for Leveraging AI on Freelance Platforms

For digital nomads looking to maximize their success on platforms like Upwork and Fiverr, it's essential to understand how to work with AI rather than against it. Here are some practical steps to take:

1. Optimize Your Profile with Keywords

- AI algorithms rely on data from freelancer profiles to match them with relevant jobs. Ensure your profile is rich with relevant keywords and descriptions that align with your skills.

- Pro Tip: Maya updated her profile to highlight specific keywords such as "e-commerce web development," "UI/UX design," and "WordPress customization." By doing this, she increased the visibility of her profile in searches, making her more discoverable to potential clients.

2. Complete AI-Assessed Skill Tests

- Take advantage of the AI-driven skill tests that many platforms offer. These assessments help you stand out and give clients confidence in your abilities.

- Practical Application: By taking Upwork's programming assessment, Maya earned a "Top Developer" badge, which was displayed on her profile and led to more project offers.

3. Use AI Tools to Automate Your Workflow

- Beyond just finding jobs, use AI tools to streamline your freelance work. From content generation with tools like Jasper AI to design automation with Canva, AI can help you scale your work.

- Pro Tip: Maya used Jasper AI to draft blog content for a client's website and Grammarly to polish the copy, speeding up her workflow significantly. This allowed her to take on more clients without sacrificing quality.

Visionary Perspectives: The Future of AI-Powered Freelancing

As AI technology continues to evolve, so too will freelance marketplaces. The future of freelance work will likely involve even more sophisticated AI systems, offering new ways for freelancers to enhance their careers and for clients to find the perfect match.

1. AI-Powered Career Coaching

- AI could evolve into a personal career coach for freelancers, analysing job performance, skill growth, and client feedback to suggest personalized learning paths and job opportunities. AI might recommend specific courses or certifications based on industry trends, helping freelancers stay competitive.

- Imagine: Maya could receive suggestions for new programming languages to learn or certifications to pursue, all based on data-driven insights from her past projects and emerging industry demands.

2. Fully Automated Client Management

- In the near future, AI might handle all aspects of client management, from contract negotiations to project updates and even dispute resolution. This would reduce the administrative workload for freelancers, allowing them to focus more on creative and strategic tasks.

- Imagine: Maya's freelance dashboard could automatically generate contracts, track project progress, and even manage client feedback loops, making the entire project lifecycle seamless and automated.

3. Global Talent Pools

- AI-driven platforms are already expanding the global talent pool, but future developments could lead to even more integrated cross-border collaborations. AI could help build global teams of freelancers who work together on large-scale projects, matching complementary skills across borders.

- Pro Tip: By expanding your network through these AI-driven platforms, you can tap into projects from all corners of the world. Platforms like Fiverr and Upwork might offer team-based projects where multiple freelancers collaborate, with AI managing task delegation and communication.

Balancing Inspiration with Caution

While AI-powered freelance marketplaces open up incredible opportunities, it's important to acknowledge the challenges that come with it. Increased automation could lead to greater competition, as more freelancers flood the market. To stay competitive, freelancers must focus on cultivating unique, high-value skills that AI cannot easily replicate —such as creative problem-solving, emotional intelligence, and strategic thinking.

Additionally, with AI handling sensitive client data, privacy and security become paramount. Freelancers must ensure the platforms they use comply with data protection regulations, such as GDPR, and be vigilant about safeguarding both their personal and client data.

Global Dimensions: AI Freelancing Across Cultures

AI-powered freelance platforms are not only a Western phenomenon. Countries like India, Brazil, and Nigeria have embraced these platforms, using AI to compete on a global scale. As these platforms grow, they are levelling the playing field, allowing freelancers from diverse cultural and economic backgrounds to participate in the global gig economy.

Example: In India, skilled developers and designers are using Upwork to connect with clients from the U.S. and Europe, providing world-class services at competitive rates. Similarly, Brazilian freelancers are leveraging Fiverr to offer creative services, like graphic design and music production, to a global audience.

Conclusion: Thriving in the AI-Powered Freelance Economy

AI-powered freelance marketplaces like Upwork and Fiverr are revolutionizing the world of digital nomads.

By automating job matching, skill assessments, project management, and payment systems, these platforms allow freelancers to focus on what they do best—delivering high-quality work.

The key to thriving in this AI-driven gig economy is to embrace the technology while continuing to develop high-value skills that set you apart. As AI continues to evolve, freelancers like Maya will be able to leverage new tools, build global careers, and achieve unprecedented levels of freedom and success. The future of freelance work is bright, and with AI as a powerful ally, the possibilities are limitless.

CHAPTER 8: DIGITAL MARKETING IN THE AI AGE

As she relaxed on the balcony of her Airbnb in Santorini, Alina marvelled at how quickly her freelance marketing business had grown. What once took hours of manual work —analysing trends, crafting campaigns, and managing client relationships—now flowed effortlessly, thanks to AI. Alina's business was thriving, and she credited much of that success to the AI tools she used to automate routine tasks, generate personalized marketing strategies, and even forecast trends. For Alina, and many digital nomads like her, AI was no longer just a tool; it had become a critical business partner, revolutionizing the world of digital marketing.

How Digital Nomads Use AI to Revolutionize Marketing

AI is reshaping how digital nomads approach marketing and branding. With the help of machine learning, predictive analytics, and automation, marketing tasks that used to be time-consuming and labour-intensive are now streamlined, allowing digital marketers to focus more on creativity and strategy.

1. Data-Driven Campaigns Powered by AI
   - AI allows digital nomads to make sense of vast amounts of data and use it to create more effective, personalized marketing campaigns. By analysing customer behaviour,

preferences, and market trends, AI helps marketers identify opportunities they would have otherwise missed.

- Case Study: Alina uses HubSpot to analyse data from her clients' websites, email campaigns, and social media channels. The AI in HubSpot automatically generates insights, such as which blog topics are driving the most engagement and what times of day are best for posting. Armed with this data, Alina can craft highly targeted campaigns that resonate with specific audience segments, leading to higher conversion rates and more satisfied clients.

2. Content Creation and Personalization at Scale

- Content creation used to be one of the most time-consuming aspects of digital marketing, but AI has changed that. Tools like Jasper AI can generate blog posts, social media updates, and even email newsletters in a matter of minutes, while still maintaining a human-like tone.

- Example: Alina recently used Jasper AI to generate a series of blog posts for a client's travel website. By feeding the AI tool a few keywords and topics, she was able to produce engaging, SEO-optimized content in a fraction of the time it would have taken manually. She then used Grammarly to polish the language, ensuring the posts were error-free and ready for publication.

3. Automated Customer Interactions

- One of the most exciting applications of AI in marketing is in customer service and engagement. AI-powered chatbots, such as Intercom and Drift, are revolutionizing how businesses interact with their customers, offering real-time responses to inquiries, solving problems, and guiding users through their purchase journey—all without the need for human intervention.

- Pro Tip: Alina integrated Intercom into her clients' websites, allowing the chatbot to handle basic customer queries, such as product availability and pricing. This freed up her time to focus on higher-level tasks like strategy and campaign planning, while still ensuring customers received timely and helpful responses.

4. Predictive Analytics for Strategic Decision-Making

- Predictive analytics, powered by machine learning, allows marketers to forecast future trends and outcomes based on historical data. This capability helps digital nomads like Alina stay ahead of the competition by anticipating changes in consumer behaviour or market conditions.

- Example: Alina used Google Analytics' AI-driven insights to predict which keywords would perform best for an upcoming campaign. By analysing historical data and current market trends, the AI provided her with a list of keywords and content ideas that were likely to drive the most traffic. This data-driven approach helped her fine-tune her strategy, leading to a significant increase in her client's website traffic and conversions.

Practical Applications of AI for Digital Marketers

For digital nomads looking to incorporate AI into their marketing strategies, the possibilities are vast. Here are some practical ways to leverage AI in your digital marketing efforts:

1. Use AI for Audience Segmentation

- AI tools like HubSpot and ActiveCampaign can help you segment your audience based on behaviour, preferences, and past interactions. By breaking your audience into specific groups, you can deliver more personalized and relevant content.

- Practical Tip: If you're running an email marketing campaign, use AI to segment your audience based on how they've interacted with your previous emails. This allows you to send targeted messages to those most likely to engage, boosting your open rates and conversions.

2. Automate Social Media Posting and Engagement

- Tools like Buffer and Hootsuite allow digital marketers to automate social media posting, while AI-driven features help optimize posting times and analyse engagement. By automating the scheduling of posts, you can maintain a consistent online presence without needing to manually post every day.

- Pro Tip: Alina uses Buffer's AI-powered scheduling feature, which determines the best times to post based on audience engagement patterns. This ensures that her clients' content reaches the maximum number of people, even when she's traveling or offline.

3. Leverage AI for Dynamic Ad Campaigns

- AI is transforming paid advertising by optimizing ad targeting and placement in real time. Tools like Facebook's AI-driven ad platform allow you to automatically adjust your ads based on performance, audience behaviour, and market trends.

- Example: Alina set up a dynamic Facebook ad campaign for a client, allowing the platform's AI to continuously optimize the ads based on real-time engagement. This led to a 30% reduction in cost-per-click and a significant improvement in conversion rates.

Visionary Perspectives: The Future of AI in Digital Marketing

As AI continues to evolve, the future of digital marketing will be driven by even more advanced capabilities. The possibilities for digital nomads are endless, as AI opens up new opportunities for efficiency, personalization, and creative strategy.

1. Hyper-Personalized Customer Experiences

- Imagine a future where AI can predict exactly what a customer wants before they even realize it. By analysing massive amounts of data, AI could offer hyper-personalized recommendations, creating marketing experiences that feel uniquely tailored to each individual.

- Imagine: Alina's clients could offer products and services to their customers based on real-time behavioural data, providing recommendations that feel almost psychic. This would create a seamless, personalized customer journey, increasing brand loyalty and driving long-term growth.

2. AI-Driven Creativity

- AI is already playing a role in content creation, but what if it could enhance creativity even further? In the future, AI tools might not only generate content but also suggest creative angles, visual elements, and storytelling techniques that resonate with specific audience demographics.

- Pro Tip: Stay ahead of the curve by experimenting with AI tools that offer creative support, such as Adobe Sensei, which uses AI to enhance design and visual content.

3. Autonomous Marketing Systems

- The future may also bring fully autonomous marketing systems that handle every aspect of a campaign, from ideation to execution, without human intervention. These systems would analyse data, create content, engage with customers, and even make real-time adjustments to strategy —all while the digital nomad focuses on more strategic, high-level decision-making.

- Visionary Question: What would your role look like if AI took care of the day-to-day marketing tasks? How could you leverage that extra time to focus on bigger, bolder ideas for your business or clients?

Balancing Opportunity and Caution

While AI offers incredible potential for digital marketers, it's essential to be mindful of the challenges and ethical considerations that come with it. For instance, AI-driven marketing systems rely heavily on user data, raising privacy concerns. Digital nomads must ensure they are using AI tools responsibly, with a commitment to data protection and transparency.

Additionally, the rise of AI in marketing could lead to increased competition as more marketers gain access to these powerful tools. To stay competitive, digital nomads must focus on cultivating skills that AI can't easily replicate, such as emotional intelligence, creativity, and strategic thinking.

Global Perspectives: AI in Digital Marketing Across Borders

AI is transforming digital marketing globally, and digital nomads are uniquely positioned to take advantage of this trend. From Asia to Europe to South America, businesses are embracing AI to reach new customers, and digital nomads like Alina are helping them do it.

In India, for example, AI-powered tools are enabling small businesses to run marketing campaigns that reach global audiences, levelling the playing field in ways that were previously unimaginable. Meanwhile, in Brazil, digital marketers are using AI to create dynamic, data-driven advertising strategies that target local and international customers alike.

Conclusion: Embracing AI to Revolutionize Your Marketing Strategy

AI is more than just a trend—it's transforming the digital marketing landscape in ways that create new opportunities for digital nomads. By automating routine tasks, enhancing creativity, and offering data-driven insights, AI enables marketers like Alina to focus on what truly matters: building relationships, creating innovative campaigns, and driving results for their clients.

As AI continues to evolve, the key to success is staying

adaptable and embracing the possibilities it offers. By leveraging AI tools, focusing on high-value skills, and keeping a global perspective, digital nomads can thrive in the AI-powered marketing world, achieving both personal fulfilment and professional success. The future of marketing is here—are you ready to embrace it?

CHAPTER 9: TECH SUPPORT IN A WORLD OF AI

As Diego sat in a small coffee shop in Buenos Aires, he was preparing to host an important virtual meeting with a new client based in the U.S. Suddenly, his laptop froze, and panic set in. Years ago, this would have meant searching for the nearest computer repair shop or calling tech support and waiting on hold for hours. But this time, Diego didn't need to worry. He opened an AI-powered tech support app on his phone, which immediately ran diagnostics on his laptop. Within minutes, the AI tool identified the issue, offered step-by-step instructions to fix it, and got him back online before the meeting started. For Diego and digital nomads around the world, AI is revolutionizing tech support, offering instant solutions wherever they are.

How AI Is Transforming Tech Support for Digital Nomads

For digital nomads, reliable tech support is not just a convenience—it's a necessity. Working remotely from various parts of the world means that technical issues can arise in locations where in-person IT support might be unavailable or difficult to access. AI has stepped in to fill this gap, offering fast, efficient, and often preventative solutions that ensure tech problems don't become career-disrupting roadblocks.

1. Instant Diagnostics and Troubleshooting

- One of the biggest advantages AI brings to tech support is its ability to diagnose and troubleshoot problems in real-time. Rather than waiting for a human technician, AI tools like Norton's AI-powered security platform or Avast's AI diagnostic tool can scan devices for issues, detect malware, and provide instant solutions.

- Case Study: Diego uses PC Doctor, an AI-based diagnostics tool, which helped him resolve a system error that could have taken hours to figure out on his own. The tool analysed his system's performance, identified memory overload, and recommended steps to clear unnecessary background processes—all within minutes. Thanks to this AI tool, Diego was able to avoid a potential setback in his workday.

2. Proactive Maintenance and Problem Prevention

- AI is not just reactive; it's proactive. Many AI-powered tech support systems offer predictive maintenance, detecting potential problems before they escalate. By analysing device usage patterns and system health, AI can alert users to issues like battery degradation, hard drive failure risks, or overheating before they cause significant damage.

- Practical Application: Diego installed Drift, an AI tool designed to monitor the health of his laptop. The software scans his system in the background and provides alerts when something isn't working as efficiently as it should. This proactive approach helps Diego avoid emergencies, saving him time and preventing costly repairs down the road.

3. AI-Powered Virtual Assistants

- Virtual assistants like Siri, Cortana, and Google Assistant are more than just voice-activated tools for setting reminders or playing music. These AI-powered systems are increasingly being integrated into tech support workflows. Users can simply ask their virtual assistant for help diagnosing problems or resolving technical issues.

- Pro Tip: Diego often uses Google Assistant to get quick answers for common tech problems. When his Wi-Fi connection was acting up during a virtual meeting, he asked Google Assistant to troubleshoot. It quickly suggested that he restart the router, and when that didn't work, it guided him through resetting his device's network settings.

4. Remote Troubleshooting Through AI Chatbots

- AI chatbots are now at the forefront of tech support. Rather than relying on human support teams, which can be costly and time-consuming, companies are implementing AI chatbots to handle basic tech inquiries. These chatbots can resolve issues such as software installation, updates, or connectivity problems without the need for a technician.

- Example: Diego's internet provider offers a 24/7 AI chatbot service that helps troubleshoot connection issues. When his internet went down in a co-working space, he quickly accessed the chatbot, which provided step-by-step instructions for resetting the router and checking local outages, all without waiting in line for human support.

Practical Applications of AI Tech Support Tools

AI has made tech support far more accessible and efficient for digital nomads. Here are some practical tips for using AI to solve tech problems:

1. Leverage AI Diagnostic Tools for Quick Fixes

- Instead of manually trying to figure out what's wrong with your system, use AI diagnostic tools to pinpoint the issue. Tools like PC Doctor and Avast can run diagnostics on your device and provide recommendations for fixes within minutes.

- Pro Tip: Diego's habit of running PC Doctor diagnostics every few weeks keeps his laptop running smoothly, reducing the likelihood of sudden crashes or slowdowns while he's working on the road.

2. Use AI-Powered Virtual Assistants for Real-Time Support

- Don't overlook the power of virtual assistants like Siri, Cortana, or Google Assistant for tech support. These AI tools are equipped to answer many tech-related questions and can guide you through basic troubleshooting steps.

- Practical Tip: If you're facing an issue with your device's software, ask your virtual assistant to search for solutions online or navigate you through fixing the issue without leaving your workflow.

3. Set Up AI-Driven Proactive Maintenance

- By using proactive maintenance tools like Drift, digital nomads can detect system failures before they become a problem. These tools run in the background, monitoring your device's performance and offering alerts when something goes wrong.

- Example: Diego set up Drift to monitor his battery health and received a warning when his battery was starting to degrade, giving him time to replace it before it failed mid-project.

4. AI Chatbots for Customer Support

- If you're using products or services that offer AI chatbot support, take advantage of these tools for instant help. Chatbots are designed to resolve a wide variety of tech issues, including software installations, system updates, or connection troubleshooting.

- Pro Tip: Diego's co-working space uses an AI chatbot to handle most of its tech issues. He uses it regularly to troubleshoot slow internet connections or adjust his device settings without needing to wait for human support.

Visionary Perspectives: The Future of AI-Driven Tech Support

As AI continues to evolve, the future of tech support is likely to become even more automated and personalized. Here are some exciting possibilities:

1. Fully Autonomous Tech Support Systems

- Imagine a world where AI tools can autonomously fix tech issues without any user intervention. AI-driven systems could detect an issue, resolve it in the background, and send a notification once the problem is fixed—all without the user needing to lift a finger.

- Imagine: Diego's laptop could fix itself by detecting a failing hard drive, ordering a replacement, and scheduling a technician visit—all automatically, allowing him to focus on his work without interruption.

2. AI-Enhanced Remote IT Support

- As AI becomes more advanced, remote IT support will become even more efficient. AI systems could work in tandem with human technicians, taking over routine tasks while escalating more complex issues to professionals.

- Future Vision: AI tools might one day be able to remotely access a user's device, perform diagnostics, and fix the problem instantly. For digital nomads, this means no more searching for a tech expert in a foreign country—AI will handle it all.

3. Predictive Tech Support for Every Device

- AI's ability to predict potential issues will continue to improve. This could lead to predictive tech support systems that monitor every aspect of a device, from battery health to software vulnerabilities, ensuring that issues are resolved before they impact performance.

- Visionary Question: How could predictive AI tech support change the way you manage your devices on the go? What if you never had to worry about sudden tech failures again?

Balancing AI-Driven Tech Support with Caution

While AI-driven tech support offers tremendous benefits, it's essential to approach it with a level of caution. Some key concerns include data privacy and the over-reliance on AI for critical tasks. Ensure that the tools you use comply with data protection regulations and that sensitive information is secured. Additionally, while AI can handle most routine issues, there will always be complex problems that require human expertise, so it's vital to maintain access to reliable tech professionals when needed.

Global and Cultural Perspectives: AI-Driven Support for Digital Nomads Worldwide

Digital nomads across the globe are benefiting from AI-driven tech support, regardless of where they work. In countries like Thailand and Mexico, AI tools offer essential support for nomads in remote locations where finding tech professionals may be difficult. Meanwhile, in Estonia, the government is leading the charge in developing AI-driven e-services for digital nomads, providing seamless tech support through digital-first policies.

Conclusion: Thriving with AI-Powered Tech Support

AI-driven tech support is a game-changer for digital nomads, offering real-time solutions, proactive maintenance, and reliable troubleshooting no matter where they are in the world. By embracing these tools, nomads like Diego are able to keep their devices running smoothly and focus on what matters most: their work, their travels, and their personal growth.

As AI continues to evolve, the future of tech support will only become more integrated, efficient, and user-friendly. Whether it's through predictive maintenance, AI chatbots, or fully autonomous tech support systems, digital nomads are at the forefront of this revolution, harnessing AI to thrive in an increasingly interconnected world.

CHAPTER 10: THE GIG ECONOMY: AI'S ROLE IN EMPOWERING NOMADS

Samantha leaned back in her chair at a cozy café in Chiang Mai, Thailand, reflecting on the journey that had brought her here. Five years ago, she was stuck in a rigid corporate job, managing tight deadlines with little flexibility. Today, she juggled multiple freelance projects in marketing and content creation, all while exploring the world as a digital nomad. What had enabled this transformation? The power of the gig economy, supercharged by AI.

Samantha's story is one that resonates with countless digital nomads who have embraced the gig economy. But it's not just the remote work opportunities that have made this lifestyle possible—it's the integration of AI into gig platforms that has allowed individuals like her to find work more efficiently, scale their freelance businesses, and optimize how they manage their time and projects. In this chapter, we'll explore how AI is amplifying the gig economy and the profound impact it's having on the lives of digital nomads around the world.

How AI Is Reshaping the Gig Economy

1. AI-Driven Platforms for Finding Work

- The foundation of the gig economy rests on platforms like Upwork, Fiverr, and Freelancer.com, which connect freelancers to clients in need of their services. AI plays a critical role here, using algorithms to match freelancers with projects that suit their skills, experience, and interests.

- Case Study: Samantha, a freelance writer and digital marketing strategist, credits her ability to maintain a steady stream of clients to AI-powered platforms. Every time she logs into Upwork, AI-driven recommendations surface projects tailored to her areas of expertise. These platforms analyse her past projects, reviews, and engagement metrics to ensure she's matched with the right opportunities, allowing her to focus on the most relevant and lucrative gigs.

2. Automation of Time-Consuming Tasks

- Beyond simply finding work, AI is also helping freelancers streamline their workflow. From administrative tasks like invoicing and scheduling to more complex operations like project management, AI is automating many aspects of freelancing, enabling digital nomads to focus on higher-value work.

- Practical Application: Samantha uses Toggl, an AI-powered time tracking and project management tool, to monitor how long she spends on each task and generate automated invoices for her clients. This has allowed her to manage multiple projects with ease, improving her productivity without getting bogged down by administrative tasks.

3. AI-Powered Content Creation and Enhancement

- For freelancers in creative fields—writing, graphic design, or marketing—AI tools are transforming the way content is created and delivered. AI can generate ideas, assist with drafting, and even automate content optimization, saving freelancers significant amounts of time.

- Example: Samantha uses Jasper AI to help her generate blog post drafts for her clients, speeding up the process while maintaining a high level of quality. Once the draft is created, she turns to Grammarly's AI-enhanced editor for suggestions on clarity, tone, and grammar, ensuring that her work is polished before it reaches the client. These AI tools allow her to handle more projects simultaneously, without sacrificing quality.

4. Gig Platforms Using AI for Payment Security
- Freelancers rely on prompt and secure payments, and AI is helping to make financial transactions on gig platforms more seamless. AI-powered systems can handle payment processing, automate invoice generation, and detect fraudulent transactions, ensuring freelancers are paid on time and without hassle.

- Pro Tip: Samantha leverages Upwork's built-in AI systems, which ensure her payments are processed securely and on time. The platform uses AI to track project milestones and automatically release payments once her clients approve the work, removing the need for lengthy invoicing processes and manual follow-ups.

Practical Applications: How Digital Nomads Can Maximize AI in the Gig Economy

1. Optimize Profiles for AI Algorithms
- AI-driven gig platforms rely heavily on profile data to match freelancers with potential clients. To increase visibility and improve the quality of job recommendations, digital nomads should optimize their profiles with relevant keywords, detailed project descriptions, and up-to-date skills.

- Pro Tip: Samantha updates her Upwork profile regularly, ensuring her top skills—such as "content marketing strategy" and "SEO writing"—are highlighted prominently. This helps the platform's AI algorithm accurately match her with clients looking for her expertise.

2. Use AI for Personal Branding and Marketing
- AI tools can also help freelancers build and maintain a strong personal brand. From social media management platforms like Buffer to SEO analysis tools like SEMrush, AI can analyse engagement data, suggest the best times to post, and even predict future trends, allowing digital nomads to market themselves more effectively.
- Example: Samantha uses Hootsuite's AI-driven scheduling feature to automatically post her latest projects and client testimonials on LinkedIn and Instagram, boosting her online presence without spending hours on social media management.

3. Leverage AI Tools for Pricing Strategy
- One of the challenges freelancers face in the gig economy is pricing their services appropriately. AI tools like Bonsai can analyse market trends, competitor pricing, and project complexity to suggest competitive rates for freelancers.
- Practical Tip: Samantha uses Bonsai to help her determine fair pricing for her services based on current market demand and her expertise level. This ensures that she remains competitive while maximizing her earnings.

Visionary Perspectives: AI's Expanding Role in the Gig Economy

As AI continues to evolve, its role in the gig economy will expand, offering even more opportunities for digital nomads. Here are some visionary possibilities for the future:

1. AI-Enhanced Global Collaboration
- In the near future, AI could enable seamless collaboration across borders by automatically translating communications, syncing time zones, and managing

projects that involve freelancers from different parts of the world. This would make it easier for digital nomads to work with clients and teams globally, regardless of language barriers or time differences.

- Imagine: Samantha could collaborate on a complex project with team members in Japan and Brazil, with AI managing the coordination and communication, allowing them to focus purely on delivering results.

2. Personalized Career Coaching Through AI

- AI could evolve into a personalized career coach for freelancers, analysing performance data, client feedback, and industry trends to suggest new skills, certifications, or niches to explore. AI-powered platforms could offer real-time insights, helping digital nomads navigate their careers more strategically.

- Visionary Question: What if AI could guide you through every step of your freelance career, offering personalized advice on which industries to target, what skills to learn, and how to grow your client base?

3. AI-Driven Gig Platforms with Full Autonomy

- As AI systems become more advanced, gig platforms could evolve to the point where they autonomously manage the entire freelancing process—from finding clients and negotiating contracts to managing projects and ensuring payments. This would allow freelancers to focus solely on their creative and strategic work, with AI handling the operational side of freelancing.

- Imagine: Samantha could focus entirely on creating high-quality content, while the platform's AI autonomously managed everything from client acquisition to final payment processing.

Balancing Opportunity and Caution

While AI amplifies opportunities in the gig economy, it's

important to acknowledge the challenges that come with it. Increased competition on gig platforms may lead to freelancers needing to continuously refine their skills to stay relevant. Furthermore, data privacy and security concerns are significant as freelancers rely more on AI systems that process sensitive information like financial transactions and personal data.

Digital nomads must take proactive steps to ensure that the platforms they use comply with data protection regulations and prioritize security.

Global and Cultural Dimensions: AI-Driven Gig Opportunities Around the World

AI-driven gig platforms are unlocking new opportunities for freelancers across the globe, particularly in emerging markets. In countries like India, Brazil, and South Africa, AI tools are enabling freelancers to compete in the global market, often with a lower cost of living but offering services at competitive international rates.

Example: In India, freelance developers are using AI-powered platforms to secure high-paying clients in the U.S. and Europe, while in Nigeria, graphic designers are leveraging AI tools to streamline their workflows and work with clients from across the globe.

Conclusion: Thriving in the AI-Enhanced Gig Economy

AI is not only empowering digital nomads but also redefining the gig economy itself. By automating routine tasks, optimizing work processes, and creating smarter connections between freelancers and clients, AI is opening up new possibilities for independent workers everywhere.

For digital nomads like Samantha, the key to thriving in this new era is adaptability—leveraging AI tools to maximize productivity, enhance client relationships, and create a sustainable, fulfilling career. The gig economy, powered by AI, is just getting started, and those who embrace this change will find themselves at the forefront of the future of work.

PART 3: THE SKILLS DIGITAL NOMADS NEED TODAY

CHAPTER 11:
LEARNING AI SKILLS:
A NOMAD'S GUIDE

As Mateo sipped his espresso in a Lisbon café, he reflected on how his career had transformed over the past year. A self-taught web developer turned digital nomad, Mateo was thriving in the remote work world. But the turning point came when he embraced AI. By learning AI-related skills, he was able to automate mundane tasks, enhance his productivity, and offer new, in-demand services to clients. The transition wasn't easy, but AI tools were gradually integrated into his workflow, unlocking opportunities he never imagined.

Mateo's story is not unique—across the globe, digital nomads are learning AI skills to remain competitive, enhance their careers, and lead the charge in an evolving work landscape. This chapter will serve as a practical guide for digital nomads looking to master AI skills that can enhance their freedom, financial security, and career prospects.

Why Learning AI Skills Is Essential for Digital Nomads

AI is becoming more pervasive across industries, and for digital nomads, understanding and utilizing AI offers immense potential. Whether you're a freelance graphic designer, marketing consultant, or software developer, incorporating AI into your skill set can lead to increased efficiency, new revenue streams, and even automation of repetitive tasks that once consumed valuable time.

For digital nomads, mastering AI skills provides more than just career advancement—it also offers the flexibility to work smarter, not harder, while continuing to pursue a life of adventure and purpose.

Essential AI-Related Skills for Digital Nomads

1. Understanding Machine Learning Basics

- Machine learning (ML) is a key pillar of AI and is applied across a wide range of industries, from marketing to software development. Learning the basics of how machines "learn" from data is crucial for digital nomads who want to integrate AI into their work.

- Practical Application: Mateo started his AI journey by taking an online course on machine learning through Coursera, where he learned the fundamentals of algorithms, data patterns, and how machines can be trained to make predictions. This knowledge allowed him to integrate AI-powered tools, like chatbots and recommendation engines, into client websites.

2. AI-Powered Automation Tools

- AI automation tools are a game-changer for digital nomads looking to streamline their work. Whether it's automating administrative tasks like scheduling, email marketing, or even content generation, learning how to leverage AI for automation can save countless hours.

- Example: After learning the ins and outs of Zapier, an AI-powered automation tool, Mateo was able to automate his project management workflow. Using Zapier, he created automated tasks that synced his Google Calendar with client reminders, invoicing, and project deadlines—allowing him to focus more on creative work and less on admin.

3. Natural Language Processing (NLP) Tools

- Natural language processing is a branch of AI focused on how computers understand and respond to human language. For digital nomads working in writing, marketing, or customer service, understanding how to use NLP tools can enhance productivity and improve communication.

- Pro Tip: Mateo uses Grammarly and Jasper AI, both of which employ NLP, to draft content for clients quickly. Grammarly ensures his writing is polished, while Jasper AI assists in generating creative ideas or refining the tone of his articles. This allows him to deliver higher quality work faster, making his services more attractive to clients.

4. AI Data Analysis Tools

- Digital nomads working in analytics, marketing, or finance will benefit immensely from understanding how to use AI data analysis tools. AI-powered data analysis enables faster decision-making by turning complex data into actionable insights.

- Example: Mateo expanded his web development business to offer AI-driven data analytics for clients. He learned how to use Google Analytics AI tools, which allowed him to provide his clients with in-depth data on website performance, traffic patterns, and user behaviour. This additional service increased his value to clients and helped him earn more revenue.

5. Building and Managing AI Chatbots

- AI-powered chatbots are becoming increasingly important in business, handling customer queries, automating responses, and providing instant feedback. Digital nomads who learn to build and manage AI chatbots can add this highly desirable skill to their portfolio.

- Practical Application: Mateo learned how to build AI chatbots using Chatfuel and ManyChat, both of which require little to no coding experience. He now integrates chatbots into his clients' websites, offering them 24/7 customer support solutions. This has become one of his most popular service offerings.

How to Start Learning AI Skills: A Step-by-Step Guide

1. Identify Your Niche and AI Relevance

- The first step in mastering AI is to determine how it relates to your field of work. Are you a content creator? Then focus on AI-driven writing tools. Are you a developer? Then machine learning or data analysis tools may be more useful. Once you identify your niche, it becomes easier to find the right learning resources.

- Pro Tip: Mateo started by identifying how AI could help automate his existing tasks in web development. He then honed in on AI-powered website optimization tools and chatbots, aligning his learning with his career goals.

2. Take Online AI Courses

- There are plenty of online resources that offer courses specifically focused on AI. Platforms like Coursera, Udemy, and LinkedIn Learning provide beginner to advanced courses on AI, machine learning, data science, and more.

- Pro Tip: Mateo took Andrew Ng's Machine Learning Course on Coursera, which helped him grasp the foundational concepts of AI. He then continued his learning with niche courses on chatbot development and AI for web optimization.

3. Practice with AI Tools

- The best way to learn AI is by doing. Once you understand the basics, experiment with AI tools that are relevant to your field. Tools like TensorFlow, IBM Watson, and Google Cloud AI offer free or low-cost platforms for hands-on learning.

- Example: Mateo started experimenting with TensorFlow for simple machine learning projects, such as creating predictive models for his clients' e-commerce websites. This helped him gain practical experience in how AI could be applied to real-world business problems.

4. Join AI Communities

- Being part of a community can provide support and insight as you learn. Join online communities of digital nomads and AI enthusiasts, such as Reddit's AI community or Kaggle, where you can collaborate on projects and share knowledge.

- Practical Tip: Mateo joined AI communities on Slack and Reddit, where he found support from other digital nomads and developers. These communities provided valuable feedback and helped him troubleshoot problems when learning new tools.

Visionary Perspectives: AI Skills for the Future

AI is evolving at a rapid pace, and the skills you learn today could lay the foundation for future innovations. Here's a glimpse of what's possible:

1. AI-Enhanced Creativity

- In the future, AI may work as an assistant that not only automates tasks but also enhances creativity. Imagine AI tools that generate design suggestions, music compositions, or creative writing ideas, acting as a partner in your creative process.

- Visionary Question: How might AI boost your creativity in ways that manual tools never could? What if AI could co-create with you, helping to unlock new ideas that align with your vision?

2. AI as a Career Mentor

- As AI systems become more sophisticated, they could act as virtual mentors, helping digital nomads map out their careers, suggest learning paths, and even connect them with the right opportunities based on their goals and interests.

- Imagine: Mateo's AI mentor could guide him on which AI skills to learn next, suggest relevant projects to apply his skills, and provide personalized insights into the evolving demands of his industry.

Balancing Opportunity with Caution

While AI offers exciting opportunities, digital nomads must approach it with a sense of responsibility. Data privacy, ethical AI use, and continuous learning will remain crucial as AI advances. Digital nomads should stay vigilant about the ethical implications of AI in their industries, ensuring that AI tools are used in ways that benefit both businesses and society.

Conclusion: Thriving in the AI Age

For digital nomads, learning AI skills is not just about staying competitive—it's about thriving in an ever-changing work landscape. By mastering essential AI tools, automating tasks, and integrating AI into their workflows, digital nomads like Mateo are not only enhancing their careers but also creating more freedom to focus on what truly matters.

AI is a powerful tool that, when used effectively, can unlock endless possibilities. For digital nomads looking to combine professional success with a life of adventure, learning AI is the gateway to a future filled with purpose, creativity, and unlimited potential. The question is: Are you ready to embrace it?

CHAPTER 12:
AI TOOLS FOR
CONTENT CREATORS

As Lucy gazed out over the serene beach in Bali, she marvelled at how technology had transformed her career. A freelance content creator, she used to spend countless hours brainstorming ideas, writing articles, and designing visuals for her clients. But since embracing AI tools, her workload had dramatically shifted. What once took days to complete could now be done in hours, leaving her with more time to focus on the parts of her job she loved—crafting stories, experimenting with new design styles, and exploring the world. For digital nomads like Lucy, AI has become the ultimate co-pilot, enabling creativity to flourish in ways previously unimaginable.

This chapter delves into the AI tools that are revolutionizing the work of writers, designers, and content creators. By exploring practical applications and real-world examples, it offers insights into how digital nomads can use AI to enhance their craft, increase productivity, and unlock new opportunities.

AI Tools Transforming Content Creation

1. AI for Writing and Copywriting

Writing is at the heart of many content creation jobs,

whether it's crafting blog posts, developing marketing copy, or producing social media content. AI-powered tools have made writing faster, more efficient, and more creative by assisting with idea generation, editing, and even drafting content.

- Jasper AI: One of the most powerful AI tools for content generation, Jasper AI can draft articles, product descriptions, and social media posts with ease. By providing a few keywords and instructions, Jasper creates content that feels human, with minimal editing required.

- Case Study: Lucy uses Jasper AI to draft the bones of her blog posts for travel companies. She inputs the destination, target audience, and key themes, and within minutes, Jasper produces a well-structured draft. Lucy then refines the tone and adds personal insights, saving her hours compared to writing from scratch.

- Grammarly: Known for its AI-enhanced grammar and style suggestions, Grammarly helps writers ensure that their content is polished and professional. Whether it's correcting grammar mistakes, enhancing readability, or adjusting tone, Grammarly provides real-time feedback.

- Pro Tip: Lucy uses Grammarly Premium to elevate the quality of her writing. Once she drafts content, Grammarly helps her fine-tune everything from word choice to sentence structure, ensuring her work is clear, concise, and error-free.

2. AI Tools for Graphic Design

Designers, whether working on logos, social media graphics, or website layouts, are using AI to speed up the design process and explore creative possibilities. AI tools are capable of generating stunning visuals, automating tedious design tasks, and offering design suggestions based on user preferences.

- Canva Pro: An intuitive, AI-powered design platform, Canva Pro allows users to create professional-quality graphics without needing advanced design skills. With AI-driven templates, users can quickly produce social media posts, presentations, and marketing materials tailored to specific audiences.

- Example: Lucy uses Canva Pro to create Instagram posts for her clients. She relies on Canva's AI suggestions to adjust colour palettes and design elements based on the brand's style, making the process not only faster but also more creative.

- Adobe Sensei: Adobe Sensei, integrated into Adobe's suite of products, uses AI to automate repetitive design tasks, enhance images, and provide intelligent design suggestions. Whether it's selecting the perfect font or making precision edits, Sensei improves the efficiency of creative projects.

- Pro Tip: For her more advanced design projects, Lucy uses Adobe Illustrator powered by Sensei to adjust photo details and generate high-quality graphics. This allows her to maintain the professional edge her clients expect, without spending hours fine-tuning small elements.

3. AI for Video and Audio Editing

With the rise of video content, digital nomads like Lucy are expanding their skill sets to include video production and editing. AI tools are making it easier than ever to create polished video content by automating time-consuming editing processes.

- Lumen5: Designed for turning text into video, Lumen5 uses AI to match video clips, images, and music to text input, creating professional-quality videos in minutes. Content creators can simply input a blog post or article, and Lumen5 generates an engaging video summary.

- Example: Lucy creates promotional videos for her clients' travel blogs using Lumen5. She pastes the article content into the platform, and within moments, Lumen5 generates a visually appealing video that she can fine-tune, saving her hours of manual editing.

- Descript: A powerful AI tool for podcast and video editing, Descript allows creators to edit audio by simply editing the transcript. The platform's AI tools also help remove filler words, adjust sound quality, and even generate voiceovers.

- Pro Tip: When Lucy started a travel podcast, she turned to Descript to handle her editing. With its AI-powered features, she can edit episodes by cutting out unwanted sections from the transcript, significantly speeding up her workflow.

4. AI Tools for Marketing and SEO

Digital nomads working as content marketers need to stay on top of SEO trends and optimize content for search engines. AI tools help automate SEO strategies, analyse content performance, and even suggest improvements.

- Surfer SEO: A leading AI tool for on-page SEO, Surfer SEO analyses top-ranking pages for a particular keyword and suggests content improvements to boost ranking potential. It offers data-driven recommendations on keyword density, word count, and internal linking strategies.

- Case Study: Lucy uses Surfer SEO to optimize her blog posts. By comparing her content to top-ranking competitors, she can adjust her articles to improve SEO performance, ensuring her clients' content ranks higher and attracts more traffic.

- BuzzSumo: AI-powered tools like BuzzSumo help

content creators discover trending topics, analyse audience engagement, and craft content that resonates with readers. It identifies what works best within specific niches and offers insights for creating shareable content.

- Example: Before crafting new content for a client, Lucy uses BuzzSumo to identify trending topics within the travel industry. By analysing popular articles, she tailors her posts to meet audience demand, ensuring her content reaches a broader audience.

Practical Application: How to Start Using AI Tools

1. Experiment with AI Tools That Fit Your Workflow
- Start by identifying AI tools that align with your current needs. Are you a writer looking to speed up your drafting process? Try Jasper AI. If you're a designer looking to streamline your workflow, explore Canva Pro or Adobe Sensei.
- Pro Tip: Lucy's approach to integrating AI was gradual. She started with basic tools like Grammarly and Canva, then progressed to more advanced options like Lumen5 and Surfer SEO as her confidence grew.

2. Leverage AI for Idea Generation
- AI can help you overcome creative blocks by generating content ideas, headlines, and even rough drafts. Tools like Jasper AI are ideal for brainstorming and automating the early stages of content creation.
- Pro Tip: Whenever Lucy feels stuck, she uses Jasper AI to generate blog post ideas based on client keywords. This gives her a starting point to build on and customize.

3. Automate Tedious Tasks with AI
- Identify areas of your work that can be automated. Whether it's scheduling posts, optimizing SEO, or editing audio, AI tools can handle these tasks, freeing up time for more creative work.

- Example: Lucy schedules social media content across multiple platforms using Hootsuite, which leverages AI to suggest the best times to post for maximum engagement.

Visionary Perspectives: AI's Future in Content Creation

Looking ahead, the role of AI in content creation will continue to evolve, offering even more opportunities for digital nomads to work smarter and faster. Some visionary possibilities include:

1. AI-Enhanced Collaboration: Imagine a world where AI tools assist teams of content creators in real time, suggesting design improvements, optimizing language for different cultures, and automatically translating content for global audiences.

2. AI-Driven Personalization: AI tools could soon tailor content to individual preferences, offering hyper-personalized experiences for readers and viewers. For content creators, this means producing content that resonates with each unique audience segment.

Conclusion: Embrace AI to Enhance Creativity

AI is transforming the work of content creators by reducing the time spent on routine tasks and enhancing the creative process. For digital nomads like Lucy, AI offers the flexibility to produce high-quality content from anywhere in the world while maximizing productivity. By experimenting with AI tools and integrating them into your workflow, you too can unlock new opportunities and thrive in the AI age. The future of content creation is here—are you ready to embrace it?

CHAPTER 13: REMOTE COLLABORATION WITH AI

As Maria settled into her workspace in a bustling café in Barcelona, she marvelled at how seamlessly her work had evolved over the past few years. A project manager for an international tech startup, Maria was coordinating with a global team of developers, designers, and marketers—all without ever stepping foot in a traditional office. Her secret weapon? AI-powered collaboration tools. Thanks to artificial intelligence, Maria and her team were able to communicate across time zones, track project progress, and manage tasks with unprecedented efficiency.

Maria's experience is increasingly common among digital nomads, as AI-enhanced tools redefine the way remote teams collaborate. Whether working from a co-working space in Bali or a mountain retreat in Colorado, digital nomads can now harness AI to streamline communication, automate project management, and foster innovation without geographical constraints.

In this chapter, we'll explore how AI is revolutionizing remote collaboration, highlighting practical examples, tools, and visionary perspectives on how AI is shaping the future of teamwork.

How AI Is Transforming Remote Collaboration

1. AI-Powered Communication Tools

For remote teams, seamless communication is critical. AI-powered communication tools are making it easier to bridge the gap between team members scattered across the globe, offering features like real-time translation, automated meeting summaries, and intelligent chatbots that assist with everything from scheduling to task delegation.

- Slack's AI Bots: Popular among remote teams, Slack uses AI to streamline communication by suggesting relevant channels, automating message sorting, and even providing intelligent chatbots that answer questions and assist with task management.

- Case Study: Maria's team uses Slack's AI bots to automate status updates and answer common questions. By using an AI assistant integrated into Slack, team members can quickly find project information or get help with technical issues without having to ping multiple colleagues, saving time and minimizing interruptions.

- Google Meet AI Features: Video conferencing tools like Google Meet are integrating AI features such as automatic transcription, real-time translation, and meeting summaries. These features help ensure that language barriers and time zone differences don't hinder communication.

- Example: Maria works with team members in Brazil, Japan, and Germany. Thanks to Google Meet's AI-powered real-time translation, they can communicate effectively in their native languages without worrying about miscommunication. After meetings, Google Meet's automatic transcription allows Maria to revisit key points and share summaries with the team.

2. AI for Project Management

Project management in the digital age has evolved with the help of AI. By automating administrative tasks like task delegation, deadline tracking, and performance analysis, AI is helping digital nomads and remote teams focus on high-impact work while ensuring that projects stay on track.

- Trello's AI Automation: Trello, a popular project management tool, has integrated AI features like Butler, an AI-powered automation tool that helps with task assignments, setting reminders, and tracking deadlines.

- Pro Tip: Maria's team uses Butler in Trello to automate recurring tasks and reminders. For example, the AI assistant automatically assigns tasks to team members based on their workload and availability, while also sending reminders when deadlines are approaching, ensuring that nothing falls through the cracks.

- Monday.com AI Insights: Monday.com, another project management tool, uses AI to provide insights into team performance and project progress. AI algorithms analyse productivity patterns and suggest ways to optimize workflow, helping managers make data-driven decisions.

- Example: Maria uses Monday.com's AI insights to monitor her team's performance. The tool highlights which tasks are taking longer than expected and suggests ways to reallocate resources to improve efficiency. This has helped Maria streamline her team's processes and avoid bottlenecks.

3. AI in Task Coordination and Time Management

Time management is a significant challenge for remote teams, especially when coordinating across different time zones. AI tools are helping digital nomads manage their time effectively, providing intelligent scheduling solutions, automating task prioritization, and even adjusting workloads based on individual productivity patterns.

- Clockwise: An AI-powered calendar assistant, Clockwise helps remote teams manage their time by automatically scheduling meetings during team members' optimal hours and protecting focus time by minimizing unnecessary meetings.

- Case Study: Maria's team uses Clockwise to automatically adjust meeting times based on time zone differences and each member's availability. The tool optimizes the team's schedule, ensuring that everyone has enough focus time for deep work, while still allowing for productive collaboration.

- RescueTime: A time management tool powered by AI, RescueTime helps digital nomads track their productivity and optimize their work habits. It analyses how users spend their time and suggests ways to improve focus and efficiency.

- Pro Tip: Maria uses RescueTime to analyse her team's work habits. By identifying periods of peak productivity, she can schedule important tasks during high-energy hours and allocate less demanding tasks to periods when team members are less focused.

Practical Applications: How Digital Nomads Can Leverage AI for Collaboration

1. Automate Repetitive Tasks
- AI-powered tools like Zapier allow digital nomads to automate repetitive tasks between different apps. For instance, you can automate the process of sending follow-up emails after meetings or generating task lists from meeting notes.
- Pro Tip: Maria uses Zapier to automatically transfer

meeting notes from Google Docs into her team's Trello boards, ensuring that no action items are missed and that everything is organized efficiently.

2. Use AI Assistants for Scheduling

- Scheduling across time zones is one of the biggest challenges for remote teams. AI assistants like x.ai help by automatically finding times that work for everyone and even sending meeting invites.

- Example: Maria's team uses x.ai to schedule meetings. The AI assistant takes into account each team member's availability, time zone, and work hours, simplifying the process and avoiding the back-and-forth often involved in manual scheduling.

3. Leverage AI for Team Building

- Building team cohesion can be challenging in a remote work environment, but AI tools like Donut in Slack help foster team culture by automating introductions and encouraging social interactions between team members who don't often work together.

- Pro Tip: Maria uses Donut to schedule virtual coffee chats for her team, ensuring that they get to know each other on a personal level, even if they're working from different parts of the world.

Visionary Perspectives: The Future of AI-Driven Collaboration

As AI continues to evolve, its role in remote collaboration will become even more powerful. Here are a few visionary perspectives on what the future might hold:

1. AI-Powered Virtual Coworking Spaces

- Imagine AI creating virtual coworking spaces where digital nomads can interact with colleagues and other professionals in real-time. AI would facilitate connections based on shared interests or projects, creating a sense of community even in a remote setting.

- Visionary Question: What if your AI assistant could recommend virtual coffee breaks with colleagues in different countries based on shared interests or work schedules?

2. AI-Driven Global Team Management
- AI could soon manage entire remote teams, from assigning tasks to tracking progress and even making hiring recommendations based on team needs and individual skill sets.

- Visionary Forecast: AI-driven team management could revolutionize how digital nomads collaborate, removing much of the administrative burden from managers and allowing them to focus solely on strategy and innovation.

Balancing Opportunity with Caution

While AI offers significant advantages for remote collaboration, there are challenges to consider. Data security, privacy concerns, and over-reliance on AI are potential risks that digital nomads must navigate. It's essential to strike a balance between leveraging AI's capabilities and ensuring that human oversight remains central to decision-making.

Conclusion: Embrace AI to Enhance Teamwork

AI is not only reshaping how digital nomads work individually but also revolutionizing how teams collaborate across borders. By automating communication, optimizing project management, and enhancing task coordination, AI is helping digital nomads like Maria lead global teams more effectively and efficiently. As AI continues to advance, the future of remote collaboration promises to be more connected, productive, and innovative than ever before.

By integrating AI tools into your workflow, you can enhance your team's productivity, foster a culture of collaboration, and create a seamless remote work experience—no matter where in the world you're working from.

CHAPTER 14: BECOMING AN AI EXPERT AS A NOMAD

As Julia sipped her morning coffee in a bustling co-working space in Lisbon, she reflected on how dramatically her career had evolved. Three years ago, she was a web developer juggling freelance projects, unsure of where her next pay check would come from. Today, she is a sought-after AI consultant, working with clients worldwide to implement cutting-edge AI solutions. Her expertise in artificial intelligence, a field that once felt out of reach, has turned her from a typical freelancer into a high-demand specialist. Like many digital nomads, Julia realized early on that the rise of AI wasn't a threat to her livelihood—it was an opportunity to future-proof her career.

In this chapter, we'll explore how digital nomads can specialize in AI fields to secure their place in the rapidly changing world of work. Through storytelling, practical applications, and visionary insights, this chapter will provide a roadmap for how you can develop AI expertise, thrive as a digital nomad, and elevate your career to the next level.

Why AI Expertise Matters for Digital Nomads

The world of work is transforming, with AI increasingly becoming a core component of most industries. From marketing and design to software development and consulting, AI tools and technologies are being adopted at a fast pace, creating new opportunities for those who master them. For digital nomads, specializing in AI offers several benefits:

1. Increased Demand for Skills: AI experts are in high demand, and this demand will only grow as companies seek to integrate AI into their processes.

   - Example: Julia leveraged her web development background and took online courses on machine learning and AI, which quickly positioned her as an expert in a growing niche. Soon after, she started landing clients who needed AI-driven solutions for their digital products.

2. Higher Earning Potential: As AI expertise becomes more valuable, those with specialized skills in this field can command higher rates for freelance work, consultations, and projects.

   - Case Study: Julia's pivot to AI allowed her to charge premium rates for her consulting services. Whereas her previous freelance gigs paid around $40 per hour, her expertise in AI now commands rates upwards of $150 per hour.

3. Future-Proofing Your Career: As AI continues to automate routine tasks, having expertise in this field ensures that your career remains relevant and adaptable to the changing demands of the job market.

   - Pro Tip: Start by learning AI tools that are already transforming your industry. Whether you're a designer, marketer, or developer, there are AI applications relevant to your field. By gaining a deep understanding of these tools, you position yourself ahead of the curve.

How to Start Specializing in AI as a Digital Nomad

1. Identify Your Niche in AI

AI is a vast field, and it's essential to narrow your focus to areas that align with your current skills and interests. As a digital nomad, you can specialize in various aspects of AI, including:

- AI-Powered Marketing: Learn how to use AI for data analysis, predictive modelling, and content generation in digital marketing.
- AI in Software Development: Explore AI-driven algorithms, machine learning, and natural language processing (NLP) to develop smarter applications.
- AI for Graphic Design: Master tools like Adobe Sensei or RunwayML, which use AI to automate and enhance the creative design process.

- Example: Julia decided to focus on AI in software development, specifically machine learning algorithms, which allowed her to offer AI-powered solutions for automating business processes for her clients.

2. Take Online AI Courses

There is a wealth of online resources to help you develop AI expertise. Platforms like Coursera, Udemy, and edX offer courses in AI, machine learning, and data science from top universities and tech companies.

- Pro Tip: Start with beginner-friendly courses like Andrew Ng's Machine Learning course on Coursera to build a foundational understanding of AI concepts. Once you're comfortable, move on to more advanced courses on deep learning and AI programming.

- Practical Application: Julia began her AI education by taking courses on Python and TensorFlow—two essential tools in AI programming. After completing several projects and obtaining certifications, she was able to integrate AI-driven solutions into her freelance services.

3. Build a Portfolio of AI Projects

To gain credibility and showcase your skills, start building a portfolio of AI projects. This could include personal projects, collaborations with other digital nomads, or case studies from client work. Displaying real-world applications of AI will help potential clients and employers see the value you bring.

- Pro Tip: Create a GitHub repository for your AI projects or build a personal website where you can share case studies, project outcomes, and insights into how you applied AI to solve problems.

4. Stay Updated on AI Trends and Tools

AI is an ever-evolving field, and staying updated on the latest trends and tools is crucial to maintaining your competitive edge. Follow AI thought leaders, attend online conferences, and subscribe to AI-focused newsletters to stay informed.

- Pro Tip: Julia subscribes to newsletters like The Batch and follows prominent AI figures like Andrew Ng and Yann LeCun to stay updated on the latest advancements in machine learning and AI ethics.

Practical Application: AI Toolbox for Digital Nomads

As you specialize in AI, here are some essential tools and technologies you should become familiar with:

- Python and TensorFlow: These are the foundational programming languages and libraries for building AI and machine learning applications.
- Hugging Face: A popular platform for natural language processing models and applications, essential for those working with language-driven AI.

- AutoML Tools: Platforms like Google AutoML and H2O.ai allow non-experts to develop machine learning models without extensive coding experience.
- AI Design Tools: For those in creative fields, AI-driven tools like RunwayML and Artbreeder allow you to create visuals and animations with the help of machine learning.

Visionary Perspectives: The Future of AI Expertise

Looking ahead, the possibilities for digital nomads with AI expertise are limitless. AI will continue to permeate every industry, from healthcare to entertainment. Those who master these technologies will have the freedom to work on the most cutting-edge projects, potentially shaping the future of AI itself.

1. AI-Driven Nomad Communities: Imagine digital nomads specializing in AI coming together to form communities, sharing knowledge, and collaborating on AI-driven startups and initiatives across the globe.

2. AI-Enhanced Skill Sharing: The future may also see AI being used to accelerate learning for nomads. AI mentors could personalize learning paths, helping digital nomads acquire new AI-related skills more efficiently.

Balancing the Opportunities with Caution

While the opportunities are vast, it's important to acknowledge some of the challenges that come with specializing in AI. Ethical concerns, such as bias in AI algorithms or data privacy issues, must be addressed. Digital nomads should not only become proficient in AI technologies but also mindful of the ethical implications of their work.

Conclusion: Your Path to AI Expertise

Specializing in AI as a digital nomad is more than just a

smart career move—it's a chance to future-proof your work and ensure you remain at the forefront of technological innovation. Like Julia, you can leverage the flexibility of the nomadic lifestyle while carving out a niche in one of the most exciting fields of the 21st century. With the right focus, education, and tools, you can become an AI expert, unlocking new opportunities and creating a fulfilling, purpose-driven career in the age of artificial intelligence.

So, are you ready to take the leap into AI and redefine your future as a digital nomad?

CHAPTER 15: AI AND THE FUTURE OF CODING

As Jackson wandered through the narrow, cobblestone streets of Prague, he couldn't help but marvel at how different his life had become. Just a few years ago, Jackson had been confined to a corporate office in San Francisco, working long hours as a software developer. Now, he was free. Free to travel the world, set his own schedule, and still get more done in less time, all thanks to the power of AI. With AI-powered coding tools at his disposal, Jackson had slashed his development time by half, allowing him to take on more clients and pursue personal projects that once seemed impossible.

This chapter delves into the transformative impact AI is having on coding, particularly for digital nomads like Jackson. As the boundaries of remote work expand, AI is making coding faster, smarter, and more efficient. By exploring the personal stories of digital nomads who have successfully integrated AI into their workflows, we'll unpack the practical tools and trends reshaping the world of development.

How AI is Revolutionizing Coding for Digital Nomads

Artificial intelligence is no longer just a futuristic buzzword —it's actively changing how developers and engineers work.

From automated code generation to intelligent debugging, AI is empowering coders to optimize their processes and produce higher-quality work with greater speed.

1. Automating Repetitive Tasks

One of the most significant ways AI is transforming coding is by automating repetitive and mundane tasks, allowing developers to focus on more complex and creative challenges. AI tools like GitHub Copilot, powered by OpenAI's Codex, can write boilerplate code, suggest snippets, and even auto-complete entire functions based on natural language input.

- Story: Jackson recalls how he used to spend hours writing repetitive code for backend applications. "It was mind-numbing work, but necessary," he says. Now, with AI tools like GitHub Copilot, those hours have turned into minutes. "I can describe what I need, and the AI writes the skeleton of the code for me. It's like having an assistant who never tires."

2. Error Detection and Debugging

Debugging is often cited as one of the most time-consuming aspects of software development. AI-powered tools are changing that. Platforms like DeepCode and TabNine are capable of detecting errors in real-time, suggesting fixes, and even predicting potential bugs before they arise.

- Practical Tip: Developers should integrate AI debugging tools into their daily workflow to catch bugs early. Tools like DeepCode analyse your code as you write, offering suggestions for optimization and error prevention, making debugging less of a hassle.

3. Learning New Languages and Frameworks

Another way AI is empowering digital nomad developers

is by making it easier to learn new programming languages and frameworks. AI-driven learning platforms like CodeSignal and LeetCode offer personalized learning experiences that help coders quickly pick up new languages based on their prior knowledge and experience.

- Case Study: For Jackson, this meant picking up Rust and Kotlin in just a few months—something he had always wanted to do but never had the time for. By using AI-powered learning platforms, he quickly became proficient in both languages and added them to his freelance skillset.

Practical Applications for Digital Nomads

As digital nomads navigate the evolving world of coding, AI tools offer numerous opportunities to work more efficiently and stay competitive in the remote work market. Below are some practical applications and tips for integrating AI into your workflow:

1. AI Code Generation Tools: Tools like GitHub Copilot, TabNine, and Kite assist in code generation by predicting and auto-completing code snippets. These tools are perfect for developers who want to speed up routine tasks or generate quick prototypes.

- AI Toolbox: Start by incorporating GitHub Copilot into your IDE (integrated development environment) like VS Code. Test how it can accelerate your coding process and free up time for more creative problem-solving.

2. Smart Refactoring and Optimization: Platforms like Refactor.ai can optimize and refactor your code, making it more efficient and easier to maintain. This is particularly useful for digital nomads working on long-term projects where maintaining clean, efficient code is essential.

- Practical Example: Julia, a digital nomad who specializes in mobile app development, uses Refactor.ai to streamline her app's performance. The AI-powered tool scans her code, identifies inefficient loops, and suggests more efficient alternatives.

3. Collaboration and Remote Teamwork: AI is enhancing collaboration for developers working remotely. Tools like Codacy and CodeClimate allow for continuous code quality monitoring across teams, while Slack bots powered by AI help manage projects by automating updates and code reviews.

- Pro Tip: If you work on collaborative projects, integrate AI-powered project management tools like Jira with GitHub Copilot to streamline team workflows, automatically generate reports, and ensure consistent code quality.

Visionary Perspectives: The Future of Coding with AI

Looking ahead, the possibilities for AI in coding are vast. The future promises even more sophisticated AI tools that can handle entire workflows—from code conception to deployment—leaving developers with the freedom to focus on innovation, strategy, and creativity.

1. End-to-End AI-Driven Development: Imagine a world where AI tools handle entire development cycles, from planning to deployment. Developers would collaborate with AI on high-level problem-solving, while AI handles the grunt work, making coding faster and more efficient.

- Visionary Question: As AI becomes more integrated into the coding process, what role will human developers play? Will AI tools eventually replace coders entirely, or will they simply enhance the creative and strategic aspects of software development?

2. AI-Enhanced Cross-Disciplinary Collaboration: AI could also act as a bridge between different fields, enabling developers to work more closely with designers, data

scientists, and business strategists. AI-driven project management tools could synthesize feedback from multiple stakeholders and create unified action plans.

- Pro Tip: Keep an eye on emerging AI tools that enhance interdisciplinary collaboration. As a digital nomad, being able to seamlessly integrate feedback from different fields into your coding process will be a valuable skill.

Balancing Innovation with Caution

While the opportunities are immense, AI in coding also brings challenges. For instance, over-reliance on AI-generated code can lead to less creativity and critical thinking. It's essential for developers to maintain a balance between leveraging AI tools and honing their foundational coding skills.

1. Ethical Considerations: As AI becomes more involved in the coding process, ethical questions arise, such as the responsibility for errors made by AI-generated code or the potential job displacement of entry-level developers.

2. Continuous Learning: The rapid advancement of AI means developers must stay vigilant and continue learning new tools and technologies. By staying adaptable and open to continuous education, digital nomads can ensure they remain relevant and competitive in the marketplace.

Conclusion: Thriving as a Digital Nomad in the AI-Powered Coding World

AI is undeniably transforming the way developers work, offering unprecedented speed, efficiency, and problem-solving capabilities. However, the human element remains crucial. As Jackson discovered, AI can't replace the creativity, strategy, and innovation that only human developers bring to the table. For digital nomads, AI is not a threat, but an opportunity—a powerful tool to enhance workflows, expand skillsets, and create more freedom in work and life.

By embracing AI, you can future-proof your coding career while continuing to enjoy the flexibility and freedom of the digital nomad lifestyle. So, whether you're developing mobile apps, building websites, or diving into machine learning, AI offers the tools you need to thrive in an ever-evolving world. Are you ready to harness the power of AI and take your coding career to new heights? The future is in your hands.

PART 4: OPTIMIZING WORK WITH AI

CHAPTER 16: PRODUCTIVITY HACKS USING AI

As the sun dipped behind the mountains in Chiang Mai, Emma sat at a cozy café, sipping a fresh coconut juice while effortlessly managing three clients across different time zones. A few years ago, this would have been impossible —juggling so many projects, meeting tight deadlines, and maintaining her travel lifestyle. But today, AI-driven productivity tools have become her secret weapon. From automating emails to scheduling content and streamlining project management, AI has revolutionized the way she works, allowing her to achieve more in less time.

For digital nomads like Emma, productivity is not just a goal —it's a necessity. Being location-independent requires the ability to work from anywhere, often with limited resources and varying internet connectivity. In this chapter, we'll explore how AI tools are helping digital nomads like Emma thrive by boosting productivity and efficiency. With real-life case studies and actionable tips, this chapter will empower readers to harness the full potential of AI for their work and lifestyle.

Engage with Storytelling: Emma's Journey

Emma is a digital marketing consultant who left her 9-to-5 job in New York to become a full-time digital nomad.

Initially, the transition was tough. She struggled with time management, client communication, and staying organized while constantly on the move. Then, she discovered the power of AI tools to automate her workflow.

One of the first tools Emma integrated into her routine was Zapier, a platform that connects apps and automates repetitive tasks. For example, every time she receives a new client email, Zapier automatically creates a task in her project management software, Asana, and schedules a follow-up. This simple automation freed up hours in her week, allowing her to focus on higher-value tasks like strategy and creativity.

Now, Emma uses AI not only to automate administrative work but also to improve her creative output. With Jasper AI, she drafts social media content for clients in minutes, while Grammarly ensures her writing is polished and error-free. As Emma's story illustrates, AI isn't just about making work easier—it's about unlocking new levels of productivity that allow digital nomads to thrive in a fast-paced, ever-changing world.

Focus on Practical Application: AI Tools for Productivity

To truly maximize productivity, digital nomads need tools that can streamline their workflow and help them focus on what matters most. Here are some of the top AI-driven tools that can help digital nomads work smarter, not harder:

1. Zapier: Automate Your Workflow
   - What It Does: Zapier connects your apps and automates workflows by setting up "Zaps" (automated tasks) between different platforms. For example, it can automatically send data from Gmail to Trello, or post social media updates when a blog is published.
   - How to Use It: Digital nomads can use Zapier to automate recurring tasks, such as creating invoices, scheduling emails,

and organizing client data. For instance, if you manage multiple clients, Zapier can create a system that tracks incoming inquiries and categorizes them by priority.

2. Trello & AI-Powered Project Management

- What It Does: Trello is a popular project management tool, and with AI integrations like Butler for Trello, you can automate common tasks such as moving cards based on due dates or assigning tasks to team members based on workloads.

- How to Use It: Butler for Trello allows digital nomads to streamline their project management by setting up rules and triggers. For example, you can automate task reminders or status updates based on card movements, keeping your projects on track without manual input.

3. Grammarly: AI Writing Assistant

- What It Does: Grammarly uses AI to improve the quality of your writing. It checks for grammar, punctuation, tone, and style, ensuring that your communications are professional and polished.

- How to Use It: Whether you're drafting client proposals, writing blog posts, or managing social media, Grammarly helps ensure your writing is error-free. Its AI-powered suggestions save time on editing and give you confidence in the clarity of your messaging.

4. Jasper AI: Content Creation

- What It Does: Jasper AI (formerly Jarvis) is an AI-powered content generation tool that can write blog posts, social media content, and marketing copy. It helps digital nomads create content faster and more efficiently by generating ideas and drafts based on prompts.

- How to Use It: Jasper AI is ideal for digital nomads who manage multiple clients or projects and need to generate content at scale. You can input a topic or keyword, and Jasper AI will create a full draft, freeing up time for strategy and refinement.

Inspire Through Visionary Perspectives: The Future of AI-Enhanced Productivity

As AI tools continue to evolve, the future of productivity for digital nomads looks more promising than ever. Imagine a world where AI acts as your personal assistant, seamlessly managing your schedule, communicating with clients, and even suggesting new business opportunities.

1. AI as a Personal Productivity Assistant

- In the near future, AI assistants like Google Duplex could schedule meetings, manage client interactions, and even book travel on your behalf. These tools will allow digital nomads to focus on creativity and strategic thinking while AI handles the logistics.

- Visionary Question: What would your ideal day look like if AI handled all the mundane tasks? How would you spend your time if you were free to focus solely on high-value activities?

2. AI-Powered Virtual Offices

- As remote work becomes more sophisticated, AI will play a key role in creating virtual offices that mimic the efficiency of physical workplaces. Tools like Slackbot and Microsoft AI are already streamlining team communication and task management, but future advancements could include fully AI-managed teams, where AI assigns tasks based on real-time analysis of workloads and skills.

- Visionary Thought: Imagine a virtual office where AI not only manages tasks but also predicts potential bottlenecks and proactively solves problems before they arise. This future could make remote collaboration seamless, no matter where in the world you are.

Balance Between Inspiration and Caution: Productivity

Challenges with AI

While AI tools offer tremendous productivity benefits, they also come with challenges. Over-reliance on automation can lead to a loss of personal touch, especially in client communications. Additionally, there's the risk of burnout if AI increases expectations for what can be accomplished in a short time.

1. Avoiding Over-Automation

- As a digital nomad, it's crucial to maintain a balance between automation and personal connection. While AI can handle administrative tasks, it's important to maintain meaningful interactions with clients, colleagues, and partners.

- Pro Tip: Use AI to streamline tasks but leave room for personal creativity and connection. Automation should enhance your work, not replace the human touch that builds strong relationships.

2. Maintaining Work-Life Balance

- AI can make us more efficient, but it can also blur the line between work and life. With tools that allow you to work faster, it's easy to fall into the trap of doing more work, rather than taking time to rest and recharge.

- Solution: Set boundaries for when and how you use AI tools. Use automation to create more free time for travel, hobbies, and personal growth—after all, that's what the digital nomad lifestyle is all about.

Motivate with Purpose: AI as a Tool for Fulfilment

AI isn't just about boosting productivity—it's about freeing up time to pursue what truly matters. For digital nomads, that might mean more time to explore new cultures, develop personal passions, or engage in meaningful projects.

- Final Thought: By using AI to optimize your work processes, you're not just becoming more efficient—you're gaining the freedom to live a more fulfilling and balanced life. Whether that means traveling the world, deepening your relationships, or simply taking a break from the hustle, AI is a powerful tool to help you create the lifestyle you desire.

Conclusion: The Productivity Revolution for Digital Nomads

AI-driven productivity tools are transforming the way digital nomads work, allowing them to achieve more in less time and with greater flexibility. By integrating automation, content creation, and project management tools into their workflows, digital nomads can unlock new levels of efficiency while maintaining the freedom and flexibility that defines their lifestyle.

As the digital landscape continues to evolve, the question isn't whether AI will enhance productivity—it's how you will use it to thrive. With the right tools and mindset, AI can be your greatest ally in the quest for balance, fulfilment, and success as a digital nomad.

CHAPTER 17: TIME MANAGEMENT WITH AI ASSISTANTS

As the sun rose over the beaches of Bali, Jake's phone buzzed with a gentle reminder from his AI assistant. His agenda for the day was simple yet efficient—three client meetings spaced out just enough to enjoy a midday surf, with a clear timeline for wrapping up his freelance project by sunset. What Jake once spent hours manually organizing now takes mere minutes thanks to the power of AI assistants. For digital nomads like Jake, time management isn't just a skill; it's the key to maintaining both productivity and the freedom to enjoy life.

In this chapter, we explore how digital nomads are leveraging AI assistants to optimize their schedules, meet deadlines, and streamline workflows—all while maintaining the flexibility and autonomy that define the nomadic lifestyle.

Engage with Storytelling: Jake's AI-Powered Routine

Jake, a web developer who has been living the digital nomad lifestyle for the past five years, used to struggle with keeping track of meetings, deadlines, and client updates while traveling. He loved the freedom of working from exotic locations, but the constant need to juggle different time zones and client expectations became overwhelming.

That changed when he discovered the power of AI-powered personal assistants.

Jake integrated Google Assistant into his workflow, and now his day-to-day activities are effortlessly managed by the AI. Whether it's reminding him about an important client meeting in a different time zone or automatically setting up his weekly planning sessions, Google Assistant ensures Jake stays on top of his work while freeing up mental energy for creative tasks.

AI assistants like Google Assistant, Cortana, and Siri are transforming how digital nomads like Jake organize their lives. These AI tools have become indispensable for time management, helping nomads stay productive without sacrificing their freedom.

Focus on Practical Application: AI Assistants for Time Management

For digital nomads, effective time management is essential for balancing client work, travel, and personal projects. Here are some practical ways AI assistants can help optimize your time:

1. Scheduling and Calendar Management
   - What It Does: AI assistants like Google Calendar and Microsoft Cortana can automatically schedule meetings, block out time for deep work, and send reminders for upcoming deadlines. They can sync across devices, ensuring you never miss an appointment, regardless of your location.
   - How to Use It: Use AI assistants to set up daily agendas, integrate time zone adjustments, and even schedule leisure activities like exercise or cultural exploration. You can also set up recurring tasks, like weekly reviews or project milestones, to keep your workflow consistent and organized.

2. Task Prioritization

- What It Does: AI tools such as Todoist use natural language processing to help prioritize tasks based on urgency and importance. They can analyse your workload and suggest the best time to tackle high-priority tasks.

- How to Use It: Input your tasks into the AI assistant and let it help prioritize them. By using AI to organize your daily to-do list, you can focus on what matters most, whether it's delivering a client project or carving out time for a personal passion.

3. Automating Repetitive Tasks

- What It Does: AI assistants can automate repetitive tasks such as sending follow-up emails, invoicing clients, and organizing files. Tools like Zapier and IFTTT allow you to create automated workflows between different apps and services.

- How to Use It: Set up automation for routine tasks like sending out client updates, organizing project files in cloud storage, or even logging your work hours. With AI handling these tasks, you can focus on creative or strategic work that requires your attention.

4. Focus and Distraction Management

- What It Does: Tools like RescueTime and Focus@Will leverage AI to help you maintain focus during work sessions. They can analyse your work habits and suggest productivity-boosting techniques, such as blocking distracting websites or scheduling deep work periods.

- How to Use It: Use AI tools to track your work patterns, eliminate distractions, and set focus blocks for uninterrupted work. AI can also recommend optimal break times to help you recharge, keeping you productive throughout the day.

Inspire Through Visionary Perspectives: The Future of AI-Assisted Time Management

The future of AI-powered time management for digital nomads is filled with exciting possibilities. As AI continues to advance, we will see increasingly intuitive and personalized time management tools that cater to the specific needs of individuals and remote teams.

1. AI as a Personalized Time Manager

- Imagine AI assistants evolving into personalized life managers that not only schedule meetings but also anticipate upcoming deadlines, suggest new learning opportunities, and provide real-time insights on how to optimize your day based on your productivity patterns. AI could monitor your workload, adjust your schedule in real-time, and even suggest when to take a break to avoid burnout.

- Visionary Question: How would your workday change if an AI assistant could proactively manage every aspect of your time, leaving you free to focus on what you love?

2. AI and Predictive Analytics for Workflow Optimization

- In the future, AI assistants could analyse your work habits over time and use predictive analytics to make workflow recommendations. For instance, AI could identify the best times of day for you to work on creative projects or suggest when to schedule meetings based on your energy levels.

- Visionary Thought: As AI tools become more intuitive, they will not only manage your current schedule but also predict future needs, helping you stay ahead of deadlines and client demands.

Balance Between Inspiration and Caution: Time Management Challenges

While AI assistants offer immense benefits for time management, there are challenges to consider. The constant availability of AI tools can make it tempting to over-schedule your day, leading to burnout. Additionally, relying too heavily on automation can cause you to lose sight of personal engagement with clients or creative spontaneity in your work.

1. Avoiding Over-Scheduling

- One of the biggest risks of using AI assistants is the temptation to over-schedule your day, leaving little room for flexibility. It's important to leave gaps in your schedule for unexpected opportunities, whether they're professional or personal.

- Pro Tip: Use AI to create a flexible, not rigid, schedule. Allow for time buffers between tasks and meetings to avoid feeling overwhelmed.

2. Maintaining a Personal Touch

- While AI assistants can handle much of the scheduling and organizing, there's still a need for human interaction. Over-automation can make your interactions feel impersonal, especially when working with clients.

- Solution: Use AI assistants for administrative work, but be mindful to maintain personal communication with clients. A quick personalized message or follow-up email can strengthen relationships and build trust.

Motivate with Purpose: AI Assistants as Tools for a Balanced Life

AI assistants aren't just about increasing productivity—they're about creating space for a more balanced and fulfilling life. By optimizing your schedule, these tools give you the freedom to focus on what truly matters—whether that's growing your business, exploring new cultures, or spending quality time with loved ones.

- Final Thought: By integrating AI assistants into your

workflow, you can unlock the potential for a more intentional and purposeful lifestyle. Whether it's finding more time for passion projects or exploring new destinations, AI can help you achieve the work-life balance you desire.

Conclusion: The Time Management Revolution for Digital Nomads

AI-powered assistants are revolutionizing how digital nomads manage their time. From automating schedules to optimizing workflows, these tools provide the structure and flexibility needed to maintain productivity while embracing the nomadic lifestyle. By harnessing the power of AI, digital nomads can achieve more in less time, all while enjoying the freedom and adventure that comes with location-independent work.

As AI continues to evolve, the future of time management is bright, promising even greater efficiencies and more personalized experiences for digital nomads. The key is to embrace these tools as enablers, allowing you to focus on the tasks that matter most while ensuring a fulfilling and balanced life on the road.

CHAPTER 18: AI-POWERED PERSONALIZATION FOR CLIENT PROJECTS

Sarah, a freelance digital marketer, found herself struggling to keep up with the diverse needs of her growing client base. Each client required unique strategies, tailored content, and personalized attention—tasks that quickly became overwhelming as her workload expanded. Then, she discovered AI tools like HubSpot, Jasper AI, and Phrasee. By leveraging these platforms, Sarah could provide hyper-personalized marketing strategies for each client without burning out. What used to take days of manual customization was now automated, allowing Sarah to focus on creativity and strategy.

For digital nomads like Sarah, AI is not just a productivity tool; it's a game-changer in how client services are delivered. In this chapter, we'll explore how AI-powered personalization is revolutionizing the freelance economy, allowing nomads to deliver exceptional, tailored services while maintaining flexibility in their work.

Engage with Storytelling: Sarah's AI-Powered Success

Sarah's workload reached a tipping point as she juggled a growing client list that spanned across multiple industries. Each business required tailored social media posts, email marketing campaigns, and SEO strategies. Personalizing these services for each client was draining her energy and time, making it impossible for her to maintain the quality of service she prided herself on.

That's when Sarah turned to AI-powered platforms like HubSpot to automate client data collection and segmentation, Jasper AI to generate personalized content for blogs and social media, and Phrasee to create customized marketing copy that resonated with her clients' specific target audiences. By integrating AI into her workflow, Sarah saw a 40% increase in productivity and was able to handle more clients without sacrificing quality.

Through AI, Sarah could automatically gather client data, analyse audience behaviour, and generate personalized marketing strategies—all within minutes. She no longer felt like she was sacrificing her personal time for work. Instead, she found a new balance that allowed her to deliver excellent results while traveling and exploring new places.

Focus on Practical Application: How to Personalize Client Services Using AI

AI offers digital nomads a suite of tools that make personalizing client services not only manageable but also scalable. Here are practical ways you can integrate AI into your workflow to deliver personalized experiences for your clients:

1. Client Data Collection and Analysis
   - What It Does: Tools like HubSpot and Salesforce use AI to automatically collect and analyse client data, segmenting audiences based on behaviour, preferences, and interactions.

This allows you to tailor services to meet specific client needs with precision.

- How to Use It: Set up automated workflows that gather insights from your clients' customers. Use these insights to create targeted marketing campaigns, personalized offers, and strategic recommendations that are relevant to your client's audience.

2. Content Personalization

- What It Does: AI tools like Jasper AI, Copy.ai, and Writesonic help digital nomads create personalized content for blogs, social media, and email marketing. These platforms generate contextually relevant content based on audience data.

- How to Use It: Input the details of your client's target audience into these tools to generate customized marketing materials. You can quickly create personalized emails, blog posts, and social media content that speaks directly to specific audience segments, increasing engagement and conversion rates.

3. Automated Communication

- What It Does: AI-powered chatbots like Intercom and Drift can engage with your client's customers 24/7, offering personalized responses based on the customer's history and preferences. These chatbots help provide real-time customer service and nurture leads.

- How to Use It: Set up AI chatbots on your client's website or social media platforms. These bots can handle customer inquiries, provide personalized product recommendations, and collect valuable customer data, freeing up your time to focus on higher-level tasks.

4. Predictive Analytics for Personalization

- What It Does: AI platforms like Google Analytics and Adobe Sensei use predictive analytics to forecast customer behaviour based on historical data. This allows you to anticipate customer needs and personalize offerings accordingly.

- How to Use It: Use predictive analytics to recommend product or service changes to your clients based on upcoming trends or forecasted customer behaviour. AI can help you predict what a client's audience is likely to want next, allowing you to stay ahead of the curve and continuously offer fresh, personalized services.

Inspire Through Visionary Perspectives: The Future of AI-Powered Personalization

The future of AI-powered personalization is bright, offering even deeper customization and client engagement than ever before. As AI tools continue to evolve, digital nomads will be able to provide highly personalized services that are not only efficient but also deeply intuitive to their client's needs.

1. Hyper-Personalization at Scale
- In the near future, AI will be able to provide hyper-personalization that goes beyond content or marketing strategies. AI could help you create tailored experiences for individual customers based on real-time data, allowing digital nomads to deliver services that feel uniquely crafted for each client.

- Visionary Question: How would your services evolve if AI could provide real-time personalization for each individual customer, adapting to their needs instantly?

2. AI-Driven Creativity
- AI is already assisting with content creation, but the future could see AI taking a more active role in shaping creative strategies based on customer feedback and engagement. Imagine AI tools that can brainstorm and generate creative concepts, offering multiple personalized versions of a marketing campaign for your client to choose from.

- Visionary Thought: As AI evolves, it will no longer be limited to automating tasks. It will actively contribute to creative processes, pushing the boundaries of what's possible in personalized client services.

Balance Between Inspiration and Caution: Personalization Without Losing the Human Touch

While AI can automate and enhance personalization, it's crucial to maintain a human touch in client interactions. Too much reliance on automation can risk alienating customers if the personalized services feel robotic or impersonal. Here's how to strike a balance:

1. Avoid Over-Automation

- Over-automation can lead to impersonal client relationships. It's important to know when to step in and add a human element, such as customizing emails or reaching out personally to clients to build rapport.

- Pro Tip: Use AI tools to handle repetitive tasks and data analysis, but keep human oversight on key decisions like finalizing creative strategies or handling complex client issues.

2. Maintaining Authenticity

- AI can help you create personalized content, but authenticity is still key. Clients and their customers can tell the difference between generic automation and thoughtful personalization.

- Solution: Use AI to support your creativity but ensure the final product has a personal touch. Whether it's tweaking copy generated by AI or adding your own insights, authenticity will help you stand out in a crowded marketplace.

Motivate with Purpose: Personalization for Meaningful

Client Relationships

AI allows digital nomads to do more than just deliver services—it enables them to create meaningful, personalized relationships with clients. By using AI to handle the technical aspects of personalization, you can focus on building deeper connections with your clients and helping them achieve their goals.

- Final Thought: AI-powered personalization isn't just about efficiency; it's about enhancing the quality of your services. By understanding your clients' unique needs and using AI to meet those needs, you're not just delivering a service— you're providing a solution that feels personal, relevant, and impactful.

Conclusion: Revolutionizing Client Services with AI

AI-powered personalization is revolutionizing how digital nomads work with clients. By using AI to gather data, create personalized content, and automate customer interactions, nomads can deliver services that are highly tailored to each client's needs without sacrificing flexibility or freedom. As AI continues to advance, the opportunities for deeper, more meaningful client engagement will only grow, allowing digital nomads to thrive in a competitive global marketplace.

The future of client services is personal—and AI is making it possible to deliver that personalization at scale. Whether you're just starting out or looking to expand your offerings, AI tools provide the foundation for building lasting, personalized client relationships that set you apart as a digital nomad.

CHAPTER 19: AI FOR SCALING BUSINESSES

As Sarah packed her bags in Chiang Mai, Thailand, for her next destination, she reflected on how far she had come. Just two years ago, she was managing a handful of freelance clients, constantly hustling to keep up with deadlines. But now, with the help of AI tools, she had grown her freelance business into a scalable digital marketing agency that handled over 30 clients from around the world. The best part? She could still live her dream of being a digital nomad, working from anywhere, without sacrificing the quality of service she provided.

For digital nomads like Sarah, scaling a business while maintaining a flexible lifestyle used to be an unattainable dream. However, AI is making that dream a reality. In this chapter, we will explore how digital nomads can use AI to scale their businesses, manage multiple clients efficiently, and automate key aspects of their operations—all while maintaining the freedom to travel and explore the world.

Engage with Storytelling: Sarah's Journey to Scaling with AI

Sarah's journey to scaling her business began when she realized she was hitting a ceiling. As a freelancer, she could only take on so many clients before her work quality began to suffer. That's when she started exploring AI tools that could help automate repetitive tasks, streamline communication, and optimize workflows.

One of her biggest challenges was managing client communication. With multiple clients in different time zones, Sarah found it overwhelming to stay on top of emails and project updates. She discovered AI-powered CRM tools like HubSpot and Zoho CRM, which allowed her to automate client communications, send personalized updates, and manage customer relationships effortlessly.

Sarah also integrated project management tools like Trello and Asana that used AI to track project progress, send reminders, and even predict bottlenecks in workflows. By automating these time-consuming tasks, Sarah was able to focus on higher-level strategy and creative work, which allowed her to onboard more clients without burning out.

Focus on Practical Application: Using AI to Scale Your Business

Scaling a business while maintaining a digital nomad lifestyle can feel daunting, but AI offers practical solutions to help you manage multiple clients, streamline processes, and expand your services. Here are actionable steps to integrate AI into your business for efficient scaling:

1. Automating Client Communication
   - What It Does: AI-powered CRM tools like HubSpot and Zoho CRM can handle client communication by automating follow-up emails, sending personalized updates, and managing client data.
   - How to Use It: Set up automated workflows that keep your clients informed at every stage of a project. For instance,

you can automate status updates, send reminders for upcoming deadlines, and even offer personalized marketing recommendations based on client data.

- Benefits: This allows you to maintain consistent communication with multiple clients without manually drafting each email, saving you time and reducing errors.

2. Streamlining Project Management

- What It Does: AI-powered project management tools like Asana and Trello help digital nomads manage multiple projects by predicting workflow bottlenecks, tracking progress, and sending reminders.

- How to Use It: Use AI-powered automation to assign tasks, track deadlines, and monitor project progress across different time zones. These tools can also help you manage team collaborations if you're working with other freelancers or contractors.

- Benefits: AI ensures that projects stay on track without constant oversight, enabling you to handle more clients and larger projects with ease.

3. Content Automation

- What It Does: AI tools like Jasper AI, Grammarly, and Writesonic can generate content, edit drafts, and provide suggestions for improving tone and readability.

- How to Use It: Use AI to automate content creation for clients, from generating blog posts to drafting social media updates. You can also use AI tools to ensure the content meets SEO standards and resonates with specific target audiences.

- Benefits: Automating content production allows you to offer high-quality, personalized content for multiple clients without being bogged down by the manual writing process.

4. Automating Financial Management

- What It Does: AI-powered financial tools like QuickBooks and Xero automate invoicing, track expenses, and manage client payments, helping digital nomads stay on top of their finances.

- How to Use It: Set up automatic invoicing systems, track expenses in real-time, and generate financial reports that give you insight into your profitability and client retention.

- Benefits: Automating your financial management allows you to scale your business without spending hours manually creating invoices or tracking payments, freeing up time for client work.

Inspire Through Visionary Perspectives: The Future of AI-Driven Scaling

AI's role in business scaling is only expected to grow. As the technology evolves, digital nomads will have access to even more advanced tools that will allow them to operate at a level previously reserved for large corporations.

1. AI as a Business Partner

- Imagine AI tools that can autonomously manage key aspects of your business—from acquiring new clients to managing customer satisfaction—allowing you to scale exponentially. In the near future, AI could act as a "virtual business partner," handling operations, marketing, and customer service while you focus on strategic growth.

- Visionary Question: What if AI could manage your entire client workflow, leaving you free to focus solely on creativity and innovation?

2. Global Expansion Made Easy

- AI is also enabling digital nomads to expand their businesses globally with ease. With translation tools like Google AI and DeepL, communication barriers are breaking down, allowing nomads to work with clients from diverse cultural and linguistic backgrounds. AI will continue to make global expansion seamless by automating compliance with international regulations and providing localized business strategies.

- Visionary Thought: In the future, scaling your business globally won't just be possible—it will be the norm, thanks to AI-driven tools that localize services for different markets around the world.

Balance Between Inspiration and Caution: Don't Lose the Human Touch

While AI offers endless possibilities for scaling your business, it's essential to balance automation with a personal touch. Relying too heavily on AI can sometimes make your services feel impersonal. Here's how to find the balance:

1. Maintain Personal Client Relationships

- Use AI for administrative tasks and client management, but always inject personal communication when it matters. AI can handle routine updates, but personal check-ins with clients build long-term relationships.

- Pro Tip: Schedule time to personally reach out to key clients, even if AI tools are handling most of the communication. A quick, thoughtful message or a personal update can go a long way in maintaining client satisfaction.

2. Customization Over Automation

- While AI can automate content and marketing strategies, it's important to ensure the final product aligns with your client's unique voice and vision.

- Solution: Use AI as a support tool, but always review and customize final outputs to maintain authenticity and creativity in your work.

Motivate with Purpose: Scaling for Freedom and Fulfilment

The beauty of using AI to scale your business isn't just in the growth potential—it's in the freedom it grants you. By automating key business functions, you can free up more time to focus on what truly matters, whether that's creative projects, travel, or personal development.

- Final Thought: Scaling your business with AI allows you to work smarter, not harder. By integrating these tools into your workflow, you can achieve greater success while maintaining the flexibility that drew you to the digital nomad lifestyle in the first place.

Conclusion: Scaling Your Business with AI

AI is reshaping the landscape for digital nomads by offering tools that make scaling a business more accessible than ever before. Whether it's automating client communication, managing multiple projects, or expanding globally, AI enables you to grow without compromising on quality or flexibility. The future of scaling lies in leveraging AI to handle the operational load, allowing you to focus on delivering exceptional services and living the lifestyle of your dreams.

As AI continues to evolve, the opportunities for digital nomads to scale their businesses will only grow. By embracing AI now, you're not just preparing for the future—you're shaping it. So, what are you waiting for? Take the first step toward scaling your business with AI, and unlock the freedom and success that come with it.

CHAPTER 20: DATA-DRIVEN DECISION MAKING

As Emma sat in a cozy café overlooking the tranquil beaches of Bali, she marvelled at how far she had come in her entrepreneurial journey. What had started as a small freelance business had evolved into a thriving consultancy. The key to her success? Harnessing the power of data through AI tools that helped her make smarter, more informed business decisions. In the past, she would have struggled with uncertainty—wondering if she should take on a new client or adjust her pricing model. But now, with AI-driven insights, she had the confidence to make decisions backed by data, allowing her business to flourish while maintaining the freedom of her digital nomad lifestyle.

For digital nomads like Emma, data-driven decision-making is revolutionizing how they operate their businesses. AI enables them to analyse large amounts of information, forecast trends, and make choices that optimize both their workflow and financial health. In this chapter, we will explore how digital nomads can leverage AI to make smarter business and financial decisions, enabling them to scale their businesses efficiently and thrive in the AI age.

Engage with Storytelling: Emma's Data-Driven Success

Emma's journey began like many other digital nomads —juggling clients, managing inconsistent cash flow, and guessing which strategies would pay off. Her breakthrough came when she integrated AI-powered tools like Tableau and Google Analytics into her workflow. These tools allowed her to track her website traffic, analyse client behaviour, and forecast which services were in high demand.

With the insights gathered, Emma made key business decisions that significantly boosted her revenue. For example, AI revealed that most of her clients came from small businesses looking for social media management services—an offering she hadn't been heavily promoting. Armed with this information, Emma restructured her website, offering specialized packages for small businesses, and doubled her income in six months.

Focus on Practical Application: How AI Enhances Decision-Making

Data is the new currency in today's world, and AI makes it easier for digital nomads to harness that currency to their advantage. Here's how you can apply AI-driven insights to make smarter business and financial decisions:

1. Analysing Client Data for Better Insights
   - What It Does: AI tools like Google Analytics and Mixpanel analyse visitor behaviour on your website, helping you understand where your traffic comes from and what your audience is most interested in.
   - How to Use It: Use AI to segment your audience based on demographics, behaviour, and preferences. This allows you to offer personalized services that cater to their specific needs, improving client satisfaction and increasing sales.
   - Benefits: By understanding your clients better, you can

create targeted marketing campaigns, adjust pricing, and even predict which services will be most in-demand.

2. Financial Forecasting with AI

- What It Does: AI-powered financial tools like QuickBooks and Xero provide real-time insights into your cash flow, expenses, and revenue. These platforms also offer predictive analytics that forecast future financial trends.

- How to Use It: Leverage AI to set financial goals, forecast upcoming expenses, and predict your income based on client bookings and historical data. These tools can help you make informed decisions on whether to hire more freelancers, expand your services, or adjust your pricing.

- Benefits: Financial forecasting enables you to plan for leaner months, allocate resources efficiently, and ensure your business remains financially healthy.

3. Making Data-Driven Marketing Decisions

- What It Does: AI-driven marketing tools like HubSpot and SEMrush help analyse data from your marketing campaigns, offering insights into which strategies are performing well and which aren't.

- How to Use It: Use AI to track the performance of email campaigns, social media ads, and content marketing. These tools also suggest improvements based on data, helping you optimize your campaigns in real-time.

- Benefits: Data-driven marketing decisions allow you to allocate your budget effectively, ensuring that you get the best return on investment (ROI) for every dollar spent.

Inspire Through Visionary Perspectives: The Future of Data-Driven Nomads

Imagine a future where every decision you make as a digital nomad is backed by AI-driven insights, allowing you to act with certainty and precision. AI's capabilities are rapidly evolving, and as they do, nomads will gain access to even more sophisticated tools for decision-making.

1. Predictive Business Insights

- As AI continues to develop, it will become better at predicting market trends, client behaviour, and even global economic shifts. Digital nomads will soon be able to use AI not only to respond to current data but to anticipate future changes. This foresight will allow them to position their businesses for success long before competitors even recognize emerging opportunities.

- Visionary Question: How would your business grow if you could predict client needs and market changes months in advance?

2. AI-Driven Personal Assistants for Financial Growth

- In the near future, AI will evolve into personal financial advisors, automatically suggesting how to invest earnings, where to cut costs, and when to take risks. These AI-driven assistants could act as both business consultants and financial planners, ensuring that your business grows sustainably while maintaining a healthy work-life balance.

- Visionary Thought: Imagine an AI assistant that handles your business's financial planning and strategy, ensuring you stay on track to achieve your goals without the stress of manual forecasting.

Balance Between Inspiration and Caution: The Human Element

While AI can significantly improve your decision-making process, it's important to balance automation with human intuition. Here's how to ensure you don't lose the human touch when relying on AI:

1. Trust Your Instincts Alongside Data

- AI can provide invaluable insights, but remember that data alone isn't everything. Trust your instincts when making decisions that involve creativity, innovation, or relationship-building. While AI can forecast trends, it's up to you to ensure that your brand remains authentic and aligned with your values.

- Pro Tip: Use AI as a guiding tool but keep your creative vision at the forefront of your business. The combination of data-driven insights and human intuition is a powerful strategy for growth.

2. Avoid Data Overload

- One challenge with data-driven decision-making is the risk of becoming overwhelmed by too much information. While AI can analyse vast amounts of data, not all of it will be relevant to your business. Focus on key metrics that align with your business goals and avoid getting bogged down by every data point.

- Solution: Set clear objectives for your AI tools to focus on. For example, prioritize client retention rates, profit margins, or marketing ROI rather than tracking every possible metric.

Motivate with Purpose: Making Decisions that Align with Your Values

AI-driven decision-making isn't just about making more money or scaling your business faster—it's about creating a life that aligns with your values and aspirations. The power of AI allows digital nomads to make smarter choices that support both their professional and personal goals.

- Final Thought: By leveraging AI to make data-driven decisions, you're empowering yourself to run a business that aligns with your lifestyle and values. Whether your goal is financial freedom, creative expression, or more time to explore the world, AI can help you make decisions that bring you closer to achieving it.

Conclusion: Leveraging AI for Smarter Decisions

Data-driven decision-making is a game-changer for digital nomads. By integrating AI into your business processes, you gain access to valuable insights that help you make smarter, more informed decisions. From analysing client behaviour to forecasting financial trends, AI tools empower you to operate at a higher level of efficiency and precision.

However, it's important to strike a balance between relying on AI and trusting your instincts. Use AI as a powerful assistant, but remember that the human element—your creativity, intuition, and unique vision—will always be central to your success. By combining data-driven insights with your personal expertise, you can make decisions that drive your business forward while staying true to your goals and values.

As AI continues to evolve, the opportunities for data-driven decision-making will only expand. By embracing these tools today, you're setting the foundation for a business that's ready to thrive in the AI age, allowing you to focus on what truly matters—living the digital nomad lifestyle on your own terms.

PART 5: THE NOMADIC LIFESTYLE IN THE AI AGE

CHAPTER 21: AI AND THE FUTURE OF CO-WORKING SPACES

As Samuel sipped his coffee in a bustling co-working space in Barcelona, he glanced at the AI-powered dashboard on his tablet. With one tap, he adjusted the room temperature to his preference, booked a quiet conference room for an upcoming client meeting, and received personalized insights on the fastest route to a popular nearby lunch spot. For Samuel, this was the future of co-working spaces—an ecosystem where artificial intelligence seamlessly enhanced his productivity, comfort, and connection to a global community of professionals.

For digital nomads like Samuel, co-working spaces have long served as vital hubs of creativity, networking, and productivity. However, with the advent of AI, these spaces are transforming rapidly, offering even greater value and functionality. This chapter delves into how AI is revolutionizing co-working spaces and what this transformation means for nomads, whose lifestyle demands flexibility, connectivity, and efficiency.

Engage with Storytelling: Samuel's AI-Enhanced Workday

Samuel had always enjoyed the freedom of the digital nomad

lifestyle, but finding the right environment to work in was often a challenge. He bounced between cafés, libraries, and co-working spaces in cities across the world, always searching for the perfect combination of peace, community, and convenience.

Then, he discovered AI-integrated co-working spaces, which elevated his productivity to new heights. One particular day in Barcelona, Samuel experienced the full power of AI at The Hive, a futuristic co-working hub. As he walked in, facial recognition software checked him in automatically. An AI-powered system had already identified his favourite desk—near the window with natural light—and reserved it for him. Throughout the day, AI assistants managed his schedule, ensuring he had time to focus deeply on work while also reminding him to take breaks and network with other professionals.

This seamless integration of AI into Samuel's work environment allowed him to work efficiently, connect with like-minded individuals, and even explore the city with recommendations generated by AI. For him, AI-enabled co-working spaces had become an indispensable part of his nomadic work life.

Focus on Practical Application: AI in Co-working Spaces

AI is revolutionizing co-working spaces in numerous ways, creating environments that are more adaptive, efficient, and personalized for digital nomads. Here are some key ways AI enhances these spaces and how you can leverage them as a nomad:

1. Smart Workstations
    - What It Does: AI can optimize workstations by adjusting lighting, temperature, and ergonomics based on individual

preferences. Many co-working spaces are now equipped with AI systems that learn your ideal work environment and automatically configure your space to fit your needs.

- How to Use It: When entering a co-working space, connect your personal profile to the AI system, allowing it to adjust the workspace according to your preferences. Whether you prefer a standing desk, a cooler temperature, or bright lighting, AI ensures your workspace is tailored to you.

- Benefits: A personalized workspace not only boosts productivity but also enhances your comfort, allowing you to work longer and more effectively.

2. AI-Powered Networking

- What It Does: AI can analyse your professional profile and interests to match you with other members in the co-working space who may share similar goals or work in complementary industries. Some co-working spaces even use AI to suggest potential collaborators or networking opportunities during events.

- How to Use It: Leverage AI-driven networking platforms within co-working spaces to connect with fellow digital nomads, freelancers, and entrepreneurs. These platforms allow you to set your networking preferences—whether you're looking for business partners, project collaborators, or simply peers to exchange ideas with.

- Benefits: AI simplifies networking by facilitating meaningful connections without the pressure of traditional networking events. This is particularly valuable for nomads looking to expand their professional network globally.

3. AI Scheduling and Booking

- What It Does: AI streamlines the process of booking conference rooms, scheduling meetings, and managing your daily agenda. Smart co-working spaces use AI-powered systems to automate these processes, ensuring availability and minimizing scheduling conflicts.

- How to Use It: Many co-working spaces provide integrated apps that allow you to book rooms, manage meeting schedules, and even track your daily goals. AI also learns your preferred times for meetings or focus sessions, optimizing your schedule for maximum productivity.

- Benefits: With AI managing your schedule, you can focus more on work and less on administrative tasks, ensuring that your time is spent efficiently.

Inspire Through Visionary Perspectives: The Future of AI in Co-working

The future of co-working spaces is intertwined with AI, and digital nomads stand to benefit from these innovations. As AI technology continues to evolve, the possibilities for AI-powered co-working spaces are endless.

1. AI-Driven Community Building

- Imagine co-working spaces where AI plays a central role in curating the community itself. By analysing the skills, goals, and preferences of members, AI could ensure that co-working spaces are filled with people who not only complement each other professionally but also foster a collaborative and supportive environment.

- Visionary Question: What would it look like to work in a space where everyone around you has been curated to help you grow both professionally and personally?

2. Global Co-working Networks

- As AI becomes more integrated, we can expect the rise of interconnected global co-working spaces. Digital nomads could seamlessly move between locations in different cities and countries, with AI recognizing their preferences and providing consistent, high-quality service no matter where they are.

- Visionary Thought: Imagine traveling from Tokyo to New

York and having every co-working space feel like a familiar, personalized environment, with AI syncing your preferences globally.

Balance Between Inspiration and Caution: The Human Element

While AI can greatly enhance co-working spaces, it's important to remember that technology is only one part of the equation. The human element—the sense of community, creativity, and connection—remains central to the appeal of these spaces.

1. Fostering Real Human Connections

- Although AI can suggest connections and enhance networking, it's essential to engage with others authentically. AI can open doors, but real relationships are built through genuine interaction and shared experiences. Use AI as a tool to facilitate connections, but be intentional about deepening those relationships beyond the digital realm.

- Pro Tip: Attend events and workshops organized within co-working spaces to build meaningful, in-person connections with others.

2. Maintaining Balance Between Automation and Personalization

- While automation is convenient, too much reliance on AI can reduce spontaneity and creativity. It's important to strike a balance between automation and maintaining a personal touch in your work environment. Engage with the community, customize your workspace to suit your mood, and allow for moments of unplanned creativity.

- Solution: Use AI tools to streamline repetitive tasks but remain open to flexibility and improvisation in your work routine.

Motivate with Purpose: Co-working Spaces as Creative Hubs

Co-working spaces have always been about more than just a place to work—they're about fostering creativity, community, and collaboration. AI's role is to enhance, not replace, the core purpose of these spaces.

- Final Thought: As AI transforms co-working spaces, they will become even more valuable as hubs for digital nomads. The ability to tailor your environment, connect with others meaningfully, and automate tedious tasks allows you to focus on what truly matters—doing your best work while living the digital nomad lifestyle.

Conclusion: The Future of Co-working is AI-Driven

AI-powered co-working spaces represent the future of work for digital nomads. From smart workstations to automated scheduling, AI is streamlining processes and making co-working environments more efficient and personalized than ever before.

However, it's important to strike a balance between leveraging technology and maintaining the human connections that make co-working spaces so appealing. By using AI to enhance your experience, while fostering real relationships and creative interactions, you can make the most of what these spaces have to offer.

As the digital nomad lifestyle continues to evolve, co-working spaces will remain essential hubs for community, collaboration, and creativity—only now, they'll be smarter, more adaptive, and more connected than ever. By embracing this AI-enhanced future, you'll position yourself to thrive in the fast-paced, ever-changing landscape of global work.

Next Steps: Before you move on, take a moment to explore some AI-powered co-working spaces in your area. Use their technology to optimize your workday and reflect: How did AI enhance your productivity and community-building experience?

CHAPTER 22: AI-OPTIMIZED TRAVEL PLANNING

As Emma stared out the window of her apartment in Bali, she felt an itch to explore a new country. But instead of spending hours juggling multiple travel apps, browsing countless blogs, and piecing together logistics, she turned to her AI-powered travel assistant, NOMAD AI. Within minutes, Emma had an itinerary for Japan tailored to her preferences —flexible working hours, affordable co-working spaces, and cultural experiences off the beaten path. What would have taken her days to organize, AI accomplished in a fraction of the time.

For digital nomads like Emma, seamless travel planning is crucial. Managing logistics while maintaining productivity is a fine balancing act, especially when work and travel intertwine. AI has transformed this process, making travel planning not just easier, but smarter and more personalized. In this chapter, we'll explore how AI-driven apps are reshaping how nomads plan travel and manage logistics, allowing them to maximize both their exploration and efficiency.

Engage with Storytelling: Emma's AI-Powered Travel Experience

Emma had always loved the thrill of discovering new places, but the planning involved often felt like a burden. As a freelance web developer traveling across Asia, she juggled client deadlines, time zone differences, and visa requirements, all while trying to find the next destination that would fuel her creativity. The process could become overwhelming, leaving little room for the joy of spontaneous travel.

Then, she discovered NOMAD AI, an AI-driven travel platform specifically designed for digital nomads. One day, Emma decided to leave Bali and explore Japan. Rather than manually searching for flights, accommodations, and workspace options, she let NOMAD AI handle it. The platform analysed her past travel habits, preferred work hours, and budget, delivering an itinerary that matched her nomadic lifestyle.

Not only did NOMAD AI handle the logistics—suggesting the best flights, visa requirements, and co-working spaces—but it also offered personalized recommendations for exploring Japan's rich culture. With AI doing the heavy lifting, Emma felt free to focus on her work, confident that the AI-assisted travel plan would support her needs.

Focus on Practical Application: How AI Optimizes Travel for Nomads

AI has revolutionized the way digital nomads plan their travel, allowing for more efficient, personalized, and flexible experiences. Here's how AI-driven apps are reshaping the travel landscape for digital nomads and how you can leverage these tools to streamline your journey.

1. AI-Powered Itinerary Building
   - What It Does: AI tools like NOMAD AI, TripIt, and Hopper

can now generate full travel itineraries based on personal preferences such as travel style, budget, and work schedules. These platforms analyse your preferences and recommend the best flights, accommodations, and activities.

- How to Use It: Sync your calendar, budget preferences, and interests with an AI-driven travel app. Let the AI map out a travel plan that fits your lifestyle, recommending everything from flights to co-working spaces in your destination.

- Benefits: Save time and reduce stress by allowing AI to handle the nitty-gritty details. Whether it's optimizing travel routes or syncing your schedule with local events, AI ensures that every aspect of your trip is handled with precision.

2. Real-Time Flight and Accommodation Insights

- What It Does: AI apps like Skyscanner and Hopper predict flight price trends and send alerts when prices drop or when a booking should be made. AI also identifies the best time to book accommodations based on demand, helping nomads stay within budget.

- How to Use It: Set up alerts for flights and accommodations using AI-driven tools. You'll receive notifications when it's the best time to book, ensuring you get the best deals for your travel needs.

- Benefits: Maximize your travel budget by using AI to predict the best booking times. No more last-minute stress—AI ensures you travel at the best possible price, with peace of mind.

3. Smart Packing and Weather Forecasting

- What It Does: AI-powered apps like PackPoint can help you pack intelligently based on the length of your trip, destination weather, and activities planned. AI also provides real-time weather updates so you can be prepared for any condition.

- How to Use It: Enter your trip details into a packing

app, and it will generate a personalized packing list tailored to your destination's weather and planned activities. Use AI weather apps to stay updated on local conditions.

- Benefits: No more overpacking or underpreparing. AI ensures you're equipped for every destination with the right gear and weather-appropriate clothing.

Inspire Through Visionary Perspectives: The Future of AI in Travel Planning

AI-driven travel planning is only scratching the surface of what's possible. As AI becomes more advanced, the future of travel for digital nomads holds even more exciting potential.

1. AI-Optimized Visa and Travel Document Assistance

- Imagine an AI assistant that automatically gathers and updates your visa requirements based on your destination, work duration, and nationality. AI could track your travel history and automatically notify you when it's time to renew your passport or apply for visas.

- Visionary Thought: What if your AI assistant could instantly generate and file visa applications for you, cutting down administrative tasks and ensuring your paperwork is always in order?

2. Personalized AI Travel Companions

- In the future, AI could create dynamic travel companions that guide you through your travels, providing local insights, language translation, and cultural context in real time. These AI travel companions would offer personalized recommendations based on your interests, learning more about your preferences with each new destination.

- Visionary Question: How would it feel to have an AI that not only plans your travels but also enriches your journey by learning your unique travel style and offering real-time tips and recommendations?

Balance Between Inspiration and Caution: The Risks of Over-Reliance on AI

While AI has undoubtedly revolutionized travel planning, there are potential pitfalls to over-relying on technology. It's important to remain aware of these risks and strike a balance between AI assistance and personal judgment.

1. Maintaining Flexibility in Travel Plans
- AI-driven itineraries can be incredibly efficient, but they may also lack the spontaneity and flexibility that many nomads value. Always leave room for adjustments—after all, part of the magic of travel is the unexpected discoveries along the way.
- Pro Tip: Use AI to structure your trip but remain open to unplanned adventures. Leave space in your itinerary for spontaneous experiences that AI might not suggest.

2. Data Privacy and Security Concerns
- AI apps that collect personal data can present privacy risks. Be mindful of the data you share with AI travel platforms, especially when using public Wi-Fi or accessing sensitive information on the go.
- Solution: Use VPNs and two-factor authentication when accessing travel apps, and review the privacy settings of AI platforms to ensure your data is protected.

Motivate with Purpose: Travel as a Means for Personal Growth

For digital nomads, travel is not just about getting from one place to another—it's about exploration, learning, and personal growth. AI can help facilitate these experiences, but it's up to you to use these tools to expand your horizons meaningfully.

- Final Thought: By using AI to streamline the logistics of travel, you'll have more time to immerse yourself in new cultures, form meaningful connections, and pursue personal projects. Travel becomes less about stress and more about experiencing the world with intention and purpose.

Conclusion: AI-Enhanced Travel for a New Era of Nomadism

AI has made travel planning simpler, smarter, and more efficient for digital nomads, but its real power lies in how it frees up time for deeper exploration and personal fulfilment. From AI-driven itinerary building to smart packing, the tools at your disposal allow you to plan with confidence and focus on what truly matters.

As AI technology continues to evolve, travel planning will become even more intuitive and personalized. For nomads, this means more freedom to roam, fewer logistics to worry about, and greater opportunities to work and play seamlessly across the globe.

- Next Steps: Before you head to your next destination, experiment with an AI travel planning app. Take note of how it simplifies your journey and ask yourself: How can you use AI to enhance your travel experience even further?

CHAPTER 23:
HEALTH AND
WELLNESS WITH AI

As a digital nomad, health and wellness can often take a backseat to tight deadlines and unpredictable travel schedules. This was the case for Mark, a freelance writer who spent years hopping between co-working spaces in Thailand, Spain, and Colombia. While he thrived on the adventure, his fitness routine and eating habits quickly deteriorated. It wasn't until Mark started using AI-driven wellness tools that he regained control of his health. Now, thanks to AI-powered fitness apps, personalized meal planning tools, and mental wellness platforms, Mark has managed to maintain his health while continuing to travel and work across the globe.

For nomads like Mark, balancing work, travel, and health is a challenge. Fortunately, the rise of AI technology has made it easier than ever for digital nomads to stay fit, healthy, and stress-free while on the move. This chapter explores the many ways AI is transforming how nomads maintain their physical and mental well-being, from personalized fitness programs to stress management tools.

Engage with Storytelling: Mark's Journey Back to Health

Mark's life as a digital nomad was full of excitement—new countries, different cultures, and endless inspiration for his writing. But as his career thrived, his health began to decline. With irregular hours, jet lag, and constantly changing environments, Mark found himself struggling to stay active and eat well. Over time, his energy levels dropped, and stress began to creep in.

One day, Mark decided to take action. He discovered Freeletics, an AI-powered fitness app that created custom workout plans based on his fitness level, goals, and schedule. The app adjusted his workouts depending on where he was and what equipment he had access to. At the same time, he began using Lifesum, an AI-driven nutrition app that offered meal plans tailored to his travel destinations and dietary preferences.

With the help of these AI tools, Mark regained control over his health. He was able to exercise regularly and eat balanced meals, even while working from various parts of the world. AI made it possible for him to maintain a healthy lifestyle without sacrificing his career or love for travel.

Focus on Practical Application: AI Tools for Staying Healthy on the Go

For digital nomads, staying healthy is about more than just working out and eating well—it's about creating a sustainable routine that fits their dynamic, often unpredictable lifestyles. AI-powered wellness tools have made it easier than ever to maintain fitness, mental health, and nutrition while traveling. Here's how you can integrate these tools into your life.

1. AI-Powered Fitness Plans
   - What It Does: AI fitness apps like Freeletics and

Aaptiv analyse your fitness level, preferences, and available equipment to create personalized workout routines. Whether you're working out in a fully equipped gym or just your hotel room, these apps adjust your routine based on what's available.

- How to Use It: Input your fitness goals, available equipment, and preferred workout duration into the app. The AI will generate a customized plan that fits your needs, adapting as you progress.

- Benefits: Stay fit no matter where you are. These apps ensure you can keep up with your fitness goals, even if your environment changes.

2. Personalized Nutrition and Meal Planning

- What It Does: AI nutrition apps like Lifesum and MyFitnessPal offer personalized meal plans based on your dietary needs, activity level, and travel location. These tools track your eating habits and make recommendations for healthy meals based on local cuisine.

- How to Use It: Enter your dietary preferences and goals, and the AI will suggest meal plans, recipes, and even local restaurant options. The apps can track your calorie intake and nutritional balance to ensure you stay on track.

- Benefits: Maintain a balanced diet no matter where you are in the world. AI tools make it easier to eat healthy, even when traveling to places where your usual food choices might not be available.

3. AI-Driven Mental Wellness Tools

- What It Does: AI-powered mental health apps like Headspace and Woebot provide guided meditation, stress relief techniques, and mood tracking. These apps are designed to help nomads manage stress, maintain focus, and stay mentally balanced despite the demands of constant travel.

- How to Use It: Set aside a few minutes each day to use AI-driven meditation apps. You can schedule regular check-ins with mood tracking apps to monitor your mental well-being and address any signs of burnout early.

- Benefits: Stay mentally healthy by incorporating mindfulness and relaxation into your daily routine. AI tools offer guided support to help you manage the unique stressors of nomadic life.

Inspire Through Visionary Perspectives: The Future of Health and Wellness for Nomads

As AI technology continues to evolve, the future of health and wellness for digital nomads is full of exciting possibilities. Imagine a world where your AI assistant not only monitors your fitness but also integrates real-time health data from wearable devices, providing instant feedback to keep you in optimal condition as you travel.

1. Real-Time Health Monitoring
    - AI-powered health trackers like Fitbit and Apple Watch are already capable of monitoring heart rate, sleep patterns, and activity levels. In the near future, these devices could work with AI to provide even deeper insights into your health, alerting you to potential health risks before they become issues.
    - Visionary Question: How will real-time health monitoring from wearables change the way digital nomads maintain their wellness? Imagine a future where your AI assistant detects early signs of burnout or dehydration and recommends immediate actions to keep you in peak condition.

2. Personalized Mental Health Support
    - In the future, AI mental health apps could become more personalized, providing one-on-one coaching based on your mood, stress levels, and environment. Imagine an AI that

understands your emotional triggers and helps you navigate the challenges of a nomadic lifestyle.

- Visionary Thought: AI mental health tools could evolve to the point where they offer daily check-ins, real-time stress-relief techniques, and instant access to therapists if needed, ensuring that digital nomads have constant support for their mental well-being.

Balance Between Inspiration and Caution: The Limitations of AI in Health

While AI tools offer incredible benefits for health and wellness, it's important to acknowledge their limitations and potential risks. Nomads should be aware of the following as they integrate AI into their health routines:

1. Over-Reliance on AI for Health Management

- While AI tools can make maintaining health easier, it's crucial not to rely on them entirely. AI apps can provide guidance, but they can't replace professional medical advice when needed.
- Pro Tip: Use AI tools as a supplement to professional healthcare. Always consult with a healthcare provider before making significant changes to your health or fitness routine.

2. Privacy Concerns with Health Data

- AI wellness tools often collect sensitive health data, raising concerns about privacy and data security. It's important to understand how your data is being used and take steps to protect it.
- Solution: Review the privacy policies of the AI tools you use and consider using encryption and secure connections when entering personal health data.

Motivate with Purpose: AI as a Tool for Holistic Wellness

Health and wellness aren't just about physical fitness—they're about achieving balance in every aspect of life. For digital nomads, wellness is the key to staying productive, creative, and resilient while living a life of freedom. AI tools provide an incredible opportunity to elevate your health, allowing you to focus on what matters most—living a fulfilling, purpose-driven life.

- Final Thought: By using AI to manage your health and wellness, you'll free up more time and energy to focus on your passions, explore new cultures, and experience life fully. Let AI handle the logistics, while you focus on living your best life.

Conclusion: AI-Driven Health for a Balanced Nomadic Life

The intersection of AI and wellness has opened up new avenues for digital nomads to maintain their health while traveling the world. From personalized fitness routines to mental health support, AI is making it easier than ever for nomads to stay fit, healthy, and stress-free. By embracing these tools, you can create a sustainable routine that supports both your career and your well-being.

- Next Steps: Explore an AI-driven fitness app and integrate it into your travel routine. Pay attention to how it improves your health and well-being, and think about how you can further optimize your wellness through AI technology.

CHAPTER 24: LIVING AS A NOMAD IN AI-ENABLED SMART CITIES

Imagine arriving in a city where everything works seamlessly to support your remote working lifestyle—where your phone guides you through real-time traffic updates, finds the quietest café with the best Wi-Fi for your morning meetings, and schedules co-working spaces tailored to your needs. This is no longer a futuristic fantasy but a reality in several AI-enabled smart cities around the globe. Cities like Singapore, Barcelona, and Tallinn are leading the charge, offering digital nomads not just a place to work but an entire infrastructure designed to meet their unique needs.

For digital nomads, smart cities are the next evolution of work-life integration. These tech-driven urban hubs leverage AI, automation, and the Internet of Things (IoT) to create an environment where convenience, connectivity, and productivity are paramount. This chapter dives into how AI-powered smart cities are reshaping the way nomads live, work, and thrive.

Engage with Storytelling and Case Studies: Mia's Experience

in a Smart City

Mia had been traveling across Europe for months, working remotely as a UX designer. When she heard about Tallinn's reputation as one of the most tech-savvy cities in the world, she decided to make it her base for a few months. The city, which prides itself on being an e-government hub and offering seamless digital services to its residents, had already attracted a strong community of digital nomads.

On her first day, Mia was amazed by how effortless everything was. Upon arriving at her Airbnb, she was immediately able to set up her e-residency, giving her access to Estonia's digital infrastructure. With this, she could open a bank account, register her freelance business, and handle everything from signing documents to paying taxes —all online. She also found that Tallinn's co-working spaces were seamlessly integrated with the city's public services. By simply scanning her e-residency card, she could book a workspace, access high-speed Wi-Fi, and even get discounts at nearby cafés.

For Mia, living in a smart city like Tallinn wasn't just about convenience—it was about being in a place where innovation and remote work coexisted harmoniously. AI-powered public transportation systems reduced her commute times, smart city apps helped her navigate the city, and automated platforms allowed her to focus on what truly mattered— growing her business.

Focus on Practical Application: How AI is Transforming Smart Cities for Nomads

The integration of AI in smart cities provides digital nomads with tools to optimize their daily lives. Here's how AI-driven smart cities are making life easier for remote workers:

1. AI-Powered Public Transportation
- What It Does: AI systems optimize public transportation by analysing real-time data from traffic patterns, weather conditions, and passenger flow to ensure efficient and timely service.
- How to Use It: In smart cities like Singapore, transportation apps powered by AI provide up-to-the-minute updates on traffic, helping nomads decide whether to take public transport, rent an e-bike, or call a ride-sharing service.
- Benefits: AI eliminates wasted time by offering faster, more efficient routes, making it easier to get to meetings, workspaces, or explore the city.

2. Smart Co-Working Spaces
- What It Does: AI enhances co-working spaces by automating everything from desk booking to climate control. Apps connected to smart city infrastructure allow you to reserve a workspace that matches your needs, ensuring you get optimal conditions for productivity.
- How to Use It: Many co-working spaces in smart cities use AI to allocate desks based on user preferences. For example, if you prefer a quiet space with ample natural light, AI algorithms will ensure you are assigned the perfect spot.
- Benefits: Nomads can focus on their work without worrying about logistics. With AI handling the details, they can enter any space and immediately start working in an environment tailored to them.

3. AI-Driven Productivity Apps and Services
- What It Does: AI-powered apps in smart cities enhance productivity by managing day-to-day tasks. These tools can automatically schedule meetings, recommend nearby cafes or spaces based on your preferences, and even manage daily errands.
- How to Use It: In cities like Seoul, AI apps use data from

your calendar and location to recommend the best nearby places to eat, work, or relax, adjusting recommendations in real-time based on traffic or crowd levels.

- Benefits: AI not only saves time but ensures that nomads can focus on their work without getting bogged down by day-to-day logistics. With AI taking care of routine decisions, digital nomads can maximize their productivity and free up time for creative pursuits or exploration.

Inspire Through Visionary Perspectives: The Future of Smart Cities for Nomads

Imagine a future where AI doesn't just make life more convenient but actively enhances your personal and professional growth. In this vision, smart cities evolve into personalized environments that adapt to the individual needs of their inhabitants. As a digital nomad, you could wake up in Tokyo, where AI anticipates your workflow for the day, suggesting collaborative spaces based on your upcoming projects and personal preferences. In the evening, AI recommends social events or cultural experiences tailored to your interests, creating a perfect work-life balance.

The potential for AI-powered smart cities to cater to digital nomads is immense. As more cities integrate these technologies, the world becomes a more accessible and accommodating place for remote workers. These cities may even begin to compete for nomads, offering specialized services like lower taxes, seamless visa processes, and innovative living solutions.

The future of AI-enabled smart cities is not just about optimizing work—it's about creating environments where creativity, connection, and innovation flourish. For digital nomads, this means a world where they are empowered to pursue their professional passions while living a life filled with purpose and exploration.

Balance Between Inspiration and Caution: Addressing the Challenges of AI in Smart Cities

While AI brings many advantages, there are important considerations to keep in mind. Privacy and data security are ongoing concerns in AI-enabled smart cities. The collection of personal data to power services like transportation, public Wi-Fi, and automated bookings raises questions about how this data is used and who has access to it.

For digital nomads, it's important to stay informed about the data practices of the cities they live in. In smart cities like Amsterdam, initiatives are in place to ensure transparency in how data is handled, but this is not always the case worldwide. Nomads should be proactive in understanding the privacy policies of the services they use and take steps to protect their information.

Another challenge is ensuring that AI does not exacerbate inequality. While smart cities offer incredible benefits, access to these resources may be unevenly distributed. As these cities continue to develop, it's critical for both governments and tech companies to focus on inclusivity, ensuring that the benefits of AI are accessible to all residents, not just the affluent or tech-savvy.

Highlight Global and Cultural Dimensions: Smart Cities Across the World

The rise of smart cities isn't confined to one region—it's a global phenomenon, with each city adapting AI to meet its unique cultural and economic context.

1. Singapore

- Known for its "Smart Nation" initiative, Singapore has long been at the forefront of AI innovation. The city's intelligent public transport systems, combined with smart living solutions, create a seamless experience for both residents and visitors. Nomads benefit from reliable Wi-Fi throughout the city and co-working spaces that cater to global professionals.

2. Tallinn, Estonia
- Estonia is often cited as the most digitally advanced country in Europe, and its capital, Tallinn, exemplifies this with e-residency programs that make it easier than ever for nomads to register businesses and work remotely. The city's AI-driven infrastructure simplifies everything from setting up a company to managing day-to-day logistics.

3. Barcelona, Spain
- Barcelona has embraced smart city technology to enhance quality of life, using AI to manage energy consumption, optimize traffic, and even monitor air quality. Digital nomads here enjoy a vibrant co-working culture supported by AI-driven tools, while the city's smart initiatives ensure sustainability and efficiency.

By understanding how different cultures and regions are integrating AI, digital nomads can choose destinations that not only offer a conducive work environment but also align with their personal values and goals.

Motivate with Purpose and Fulfilment: Smart Cities as a Pathway to a Balanced Life

For many digital nomads, the decision to live and work remotely is driven by a desire for more than just financial freedom. They seek a life rich in experiences, connections, and purpose. AI-enabled smart cities offer a unique opportunity to achieve this balance. By automating mundane tasks and optimizing daily workflows, these cities allow nomads to focus on what truly matters—whether that's building meaningful relationships, pursuing passion projects, or exploring new cultures.

By embracing smart cities, digital nomads can live a life of intention, where their work serves as a means to a fulfilling and purpose-driven existence.

Conclusion: Smart Cities and the Future of Digital Nomadism

As AI continues to transform cities across the globe, digital nomads stand at the forefront of this change. Smart cities offer a glimpse into a future where technology enhances both professional and personal life, providing nomads with the tools they need to thrive. From optimizing productivity to creating environments that foster creativity and connection, smart cities are not just shaping the future of work—they're shaping the future of living.

As a digital nomad, the rise of AI-enabled smart cities presents an unparalleled opportunity to experience the world in a new way, where every city is a potential home and every day is filled with possibilities.

By choosing to embrace this future, digital nomads can lead a life where their work and passions intersect, creating a lifestyle that is both fulfilling and exciting in the AI age.

CHAPTER 25: AI AND THE RISE OF DIGITAL NOMAD VILLAGES

The rise of digital nomadism has sparked the creation of a unique global network of communities where like-minded individuals gather to live, work, and explore. These digital nomad villages, often located in scenic or culturally rich destinations, offer more than just co-working spaces—they create thriving ecosystems for work and life balance. As artificial intelligence (AI) continues to reshape industries, it's playing a pivotal role in the development and operation of these nomad hubs, making them more efficient, innovative, and attractive to remote workers.

In this chapter, we'll explore how AI is accelerating the growth of digital nomad villages, providing opportunities for connectivity, enhancing the lifestyle experience, and supporting the infrastructure of these dynamic communities.

Engage with Storytelling and Case Studies

Take Sarah, for instance, a freelance web developer who had spent years hopping between cities, trying to find a rhythm that suited her digital nomad lifestyle. The constant changes in environment—new cultures, languages, time zones—while exciting, were draining. Sarah wanted to be part of a community, a place where she could find a sense of belonging without sacrificing the freedom to move.

That's when she discovered the digital nomad village in Madeira, Portugal. Powered by AI-driven systems, the village offered more than just high-speed Wi-Fi and co-working spaces. It provided an ecosystem tailored to digital nomads, where the housing, transportation, and social experiences were integrated with AI tools that simplified her daily life. From personalized event recommendations to optimized workflows in shared workspaces, the technology surrounding Sarah enabled her to focus on her passion projects without the usual distractions. What would have taken hours to manage—finding the best accommodation, organizing her work schedule, or discovering local community events—was done in a few clicks.

By removing the logistical headaches of nomadic living, Sarah's productivity soared. The AI tools that operated behind the scenes empowered her to achieve work-life balance in ways she hadn't thought possible before.

Focus on Practical Application

For digital nomads like Sarah, AI is transforming the concept of living and working abroad. But how exactly is AI helping to shape these nomad villages?

1. Personalized Workspaces: Many digital nomad hubs now use AI-powered platforms to help remote workers find the ideal workspace for their needs. AI can analyse your work habits, preferences, and even the type of projects you're working on to recommend the best environment. For instance, some nomads may prefer quiet spaces with minimal distraction, while others thrive in more social environments. AI tools provide that personalized touch.

2. Community Building: Digital nomad villages thrive on community. AI is helping to foster stronger connections by

recommending relevant events, networking opportunities, and even social groups based on individual interests. For instance, if you're a writer working on a new project, AI might suggest a nearby writer's group or workshops happening in the area. The algorithm curates activities that resonate with your passions and professional goals, making the nomad experience far more enriching.

3. Smart Infrastructure: Managing resources like electricity, water, and internet bandwidth is crucial in these villages, especially when accommodating hundreds of remote workers with varying demands. AI is optimizing this infrastructure, predicting needs based on user patterns and ensuring that resources are distributed efficiently. This sustainable approach not only enhances the comfort of living in these communities but also minimizes their environmental impact.

4. Remote Healthcare Access: Nomad villages are often in more remote areas, far from urban healthcare systems. AI has enabled access to telemedicine services, where digital nomads can consult with doctors virtually, schedule appointments, and manage their health without leaving the village. This is especially important for those traveling long-term and needing consistent healthcare services.

5. AI-Powered Transportation Solutions: One of the most challenging aspects of living and working in new places is navigating transportation systems. AI tools in nomad villages are streamlining transportation, from local bike-sharing schemes to AI-driven ride-hailing services that operate based on real-time traffic patterns, reducing waiting times and making daily commutes hassle-free.

Inspire Through Visionary Perspectives

Imagine a future where entire cities, not just small villages, are designed specifically for digital nomads. AI would be the backbone of such cities, with real-time analytics driving every aspect of life, from work to leisure. These cities would be fully integrated with AI-powered co-living and co-working spaces, ensuring that digital nomads have seamless access to what they need, whenever they need it.

As more countries recognize the economic and cultural value of attracting digital nomads, we could see AI-driven nomad villages and hubs becoming more common. These future-forward cities would cater specifically to nomads, offering fully automated services, dynamic housing solutions, and tailored workspaces that evolve as the needs of the workforce change.

Nomadism wouldn't just be about traveling from place to place—it would be about plugging into a network of AI-enabled cities where you can thrive professionally while experiencing the world in meaningful ways.

Balance Between Inspiration and Caution

While the potential of AI-powered nomad villages is exciting, there are challenges that come with this innovation. The reliance on AI in these communities raises concerns about privacy and data security. As AI collects vast amounts of data to optimize your living and working experience, it's crucial for digital nomads to understand how their personal information is being used and protected.

Additionally, as AI takes over more operational roles in these villages, there's the potential for a loss of human connection. For instance, while AI-driven networking tools can bring people together, the reliance on algorithms could unintentionally isolate people based on data points rather than fostering organic connections. A balance between automation and authentic human experience is essential for maintaining the sense of community that makes these villages so appealing.

Highlight Global and Cultural Dimensions

AI-powered digital nomad villages are popping up all over the world, from the mountains of Bali to the beaches of Mexico. Each region brings its own cultural influence to these hubs, creating diverse environments where technology meets tradition.

For instance, in Bali, you'll find eco-conscious nomad villages that blend AI-powered smart infrastructure with sustainable living practices. Meanwhile, in Mexico, the focus might be on creating vibrant communal spaces where culture, collaboration, and creativity intersect, supported by AI technologies that optimize everything from workspace lighting to communal dining schedules.

These villages highlight how AI can be adapted to fit different cultural and regional contexts, making the digital nomad lifestyle a truly global experience.

Motivate with Purpose and Fulfilment

At the core of the digital nomad lifestyle is the desire for freedom, purpose, and connection. AI-powered nomad villages offer the opportunity to live a life that blends work and personal fulfilment seamlessly. By removing the barriers of logistics, community building, and resource management, AI is enabling nomads to focus on what truly matters—exploring new cultures, pursuing passion projects, and building meaningful relationships.

In these villages, work isn't just something you do; it's part of a larger, purpose-driven lifestyle where AI helps you live more intentionally. The rise of these communities represents a shift toward a more balanced, connected, and fulfilled way of living.

Conclusion

As AI continues to shape the future of digital nomadism, the rise of AI-powered nomad villages is creating unprecedented opportunities for remote workers to live, work, and thrive in global communities. From personalized workspaces to AI-driven healthcare, these villages represent the next step in the evolution of the digital nomad lifestyle.

For those looking to embrace this future, now is the time to explore these AI-enabled communities and see how they can enhance your life—both personally and professionally. As digital nomads, we stand at the crossroads of technology and freedom, and AI is the tool that will allow us to navigate this exciting new world.

PART 6: OVERCOMING CHALLENGES IN THE AI ERA

CHAPTER 26: NAVIGATING JOB LOSS AND AI AUTOMATION

The world of work is rapidly changing, and digital nomads, who thrive on flexibility and adaptability, are often at the forefront of these shifts. As artificial intelligence (AI) continues to advance, it's not only reshaping how tasks are done but also posing challenges to job security across industries. For digital nomads, this creates a dual reality: while AI can unlock incredible opportunities for growth and efficiency, it also carries the risk of job loss through automation. How can nomads navigate these waters, protect their careers, and even leverage AI for their benefit?

This chapter explores the strategies digital nomads can adopt to mitigate the risks of job loss due to AI automation, while also focusing on how they can proactively evolve and stay ahead of the curve.

Engage with Storytelling and Case Studies

Meet Daniel, a freelance virtual assistant who spent years working with clients across multiple continents. His work mainly consisted of organizing schedules, managing emails, and handling customer inquiries. As AI tools became more sophisticated, Daniel noticed a shift—clients began turning to AI-powered virtual assistants like Siri, Google Assistant, and ChatGPT to handle the tasks he had spent years perfecting.

At first, Daniel panicked. Was his career over? Would the work he depended on be taken over entirely by machines?

Instead of giving up, Daniel took a proactive approach. He studied the ways in which AI was transforming his industry and learned how to use these tools to enhance his services rather than replace them. He became adept at integrating AI into his workflows, managing AI tools for his clients, and focusing on the more complex, human aspects of his work that AI couldn't replicate—relationship management, creative problem-solving, and strategic planning.

Within months, Daniel was offering more comprehensive services, positioning himself not as a competitor to AI but as a complementary force that made AI even more effective. As a result, his client base expanded, and he found new ways to thrive in a world where AI automation was a growing presence.

Daniel's story is a testament to the power of adaptation. Instead of being replaced, he found ways to upskill and integrate AI into his work, ensuring he stayed relevant in an evolving marketplace.

Focus on Practical Application

The lessons from Daniel's story are applicable to all digital nomads. While the fear of automation is real, it's possible to future-proof your career with the right approach. Here's how digital nomads can navigate the risks of job loss due to automation:

1. Upskill Continuously: AI is an ever-evolving technology, and staying relevant means constantly learning new skills.

Whether it's learning how to use AI-powered software, developing proficiency in data analysis, or mastering AI-enhanced marketing tools, continuous education is key. Platforms like Coursera and Udemy offer courses specifically geared toward understanding and leveraging AI in various fields.

2. Focus on What AI Can't Replace: While AI excels at handling repetitive and data-heavy tasks, it falls short in areas requiring emotional intelligence, creativity, and deep strategic thinking. Digital nomads should lean into these human-centric skills—whether it's writing, design, consultancy, or personal coaching. By offering services that AI can't fully automate, you maintain your value in the workforce.

3. Integrate AI Tools into Your Workflow: Rather than viewing AI as a threat, consider it an enhancement. Tools like Grammarly for writing, Jasper AI for content creation, or Zoho CRM for customer management can make your work faster, more efficient, and of higher quality. Becoming an expert in managing these tools allows you to offer clients a more sophisticated level of service.

4. Diversify Your Income Streams: Relying on one source of income is risky, especially in the face of AI automation. Digital nomads can mitigate this by creating multiple income streams. This could mean offering online courses, creating digital products, or branching into new niches that aren't as susceptible to AI disruption.

Inspire Through Visionary Perspectives

The future of work is uncertain, but it's filled with exciting possibilities. Rather than fearing automation, digital nomads have the unique opportunity to harness the power of AI to elevate their careers and redefine the way they work.

Imagine a future where AI takes care of all the tedious tasks, allowing you to focus solely on high-level strategy, innovation, and creative pursuits. This future is already beginning to unfold, and digital nomads who embrace AI will find themselves not only surviving but thriving in this new landscape.

In a fully AI-powered world, the skills that will matter most are those that involve human connection, empathy, and vision. By preparing now, you can position yourself to be at the forefront of this shift, enjoying a work-life balance where technology enhances your freedom, not limits it.

Balance Between Inspiration and Caution

While the future is bright, it's important to remain realistic about the challenges AI presents. Job displacement is real, and entire industries may be disrupted. However, the key to overcoming these challenges lies in adaptability.

For every challenge AI brings, there is a solution. Worried about job loss? Upskill. Concerned about losing clients to automation? Offer services that AI can't replicate. The more proactive digital nomads are about preparing for these changes, the less likely they'll be caught off guard.

At the same time, it's crucial to remain informed about the ethical implications of AI. As digital nomads, you must be aware of how AI is being used, not just for efficiency but in ways that could potentially harm privacy or contribute to inequality. Understanding these issues allows you to make more conscious decisions in your work and advocate for responsible AI use.

Highlight Global and Cultural Dimensions

The impact of AI automation is being felt differently across the globe. In developing regions, AI is creating opportunities for small businesses to reach global markets more easily. In tech hubs like Estonia, governments are adopting AI-first policies to attract digital nomads through seamless digital infrastructures.

In countries where job displacement is more pronounced, governments are starting to implement reskilling programs to help workers transition to AI-driven economies. As a global citizen, understanding how AI is transforming different regions gives you the insight to adapt and seize opportunities wherever they arise.

Motivate with Purpose and Fulfilment

At its core, the digital nomad lifestyle is about more than just work—it's about living a life of purpose, adventure, and connection. AI can enhance that by freeing up time and mental energy, allowing you to focus on what truly matters. Whether it's spending more time with loved ones, pursuing passion projects, or exploring new cultures, AI can be a tool that supports your journey toward a more fulfilling life.

By embracing AI, digital nomads can turn the challenges of automation into opportunities for growth, ultimately leading to greater career satisfaction and personal fulfilment.

Conclusion

AI automation doesn't have to be the end of opportunity —it can be the beginning of something even greater. By upskilling, integrating AI into your workflow, and focusing on what makes you uniquely human, you can future-proof your career and thrive in the AI age. Embrace the changes, stay ahead of the curve, and turn challenges into opportunities. The world of digital nomadism is evolving, and with the right mindset, AI can be your greatest ally in navigating this exciting new landscape.

CHAPTER 27: AI AND INCOME INEQUALITY IN THE DIGITAL NOMAD LANDSCAPE

In the evolving world of digital nomads, artificial intelligence (AI) offers incredible possibilities—greater efficiency, new career opportunities, and unprecedented freedom. However, with these opportunities comes a deeper question: does AI reduce or exacerbate income inequality among digital nomads? While AI has the potential to level the playing field for many, its rapid rise also risks creating a wider gap between those who can fully leverage these tools and those left behind.

This chapter explores how AI affects income inequality among digital nomads and how individuals can navigate this shifting landscape to thrive, regardless of their starting point.

Engage with Storytelling and Case Studies

Let's start with the story of two digital nomads—Ana and Mark—who are both freelance writers traveling the world while building their careers. Ana quickly adopted AI tools such as Jasper AI and Grammarly, using them to streamline her content creation, automate research, and improve the quality of her writing. With these tools, she was able to take on more clients, boost her income, and even diversify into new areas like content marketing and copywriting.

Mark, on the other hand, was more resistant to adopting AI. He stuck with his traditional methods, which involved more manual work. As clients began to expect faster turnaround times and higher-quality content, Mark struggled to keep up. He found it harder to compete for high-paying jobs and noticed a decline in his earnings as AI-enhanced freelancers like Ana thrived.

Ana and Mark's stories reflect the growing divide between digital nomads who embrace AI and those who do not. The difference in income, workload, and opportunities between these two types of nomads illustrates a key challenge in the AI age—those who leverage AI effectively are seeing their careers and incomes skyrocket, while others risk falling behind.

Focus on Practical Application

The key takeaway from Ana and Mark's stories is clear: digital nomads who actively adopt AI into their workflows are better positioned to succeed in the future. Here's how you can use AI to reduce your risk of falling behind and ensure that your income grows alongside technological advancements:

1. Embrace AI Tools Early: The earlier you adopt AI tools in your field, the better. Tools like ChatGPT for content generation, Canva AI for design, or Notion AI for organizing tasks can increase efficiency and improve the quality of your work. The sooner you integrate these tools, the greater your advantage in staying ahead of your peers.

2. Invest in AI Skills: Upskilling is essential in the AI age. Learning how to work with AI, whether through coding,

data analytics, or simply mastering the latest AI-enhanced platforms, will make you more marketable and ensure your services remain relevant. Websites like Coursera and LinkedIn Learning offer affordable courses on AI basics, automation, and machine learning.

3. Create AI-Enhanced Offerings: Use AI to diversify your service offerings. As Ana did, you can expand into areas like content strategy, SEO optimization, or data analysis by integrating AI tools that simplify these tasks. Offering a broader range of services will help increase your earning potential and reduce reliance on a single income stream.

4. Stay Flexible: One of the most significant advantages of being a digital nomad is the ability to pivot quickly. Keep a close eye on AI developments in your industry and be ready to adapt your skills, services, and tools as the technology evolves.

By embracing these strategies, you can ensure that AI works for you, not against you. Rather than widening income inequality, AI can become a tool that helps you break into higher-paying jobs, access more clients, and scale your work.

Inspire Through Visionary Perspectives

Looking toward the future, AI has the potential to be a great equalizer, but only if digital nomads take full advantage of the opportunities it presents. Imagine a future where AI removes the barriers of entry for those starting with minimal resources, allowing anyone with a laptop and internet connection to compete globally. AI tools can turn a solo freelancer into a one-person agency capable of handling complex tasks at scale.

However, there's a cautionary side to this vision. AI can just as easily deepen the divide between those with access to technology and skills, and those without. If left unchecked, income disparities could widen as high-paying clients flock to AI-savvy nomads, while others struggle with obsolete workflows.

As digital nomads, the challenge is to actively participate in this AI-powered future, ensuring it brings benefits to all rather than a select few. By taking ownership of your learning and ensuring you stay ahead of the curve, you can be part of a global workforce that thrives on technological advancements, rather than becoming marginalized by them.

Balance Between Inspiration and Caution

While the future promises incredible opportunities, it's crucial to approach AI with both optimism and caution. Automation has the potential to displace many jobs, and digital nomads are not immune. However, unlike traditional workers, nomads have the flexibility and adaptability needed to navigate these challenges.

For every AI tool that threatens to replace a certain task, there's an opportunity to pivot into more creative, human-centred work. Instead of focusing on what might be lost, digital nomads should concentrate on the new skills and services AI enables. Automation may take over routine tasks, but it can never replace the creativity, empathy, and strategic thinking that make humans unique.

Highlight Global and Cultural Dimensions

The impact of AI on income inequality is not just felt on an individual level—it varies widely across different regions and cultures. In countries with strong technological infrastructure, digital nomads may find it easier to access the tools and resources needed to compete globally. In contrast, nomads in developing countries may struggle with poor connectivity, limited access to AI platforms, and fewer opportunities for upskilling.

However, AI also presents unique opportunities for global inclusion. AI-powered translation tools, for example, allow nomads from non-English-speaking countries to work with international clients without language barriers. Similarly, AI tools that automate administrative tasks can help nomads with limited financial resources compete in global markets by lowering overhead costs and reducing time spent on non-billable work.

Motivate with Purpose and Fulfilment

AI isn't just about earning more money—it's about creating a life of purpose and fulfilment. By embracing AI, digital nomads can free up more time for what truly matters. Automation can take over the mundane, repetitive tasks, leaving you with more space for passion projects, travel, learning new skills, or engaging with causes you care about.

Ultimately, the goal is not just to survive but to thrive in the AI age. By staying informed, flexible, and proactive, digital nomads can ensure that AI enhances their lives, rather than diminishing them.

Conclusion

AI is both a challenge and an opportunity for digital nomads. While it has the potential to exacerbate income inequality, those who embrace AI tools, invest in upskilling, and adapt their services can thrive in this new landscape. Rather than fearing automation, use it as a catalyst to enhance your career, create more fulfilling work, and secure your place in the future of the global digital economy.

CHAPTER 28: LEGAL ISSUES FOR DIGITAL NOMADS IN THE AI-POWERED GLOBAL ECONOMY

In the increasingly borderless world of digital nomads, the rise of AI has unlocked incredible opportunities for location-independent professionals. However, with these opportunities come significant legal complexities that digital nomads must navigate. Whether it's working across multiple jurisdictions, understanding intellectual property rights in AI-generated work, or dealing with evolving regulations around data privacy, the legal landscape can be both confusing and ever-changing.

In this chapter, we'll explore some of the key legal issues digital nomads face in the AI-powered global economy and how to address them.

Engage with Storytelling and Case Studies

Take the case of David, a digital nomad based in Portugal but working with clients across Europe, Asia, and North America. David uses AI-powered tools like Copy.ai and ChatGPT to help him generate marketing copy, create presentations, and even manage client relations. For a while, things were going smoothly—until one of his clients in Germany flagged a compliance issue around data privacy. It turned out that David had unknowingly used a tool that wasn't compliant with the European Union's General Data Protection Regulation (GDPR), and his client was potentially facing fines.

The incident served as a wake-up call. David realized that as a digital nomad, legal responsibilities don't disappear simply because you're moving across borders. Instead, they can multiply. From data protection laws to intellectual property rights for AI-generated content, digital nomads must stay vigilant in understanding the legal frameworks in the regions where they operate.

Focus on Practical Application

Here are some practical tips for digital nomads navigating the legal landscape in an AI-driven economy:

1. Understand Cross-Border Regulations: Digital nomads are often working across multiple jurisdictions simultaneously. For example, if you're offering services to clients in the EU, familiarize yourself with the GDPR. If you're working with American companies, you should be aware of regulations like the California Consumer Privacy Act (CCPA). Stay up to date on evolving regulations in countries where your clients are based.

2. Use AI Tools with Privacy Compliance: Ensure that the AI tools you use are compliant with relevant privacy regulations. Some AI tools may collect or process data in ways that could breach data protection laws in certain regions. Platforms like Jasper or Notion AI typically provide information on their compliance with international regulations, so review this before integrating them into your workflow.

3. Intellectual Property (IP) Rights: One of the most common legal concerns surrounding AI is the issue of intellectual property. Who owns the content created by AI tools? While some jurisdictions offer clearer guidance than others, you should always check the terms of service for any AI platform you use. In many cases, the AI tool may claim ownership of any output it produces, or it may be shared between the user and the company. Make sure your client agreements clearly define ownership of AI-generated content.

4. Tax Considerations: Digital nomads must also be mindful of tax obligations, especially when living in one country and working in another. AI has made it easier than ever to automate invoicing, track earnings, and report taxes, but the legal obligations remain complex. Some countries have double-taxation agreements, while others may impose hefty penalties for failing to file the right paperwork. Consult with a tax expert familiar with international laws for digital nomads to ensure compliance.

5. AI-Generated Contracts and Legal Documents: Many nomads are using AI to generate contracts, invoices, and other legal documents. While AI tools like LegalZoom and DocuSign can be useful for streamlining administrative tasks, it's important to have these documents reviewed by a qualified legal professional. AI-generated contracts might miss nuances that a human lawyer would catch, which could leave you vulnerable to legal disputes later on.

6. AI and Employment Laws: As AI blurs the line between employee and freelancer roles, it's essential to understand how employment laws apply to digital nomads. In some countries, even freelancers are subject to employment regulations, such as mandatory benefits, workers' compensation, or restrictions on working hours. AI may also raise questions about whether some work performed by a

human (a freelancer or contractor) can be outsourced to AI, further complicating labour laws.

By proactively addressing these issues, digital nomads can protect themselves from legal complications and ensure their operations run smoothly no matter where they're working from.

Inspire Through Visionary Perspectives

Looking toward the future, AI and the digital nomad lifestyle will likely become even more intertwined, with more complex legal challenges to match. As AI continues to evolve, it may soon take on more tasks traditionally reserved for human workers, which will raise new legal questions. For example, if a digital nomad relies entirely on AI to complete a client project, who holds legal responsibility if something goes wrong?

The visionary perspective here is to embrace AI as a tool for empowerment while staying aware of the evolving legal landscape. Imagine a world where AI handles all the administrative and legal hurdles of cross-border work, allowing digital nomads to focus entirely on their creative and strategic efforts. But to make that future a reality, nomads must remain educated about their legal responsibilities and work to ensure they stay compliant in a rapidly changing world.

Balance Between Inspiration and Caution

It's important to maintain a balanced view of AI and its role in the digital nomad community. While AI can significantly reduce the burden of legal paperwork, streamline workflows, and open up new global markets, it can also introduce risks if not managed carefully. AI is still a tool, and tools must be used correctly to avoid pitfalls.

For instance, relying too heavily on AI without

understanding the legal ramifications could lead to costly mistakes. Just as David discovered with his GDPR compliance issue, digital nomads should always be proactive in assessing the legal impact of their AI usage.

Highlight Global and Cultural Dimensions

Legal challenges are not uniform around the globe. Different countries have different perspectives on data privacy, intellectual property, taxation, and labour laws. Digital nomads who work in multiple countries must be aware of these regional differences.

For example, Europe's stringent data privacy regulations, such as the GDPR, are in stark contrast to more lenient policies in other parts of the world. Similarly, intellectual property laws vary significantly, particularly when it comes to AI-generated content. In Japan, for instance, AI-generated works are explicitly recognized as copyrightable, whereas in other countries, this issue remains unresolved.

Navigating these different legal frameworks requires flexibility and a commitment to staying informed. Digital nomads who work across borders should continuously educate themselves on the specific legal requirements of the regions they operate in.

Motivate with Purpose and Fulfilment

The ultimate goal for digital nomads using AI is not just to avoid legal issues but to create a thriving, purpose-driven career. By addressing these legal challenges head-on, nomads can focus on what truly matters—building a lifestyle that brings them freedom, creativity, and fulfilment. AI offers the possibility of achieving more while working less, allowing nomads to spend more time on passion projects, travel, and personal growth.

Conclusion

Legal challenges are inevitable for digital nomads working in the AI age, but they are not insurmountable. By staying informed, adopting best practices, and leveraging AI tools responsibly, digital nomads can navigate these complexities with confidence. As the legal landscape continues to evolve alongside AI, proactive education and compliance will be key to thriving in the global economy. Ultimately, by embracing both AI and the legal challenges it brings, digital nomads can ensure they're well-positioned for a future that is as legally sound as it is exciting.

CHAPTER 29:
AI SECURITY
AND PRIVACY –
NAVIGATING THE
DIGITAL NOMAD
LANDSCAPE

As the digital nomad lifestyle continues to rise, the growing reliance on AI tools for work, travel, and personal management presents new challenges. One of the biggest concerns in this digital age is the security and privacy of data. With AI powering most of the tools nomads use daily, understanding the risks and addressing privacy concerns becomes crucial.

A Case Study: Jack's Journey with Data Vulnerabilities

Jack, a freelance software developer, was living the dream life of a digital nomad. Hopping from Bali to Lisbon, he relied heavily on AI-powered tools to manage his freelance contracts, communicate with clients, and even book his flights. His productivity skyrocketed as AI automated mundane tasks, allowing him more time to explore new cultures.

However, during a project involving sensitive client data, Jack's account with a popular AI-powered project management tool was hacked. The intrusion exposed sensitive client information, which led to a loss of trust and even cost him a few contracts. Jack quickly realized that while AI made his work easier, it also came with a steep security risk if not handled properly. From this experience, Jack learned how important it is to secure his digital life and carefully choose the tools he uses.

Jack's story is a wake-up call for digital nomads relying on AI—understanding the risks around data privacy, security breaches, and the vulnerabilities that come with advanced technologies is essential for avoiding disastrous outcomes.

Why AI Poses Privacy and Security Risks

AI tools work by processing vast amounts of data. This data can range from mundane work files to sensitive personal information, like your location history or financial records. For digital nomads who are constantly on the move, using public Wi-Fi and multiple devices, the risks multiply.

Here are some of the key privacy concerns digital nomads face when using AI-powered tools:

1. Data Collection: Most AI tools require a substantial amount of personal and professional data to function. Whether it's a virtual assistant learning your preferences or a financial app managing your expenses, the volume of data collected can pose a risk if it's not adequately protected.

2. Cloud-Based Vulnerabilities: Many AI-powered tools operate on the cloud, which, while convenient, also means data is stored on servers accessible over the internet. These cloud environments can be vulnerable to cyberattacks if not properly secured.

3. Public Wi-Fi Risks: Digital nomads frequently connect to public Wi-Fi networks, which are notorious for their weak security. Without proper encryption, data transmitted through these networks can be intercepted, leaving sensitive information exposed.

4. AI's Autonomous Learning: Some AI tools learn from your data and behaviour patterns to improve their functionality. However, without proper controls, this can lead to excessive data collection and potential misuse, such as unauthorized tracking or profiling.

Practical Tips for Securing Your Digital Life as a Nomad

Understanding the risks is only half the battle. To truly thrive as a digital nomad, it's vital to take proactive steps in securing your data and ensuring privacy while using AI tools. Here are some practical strategies:

1. Use VPNs (Virtual Private Networks): A VPN encrypts your internet connection, ensuring that data sent over public Wi-Fi networks is protected from prying eyes. Always use a trusted VPN when accessing sensitive data or connecting to public Wi-Fi.

2. Two-Factor Authentication (2FA): Enable two-factor authentication on all AI tools and platforms you use. 2FA adds an extra layer of security by requiring a second form of verification, such as a text message or authentication app, before logging in.

3. Data Encryption: Ensure that the tools and platforms you use employ encryption for data storage and transmission. This makes it harder for cybercriminals to access or steal your information.

4. Choose Privacy-Focused Tools: Not all AI tools are created equal when it comes to privacy. Opt for platforms that

prioritize data security and give you control over what information is collected and how it's used. Tools like Signal for encrypted communication or ProtonMail for secure emails are great alternatives for maintaining privacy.

5. Regularly Update Software: Always keep your software, apps, and AI tools up to date. Cybercriminals often exploit vulnerabilities in outdated software, so by staying up to date, you reduce the risk of being hacked.

6. Understand Data Permissions: Before using any AI tool, carefully read the terms and conditions, focusing on the data permissions. Limit the amount of data you share and only use tools that give you transparency and control over your data.

AI: Balancing Convenience and Caution

While AI tools offer immense convenience for digital nomads, it's essential to maintain a balanced approach. Sarah, a digital marketer based in Thailand, uses AI-powered platforms for everything—from automating social media posts to tracking her clients' analytics. While these tools save her hours every day, Sarah is also meticulous about how her data is handled. She uses a password manager for creating strong passwords and conducts regular audits of the AI tools she integrates into her workflow.

Her secret to success? Balancing the adoption of cutting-edge AI tools with a cautious and informed approach to data privacy and security.

Visionary Perspectives: The Future of AI Security for Digital Nomads

As AI continues to evolve, so too will the tools to protect your data. Emerging technologies such as blockchain are being explored for securing data in decentralized ways, reducing the risk of single points of failure. In the future, AI itself may be harnessed to detect and mitigate cyber threats in real time, using its pattern-recognition capabilities to thwart hackers before they can access sensitive information.

Imagine a future where digital nomads like Sarah and Jack can navigate the world freely without worrying about data breaches or security risks. AI-driven security tools might even proactively shield nomads from cyber threats based on predictive analytics, ensuring that privacy and convenience go hand in hand.

Final Takeaway

AI opens up incredible possibilities for digital nomads, but it's crucial to remain vigilant about the security risks it introduces. By taking proactive measures, you can enjoy the full benefits of AI while keeping your data secure and your privacy intact. In the AI-powered world, digital nomads have the potential to thrive safely, balancing innovation with security.

CHAPTER 30: DEALING WITH BURNOUT IN THE AI AGE – STAYING BALANCED AS A DIGITAL NOMAD

In a world where AI tools promise unprecedented productivity and efficiency, it's easy for digital nomads to fall into the trap of constantly working. The allure of automation, instant responses, and seamless workflows can blur the lines between work and personal life, making it harder to unplug. However, with the ever-present digital demands, burnout has become a real challenge for many digital nomads in the AI age.

Sarah's Story: From Productivity to Burnout

Take Sarah, for example, a successful freelance copywriter who began her journey as a digital nomad three years ago. At first, Sarah thrived using AI-powered writing tools like Jasper AI to generate ideas, structure her content, and automate repetitive tasks. Her output doubled, and she took on more clients. She was living the dream, traveling across Europe and Southeast Asia while maintaining a steady income. But soon, Sarah found herself glued to her laptop—AI had made her more efficient, but it also enabled her to take on far more work than she could handle. The pressure to stay competitive in the AI-driven gig economy led her to work 12-hour days, and weekends started blending into weekdays.

Before long, Sarah hit a wall. The joy of digital nomadism, which had been about freedom and exploration, was overshadowed by constant deadlines and an unrelenting workload. Despite the support AI provided, she was burned out.

Sarah's story resonates with many digital nomads who rely on AI tools to optimize their workflows but struggle to maintain a balance. AI can enhance productivity, but without boundaries, it can also push individuals toward burnout.

Understanding Burnout in the AI Age

Burnout is often associated with chronic stress, and in the AI-driven world, that stress can be exacerbated by the constant connectivity and the pressure to be always "on." AI tools help automate tasks and provide incredible convenience, but they also create expectations of immediate responses and heightened output, particularly for digital nomads who work across multiple time zones.

The key triggers of burnout among AI-driven digital nomads include:
1. Over-Optimization: The belief that AI tools will help you do everything faster, leading to taking on more tasks than you can reasonably manage.
2. Lack of Boundaries: AI tools work 24/7, which can push nomads to feel like they should be working all the time too.
3. Client Expectations: AI-driven tools can make clients expect faster turnarounds and more polished results,

increasing pressure on freelancers and remote workers.

4. Isolation: Digital nomads often work alone, and even though AI tools streamline communication, they can't replace the benefits of human interaction, leading to feelings of isolation.

Practical Applications: Managing AI to Prevent Burnout

While AI can amplify productivity, it's crucial to manage how you use these tools to avoid burnout. Here are several practical strategies digital nomads can use to maintain balance:

1. Set Clear Boundaries with AI: Just because AI can work around the clock doesn't mean you should. Define clear working hours and ensure that you're not always reachable by clients or colleagues. Use AI assistants to help schedule focused work time and breaks.

Example: "Sarah started using an AI-powered time management tool, Clockwise, to block out time in her calendar for focused work and personal downtime. This allowed her to balance work without overcommitting."

2. Automate Responsibly: Use AI to streamline repetitive tasks, but resist the temptation to take on more work than you can handle. Be selective about how you use AI —automate what's necessary, but don't sacrifice your well-being for additional projects.

AI Toolbox: "Use tools like Zapier to automate non-essential tasks like sending routine client updates or managing social media posts, freeing up time for creative work or relaxation."

3. Practice Digital Detox: Regularly disconnect from AI tools and work. Set aside time where you're completely unplugged from your devices to recharge. AI might make it easier to stay connected, but intentional disconnection is essential for

mental health.

AI Toolbox: "Consider using apps like RescueTime to monitor your AI tool usage and schedule time away from screens. Set boundaries for how long you're willing to work each day."

4. Leverage AI for Self-Care: AI isn't just for work—it can also be used to enhance your well-being. Use AI-powered meditation apps, wellness trackers, or fitness programs to prioritize your health.

Example: "Sarah discovered Headspace, an AI-powered meditation app, which helped her carve out moments of mindfulness during her busy schedule, alleviating some of her stress."

5. Outsource to AI Intelligently: Learn to delegate specific tasks to AI assistants. Whether it's answering routine emails, managing your calendar, or conducting research, AI can take these off your plate, allowing you to focus on high-priority tasks.

Example: "Sarah used AI writing assistants to handle repetitive blog posts, allowing her to focus on more creative, high-level projects."

Visionary Perspectives: AI and the Future of Work-Life Balance

The future of AI promises even greater integration into the digital nomad lifestyle, but this also calls for greater awareness of how we manage our interaction with it. As AI evolves, it's not inconceivable that more sophisticated AI tools could help monitor your stress levels, mental health, and work habits in real time. Imagine an AI assistant that not only schedules your meetings but also alerts you when you're working too much, suggesting wellness breaks based on your cognitive load.

Visionary Example: "In the near future, we might see AI-driven wellness coaches, powered by real-time data, helping digital nomads balance productivity and health by learning individual behaviour patterns and adjusting work schedules accordingly."

Balancing Inspiration with Caution

While the opportunities AI presents are immense, it's essential to strike a balance between leveraging the technology and recognizing its potential drawbacks. Burnout is preventable, but it requires setting limits on how we use AI to avoid overwhelming ourselves.

Inspiration: "AI is not just a tool for productivity; it's a partner in achieving a better, more balanced life. By using AI to automate work and create efficiencies, we can also create space for the things that truly matter—personal growth, travel, relationships, and well-being."

Final Takeaway: Embrace AI, but on Your Terms

AI has become an integral part of the digital nomad lifestyle, allowing individuals to work smarter and live more freely. However, without mindful use, it can lead to burnout and diminished well-being. The key is to embrace AI as a tool that serves you, not one that defines your work or life.

By integrating boundaries, practicing mindful tech use, and leveraging AI for both productivity and well-being, digital nomads can thrive in the AI age without succumbing to burnout.

PART 7: CASE STUDIES OF DIGITAL NOMADS USING AI

CHAPTER 31: FREELANCERS THRIVING WITH AI – REAL-WORLD EXAMPLES OF SUCCESS

For freelancers in the AI age, technology is no longer just a tool; it's a partner. It's transforming the way they work, allowing them to be more productive, creative, and efficient, all while opening new doors for income generation. In this chapter, we dive into the stories of freelancers who are thriving thanks to AI, showing how they've leveraged AI tools to elevate their businesses and improve their lives. These real-world examples will inspire you to see the potential AI holds for enhancing your freelance career.

Sarah's Journey: Scaling a Graphic Design Business with AI

Let's start with Sarah, a freelance graphic designer who once struggled to keep up with client demands while maintaining the quality of her work. Like many freelancers, she was hesitant to use AI at first, fearing that automation might dilute the creative aspect of her job. However, as her workload increased, she found herself overwhelmed, spending more time on routine tasks like image editing, resizing, and layout adjustments than on actual design work.

That's when Sarah discovered Canva Pro, a tool that integrates AI into design. With its AI-powered features, she was able to automate many of the repetitive tasks that had been consuming her time. Canva's AI could generate templates, suggest colour palettes, and even recommend designs based on previous projects. Sarah's workflow transformed almost overnight. Tasks that once took her hours now took minutes, and she could spend more time on the creative elements that her clients loved her for.

As a result, Sarah's income doubled. She took on more clients without sacrificing quality and even launched her own online course teaching others how to use AI-driven design tools. By embracing AI, she not only improved her business but also expanded into new revenue streams.

Practical Applications for Freelancers

Sarah's story is just one example of how AI can reshape a freelancer's career. Now, let's explore how you can incorporate AI into your own workflow, no matter your industry or skill set.

1. AI-Powered Writing Assistants

If you're a freelance writer or content creator, tools like Jasper AI or ChatGPT can help you generate content ideas, draft outlines, and even write articles. While these tools don't replace the human touch, they can streamline the research and ideation process, allowing you to focus on refining and personalizing the content.

Practical Tip: Use Grammarly's AI-enhanced editor to improve your writing's clarity and tone. Not only will it save time on editing, but it will also provide real-time feedback on grammar and style.

2. Automating Administrative Tasks

Freelancers often wear multiple hats, from project manager to accountant. AI tools like HoneyBook and Dubsado can help automate invoicing, contracts, and client communications, freeing up valuable time that you can spend on the work that matters most. These platforms even allow you to create workflows that automatically follow up with clients or remind you of deadlines.

Practical Tip: Set up AI-driven workflows to handle recurring tasks. For example, use Zapier to connect your email with project management tools like Trello or Asana, ensuring that tasks are automatically created based on incoming client requests.

3. Optimizing Social Media with AI

Social media is a key marketing tool for freelancers, but managing it can be time-consuming. AI-powered tools like Buffer and Hootsuite allow you to schedule posts, analyse engagement, and even generate hashtags based on trending topics. By using AI, you can maintain a consistent online presence without spending hours manually posting content.

Practical Tip: Use Lately.ai, an AI social media tool that repurposes long-form content into bite-sized posts. If you've written a blog or newsletter, Lately.ai can turn it into multiple social media updates with optimized hashtags and formats for each platform.

Inspiring Visionary Perspectives: The Future of Freelance Work with AI

As AI continues to evolve, it's poised to create even more opportunities for freelancers. Imagine a future where AI not only assists with mundane tasks but actively enhances your creative process. For writers, AI could suggest innovative story arcs or unique characters based on market trends. Designers might collaborate with AI to produce entirely new forms of digital art, with the technology learning from their unique style and preferences.

Even more exciting is the potential for AI to connect freelancers with clients on a global scale. AI-driven platforms like Upwork and Fiverr are already using algorithms to match freelancers with clients, but as AI advances, these platforms could evolve into personalized talent agents, learning from your past work and preferences to find the perfect projects.

Visionary Question: How might your freelance career evolve if AI could predict client needs and automatically propose new services that align with emerging trends? What if AI could help you stay ahead of the curve, suggesting the next big opportunity before it even becomes mainstream?

Balancing Inspiration and Caution

While AI offers tremendous potential for freelancers, it's important to approach it with a balanced perspective. The fear of automation replacing human jobs is real, but for freelancers, the key is to see AI as an enhancement, not a replacement. AI tools can handle repetitive tasks, but creativity, problem-solving, and emotional intelligence remain human strengths that can't be replicated.

The best way to future-proof your career in the age of AI is to continuously upskill. Stay informed about new AI tools, learn how to use them effectively, and focus on developing skills that complement what AI can't do—like relationship-building, complex decision-making, and creative ideation.

Global and Cultural Dimensions: AI in Freelancing Across the World

Freelancers from different parts of the world are embracing

AI in unique ways. In countries like India, AI is helping freelancers tap into international markets by automating payment processes, translating content, and even managing cross-border legalities. In Europe, AI-driven tools are being used to navigate complex tax systems and regulatory environments, making it easier for freelancers to operate across borders.

In Estonia, a digital-first country known for its e-residency program, AI plays a significant role in supporting the nomadic freelance community. Freelancers there can automate everything from client contracts to tax filing through the government's digital platforms, enabling seamless remote work from anywhere in the world.

Motivating with Purpose and Fulfilment

As freelancers, many digital nomads pursue this lifestyle not just for financial independence but for the freedom to live life on their own terms. AI can help you reclaim time for your passions, whether that's traveling, exploring new hobbies, or building a deeper connection with your clients.

By integrating AI into your freelance business, you're not only optimizing your work—you're creating more space to live a fulfilling, purpose-driven life. Imagine being able to take on fewer, higher-paying clients while spending more time on the things that matter most to you.

Final Takeaway: Thriving with AI

AI is a powerful ally for freelancers looking to boost productivity, income, and creative potential. By embracing AI tools and integrating them into your workflow, you can not only improve efficiency but also open the door to new opportunities. The key to thriving in this AI-powered freelance world is balance—using technology to enhance your work while staying true to the human aspects of creativity, empathy, and innovation.

Remember, AI is here to help you thrive, not to replace you. Embrace it, adapt, and use it as a tool to unlock your full potential as a freelancer in the AI age.

CHAPTER 32: ENTREPRENEURS BUILDING AI-DRIVEN STARTUPS – DIGITAL NOMADS INNOVATING THE FUTURE

As the world of work continues to evolve with artificial intelligence, a new breed of digital nomad is emerging—entrepreneurs who are using AI to create disruptive startups. These innovators are not only embracing the flexibility and freedom that comes with being a digital nomad but are also leveraging AI to solve real-world problems, scale their businesses, and reach global markets. In this chapter, we'll explore the stories of digital nomad entrepreneurs who have harnessed AI to build successful startups, illustrating the immense potential AI holds for innovation.

Case Study: Emily's AI-Powered E-Commerce Startup

Emily was a marketing professional traveling through Europe when she noticed a gap in the market for personalized e-commerce experiences. She realized that while online shopping had exploded globally, most platforms were still offering cookie-cutter experiences that didn't cater to individual tastes. Emily saw an opportunity to use AI to bridge this gap and create something revolutionary.

With a passion for technology and a strong marketing background, Emily launched ShopSmart, an AI-driven e-commerce platform that uses machine learning to personalize product recommendations based on user behaviour. Leveraging AI algorithms, ShopSmart analyses customers' browsing and purchasing habits to curate product suggestions tailored to their preferences. This innovation not only improved customer satisfaction but also increased sales for the merchants on the platform.

Operating her startup as a digital nomad, Emily worked with AI developers from around the world, using platforms like Upwork to build her team. ShopSmart quickly gained traction, and within a year, Emily expanded her client base from Europe to North America and Asia. AI allowed her to scale globally without the traditional limitations of a brick-and-mortar business. Her story showcases how AI can empower digital nomad entrepreneurs to innovate, scale, and achieve global reach.

How Digital Nomads Are Building AI Startups

Like Emily, many digital nomad entrepreneurs are leveraging AI to build scalable businesses. Here are some ways they are doing it and how you can apply these insights to your own entrepreneurial journey.

1. AI-Powered Product Development

For many startups, product development can be one of the most resource-intensive aspects of building a business. AI tools like TensorFlow and IBM Watson are enabling digital nomads to develop smarter products faster. Whether it's automating code writing, optimizing user interfaces, or building AI-driven apps, these tools allow entrepreneurs to innovate at a fraction of the cost.

Practical Tip: Use platforms like Google Cloud AI or Amazon Web Services (AWS) AI to develop, test, and deploy machine learning models for your startup, giving you access to enterprise-level resources without the high costs.

2. Data-Driven Business Decisions

AI isn't just about product development; it's also about making smarter business decisions. Digital nomads are using AI to analyse market trends, customer data, and financial reports to make data-driven decisions. Tools like Looker and Power BI offer advanced analytics, allowing entrepreneurs to visualize complex data in an accessible way. This capability is especially valuable for digital nomads who operate in diverse markets and need to stay ahead of trends.

Practical Tip: Incorporate AI analytics tools into your startup to track customer behaviour, monitor market shifts, and optimize your pricing or product offerings based on real-time data.

3. AI-Driven Customer Support

One of the key challenges for any startup is maintaining high-quality customer service while scaling. AI tools like Chatbot and Zendesk AI are allowing digital nomads to automate customer support, handling inquiries and resolving issues with minimal human intervention. This automation reduces costs and improves customer experience by providing immediate responses to common questions or concerns.

Practical Tip: Use AI chatbots to handle customer inquiries 24/7, ensuring that your startup can support a global client base even when you're on the move.

Visionary Perspective: The Future of AI-Driven Startups

As AI continues to evolve, the possibilities for digital nomads in the startup world are expanding. In the near future, AI may evolve to a point where startups can operate almost autonomously, with founders focusing solely on strategic decision-making while AI handles the execution. Imagine a startup where AI runs everything from product development and marketing to logistics and customer service, leaving entrepreneurs with the freedom to focus on innovation and growth.

Visionary Question: What would your life look like if your AI-driven startup could scale globally with minimal human oversight? How would you use this newfound freedom to innovate and explore new business opportunities?

Balancing Inspiration and Caution

While the potential for AI-driven startups is immense, it's essential to acknowledge the challenges. AI brings with it concerns about data privacy, job displacement, and the ethical use of technology. Entrepreneurs must navigate these challenges carefully, ensuring that their startups use AI in ways that are transparent, fair, and beneficial to society.

One example is the debate surrounding AI in hiring. Many startups are using AI to automate parts of the hiring process, but there's a risk of bias in the algorithms. As an entrepreneur, you must remain vigilant and ensure that the AI tools you use are ethical and inclusive.

Global and Cultural Dimensions: AI Startups Around the World

AI is transforming entrepreneurship globally, but each region is embracing it differently. In Southeast Asia, for example, AI is being used to solve logistical challenges in e-commerce. In Africa, digital nomads are using AI to create startups that address local issues, such as access to healthcare and education.

In Estonia, one of the world's most digital-forward countries, the government has implemented AI-driven platforms that allow digital nomads to establish and operate businesses entirely online. Estonia's e-residency program, paired with AI tools, makes it easier than ever for nomadic entrepreneurs to manage their startups from anywhere in the world.

Practical Tip: If you're considering launching a startup as a digital nomad, explore e-residency programs like those in Estonia to streamline your business operations and take advantage of global opportunities.

Motivating with Purpose and Fulfilment

At the heart of every successful startup is a purpose. For many digital nomads, entrepreneurship isn't just about financial freedom—it's about creating something meaningful. AI can help you build a business that not only scales but also makes a positive impact on the world. Whether it's solving a global challenge or creating a product that improves lives, AI enables you to fulfil your entrepreneurial dreams while maintaining your values.

Inspiration Question: How can your AI-driven startup not only succeed financially but also contribute to making the world a better place?

Simple Language for Complex Topics

AI can be an intimidating concept for many aspiring entrepreneurs, but it doesn't have to be. Think of AI as a tool that amplifies your strengths. Just as a hammer makes building a house easier, AI makes building a business more efficient. Don't worry about understanding every technical detail—focus on how AI can support your vision and help you achieve your goals.

Engaging Content and Takeaways

Before wrapping up this chapter, reflect on how AI could revolutionize your entrepreneurial journey. Take some time to explore AI tools that align with your startup idea. Experiment with them, and think about how you could integrate them into your business model to accelerate growth.

Final Takeaway

AI is opening doors for digital nomad entrepreneurs like never before. From product development to customer support and beyond, the possibilities are endless. The key to success is embracing AI as a partner in your journey and using it to build something that aligns with your vision. As an entrepreneur in the AI age, you have the unique opportunity to shape the future—one startup at a time.

CHAPTER 33: NOMADIC EDUCATORS LEVERAGING AI

In the age of digital transformation, education is no longer confined to physical classrooms or local geography. With the rise of AI and digital nomadism, educators and coaches are finding new ways to deliver learning and mentorship services across borders, time zones, and cultures. Whether you're a language tutor, a business coach, or an online course creator, artificial intelligence is opening doors to streamline operations, reach more students, and offer personalized learning experiences. In this chapter, we'll explore how nomadic educators are leveraging AI tools to create impactful and scalable online learning environments.

Case Study: Kate's Journey as a Nomadic Language Educator

Kate had always been passionate about teaching languages. Before embracing the digital nomad lifestyle, she worked in a traditional classroom setting. However, as her wanderlust grew, she realized that the constraints of a physical location were limiting her potential. Determined to combine her love for travel with her career, Kate transitioned to becoming a digital nomad, offering language lessons online.

At first, managing a global student base was a challenge. With students from all corners of the world, Kate struggled to keep track of individual progress and customize her lessons based on each student's needs. That's when she discovered AI-powered educational platforms like Duolingo for Educators and Linguist, which allowed her to integrate AI into her teaching process.

Using AI-powered learning tools, Kate was able to offer personalized lessons based on her students' learning pace, strengths, and weaknesses. The AI helped her analyse student data and tailor her teaching strategies. She also incorporated chatbots as virtual teaching assistants, offering students immediate feedback on their homework, while she focused on more complex aspects of the curriculum.

Through these AI-powered tools, Kate saw an improvement in her students' language proficiency, which in turn allowed her to grow her online teaching business while continuing her travels. Kate's story shows how AI can empower nomadic educators to optimize their teaching methods, save time, and offer a more personalized and impactful learning experience.

Practical Applications of AI for Educators and Coaches

AI provides several practical tools for nomadic educators and coaches. Here's how you can use these tools to improve your online learning services and scale your educational business:

1. AI-Driven Content Personalization
   AI can analyse a student's learning history and suggest customized learning paths. For instance, platforms like Edmodo and Coursera use AI to recommend personalized courses based on a student's interests, previous learning, and progress. For language tutors like Kate, AI provides personalized grammar lessons, quizzes, and practice modules, making it easier to cater to students of different

levels.

Practical Tip: Use AI-powered platforms like Thinkific or Teachable to offer personalized content recommendations to your students. These tools can help you tailor the learning experience for each individual, increasing engagement and retention.

2. Automating Administrative Tasks

Running an online education business means juggling multiple administrative tasks—scheduling, feedback collection, and grading can take up valuable time. AI-based solutions such as Grammarly and Otter.ai automate grading, feedback generation, and note-taking, allowing educators to focus on teaching and growing their businesses.

Practical Tip: Automate grading and administrative tasks by using AI tools like Quizlet for creating self-assessing quizzes and Grammarly for offering instant writing feedback to your students.

3. Enhanced Student Interaction Through AI Chatbots

AI chatbots can assist students with 24/7 support, answering questions about course material, deadlines, or assignments. This ensures that students have access to immediate guidance, even when you're unavailable due to time zone differences or travel. Tools like Ada and ManyChat allow educators to integrate chatbots into their websites or communication platforms to handle repetitive student queries.

Practical Tip: Implement AI-driven chatbots to handle FAQs, assignment inquiries, and other routine communication, leaving you with more time to address high-level teaching concerns.

4. Virtual Coaching Sessions with AI-Driven Feedback

AI is revolutionizing coaching by offering real-time

analysis of sessions. Platforms like CoachAccountable use AI to analyse coaching sessions, providing insights into how clients are progressing and areas they need to focus on. For business or life coaches, this allows you to track the progress of clients and adjust strategies based on real-time data.

Practical Tip: Use AI-driven coaching platforms to track your clients' progress and make data-informed adjustments to their learning plans, improving overall outcomes.

Visionary Perspective: The Future of AI in Education and Coaching

Imagine a world where AI doesn't just assist in lesson planning or administration but co-teaches with you. AI can analyse a student's mood, attention span, and learning preferences in real time, adjusting lessons to maximize engagement and retention. In this future, the role of educators will evolve from providing content to curating experiences that blend human mentorship with AI's capacity for infinite customization.

Visionary Question: How would your teaching methods change if AI could monitor student engagement in real-time and adjust lessons accordingly? How would that redefine personalized education?

Balancing Inspiration and Caution

While the use of AI in education offers incredible possibilities, it's crucial to address potential concerns. Over-reliance on AI can sometimes lead to depersonalized learning, where students feel they are engaging with machines rather than humans. There is also the risk of data privacy issues when student information is collected and analysed by AI tools.

Practical Tip: Balance AI automation with the human touch. Use AI to handle repetitive tasks, but make sure to engage with your students or clients on a personal level to maintain a human connection.

Global and Cultural Dimensions of AI-Powered Education

AI-powered education is taking off globally, but its impact varies across regions. In developing countries, AI is helping bridge educational gaps by providing access to quality learning resources in areas with limited human educators. In contrast, in developed countries, AI is being used to enhance already robust educational systems, offering hyper-personalized learning and innovative coaching methods.

For digital nomads, the ability to deliver AI-enhanced education across borders allows them to tap into global markets. Language tutors, business coaches, and online educators are leveraging AI to connect with students from Africa to Asia, breaking down geographical barriers.

Practical Tip: Consider offering your educational services in multiple languages and targeting diverse regions by using AI tools that translate and adapt your content to various cultural contexts.

Motivate with Purpose and Fulfilment

Education is more than a profession—it's a calling. By embracing AI, nomadic educators and coaches can focus more on the purpose behind their work: transforming lives through learning. AI provides you with the freedom to scale your teaching, reach more students, and make a greater impact without sacrificing the personal fulfilment that comes with helping others grow.

Inspiration Question: How can AI help you reach more students and make a larger impact while allowing you to stay connected to the heart of teaching—helping individuals achieve their personal and professional goals?

Keeping AI Simple and Accessible

AI can seem daunting, especially for those without a technical background. However, educators and coaches don't need to be AI experts to benefit from these tools. Think of AI as an extension of your capabilities—a tool that amplifies what you're already great at. You don't need to understand the algorithms; you just need to know how to use AI tools effectively to achieve your teaching or coaching goals.

Interactive Content: Try It Yourself

Before you wrap up this chapter, consider integrating an AI tool into your teaching or coaching services. Explore AI-powered platforms like Teachable, Thinkific, or CoachAccountable, and see how they can streamline your operations and enhance the learning experience for your students or clients.

Final Takeaway

The integration of AI in education and coaching is revolutionizing the way digital nomads operate. AI tools provide the flexibility, scalability, and efficiency to deliver quality education across borders while freeing up educators and coaches to focus on their true purpose—helping others grow. Whether you're just starting or scaling your online education business, AI can help you thrive in the digital nomad landscape, allowing you to teach, coach, and mentor from anywhere in the world.

CHAPTER 34: AI-DRIVEN DIGITAL AGENCIES: SCALING SUCCESS IN THE NOMADIC LIFESTYLE

For digital nomads, the rise of AI has opened up new avenues to create and scale digital marketing agencies that offer services across the globe. Whether it's automating campaigns, enhancing data analysis, or managing multiple clients simultaneously, AI is transforming how digital nomads approach the world of digital marketing. In this chapter, we will explore the transformative power of AI in building digital agencies, the tools digital nomads use to run their businesses, and real-world case studies of entrepreneurs who have scaled their agencies while traveling the world.

Case Study: Emma's Journey to a Thriving AI-Driven Marketing Agency

Emma was an SEO and social media marketing expert who had spent years working for a corporate agency. However, she always dreamed of becoming a digital nomad, combining her love for travel with her passion for marketing. After leaving her 9-to-5 job, she decided to start her own digital marketing agency while traveling across South America.

At first, Emma struggled to manage her new agency. She found it challenging to handle multiple clients, analyse large volumes of data, and scale her operations without hiring a large team. But once she incorporated AI tools into her agency's operations, everything changed. Emma started using platforms like HubSpot for automated customer relationship management (CRM) and Jasper AI for automating content creation. These AI tools allowed her to create personalized campaigns for clients, optimize social media posts, and generate reports with a fraction of the time and effort.

Within a few months, Emma's agency began to thrive. She could handle more clients than she had ever imagined, all while exploring the vibrant streets of Rio de Janeiro or the breathtaking landscapes of Patagonia. By leveraging AI, Emma expanded her agency's reach globally, offering services to clients in the United States, Europe, and Asia, all while living her dream of being a nomadic entrepreneur.

How Digital Nomads Are Leveraging AI to Build and Scale Agencies

For digital nomads looking to build and scale digital marketing agencies, AI offers a range of practical applications that make operations more efficient, allowing them to focus on high-level strategy and client relationships rather than getting bogged down in routine tasks.

Here are some key ways AI is empowering nomadic entrepreneurs in the digital marketing space:

1. Automated Customer Relationship Management (CRM)
   Managing relationships with multiple clients across time zones can be challenging for any digital nomad. AI-driven CRM systems like HubSpot, Salesforce, or Zoho

CRM are essential for keeping track of leads, managing communications, and automating follow-up emails. These platforms allow digital nomads to build deeper relationships with clients while streamlining administrative tasks.

Practical Tip: Set up automated workflows within your CRM to nurture leads and send personalized messages at key points in the customer journey. This keeps potential clients engaged without requiring manual follow-ups.

2. AI-Powered Content Creation

One of the most time-consuming aspects of running a digital agency is generating high-quality content. AI tools like Jasper AI and Copy.ai have revolutionized content creation, enabling digital nomads to generate blog posts, social media captions, and even email newsletters quickly and efficiently. These tools use machine learning to analyse previous content, client goals, and audience preferences to create optimized content.

Practical Tip: Use AI writing tools to draft initial content, then refine and personalize it to ensure it aligns with your client's voice and brand tone. This speeds up content production while maintaining quality.

3. Data Analysis and Reporting

Data is at the core of any successful digital marketing campaign. AI tools like Google Analytics powered by machine learning algorithms help marketers analyse vast amounts of data, spot trends, and provide actionable insights to improve campaign performance. AI-driven platforms like Supermetrics or Domo can automatically pull data from multiple channels, giving digital nomads the ability to deliver detailed reports to clients with minimal effort.

Practical Tip: Set up automated reports using AI-powered tools that compile key metrics from different platforms (social media, PPC, SEO) and deliver them directly to your inbox or dashboard, allowing you to quickly assess and optimize campaigns.

4. Predictive Analytics for Campaign Optimization

AI tools such as AdRoll and Albert use predictive analytics to optimize digital marketing campaigns in real time. These tools analyse past campaign performance, market conditions, and audience behaviours to suggest the best course of action, from ad placement to content personalization.

Practical Tip: Integrate AI-powered predictive analytics into your PPC and social media advertising strategies. Let AI suggest budget allocations and audience targeting to maximize return on investment (ROI) for clients.

5. Automated Customer Service and Chatbots

Customer service can be time-consuming, but AI-powered chatbots like Drift or Intercom can automate much of this process, offering instant responses to client inquiries and freeing up time for nomadic entrepreneurs to focus on more critical tasks. These bots can handle FAQs, schedule meetings, and even collect feedback from clients, ensuring they feel supported 24/7.

Practical Tip: Use AI chatbots to manage client inquiries and automate scheduling, giving your clients immediate support while you focus on higher-level strategy.

Visionary Perspective: The Future of AI-Driven Digital Agencies

As AI tools evolve, the digital marketing landscape is on the brink of even greater transformation. Imagine a future where AI doesn't just suggest campaign improvements but fully manages campaigns autonomously. AI could create content, optimize targeting, and analyse real-time data, allowing digital nomads to focus entirely on high-level strategy, creativity, and client relationships. This level of automation will enable digital nomad entrepreneurs to scale their agencies without the need for large teams.

Visionary Question: What could your agency look like if 90% of your operations were handled by AI? How would you redefine your role as a strategist and creative visionary?

Balancing Inspiration and Caution

While AI offers exciting possibilities, it's essential to remain mindful of the potential challenges. The rise of AI could lead to an over-reliance on automation, where the human touch in marketing is lost. Clients still value creativity, personal connection, and the ability to think outside the box. Therefore, it's crucial for digital nomads to strike a balance between AI-driven efficiency and personalized client relationships.

Practical Tip: Automate routine tasks, but maintain personal client interactions and a hands-on approach to creative strategy to build long-term relationships and trust.

Global Impact and Cultural Dimensions

AI-driven digital marketing is a global phenomenon, enabling nomadic entrepreneurs to offer services to clients in diverse markets. In developing regions like Africa and Southeast Asia, AI is helping businesses reach new audiences online with limited resources. Meanwhile, in tech-savvy regions like North America and Europe, AI is being used to scale already established digital marketing infrastructures.

For digital nomads, this global approach to marketing means there are no limits to where your clients can be located, allowing you to work with diverse businesses across continents.

Global Tip: Expand your services by offering AI-driven solutions to clients in emerging markets. Use AI tools to adapt campaigns for different cultural contexts and languages, ensuring global reach and relevance.

Motivate with Purpose and Fulfilment

At its core, running an AI-driven digital agency as a digital nomad is about more than just scaling a business—it's about creating freedom, flexibility, and purpose. AI allows digital nomads to work less on mundane tasks and more on what truly matters: traveling, exploring new cultures, and making meaningful connections with clients around the world.

Inspiration Question: How can AI help you not only grow your business but also achieve the freedom to live life on your terms, exploring the world and creating meaningful impact?

Final Thoughts

The rise of AI has transformed how digital nomads build and scale digital agencies. From automating client management and content creation to predicting campaign outcomes, AI offers a world of opportunities for those ready to embrace it. As you continue on your journey as a digital nomad entrepreneur, remember to strike a balance between automation and creativity, using AI to enhance your business while staying connected to your clients and purpose.

The future is bright for AI-driven digital marketing agencies—allowing digital nomads to thrive in a globalized, tech-enabled world.

CHAPTER 35: CONTENT CREATORS AND AI TOOLS: REVOLUTIONIZING CREATIVITY IN THE DIGITAL AGE

The rise of AI has brought a transformative shift in how content creators—bloggers, vloggers, and influencers —approach their work. For digital nomads in the content creation space, AI tools have become indispensable for streamlining tasks, increasing productivity, and enhancing creativity. Whether it's automating video editing, optimizing SEO for blogs, or generating social media content, AI is reshaping the creative process, allowing creators to focus more on storytelling and less on routine tasks. This chapter dives into how AI is empowering digital nomad content creators to thrive in the competitive world of online media.

Case Study: Jason's Journey as a Digital Nomad Vlogger

Jason, a travel vlogger, had spent years documenting his adventures as a digital nomad across the globe. While his

YouTube channel had grown steadily, he struggled with the time-consuming process of editing videos, optimizing SEO, and keeping up with social media trends. Managing all these tasks while traveling from Bali to Tokyo left him overwhelmed.

However, when Jason integrated AI tools into his workflow, his entire approach transformed. Using Descript for automated video editing, Jason was able to trim, edit, and caption his videos in a fraction of the time it once took. For SEO optimization, he turned to MarketMuse, an AI-powered tool that helped him identify the best keywords, ensuring his videos ranked higher on YouTube and Google searches. AI-driven platforms like Later scheduled his social media posts, allowing him to engage with followers around the clock while he continued his travels.

Within months, Jason saw a significant increase in views, followers, and engagement across platforms. By leveraging AI, Jason not only streamlined his creative process but also unlocked more time to focus on content ideation, storytelling, and audience interaction—all while continuing his digital nomadic journey.

How AI is Empowering Content Creators

AI tools have revolutionized the way digital nomad content creators work. These tools automate tedious tasks, provide powerful insights, and enhance creative output. Here are some key ways AI is enabling bloggers, vloggers, and content creators to elevate their work:

1. AI-Powered Writing and Editing for Bloggers

For bloggers, AI tools like Jasper AI and Grammarly have become essential for content generation and editing. Jasper AI helps creators brainstorm blog topics, write drafts, and generate SEO-optimized content. Meanwhile, Grammarly's AI-driven grammar and style checker ensures that the writing is polished and professional. These tools help bloggers save time and focus on creativity.

Practical Tip: Use Jasper AI to generate blog post outlines, then refine the draft using your voice and style. Combine this with Grammarly to ensure clarity and error-free content before publishing.

2. Automated Video Editing for Vloggers

Video editing is often one of the most time-intensive tasks for vloggers. AI tools like Descript and Pictory simplify this process by offering automated video transcription, editing, and captioning. With these tools, creators can edit videos by simply editing the transcript, saving time on cutting clips manually. AI algorithms can also identify the best scenes, add captions, and enhance the overall video quality.

Practical Tip: Use Descript to edit your vlogs by removing filler words, trimming unnecessary parts, and adding captions—all through an intuitive, text-based interface.

3. SEO Optimization for Increased Reach

Content creators rely heavily on search engine optimization (SEO) to increase their visibility online. AI-driven tools like Surfer SEO and MarketMuse analyse top-ranking content and provide keyword suggestions, content structure recommendations, and optimization tips to help creators rank higher on search engines. These tools take the guesswork out of SEO, ensuring that every blog or video is optimized for searchability.

Practical Tip: Use Surfer SEO to analyse the top 10 search results for your topic, and implement AI-driven recommendations for headings, keyword usage, and word count to improve your ranking.

4. AI-Driven Social Media Management

For content creators, managing social media across

multiple platforms can be exhausting. AI tools like Buffer and Later help automate the scheduling of posts, analyse engagement metrics, and suggest the best times to post. These platforms allow creators to plan and automate their content distribution, ensuring they remain active and engaged with their audience without constantly being online.

Practical Tip: Use Later to schedule a week's worth of Instagram posts in advance, ensuring that your content goes live at peak engagement times without interrupting your travel or work.

5. Content Personalization and Audience Insights

AI has enhanced how content creators understand and engage with their audiences. Platforms like Hootsuite Insights and Sprinklr analyse social media engagement, track trends, and provide real-time data on audience preferences. This allows creators to tailor their content to meet the expectations of their followers, ensuring higher engagement and more meaningful connections.

Practical Tip: Use Hootsuite Insights to monitor audience sentiment and adapt your content strategy based on what resonates most with your followers.

Inspiring a Visionary Future for Content Creators

The future of AI-driven content creation holds incredible potential. Imagine a world where AI can autonomously generate blog posts, edit vlogs, and manage entire social media platforms—all while maintaining the unique voice of the creator. With advancements in natural language processing (NLP) and machine learning, AI could soon become a co-creator, collaborating with content creators to develop innovative ideas and execute them in real-time.

Visionary Question: What new creative possibilities could

you explore if AI handled 80% of your content production tasks, leaving you free to focus entirely on storytelling and strategy?

Balancing Inspiration and Caution

While AI offers exciting opportunities, creators must be mindful of the potential risks. Over-reliance on automation can result in content that feels impersonal or lacks the creator's unique voice. It's crucial for digital nomads to strike a balance between AI-driven efficiency and maintaining an authentic connection with their audience.

Practical Tip: Use AI to streamline repetitive tasks but ensure that the heart of your content—your unique perspective and storytelling—remains intact. AI should enhance creativity, not replace it.

Global and Cultural Dimensions of AI-Driven Content

As digital nomads travel and work across different cultures, AI tools offer the potential to tailor content for global audiences. Tools like DeepL provide AI-powered translations, allowing creators to reach new audiences by translating their content into multiple languages. Additionally, AI tools can analyse cultural trends, enabling creators to localize content for specific regions.

Global Tip: Use DeepL to translate your blog posts or videos into the language of the local audience you're targeting. Combine this with culturally relevant imagery and examples to create a deeper connection with international followers.

Motivating Purpose and Fulfilment in Content Creation

For digital nomads, content creation is more than just a job—it's a way to share experiences, inspire others, and live a life of adventure and purpose. By embracing AI, content creators can free up time for travel, passion projects, and deeper engagement with their audience. AI tools allow creators to focus on what truly matters: connecting with others, telling meaningful stories, and pursuing personal fulfilment.

Inspiration Tip: Reflect on how AI can help you achieve a balance between professional success and personal fulfilment. Use AI tools to manage the operational side of content creation, while dedicating more time to exploring new cultures, building relationships, and living out your digital nomadic dreams.

Conclusion: AI as the Ultimate Co-Creator

AI has reshaped the landscape for digital nomads in the content creation world. From automating video editing and SEO optimization to personalizing content and managing social media, AI tools enable creators to scale their efforts while remaining true to their creative vision. By finding the right balance between AI-driven efficiency and human creativity, digital nomads can build thriving content creation businesses that allow them to live life on their own terms.

As you continue on your journey as a digital nomad, remember that AI is your co-creator—empowering you to achieve more while staying connected to the stories, cultures, and communities that inspire your content. The future of content creation is bright, and AI is the key to unlocking new levels of creative potential.

PART 8: AI AND THE FUTURE OF DIGITAL NOMADS

CHAPTER 36: AI'S ROLE IN THE FUTURE OF WORK

The future of work is no longer a distant concept—it is unfolding now, and AI is at the centre of this transformation. As digital nomads, we stand on the front lines of this evolution, embracing technologies that allow us to work from anywhere in the world while remaining deeply connected to the global economy. The way we work, collaborate, and create value is shifting as AI continues to reshape industries and job functions. But what exactly does the future of work look like in an AI-dominated landscape? More importantly, how can digital nomads not only survive but thrive in this new era?

In this chapter, we explore the broad implications of AI on work, grounded in real-life stories, practical tips, and a vision for the future that inspires and empowers.

Case Study: How AI Transformed Luis's Freelance Career

Luis was a digital nomad with a background in graphic design. He had been working on freelance projects for years, managing a steady income but always struggling with the manual aspects of his job. From designing marketing collateral to tweaking client logos, the process was slow and repetitive. It wasn't until Luis adopted AI-powered design tools like Canva Pro and Adobe Sensei that his workflow underwent a dramatic transformation.

With AI handling much of the mundane design work —suggesting layouts, automating colour adjustments, and even generating design templates—Luis found that he could now complete projects in half the time. The time he saved allowed him to focus on building relationships with new clients and even launching a side business offering AI-enhanced design services. His revenue soared as a result, but more importantly, Luis felt liberated from the mechanical tasks that once drained his energy.

Luis's journey demonstrates the profound impact AI can have on freelancers and digital nomads. AI isn't just an assistant; it can become a powerful co-creator, allowing digital nomads to scale their businesses and offer cutting-edge services with minimal effort.

How AI is Reshaping the Future of Work

The future of work will not revolve around a traditional office setup or fixed schedules. Instead, it will emphasize flexibility, creativity, and human-AI collaboration. As AI tools continue to advance, they will not only automate repetitive tasks but also enhance creative work, decision-making, and strategy.

1. AI-Powered Automation and Efficiency

One of AI's most significant contributions to the future of work is its ability to automate time-consuming and repetitive tasks. Whether it's data entry, email marketing, or video editing, AI tools can now handle tasks that once took hours. This allows digital nomads to focus on higher-level activities such as strategic thinking, creativity, and innovation.

Practical Tip: Use tools like Zapier to automate routine processes such as sending emails or updating project management tools. This frees up valuable time for more impactful tasks.

2. Collaboration Across Borders

AI is breaking down barriers to collaboration by enabling seamless communication across time zones and languages. Tools like Otter.ai for real-time transcription and DeepL for AI-driven translations allow digital nomads to work with global clients and teams without the friction of language barriers or time zone differences.

Practical Tip: For international projects, use DeepL to instantly translate communications or blog posts into multiple languages, broadening your reach and client base.

3. Remote Team Management

As remote work becomes the norm, AI-powered project management tools like Trello and Monday.com help digital nomads manage teams, delegate tasks, and track progress in real-time. AI can provide insights into project timelines, resource allocation, and bottlenecks, making it easier to manage multiple clients and teams.

Practical Tip: Use AI-driven project management platforms to get real-time analytics on team productivity, ensuring you're always one step ahead in managing deliverables.

4. AI-Powered Upskilling

In the AI-driven future of work, continuous learning will be essential. Fortunately, AI is making it easier than ever to acquire new skills through personalized learning platforms like Coursera and LinkedIn Learning, which use AI to recommend courses based on your career goals and learning preferences.

Practical Tip: Set aside time each week to engage in AI-driven learning platforms that align with your career trajectory. This proactive approach will ensure that you stay relevant and competitive in the job market.

Inspiring a Vision for the Future

What does the future hold for digital nomads as AI continues to evolve? Imagine a world where AI assistants not only handle mundane tasks but also provide strategic insights, enabling digital nomads to run fully autonomous businesses while traveling the world. AI could optimize everything from financial management to creative content production, allowing nomads to focus on exploring new cultures, engaging in passion projects, or pursuing lifelong learning.

Visionary Question: What would your life look like if AI could handle 80% of your business operations? How would that newfound freedom impact your creativity, work-life balance, and fulfilment?

Balancing Innovation with Ethical Concerns

While the future of work with AI is promising, it also raises important questions around job displacement, data privacy, and work-life balance. Many jobs will undoubtedly be transformed or eliminated by automation. However, new opportunities will arise for those willing to adapt and upskill.

It's essential to approach AI with both optimism and caution. While AI will increase productivity and create new career paths, it's equally important to ensure that we do not lose sight of ethical considerations, including fair compensation, privacy, and the preservation of human creativity.

Practical Tip: Stay ahead of AI-related disruptions by continuously learning new skills and staying informed about ethical AI practices. Engage in discussions around AI's societal impact to ensure that your work aligns with ethical and sustainable practices.

Global and Cultural Impacts of AI

As digital nomads, we have the unique opportunity to observe how AI is impacting different regions of the world. In some countries, AI is being leveraged to provide essential services, while in others, it is enhancing business operations and driving innovation. Understanding how AI is shaping the global landscape will give digital nomads a competitive edge as they work across borders.

For example, in Estonia, AI is powering e-residency programs, allowing digital nomads to establish businesses and manage their taxes remotely. In Southeast Asia, AI is being used to support small businesses by automating supply chains and improving customer service.

Global Tip: Stay attuned to how AI is being implemented in different countries to understand global trends and position your business to take advantage of regional AI advancements.

Motivating a Purpose-Driven Career in the AI Age

AI will undoubtedly play a significant role in the future of work, but its true power lies in its ability to free up time for humans to focus on what truly matters: purpose, creativity, and human connection. For digital nomads, AI provides the tools to not only achieve financial freedom but also pursue meaningful and fulfilling careers.

Inspiration Tip: Reflect on how AI can help you achieve a balance between work and personal fulfilment. By using AI to handle the operational side of your business, you can focus on making a positive impact in the world—whether through creative endeavours, charitable work, or cultural exploration.

Conclusion: Embracing the AI Revolution

The future of work in an AI-dominated landscape is one of unprecedented opportunity. AI is not here to replace digital nomads but to empower them—to elevate their work, enhance their creativity, and allow them to live lives of freedom and purpose. By embracing AI, digital nomads can shape their careers on their own terms, contributing to a future that values both technological innovation and human connection.

As you move forward in your digital nomad journey, remember that AI is not just a tool; it's a partner in your success. The possibilities are limitless, and the future is yours to create.

CHAPTER 37: WILL AI REPLACE DIGITAL NOMADS?

In a world increasingly shaped by artificial intelligence, the question that looms large for digital nomads is: Will AI replace us? As AI-powered automation transforms industries, the idea of machines taking over jobs traditionally done by humans is no longer a futuristic fantasy—it's a real possibility. For digital nomads, who often rely on freelance work, remote collaboration, and niche expertise, understanding the impact of AI on their careers is essential. In this chapter, we'll explore whether AI will replace digital nomad roles, which jobs are most at risk, and how nomads can future-proof their careers.

To ground this discussion, let's begin with a story of adaptation and survival in the age of AI.

Case Study: Emma's Journey from Copywriter to AI Consultant

Emma, a digital nomad, spent the last five years working as a freelance copywriter. She travelled the globe while crafting marketing content for clients across different industries. However, as AI writing tools like Jasper AI and Copy.ai became more advanced, Emma noticed a drop in demand for her services. Many of her clients were turning to AI to generate blog posts, product descriptions, and social media content at a fraction of the cost.

Initially, Emma was worried about the future of her career. She wondered, Will AI take over my job entirely? But instead of seeing AI as a threat, Emma decided to embrace it. She started using AI tools to enhance her work, allowing her to write faster and more efficiently. Soon, she pivoted her business, offering a unique service: AI-powered copywriting consultancy. Emma didn't just write content; she trained her clients to use AI tools effectively, bridging the gap between machine-generated content and human creativity.

Today, Emma's income has tripled, and she's never been more in demand. Her story shows that while AI might disrupt certain roles, those who are adaptable and willing to embrace AI as a tool rather than a replacement can thrive.

Understanding the AI Threat: Which Roles Are at Risk?

While not all digital nomad roles will be replaced by AI, certain jobs are more vulnerable to automation than others. Roles that involve repetitive tasks, data processing, and pattern recognition are the most susceptible. Here are a few examples:

1. Content Creation and Writing
   As Emma's story highlights, AI is already capable of generating written content at scale. Tools like Jasper AI and Copy.ai can produce high-quality blog posts, marketing copy, and product descriptions in seconds. For digital nomads who rely solely on writing services, this could mean fewer opportunities as clients opt for cheaper, AI-generated alternatives.

2. Graphic Design and Visual Content
   AI-driven design tools like Canva and Adobe Sensei are revolutionizing the graphic design industry. These tools automate tasks such as layout design, colour correction,

and even logo creation, making it easier for non-designers to produce professional-quality visuals. Digital nomads who specialize in basic design tasks may find themselves competing with AI-powered tools that offer similar services at lower costs.

3. Customer Support

Many companies are adopting AI chatbots and virtual assistants to handle customer service queries. For digital nomads who provide remote customer support, this shift could mean fewer job opportunities as AI systems like Intercom and Zendesk become more sophisticated.

The Human Advantage: Why AI Won't Replace All Nomads

Despite AI's rapid advancement, there are several areas where digital nomads still hold a competitive edge. AI may be great at processing data and automating routine tasks, but it lacks emotional intelligence, creativity, and critical thinking. These uniquely human traits are irreplaceable in many fields.

1. Creativity and Innovation

While AI can generate content or design logos, it doesn't possess the ability to create something truly original or innovative. Digital nomads who work in creative industries —such as art, branding, and product design—will continue to thrive because creativity requires human intuition, context, and emotional understanding that AI cannot replicate.

2. Strategic Thinking and Problem Solving

AI can analyse vast amounts of data, but interpreting that data and applying it to complex business strategies is still a human domain. Digital nomads who offer consulting, project management, and strategic planning services are likely to see continued demand, as these roles require a deep understanding of context, market dynamics, and human behaviour.

3. Building Relationships

In the freelance world, building and maintaining client relationships is key to success. While AI can automate communication, it cannot forge the trust and rapport that come from human interaction. Digital nomads who excel at client management, sales, and networking will continue to have a competitive advantage.

How to Future-Proof Your Digital Nomad Career

If AI is set to disrupt many digital nomad roles, how can you ensure that your career remains relevant? Here are some practical strategies to safeguard your future:

1. Embrace AI as a Tool, Not a Threat

Just like Emma, the best way to future-proof your career is to integrate AI into your workflow. AI should be seen as a tool that enhances your productivity and creativity, rather than something to compete with. By using AI to automate repetitive tasks, you can free up time to focus on higher-level work that requires human ingenuity.

Practical Tip: Start by incorporating AI tools like Grammarly for editing or Jasper AI for content generation into your workflow. These tools will improve your efficiency while allowing you to maintain creative control.

2. Upskill and Diversify

The future belongs to those who are adaptable and constantly learning. Digital nomads should invest in acquiring new skills that complement their existing expertise. For example, if you're a content creator, learning about AI-driven marketing strategies or data analysis will make you more versatile and valuable in the job market.

Practical Tip: Platforms like Coursera and LinkedIn Learning offer AI-related courses that can help you stay ahead of the curve. Focus on areas like machine learning, AI ethics, and AI-driven marketing.

3. Focus on Human-Centred Services

Jobs that require emotional intelligence, creativity, and interpersonal skills will be the least affected by AI. If you can provide services that involve building relationships, offering personalized advice, or creating unique solutions, you'll remain indispensable in a world dominated by AI.

Practical Tip: Consider shifting your focus to client-based roles such as coaching, consulting, or project management— fields where human interaction and empathy are key.

The Visionary Future: AI and the Digital Nomad of Tomorrow

Imagine a future where AI handles all the mundane aspects of work—admin, scheduling, data analysis—while digital nomads focus entirely on creative projects, innovation, and building meaningful connections. Rather than replacing digital nomads, AI will empower them to pursue passion projects, collaborate on a global scale, and explore new dimensions of creativity.

Visionary Question: How can you leverage AI to maximize your time, creativity, and potential? What will your career look like if AI handles the repetitive tasks, freeing you to focus on your true passions?

Conclusion: Adapting to Thrive

The rise of AI will undoubtedly change the digital nomad landscape, but it doesn't have to be a threat. By embracing AI, continuously learning, and focusing on uniquely human skills, digital nomads can not only survive but thrive in this new era of work. The future isn't about AI versus humans —it's about collaboration. Together, we can shape a future where AI enhances our capabilities and enables us to live more fulfilling, purpose-driven lives.

Let AI handle the tasks, while you focus on what matters most—creating, innovating, and living the digital nomad dream.

CHAPTER 38: THE NEW GLOBAL WORKFORCE – HOW AI AND GLOBALIZATION WILL SHAPE THE FUTURE OF REMOTE WORK

As the digital landscape continues to evolve, the forces of AI and globalization are reshaping the future of remote work, and with it, the lifestyle of digital nomads. The ability to work from anywhere is no longer just a niche lifestyle; it's becoming a dominant global trend. Coupled with AI's incredible advancements in automation and optimization, digital nomads now have more tools and opportunities to thrive than ever before. But what does this future look like, and how will AI and globalization create a new global workforce?

In this chapter, we will explore how AI is transforming

the digital nomad lifestyle, breaking down borders and expanding opportunities. From storytelling that showcases real-world successes to practical applications and visionary forecasts, we'll chart a course for how digital nomads can not only survive but thrive in this new age of work.

Engage with Storytelling and Case Studies

Meet Sophie, a digital marketing strategist from France. Like many digital nomads, she began her journey freelancing while traveling, seeking the freedom to work from anywhere. But as her client list grew, Sophie found herself stretched thin. She was spending hours managing campaigns, optimizing content, and handling client feedback manually. It wasn't long before she realized something had to change.

Enter AI. Sophie integrated AI-powered tools like HubSpot for automating email marketing campaigns, Jasper AI for generating content, and Hootsuite's AI features to schedule social media posts. Suddenly, what once took hours could now be completed in minutes. Sophie's business transformed from a solo freelance gig into a full-fledged agency. She now manages teams across different continents, all while exploring the beaches of Bali.

Sophie's story is one of many examples of how AI is empowering digital nomads to scale their businesses and operate across borders with ease. AI is enabling nomads to not just survive in the remote work landscape but to build sustainable, scalable careers that flourish no matter where they choose to live.

Focus on Practical Application

AI offers a multitude of practical tools for digital nomads, helping streamline processes and improve productivity. Here's how you can leverage AI to thrive in a rapidly globalizing world:

1. Automating Administrative Tasks:
For digital nomads, time is a precious resource. AI-driven platforms like Zapier can automate mundane tasks such as invoicing, email responses, and scheduling. This allows nomads to spend more time on strategic work, networking, and enjoying the freedom that comes with remote work.

Practical Tip: Use Zapier to create workflows that connect your apps. For example, automate the creation of invoices in QuickBooks when a client project is marked complete in Asana.

2. Enhanced Communication and Collaboration:
Remote teams often face challenges in collaboration, especially when working across time zones. AI-powered tools like Slack and Zoom's AI integrations can bridge the gap by scheduling meetings automatically and suggesting collaboration times based on team members' locations.

Practical Tip: Leverage Google Translate and AI-powered transcription tools to facilitate communication across language barriers, making it easier to collaborate with international clients or teammates.

3. Predictive Analytics for Business Growth:
With the rise of data-driven decisions, AI can provide digital nomads with predictive insights into market trends. Tools like Google Analytics AI can track and predict traffic, giving freelancers and entrepreneurs key insights on where to focus their efforts.

Practical Tip: Use Google Analytics AI to predict website traffic spikes or dips, enabling you to plan marketing campaigns or content production accordingly.

Inspire Through Visionary Perspectives

As AI continues to evolve, the possibilities for remote work seem limitless. Imagine a world where AI assistants manage all mundane tasks—from handling client communication to optimizing your personal brand's SEO—leaving you to focus entirely on creative and strategic work.

In the near future, digital nomads could work seamlessly across global teams without the constraints of language or time zones. AI-driven translation tools could make real-time conversations across languages a breeze, while AI assistants would handle time zone management, ensuring meetings are scheduled at the perfect time for everyone involved.

Visionary Question: What could your business or career look like if AI took over 90% of your administrative tasks? How would that free you up to pursue bigger, more creative projects?

Balance Between Inspiration and Caution

While AI brings enormous opportunities, it also presents challenges. The rise of AI is poised to disrupt certain job markets, especially roles that involve repetitive tasks. For digital nomads, staying ahead of these changes means continuously upskilling and staying adaptable.

For instance, some administrative jobs may be automated, but this opens doors for nomads to pivot into high-value roles like consulting, AI tool implementation, or strategy development. The future will reward those who are proactive in learning and embracing new technologies.

Balanced Tip: To stay relevant, invest in learning AI-related skills like machine learning basics, data analysis, or AI tool management. Continuous learning will keep you ahead of the curve as the remote work landscape evolves.

Highlight Global and Cultural Dimensions

The digital nomad movement has always been a global one, and AI is amplifying this trend. Countries like Estonia and Thailand are leading the way in creating digital nomad-friendly ecosystems. In Estonia, the government's digital-first approach allows nomads to set up businesses remotely, while Thailand is working on visa programs to attract tech-savvy workers.

In countries like India, AI is transforming small businesses, giving entrepreneurs access to global markets. Digital nomads who offer AI-driven services, such as marketing or data analysis, are helping businesses in these regions scale, creating new opportunities for cross-border collaboration.

Motivate with Purpose and Fulfilment

At the core of the digital nomad lifestyle is the pursuit of freedom, purpose, and fulfilment. AI amplifies this by enabling nomads to work more efficiently and focus on what truly matters—whether that's creative pursuits, travel, or contributing to causes they care about.

Inspirational Thought: By automating your workload with AI, you're not just optimizing your business—you're creating space for meaningful, purpose-driven work. The freedom to live anywhere and work globally allows you to design a life that aligns with your passions and values.

Use Accessible, Simple Language for Complex Topics

AI can seem intimidating, but it doesn't have to be. Think of AI as your highly efficient assistant. It's there to sort through data, automate tasks, and help you focus on creative or strategic aspects of your work.

Analogy: Imagine AI as a digital assistant who can sift through piles of information in seconds, leaving you free to focus on the things only humans can do—like brainstorming innovative ideas, forming client relationships, and developing creative content.

Interactive and Engaging Content

To fully embrace AI's potential, it's essential to get hands-on experience. Before moving on to the next chapter, spend 15 minutes exploring one of the AI tools mentioned. Try out Jasper AI for content creation or Grammarly for editing. Experiment with it in your work, and reflect: How did it change your workflow? What surprised you?

Conclusion: Embrace the Future of Work with AI

As AI continues to evolve, so too will the opportunities for digital nomads. The future of work is global, borderless, and powered by AI. By embracing these changes, digital nomads can thrive in ways that were previously unimaginable. Now is the time to adapt, learn, and leverage AI to shape a career—and a life—that is both fulfilling and future-proof.

CHAPTER 39: ETHICAL AI AND DIGITAL NOMADS – NAVIGATING THE MORAL IMPLICATIONS OF AN AI-DRIVEN WORLD

The rise of artificial intelligence (AI) has not only reshaped how digital nomads work but has also introduced a new set of ethical challenges. As more nomads leverage AI to automate workflows, enhance productivity, and scale their businesses, there are deeper moral questions that must be addressed. What are the ethical implications of working with AI? How can digital nomads ensure that the AI tools they rely on are used responsibly and ethically? In this chapter, we will explore these questions and provide a comprehensive guide to the ethical considerations digital nomads must be mindful of in an AI-powered world.

Engage with Storytelling and Case Studies

Let's begin with James, a freelance data analyst and digital nomad from the UK. For years, James travelled across Europe while providing data insights to clients around the world. Recently, he adopted AI-driven data analysis tools to automate much of his work. These tools processed enormous amounts of personal data, offering powerful insights for his clients.

However, James soon realized a problem: some of the data his clients collected and fed into AI tools came from questionable sources. It included sensitive information that lacked proper user consent. James faced an ethical dilemma. Was it right to continue using AI tools that might be processing data unethically, even if his clients benefited from the insights? After all, in his hands, AI could make his work more efficient, but at what cost to privacy?

James decided to take a stand. He educated his clients on responsible data collection and implemented strict guidelines for how data should be gathered and used. By setting a precedent for ethical AI usage, James safeguarded his clients' reputation and his own while ensuring that his work aligned with his personal values.

Focus on Practical Application

AI is incredibly useful for digital nomads, but how can you ensure that the AI tools you use are ethical? Here are some practical steps you can take to integrate ethical practices into your work:

1. Data Privacy and Consent:
   When working with AI tools, particularly those handling

data (such as customer profiles, analytics, or marketing insights), ensure that the data being processed has been collected ethically. Users must have provided informed consent for their data to be used in AI systems.

Practical Tip: Use privacy-focused tools like DuckDuckGo for search analysis and ensure that any AI systems you use comply with global regulations such as GDPR. Additionally, always seek transparent user consent for data collection.

2. Avoiding Algorithmic Bias:

AI algorithms are only as unbiased as the data they're trained on. If an AI tool is trained on biased data, it can produce skewed results, often to the detriment of certain groups. As a digital nomad, whether you're using AI for recruitment, content generation, or analytics, it's essential to audit the tools you're using to avoid perpetuating bias.

Practical Tip: Conduct regular audits on AI tools like Google Analytics or LinkedIn Recruiter to ensure that the insights generated are fair, inclusive, and representative. Keep an eye on any trends that seem disproportionately skewed and flag any suspicious results.

3. Environmental Considerations:

AI systems, particularly those involving machine learning and large data processing, consume vast amounts of energy. Digital nomads who value sustainability should consider the carbon footprint of the AI tools they use and seek greener alternatives.

Practical Tip: Choose AI services powered by renewable energy or with a lower environmental impact, such as Google Cloud AI, which runs on carbon-neutral infrastructure.

Inspire Through Visionary Perspectives

As AI continues to evolve, it's crucial for digital nomads to think ahead. How will ethical AI shape the future of remote work? Imagine a world where digital nomads not only leverage AI to scale their businesses but also advocate for fair, responsible AI development on a global level. By embracing the ethical implications of AI, digital nomads can lead a movement toward more responsible tech innovation.

In the near future, digital nomads may serve as ethical gatekeepers—working across borders and cultures to ensure that AI tools are developed with inclusivity, fairness, and transparency in mind.

Visionary Question: As a digital nomad, how can you contribute to shaping the ethical landscape of AI? What steps can you take today to advocate for responsible AI development in your work and industry?

Balance Between Inspiration and Caution

AI offers tremendous opportunities, but it also has a darker side. The potential for AI-driven mass surveillance, misuse of personal data, and job displacement is real. Digital nomads must be proactive, not only in using AI responsibly but also in pushing back against unethical practices.

For example, facial recognition technologies used in some countries to monitor citizens have sparked global debates. As a digital nomad, consider the implications of working with clients who employ such technologies. While the financial gain may be tempting, the ethical cost could be much higher.

Balanced Tip: If you're unsure whether a client or AI tool aligns with your values, do your research. Platforms like AI Ethics Lab or AlgorithmWatch can provide insights and guidelines on the responsible use of AI technologies. If needed, decline projects that compromise ethical standards.

Highlight Global and Cultural Dimensions

Ethical considerations around AI vary significantly across the globe. In Europe, stringent data privacy regulations like GDPR set a high bar for how AI tools handle personal data. In contrast, some countries prioritize innovation and may not impose similar levels of regulation, which could create ethical gray areas for digital nomads.

For example, in China, AI is at the forefront of technological innovation but is also used extensively for surveillance. As a digital nomad, navigating these cultural differences requires an understanding of how AI regulations and ethical standards differ globally.

Global Insight: Research the legal and ethical frameworks surrounding AI in the regions where you work. By understanding the local context, you can make more informed decisions about which AI tools and projects to engage with.

Motivate with Purpose and Fulfilment

Ultimately, the goal of ethical AI use is to align your work with your values. By using AI responsibly, digital nomads can contribute to a world where technology empowers people without exploiting them. AI doesn't have to come at the cost of privacy, fairness, or ethics.

Inspirational Thought: By adopting ethical AI practices, you're not just optimizing your business—you're aligning your career with a higher purpose. Ethical AI allows you to build a career that not only thrives in the present but contributes to a more responsible and equitable future.

Use Accessible, Simple Language for Complex Topics

Ethical AI can be daunting, but it's really about asking the right questions. Think of ethical AI as a compass that helps guide you through the complex landscape of remote work and technology. It's about ensuring that your digital footprint leaves a positive mark.

Analogy: Just as you wouldn't compromise your personal ethics for short-term gains, ethical AI practices ensure that the technology you use reflects your values—like making sure your digital path is one you can be proud of.

Interactive and Engaging Content

Before you move on, take a moment to reflect on your own use of AI tools. Ask yourself:

- Are the AI tools I'm using aligned with my ethical values?
- Am I confident that these tools handle data responsibly?
- What steps can I take to ensure I'm using AI ethically?

Make a list of AI tools you currently use, research their ethical practices, and take action where necessary.

Conclusion: Building a More Ethical Future with AI

As digital nomads, we are in a unique position to shape the future of work through the ethical use of AI. By asking the right questions and staying vigilant, we can ensure that the technology we rely on contributes to a fairer, more inclusive world. Let's lead the way in making ethical AI the standard, not the exception.

CHAPTER 40: NOMADS IN A POST-AI ECONOMY – ESSENTIAL SKILLS AND TOOLS FOR THE FUTURE

As the AI revolution continues to transform industries and the global economy, digital nomads are at the forefront of this wave of change. In a post-AI economy, where automation takes over many routine tasks, the question is no longer whether AI will replace jobs, but how digital nomads can thrive by adapting their skills and embracing new tools. This chapter explores the critical skills and AI-powered tools that will be essential for digital nomads to not just survive but flourish in the evolving work landscape.

Engage with Storytelling and Case Studies

Take Clara, a marketing consultant and digital nomad from Brazil, who was initially overwhelmed by the rapid changes in AI. As automation took over many of the tasks she used to do manually, such as data analysis and social media scheduling, she worried about being left behind. But instead of resisting, Clara chose to embrace AI tools like Hootsuite Insights for social media analytics and Jasper AI for generating content ideas.

As a result, she transformed her business. What used to take hours of manual work—like creating tailored marketing strategies—now took a fraction of the time with the help of AI tools. Clara not only saved time but also expanded her client base, offering more sophisticated insights and services thanks to AI. Her journey is a testament to how digital nomads who lean into AI can carve out new niches in a fast-changing economy.

Focus on Practical Application

To succeed in a post-AI economy, digital nomads will need to cultivate a blend of skills that complement AI technologies. Here's a breakdown of the most valuable skills and tools:

1. AI Literacy and Critical Thinking
    Understanding AI basics—how it works, its strengths, and limitations—is crucial for staying relevant. More importantly, digital nomads must become skilled in leveraging AI to enhance creativity and strategy. Knowing how to ask the right questions and critically interpret AI outputs will set you apart from those who blindly rely on automation.

    Practical Tip: Use platforms like Coursera and edX to develop your understanding of AI fundamentals. Courses like "AI for Everyone" by Andrew Ng provide a solid foundation in AI, tailored for non-technical users.

2. Automation and Workflow Optimization
    Digital nomads who can master automation will be able to scale their businesses more efficiently. Tools like Zapier

and IFTTT allow you to automate repetitive tasks, freeing up time for more meaningful work. Whether you're automating client emails or syncing tasks between different platforms, the ability to streamline your workflow is key.

Practical Tip: Experiment with automation by setting up basic workflows on Zapier. For example, create an automation that sends your new blog posts to all your social media platforms without manual intervention.

3. Data Interpretation and AI-Driven Analytics

AI tools can analyse massive datasets, but humans are still needed to interpret that data and turn it into actionable insights. Being able to read AI-generated analytics and apply them to your projects is an invaluable skill. Whether you're using AI to optimize ad campaigns or fine-tune your digital products, understanding how to draw conclusions from data is essential.

Practical Tip: Use Google Analytics and Tableau to familiarize yourself with data visualization and reporting. Learn how to use AI-powered tools to predict trends, track performance, and optimize strategies.

4. Personal Branding and AI-Powered Content Creation

In the post-AI economy, personal branding will become even more important as AI commoditizes certain tasks. Digital nomads can differentiate themselves by building strong personal brands and using AI tools to produce high-quality content at scale. Tools like Jasper AI and Canva Pro enable content creation with AI assistance, streamlining everything from blog posts to graphic design.

Practical Tip: Experiment with AI-powered writing tools like Jasper AI to generate blog ideas and first drafts. Use Grammarly to polish your writing, and Canva Pro for quick, visually appealing designs that can boost your brand.

5. Agility and Continuous Learning

The AI landscape evolves quickly, and digital nomads who are adaptable and committed to continuous learning will stay ahead. Whether it's mastering new AI tools or picking up adjacent skills like coding or project management, being agile will ensure you can pivot and adjust to new market demands.

Practical Tip: Dedicate a portion of your workweek to learning new skills. Platforms like Udemy or Skillshare offer bite-sized courses on AI, business, and more. Stay open to new fields like AI ethics, digital project management, or blockchain, which will shape the future.

Inspire Through Visionary Perspectives

Imagine a future where AI not only automates the mundane but also enhances your creativity, allowing you to focus on big-picture strategies and passion projects. In this world, digital nomads who fully embrace AI will operate more like "cyborgs"—combining human ingenuity with machine efficiency to offer unprecedented value to clients.

The ability to handle complex tasks with the aid of AI will make digital nomads indispensable in the global workforce. As AI continues to advance, it won't just be about using tools but co-creating with them, where human intuition meets machine precision.

Visionary Question: What new possibilities could open up if AI handled the majority of your operational tasks? How much more time would you have to focus on innovation and personal growth?

Balance Between Inspiration and Caution

While AI offers vast opportunities, it also presents risks, particularly regarding job displacement. Certain digital nomad roles—such as entry-level content writing or data entry—may be fully automated. However, this isn't a cause for alarm. Instead, it's an invitation to upskill and pivot towards roles that require human creativity, strategic thinking, and emotional intelligence—things AI cannot replicate.

Balanced Tip: If you're in a field at high risk of automation, consider transitioning to higher-level roles that involve managing AI systems, interpreting data, or providing creative direction.

Highlight Global and Cultural Dimensions

The post-AI economy is global by nature, and digital nomads are uniquely positioned to leverage this interconnectedness. Different regions are adopting AI at varying speeds, offering digital nomads the chance to work across diverse cultural and technological landscapes. For instance, Estonia's digital-first policies provide seamless e-residency options for nomads, while countries like India are leveraging AI to scale their growing entrepreneurial ecosystems.

Global Insight: As a digital nomad, keep an eye on emerging AI hubs around the world. Opportunities are abundant in countries pushing digital transformation, such as Estonia, Singapore, and Kenya. You can thrive by connecting with local tech ecosystems and expanding your network globally.

Motivate with Purpose and Fulfilment

In a post-AI economy, thriving as a digital nomad isn't just about keeping pace with technology. It's about using AI to align your career with a deeper sense of purpose. AI can free you from repetitive tasks, giving you more time to focus on what truly matters—whether that's creative work, spending time with loved ones, or contributing to causes you care about.

Inspirational Thought: By embracing AI, you're not only optimizing your career; you're creating space for fulfilment, passion, and purpose. What would you do if AI freed up 50% of your workweek?

Use Accessible, Simple Language for Complex Topics

Think of AI as an incredibly efficient assistant. It can sift through mountains of data in seconds, highlight important trends, and even suggest creative ideas. While it may seem complex, AI is really just a powerful tool that amplifies your own skills and talents. And like any tool, its value comes from how well you use it.

Interactive and Engaging Content

Before you move on to the next chapter, take a few minutes to reflect on your current skills. Ask yourself:
- How can AI help me improve my workflow or scale my business?
- What new AI-powered tools can I integrate into my current projects?
- What skills can I develop to stay relevant in a post-AI economy?

List three AI tools you'd like to explore and set aside time to experiment with them in your own work.

Conclusion: Embracing the Future with AI

The post-AI economy offers endless opportunities for digital nomads who are willing to adapt, learn, and evolve. By focusing on the right skills and tools, you can not only secure your place in the future of work but also thrive in ways that weren't possible before. Let AI handle the routine while you focus on what truly matters—creativity, strategy, and personal fulfilment.

PART 9: AI AND CULTURAL SHIFTS FOR DIGITAL NOMADS

CHAPTER 41: AI AND THE REMOTE WORK REVOLUTION – HOW AI ACCELERATED THE GLOBAL SHIFT TO REMOTE WORK

In recent years, the rise of artificial intelligence (AI) has dramatically reshaped how and where we work. For digital nomads, who thrive on the flexibility of remote work, AI has been a game-changer, enabling them to stay competitive, productive, and agile while working from anywhere in the world. As businesses around the globe adapt to a more decentralized workforce, AI is proving to be one of the key forces driving this transformation. In this chapter, we explore how AI has accelerated the remote work revolution, the tools enabling this shift, and what this means for the future of work for digital nomads.

Engage with Storytelling and Case Studies

Consider Tomás, a freelance software developer from Portugal who started his digital nomad journey long before the pandemic forced companies to shift to remote work. In the beginning, Tomás struggled with time zone differences, communication delays with clients, and managing a growing workload. However, when he integrated AI-powered project management tools like Monday.com and Trello, everything changed.

These tools used AI to predict deadlines, assign tasks automatically, and even suggest solutions to bottlenecks in his projects. What used to be hours of manual planning and follow-up became automated, leaving Tomás free to focus on coding and client meetings. Soon, his ability to deliver projects faster and with more precision led to increased client satisfaction and an expanding portfolio of remote clients across the globe. AI didn't just make remote work easier for Tomás—it allowed him to scale his career while living the lifestyle he dreamed of.

Focus on Practical Application

For digital nomads, AI-powered tools have become indispensable in navigating the demands of remote work. From optimizing time management to enhancing communication across borders, here are some practical applications that digital nomads should consider; to thrive in the AI-powered remote work era:

1. Task Automation and Project Management

AI has significantly improved task management for remote workers. Platforms like Trello, Asana, and Monday.com now offer AI-driven features that automate task assignments, track progress, and provide real-time insights into project performance. These tools are particularly helpful for digital nomads who work with clients across time zones, ensuring that deadlines are met without the need for constant check-ins.

Practical Tip: Set up AI-driven task tracking to manage multiple clients more efficiently. Use AI to predict project timelines and flag potential delays, so you stay ahead of deadlines.

2. AI-Powered Communication Tools

Remote work relies heavily on seamless communication, and AI has improved how we connect across borders. AI-powered chatbots and virtual assistants like Slack's Workflow Builder and Zoom's AI transcription streamline conversations, automate responses, and ensure that nothing falls through the cracks. AI tools also help translate languages in real-time, making it easier to collaborate with international teams.

Practical Tip: Use Otter.ai for meeting transcription and summarization. It's an AI-powered tool that automatically transcribes conversations in real-time and provides summaries, ensuring that every meeting is productive, even across different time zones.

3. Time Zone Management

One of the greatest challenges for digital nomads is managing clients and teams across different time zones. AI-powered scheduling tools like Calendly and Google Calendar now offer smart scheduling features that consider multiple time zones, making remote meetings easier to organize.

Practical Tip: Automate your calendar to suggest optimal meeting times across time zones, and use AI assistants to manage meeting scheduling, reminders, and follow-ups.

Inspire Through Visionary Perspectives

Looking into the future, AI is set to make remote work even more seamless. As technology evolves, AI will go beyond just facilitating communication and task management—it will become a co-creator in many fields. Imagine a world where digital nomads collaborate with AI systems that generate creative solutions, streamline their workflow, and even predict market trends, allowing them to focus on strategy and high-level decision-making.

Visionary Question: How will your work evolve if AI takes over the repetitive aspects of your job, leaving you to focus solely on innovation and creativity?

Balance Between Inspiration and Caution

While AI is accelerating the remote work revolution, it also brings new challenges, particularly around data security, privacy, and the potential for job displacement. Digital nomads must be cautious about over-reliance on AI for decision-making without understanding the underlying data and ethical implications. Moreover, with an increasing amount of sensitive information being shared across AI-powered platforms, ensuring the security of client data is paramount.

Balanced Tip: Familiarize yourself with cybersecurity best practices for remote work and consider using AI-powered security tools like LastPass or 1Password to manage passwords and protect sensitive data.

Highlight Global and Cultural Dimensions

AI has made it easier for digital nomads to work across borders and engage with global clients. In regions like Southeast Asia, Africa, and South America, AI is playing a critical role in bridging gaps in communication and infrastructure, enabling more people to participate in the global workforce. For example, Estonia's e-residency program has attracted digital nomads by allowing them to easily set up businesses and access the European market remotely.

Meanwhile, countries like India are seeing rapid AI adoption in sectors like customer service, where AI chatbots are enabling companies to serve international clients around the clock. For digital nomads, the rise of these AI-driven ecosystems means more opportunities to tap into emerging markets.

Global Insight: Consider regions where AI infrastructure is rapidly developing, such as Southeast Asia or Africa, and explore opportunities to work with local businesses that are embracing AI for remote collaboration.

Motivate with Purpose and Fulfilment

For digital nomads, remote work is more than just a job —it's a lifestyle. AI's role in enabling this lifestyle goes beyond efficiency and productivity; it's about unlocking new possibilities for personal growth, creativity, and work-life balance. By automating mundane tasks, AI allows digital nomads to focus on what truly matters, whether that's pursuing passion projects, spending more time with loved ones, or exploring the world.

Inspirational Thought: AI gives you the freedom to work smarter, not harder. What will you do with the extra time and mental energy that AI tools can offer?

Use Accessible, Simple Language for Complex Topics

AI might sound complex, but at its core, it's simply a tool that helps you get more done in less time. Think of AI as your personal assistant—whether it's scheduling your meetings, organizing your projects, or even writing your next blog post, AI is there to support your work, not replace you.

Interactive and Engaging Content

Before you move on to the next chapter, take a moment to reflect on how you can integrate AI into your remote work setup. Ask yourself:
- What are the most repetitive tasks I could automate with AI?
- How can AI-powered communication tools help me stay better connected with my clients?
- What skills should I develop to stay ahead in an AI-driven remote work environment?

Take 10 minutes to explore one of the AI tools mentioned in this chapter, and try integrating it into your workflow this week.

Conclusion: Thriving in the AI-Powered Remote Work Era

AI has rapidly accelerated the shift to remote work, offering unprecedented opportunities for digital nomads to thrive. By automating routine tasks, facilitating communication across borders, and helping manage complex schedules, AI is transforming the way we work from anywhere in the world. As digital nomads, the key to thriving in this new era is not just in adopting AI tools, but in leveraging them to enhance your creativity, productivity, and sense of fulfilment. Let AI handle the logistics, while you focus on building a life that's both meaningful and flexible, anywhere in the world.

CHAPTER 42:
CULTURAL
ADAPTATION IN AN
AI-DRIVEN WORLD

How Digital Nomads Are Thriving Amid Cultural Shifts Brought on by AI

As the digital nomad movement grows, artificial intelligence (AI) is transforming not only how people work but also the cultural landscapes they navigate. From the bustling streets of Bali to the tech-savvy co-working spaces of Berlin, digital nomads are riding the wave of AI-fuelled shifts in global work culture. In this chapter, we'll explore how digital nomads are adapting to the cultural changes brought on by AI, leveraging technology to enhance their experiences across borders, and thriving in an increasingly automated world.

Engage with Storytelling and Case Studies

Take the story of Amina, a digital nomad originally from Kenya, who has been traveling the globe for the past five years. Amina's passion lies in social media marketing, and like many digital nomads, she relies heavily on AI to stay competitive in the industry. AI-powered tools such as Hootsuite and Buffer help her manage clients' social media accounts across various time zones. But for Amina, AI's impact goes beyond automation. It has allowed her to work seamlessly in different cultural environments, providing her with insights into local trends and behaviours through AI-driven analytics.

For example, when she arrived in Mexico, Amina used Google Trends to track regional interests, and AI translation tools like DeepL to communicate effectively with local clients. AI not only allowed her to adapt quickly to the new market but also gave her the cultural fluency needed to thrive. For digital nomads like Amina, AI has become an essential partner in navigating the intricacies of cultural adaptation while maintaining a competitive edge in the global marketplace.

Focus on Practical Application

For digital nomads, adapting to cultural shifts in an AI-driven world requires more than just learning how to use new tools—it involves understanding how these tools affect communication, work habits, and even local economies. Below are practical tips for digital nomads to leverage AI as they adapt to different cultures:

1. Leveraging AI for Cultural Insights

Digital nomads often find themselves working with clients from diverse cultures, and understanding those cultures is key to building successful relationships. AI-powered analytics platforms, such as Brandwatch and Sprout Social, can provide insights into local trends, consumer behaviour, and cultural preferences, helping digital nomads tailor their services accordingly.

Practical Tip: Use AI to analyse social media trends specific to the regions where you're working. These tools can help you understand local customer sentiment, making your marketing or business efforts more effective.

2. Real-Time Language Translation

Language barriers are a common challenge for digital nomads working in different regions. AI-powered translation tools like Google Translate and DeepL offer real-time, accurate translations that allow for smooth communication with clients, partners, and vendors worldwide.

Practical Tip: Use AI translation tools not just for business communications but also for immersing yourself in the local culture. Learning key phrases in the local language can open doors and foster better relationships with the communities where you live and work.

3. AI for Remote Collaboration Across Cultures

AI tools like Grammarly, Notion, and Slack help digital nomads collaborate effectively across borders. These tools enhance communication by offering suggestions that adapt to local linguistic nuances, ensuring clarity and professionalism when working with international teams.

Practical Tip: Customize AI communication tools to align with cultural norms. For example, in some cultures, formal language is preferred in business settings. Ensure that your communication style aligns with the expectations of the region you're working in.

Inspire Through Visionary Perspectives

AI is transforming cultural boundaries in unprecedented ways. The future of work for digital nomads is one where AI blurs the lines between cultures, making the world more interconnected than ever before. Imagine a world where AI not only automates mundane tasks but also provides personalized insights on how to engage with specific cultural norms. From suggesting local customs for business meetings to advising on region-specific business strategies, AI will become an indispensable cultural guide.

Visionary Thought: What if, in the near future, AI could analyse not just data but the emotional and social cues of different cultures, helping you adapt seamlessly to any environment? As AI evolves, so too will our ability to work harmoniously in the diverse, global workspace of tomorrow.

Balance Between Inspiration and Caution

While AI offers enormous potential for cultural adaptation, it's essential to approach it with caution. AI is a tool, not a replacement for genuine human interaction. It's important for digital nomads to strike a balance between leveraging AI's capabilities and engaging authentically with the cultures they encounter.

Over-reliance on AI for communication, for example, may lead to misunderstandings or the loss of personal connections. Cultural nuances—such as humor, gestures, or local etiquette—are not always easy for AI to interpret. Digital nomads should use AI as a complement to their cultural experiences, not a crutch.

Balanced Tip: While AI can provide valuable insights, always prioritize human connection. Make an effort to learn about the local culture firsthand by engaging with people, exploring traditions, and immersing yourself in local experiences.

Highlight Global and Cultural Dimensions

AI is impacting cultures worldwide in unique ways. In Japan, AI is being integrated into traditional businesses, modernizing centuries-old practices while preserving cultural values. In Estonia, AI is helping streamline government services, making it easier for digital nomads to establish businesses remotely. And in Africa, AI is creating opportunities for tech startups, empowering local entrepreneurs to compete on the global stage.

For digital nomads, this global cultural shift presents unprecedented opportunities. By leveraging AI, they can tap into local economies, contribute to emerging markets, and build cross-cultural partnerships in ways that were previously unimaginable.

Global Insight: Explore how different regions are adopting AI. Whether it's working in tech-forward cities like Singapore or tapping into emerging markets in South America, AI is creating pathways for digital nomads to work globally, while respecting local customs and values.

Motivate with Purpose and Fulfilment

AI is more than just a tool for efficiency—it's an enabler of purpose. For digital nomads, the lifestyle is about more than just working remotely; it's about creating meaningful connections and exploring new opportunities. AI can help them achieve this by freeing up time from mundane tasks and allowing them to focus on personal growth, travel, and cultural exploration.

Inspirational Thought: How can you use the time saved through AI automation to pursue deeper connections with the cultures and people around you? Let AI handle the logistics, while you focus on living a life rich in purpose and experience.

Use Accessible, Simple Language for Complex Topics

AI can seem overwhelming, but it doesn't have to be. Think of AI as your virtual assistant—helping you communicate, collaborate, and stay productive no matter where you are. It's like having a personal guide that helps you understand cultural differences, enabling you to adapt and thrive in new environments. AI is not here to replace your skills or intuition—it's here to enhance them.

Interactive and Engaging Content

To fully embrace cultural adaptation with AI, take a moment to reflect on how you've adapted to new cultures in the past. Think about your most recent travels:
- How did you learn about the local customs?
- How could AI have enhanced that experience?

Now, choose one of the AI tools mentioned in this chapter and experiment with it in your current location. How does it help you navigate your environment or communicate more effectively with locals?

Conclusion: Adapting with AI to a Culturally Fluid World

AI is shaping how digital nomads adapt to and interact with diverse cultures, providing new opportunities to thrive in an increasingly globalized world. By leveraging AI tools, digital nomads can not only improve their productivity but also deepen their cultural connections, ultimately leading to a more enriching and purposeful lifestyle. As the world continues to evolve, digital nomads who embrace AI will find themselves at the forefront of a new, culturally fluid work paradigm—one where they can seamlessly navigate both technological and cultural landscapes, no matter where they go.

CHAPTER 43:
AI, TRAVEL, AND CULTURAL EXCHANGE

How AI is Shaping the Way Digital Nomads Experience Travel and Cultural Exchange

In today's increasingly interconnected world, digital nomads have unprecedented access to global opportunities. Artificial intelligence (AI) is playing a pivotal role in enhancing these experiences, from planning travel to fostering deeper cultural exchanges. AI empowers nomads to navigate new environments with ease, explore new cultures, and seamlessly manage both work and play while traveling. This chapter will explore how AI has transformed the travel experiences of digital nomads and opened up new possibilities for cultural exchange.

Engage with Storytelling and Case Studies

Let's take the story of Paul, a software developer who had always dreamed of exploring the world while working remotely. However, managing his workflow and travel plans simultaneously seemed overwhelming until he discovered how AI could simplify both. He began using AI-powered tools such as Skyscanner to find affordable flights and Google Maps to navigate unfamiliar cities.

But Paul's journey in Japan revealed the true power of AI in fostering cultural exchange. He used Google Translate to communicate with local vendors, which broke the language barrier and allowed him to build genuine connections with people he otherwise might not have been able to converse with. By using AI to bridge the gap, Paul felt more connected to the culture than ever before, even attending local community events that he learned about through AI-driven social platforms.

Paul's experience is just one example of how AI has made it easier for digital nomads to travel, work, and engage meaningfully with new cultures. The barriers of language, location, and logistics are increasingly mitigated by AI, making travel more accessible and enriching for digital nomads like Paul.

Focus on Practical Application

AI can make the travel experiences of digital nomads more efficient and rewarding, enhancing both their work and personal lives. Below are several practical applications of AI that are redefining travel and cultural exchange for nomads:

1. AI-Powered Travel Planning

Platforms like Skyscanner, Kayak, and Hopper use AI algorithms to provide real-time updates on flight prices, recommend the best booking times, and even suggest alternative travel routes. This allows digital nomads to be more flexible and cost-efficient in their travel plans.

Practical Tip: Use AI-powered travel platforms to set up alerts for flight and hotel deals. By monitoring your travel preferences, AI will notify you when the best prices are available, allowing you to make smarter, more budget-friendly travel decisions.

2. AI for Language Translation and Learning

Tools like Google Translate and Duolingo enable digital nomads to break through language barriers. Whether you need instant translations or are learning a new language to immerse yourself in the local culture, AI can make communication much smoother.

Practical Tip: Use AI tools to learn key phrases in the local language before arriving in a new country. Even if you rely on AI for translations, a few basic phrases can go a long way in creating more authentic connections with locals.

3. AI for Cultural Exploration

AI algorithms on platforms like Instagram and TripAdvisor recommend local attractions, cultural landmarks, and events based on your preferences and past behaviour. This enables digital nomads to discover unique, culturally significant experiences that may not be in the mainstream travel guides.

Practical Tip: Use AI to explore off-the-beaten-path cultural experiences by setting your preferences to highlight local traditions, events, and hidden gems. This allows for a deeper engagement with the culture beyond typical tourist hotspots.

Inspire Through Visionary Perspectives

As AI technology continues to evolve, the future of travel and cultural exchange for digital nomads will expand in remarkable ways. Imagine AI-driven virtual reality experiences that allow nomads to "preview" cultural events or festivals in a location before arriving. Or AI that can predict your ideal travel destinations based on your personal interests, work needs, and cultural inclinations.

Visionary Thought: What if AI could not only translate languages but also interpret cultural nuances in real time? In the future, AI might help digital nomads navigate cultural norms with ease, suggesting appropriate greetings, attire, or even guiding them through cultural taboos.

Balance Between Inspiration and Caution

While AI offers transformative tools for travel and cultural exchange, it's important to remember that technology should enhance—not replace—authentic experiences. Relying too much on AI for communication, for example, can distance digital nomads from the richness of human interaction. Face-to-face engagement, without the mediation of technology, remains a crucial part of truly understanding a culture.

Moreover, the rise of AI in travel raises ethical questions around data privacy and surveillance. Travelers need to be cautious about sharing personal information with AI-driven platforms and ensure that they use secure, trustworthy services.

Balanced Tip: Use AI to support your travel and work experience, but always prioritize human connection. Engage with locals, attend cultural events, and embrace opportunities to step outside the digital world to truly immerse yourself in the cultural landscape.

Highlight Global and Cultural Dimensions

AI is shaping how cultures are experienced and shared across borders. For instance, in Estonia, the government's innovative e-residency program, powered by AI, allows digital nomads to register businesses remotely while enjoying the flexibility of living anywhere in the world. In Japan, AI is being used to preserve traditional crafts and arts, offering digital nomads a chance to learn about ancient practices through modern technology.

In China, AI is revolutionizing tourism by offering intelligent guides that provide detailed information about cultural landmarks. This technology is not only improving the travel experience but also deepening cultural exchange by making cultural history more accessible to foreign visitors.

Global Insight: As AI continues to be adopted in different parts of the world, it's important for digital nomads to understand how technology is influencing local cultures. In many cases, AI serves as a bridge that helps preserve and share cultural heritage while making it easier for nomads to engage with and learn from these traditions.

Motivate with Purpose and Fulfilment

At its core, the digital nomad lifestyle is about freedom, exploration, and personal fulfilment. AI enhances this by freeing up time and resources, enabling digital nomads to focus on what truly matters—whether it's pursuing creative projects, connecting with new communities, or making a meaningful impact on the world.

Inspirational Thought: How can AI free up your time so that you can engage more deeply with the cultures and places you visit? By automating mundane tasks, AI allows you to live a more purpose-driven, culturally immersive life.

Use Accessible, Simple Language for Complex Topics

AI may seem like a complicated concept, but think of it as your travel companion—an assistant that helps you navigate the world more easily. Whether you're booking flights, learning a new language, or finding the best local experience, AI is there to support you. It's like having a personal guide that helps you understand and engage with different cultures, so you can focus on enjoying your journey.

Interactive and Engaging Content

Reflect on a recent trip you took:
- How did you use technology to enhance your travel experience?
- How could AI have made it even better?

Take a moment to explore one of the AI tools mentioned in this chapter. Spend 15 minutes researching the next destination you want to visit. How can AI help you get the most out of your experience?

Conclusion: AI and the Future of Travel and Cultural Exchange

AI is redefining how digital nomads travel and engage with new cultures, making the world more accessible while enhancing the richness of cultural experiences. By leveraging AI, digital nomads can immerse themselves more deeply in the places they visit, break down language barriers, and enjoy personalized travel experiences that foster cultural exchange. As the technology continues to evolve, the potential for digital nomads to explore the world in more meaningful ways will only grow. Embrace AI, and let it be your bridge to deeper cultural connections and enriching travel experiences.

CHAPTER 44: HOW AI IS RESHAPING GLOBAL ECONOMIES

How AI is Impacting the Economies of Countries that Host Digital Nomads

The rise of artificial intelligence (AI) is not only transforming the way we work but also reshaping global economies, particularly in countries that attract digital nomads. As more remote workers flock to destinations with favourable digital infrastructure and visa policies, the interplay between AI and these local economies is becoming increasingly important. AI-powered technologies are creating new business opportunities, streamlining processes, and enhancing the economic contributions of digital nomads. This chapter explores how AI is reshaping global economies, with a focus on the countries that host digital nomads and how these changes are unlocking new potentials for both individuals and nations.

Engage with Storytelling and Case Studies

Consider the case of Lucas, a web developer from Brazil, who decided to live and work remotely from Bali, Indonesia. When he arrived, Lucas was amazed at how the island had embraced AI to cater to the needs of the growing digital nomad community. He quickly realized that many local businesses had incorporated AI-driven tools to attract and retain foreign workers like him. Restaurants used AI algorithms to provide personalized menus based on dietary preferences, while co-working spaces implemented AI to optimize desk allocation and energy consumption.

As a digital nomad, Lucas also benefited directly from AI. With the help of AI-powered project management platforms like Trello and AI coding assistants like GitHub Copilot, Lucas was able to streamline his work and focus on what mattered most—building meaningful software solutions. The local businesses and economy thrived as digital nomads like Lucas spent their money on food, accommodation, and services, driving growth in a tech-enabled marketplace.

Bali's economy, like many other popular digital nomad destinations, has embraced AI not only as a tool to enhance the experience of remote workers but as a driver of economic development. AI is no longer just a technological trend but a powerful economic force that is transforming how countries host and benefit from digital nomads.

Focus on Practical Application

AI's impact on the economies of countries hosting digital nomads is tangible and wide-reaching. By leveraging AI-driven tools, local businesses can cater to a more tech-savvy, mobile workforce, boosting their own profitability while attracting more remote workers. Below are practical ways AI is reshaping the global economy and how digital nomads can engage with these changes:

1. AI-Powered Infrastructure for Digital Nomads

Many popular digital nomad destinations, like Thailand, Portugal, and Estonia, are using AI to improve infrastructure and attract nomads. From AI-enhanced public Wi-Fi networks to smart urban planning that anticipates the needs of transient workers, these countries are building the foundation for an AI-driven economy that supports remote workers.

Practical Tip: Digital nomads should research the AI infrastructure available in potential destinations. Countries that are heavily investing in AI technologies—like Estonia's e-residency program—can offer smoother, more efficient experiences for nomads.

2. Local AI-Powered Businesses

Many small- and medium-sized businesses (SMEs) in nomad-friendly countries are integrating AI to boost productivity and attract more digital nomads. AI tools for personalized marketing, inventory management, and customer service are helping these businesses thrive in a competitive global market.

Practical Tip: Support local businesses by seeking out AI-enabled services. For example, book accommodations through platforms that use AI to recommend lodging options based on your preferences or visit cafes that offer AI-driven ordering systems to speed up service.

3. AI-Enhanced Government Services

In many digital nomad hubs, governments are increasingly turning to AI to streamline administrative processes. Countries like Georgia and Estonia have introduced e-visa services powered by AI that allow nomads to apply for residency and work permits in a matter of minutes.

Practical Tip: Before moving to a new country, explore the digital services available for remote workers. AI-powered e-residency and visa programs can simplify bureaucratic procedures, allowing nomads to focus more on their work and less on paperwork.

Inspire Through Visionary Perspectives

AI's influence on the global economy extends far beyond the present day. Looking into the future, it's clear that AI will further accelerate the movement of digital nomads, while creating new opportunities for both workers and countries. Imagine a world where AI predicts the best locations for nomads based on real-time data—everything from local job opportunities to optimal work-life balance conditions.

What if AI could analyse local economies and offer personalized recommendations for the best places to invest or start a business as a nomad? This future isn't far off. AI will continue to push the boundaries of economic potential, empowering both nomads and the countries that host them.

Visionary Thought: As AI evolves, we may see the rise of fully autonomous nomad cities that cater to the specific needs of digital workers, from AI-driven transportation to smart housing and AI-enhanced workspaces.

Balance Between Inspiration and Caution

While AI is driving economic growth and innovation, it also presents challenges that need to be managed. In countries that rely heavily on digital nomads, there are concerns about over-dependence on AI-driven industries and the displacement of traditional jobs. Automation powered by AI could reduce the demand for certain roles, particularly in industries like hospitality and customer service, where AI is being used to replace human workers.

However, countries that prepare for these changes by reskilling their workforce and investing in AI education can mitigate the risks. Nomads should also be mindful of their role in these shifting economies and look for ways to contribute to the local workforce by sharing AI expertise or creating new job opportunities.

Balanced Advice: As digital nomads, you should embrace AI's benefits while being conscious of its potential effects on local economies. Collaborate with local communities to build skills and avoid contributing to economic inequality.

Highlight Global and Cultural Dimensions

AI's role in reshaping global economies is particularly evident in how different countries have embraced it. In Estonia, the e-residency program powered by AI has positioned the country as a digital hub for nomads, generating significant economic activity. In Thailand, AI-driven tourism platforms are helping local businesses better market themselves to remote workers, while in Portugal, AI is being used to forecast the economic impact of digital nomads on the housing market.

By understanding these regional differences, digital nomads can make more informed decisions about where to live and work, while also appreciating the unique economic contributions they can make in each location.

Global Insight: The opportunities AI brings to global economies are vast, but they also require digital nomads to adapt to the local culture, policies, and economic landscapes of each country they visit. Recognize the local impact of your presence as a remote worker.

Motivate with Purpose and Fulfilment

At the heart of the digital nomad lifestyle is the desire for freedom, adventure, and personal fulfilment. AI offers the tools to achieve these goals more efficiently, but it's up to nomads to use this technology in ways that benefit both themselves and the economies they engage with.

By contributing to the development of local businesses, embracing AI to improve their own productivity, and actively participating in local economies, digital nomads can create a positive and lasting impact wherever they go.

Inspirational Thought: How can you leverage AI to not only benefit your work but also contribute to the economies and cultures of the places you visit? AI provides endless opportunities to make a meaningful impact on a global scale.

Conclusion: AI's Lasting Impact on Global Economies

AI is undeniably transforming the global economies that digital nomads interact with, from improving infrastructure and local business services to streamlining government processes. As the digital nomad movement continues to grow, AI will be a crucial driver of economic development in countries that embrace it. For digital nomads, understanding how AI impacts the local economies they engage with is not just beneficial but essential to ensuring a harmonious, productive, and fulfilling lifestyle. Through the conscious use of AI, nomads can thrive while contributing to the economic prosperity of the countries they call home.

CHAPTER 45: DIGITAL NOMADS AS GLOBAL CITIZENS

How Digital Nomads Are Evolving into Global Citizens in the AI Age

The digital nomad movement has come a long way, evolving from a niche lifestyle into a powerful global trend. Today, AI is not only enabling digital nomads to work more efficiently, but it's also transforming how they connect with the world. These nomads are no longer just remote workers traveling from place to place; they are evolving into true global citizens, bridging cultures, industries, and economies in ways that were once unimaginable. This chapter explores how AI is helping digital nomads embrace the world as their home, redefine their roles, and make an impact across borders.

Engage with Storytelling and Case Studies

Meet Sophie, a digital marketer from the UK, who has spent the last three years living and working across Asia, Europe, and South America. What sets Sophie apart is her ability to seamlessly integrate into different cultures, making her feel at home wherever she goes. She credits AI for this newfound flexibility and connection.

In Bali, she used AI-powered language translation tools like Google Translate and DeepL to communicate with locals and bridge cultural gaps. When she moved to Colombia, she leveraged AI-powered co-working platforms that connected her with fellow digital nomads and local businesses, creating opportunities for collaboration.

AI not only helped Sophie work more efficiently by automating her routine tasks but also allowed her to immerse herself in new cultures, learn from local perspectives, and contribute to the communities she joined. Her story represents a broader trend: digital nomads using AI to foster deeper global engagement, positioning themselves as ambassadors of a new, interconnected world.

Focus on Practical Application

AI is playing a vital role in empowering digital nomads to transition from remote workers to global citizens. Here are practical ways in which AI is reshaping this transition:

1. AI-Powered Cultural Integration

Language barriers are often one of the biggest challenges digital nomads face when moving to new countries. AI-powered translation tools like Google Lens and translate can help bridge these gaps by offering real-time translation, enabling digital nomads to interact with locals in meaningful ways.

Practical Tip: Use AI translation tools not only for daily interactions but also to explore local cultures. Attend local events, markets, or community gatherings where you can practice using AI to assist you in communication.

2. AI-Enhanced Networking

Networking is essential for digital nomads, not just for business purposes but for creating connections across cultures. AI-driven platforms like Meetup and Nomad List use algorithms to suggest events, co-working spaces, and communities that align with a nomad's interests. These platforms help nomads find their tribe wherever they go.

Practical Tip: Regularly engage with AI-powered networking platforms to expand your personal and professional connections globally. By attending AI-recommended events, you can meet like-minded people and foster long-term global relationships.

3. Digital Visas and Residency

Some countries, like Estonia and Georgia, have leveraged AI to streamline their digital nomad visa processes. AI-based systems analyse applications faster, allowing nomads to apply for visas or e-residencies with ease. Estonia's e-residency program is a prime example, enabling nomads to register businesses and pay taxes online, no matter where they are.

Practical Tip: Look for countries that offer AI-enhanced e-residency or visa programs. These programs make it easier for you to manage the administrative side of being a digital nomad while focusing on your work and cultural experiences.

Inspire Through Visionary Perspectives

As AI continues to evolve, so too will the digital nomad lifestyle. Imagine a world where AI doesn't just assist with language translation and networking, but helps nomads fully immerse themselves in new cultures. AI-powered virtual reality (VR) could offer immersive cultural training before a nomad even sets foot in a new country. Machine learning algorithms could curate personalized travel and work recommendations based on past experiences and cultural preferences.

In this future, digital nomads won't simply be passing

through countries—they'll be fully integrated into the global fabric, moving between regions with ease and contributing to local economies, businesses, and cultural exchanges in meaningful ways. AI will enable nomads to balance work and cultural enrichment seamlessly, reinforcing the idea that we are all part of a global community.

Visionary Thought: How will AI shape the role of digital nomads as connectors in a globalized world? Imagine a future where AI enables deeper cultural understanding and helps create a global network of nomads working together to solve pressing global challenges.

Balance Between Inspiration and Caution

While AI offers many opportunities for digital nomads to evolve into global citizens, it's important to be mindful of potential pitfalls. With AI automating many tasks and streamlining experiences, there is a risk of becoming overly reliant on technology and losing the authentic human connections that are at the heart of cultural exchange.

Moreover, while AI is making the world more accessible to digital nomads, it is also raising concerns about data privacy and surveillance. As digital nomads move from country to country, they must be aware of how their data is being collected and used by the AI systems they rely on.

Balanced Advice: Use AI to enhance your experiences, but don't let it replace genuine human interactions. Make sure to engage with local communities in meaningful ways, and stay informed about the data privacy laws in the countries you visit.

Highlight Global and Cultural Dimensions

AI's ability to reshape the world goes beyond individual nomads; it is also impacting the countries and cultures they engage with. In Portugal, AI is being used to assess the economic impact of digital nomads on local economies, helping to ensure that the influx of remote workers benefits both the nomads and the communities they join. In Japan, AI is assisting businesses in offering more personalized experiences to international workers, fostering deeper cultural connections.

As digital nomads move between these AI-enabled regions, they become part of a global ecosystem where their presence influences local economies, industries, and cultures. AI serves as a tool that connects these diverse cultural elements, ensuring that nomads contribute to the communities they inhabit while also learning from them.

Global Insight: Be mindful of how your presence as a digital nomad impacts local economies and cultures. Use AI tools to engage with local communities, but also make a conscious effort to give back by sharing your skills, knowledge, or resources.

Motivate with Purpose and Fulfilment

Digital nomads are not just searching for adventure or financial freedom—they are seeking purpose. AI allows them to pursue this deeper mission by freeing up time and energy, which can then be redirected into passion projects, volunteering, or cultural contributions. Whether you're a freelancer, entrepreneur, or remote worker, AI can help you find the balance between work and fulfilment.

By automating mundane tasks, AI empowers nomads to focus on what truly matters: building meaningful relationships, exploring new cultures, and making a positive impact in the world. The journey of a digital nomad is no longer just about working from beautiful locations— it's about becoming a global citizen with a purpose-driven mindset.

Inspirational Thought: How can you use AI to live a more purpose-driven life? Consider ways AI can streamline your work and create space for you to engage more deeply with the cultures and communities you encounter.

Conclusion: Digital Nomads as Global Citizens in the AI Age

In this new era, digital nomads are becoming more than just remote workers—they are evolving into global citizens. With AI at their disposal, they are able to move seamlessly between cultures, contributing to global economies, bridging cultural gaps, and making meaningful connections. The AI-powered future offers endless possibilities, not only for work but also for a deeper, more purposeful engagement with the world.

By harnessing the power of AI, digital nomads can redefine their roles as global citizens, contributing positively to the countries and cultures they engage with while enjoying the personal and professional freedoms this lifestyle offers. As the digital nomad movement grows, so too will the opportunities for individuals to make a global impact—one AI-driven step at a time.

PART 10: THE PERSONAL IMPACT OF AI ON NOMADS

CHAPTER 46: WORK-LIFE BALANCE FOR DIGITAL NOMADS

How Digital Nomads Can Maintain a Healthy Work-Life Balance with AI Tools

As the digital nomad lifestyle continues to gain momentum, the boundaries between work and life often blur. While the freedom to work from anywhere in the world offers flexibility, it also brings challenges in maintaining a healthy balance between professional commitments and personal well-being. With AI becoming increasingly embedded in the tools that digital nomads use daily, achieving work-life balance is not only possible but can be optimized like never before. This chapter explores how digital nomads can leverage AI to create harmony between work and play, productivity and relaxation, by making the most of automation, personalization, and time management.

Engage with Storytelling and Case Studies

Meet Emma, a freelance writer and content strategist from Australia, who's spent the last year traveling through Latin America while managing a steady stream of international clients. In her early days as a digital nomad, Emma struggled to maintain a consistent work-life balance. She found herself working late into the night, missing out on the adventures that originally inspired her to live the nomadic lifestyle.

That changed when she started using AI-powered time management and productivity tools. With the help of apps like RescueTime and Trello's AI-enhanced task automation, Emma was able to regain control of her schedule. AI analysed her work habits, identified time-wasting activities, and suggested more productive ways to organize her tasks. Now, she works fewer hours but gets more done. Instead of working into the late evening, Emma spends her afternoons exploring the culture, history, and beauty of the cities she visits.

Emma's experience highlights how AI can help digital nomads find balance, allowing them to maximize their productivity while still enjoying the freedom and adventure that comes with their lifestyle.

Focus on Practical Application

For digital nomads, finding work-life balance is often about managing time, minimizing distractions, and streamlining workflows. AI can provide practical solutions to achieve this balance. Here are some ways AI can help:

1. Time Management with AI

AI-driven apps like RescueTime and Clockify analyse how you spend your work hours. These tools can break down the time spent on different tasks, flag distractions, and offer insights into your most productive hours. By harnessing this data, you can adjust your work schedule to make the most of your day while carving out time for relaxation.

Practical Tip: Use AI time-tracking tools to identify when you're most productive and when distractions creep in. Schedule your work during your peak performance hours and reserve off-peak hours for leisure or exploration.

2. AI-Powered Task Automation

Managing multiple projects across different clients or businesses can be overwhelming for digital nomads. AI tools like Zapier and Trello can automate repetitive tasks, such as sending emails, updating project boards, or tracking deadlines. By automating routine tasks, digital nomads can focus more on creative and strategic work while enjoying more downtime.

Practical Tip: Identify tasks that you regularly perform and set up AI automation workflows to handle them. Use Trello's automation features or Zapier's integrations to keep your projects organized with minimal manual effort.

3. AI-Enhanced Focus Tools

AI tools like Focus@Will and Brain.fm offer personalized music and soundtracks designed to improve focus and productivity. These tools use algorithms that adapt to your brain's rhythms, helping you concentrate during work hours and relax during breaks.

Practical Tip: Use AI-powered focus tools during work sprints to maximize productivity. Then, switch to relaxing soundtracks or guided meditation apps like Headspace to unwind after your workday.

Inspire Through Visionary Perspectives

As AI continues to evolve, the future of work-life balance for digital nomads looks even more promising. Imagine a future where AI not only helps manage your tasks and time but also acts as a personal wellness coach. AI could analyse your work patterns, sleep habits, and activity levels to create a completely personalized routine, ensuring you maintain optimal work-life balance.

Picture an AI assistant that schedules your work hours around your peak productivity, reminds you to take breaks, and suggests leisure activities based on your location and interests. With AI as a co-pilot, digital nomads can thrive professionally without sacrificing the joy of exploration and personal growth.

Visionary Thought: As AI becomes more sophisticated, how will it reshape our understanding of productivity and leisure? Will it enable digital nomads to achieve the perfect blend of work and life, allowing them to live more fulfilling lives without burning out?

Balance Between Inspiration and Caution

While AI offers incredible opportunities for enhancing work-life balance, it's important to remember that technology should serve as a tool, not a crutch. Relying too heavily on AI to manage every aspect of your life can lead to a lack of personal agency and awareness.

Moreover, using AI tools requires a certain level of data sharing. Digital nomads need to be aware of how their data is being collected and used by the AI applications they rely on. Ensuring that you choose trustworthy platforms with clear privacy policies is essential.

Balanced Advice: Use AI as a tool to enhance your productivity and work-life balance, but make sure you maintain control over your schedule and personal choices. Be mindful of data privacy and ensure you understand the trade-offs involved when using AI tools.

Highlight Global and Cultural Dimensions

AI is also impacting how digital nomads engage with global cultures and communities. In countries like Thailand, Indonesia, and Portugal, where co-working spaces are booming, AI-driven tools are helping digital nomads connect with local professionals and fellow nomads. Platforms like Nomad List and Workfrom use AI to suggest co-working spaces and events, making it easier for nomads to blend work and life, and even network across different cultures.

By integrating AI tools into their routines, nomads can navigate new cultures more efficiently, learn local customs, and form global connections that enrich their personal and professional lives.

Global Insight: Take advantage of AI-driven community platforms to meet other digital nomads and locals. Use AI to help you discover local events, co-working spaces, and cultural experiences, ensuring a balanced approach to both work and cultural immersion.

Motivate with Purpose and Fulfilment

For many digital nomads, the journey is about more than just earning a living—it's about seeking purpose, fulfilment, and adventure. AI can help digital nomads free up time to focus on what truly matters, whether that's pursuing passion projects, volunteering, or engaging in personal development.

By offloading mundane tasks and optimizing work schedules, AI enables nomads to dedicate more time to fulfilling activities—whether it's hiking in the mountains of Peru, working on a novel, or volunteering for environmental causes in Costa Rica.

Inspirational Thought: What could you achieve with the extra time AI saves you? Consider how you can use AI to minimize distractions and create space for passion projects or personal goals that bring meaning to your nomadic life.

Conclusion: AI as the Key to Work-Life Balance

In a world where digital nomads are constantly balancing work and travel, AI offers a path to a more harmonious lifestyle. By automating routine tasks, enhancing focus, and helping manage time, AI enables nomads to work efficiently while enjoying the freedom that drew them to this lifestyle in the first place.

However, achieving a healthy work-life balance also requires intention. It's essential to use AI mindfully, ensuring that it supports—not dominates—your life. As you continue your journey as a digital nomad, remember that AI is a tool to help you thrive, both professionally and personally. By leveraging its capabilities, you can create the life you've always dreamed of, where work and play coexist in perfect balance.

CHAPTER 47: THE PSYCHOLOGICAL IMPACT OF AI ON REMOTE WORKERS

How AI is Influencing Mental Health and Wellbeing Among Digital Nomads

As the world of work continues to evolve, digital nomads are at the forefront of a shift fuelled by technology. AI has been a game-changer for remote workers, providing tools that enhance productivity, streamline workflows, and even manage personal finances. However, like any powerful tool, AI has a multifaceted impact—not just on productivity, but also on the psychological well-being of those who use it.

In this chapter, we'll explore how AI is reshaping mental health among digital nomads, touching on both the positive effects and the potential challenges. By examining real-life stories and offering actionable insights, we aim to provide a balanced perspective on how digital nomads can navigate the psychological landscape of working in an AI-driven world.

Engage with Storytelling and Case Studies

Sofia, a graphic designer from Italy, embarked on her digital nomad journey three years ago, armed with an impressive portfolio and boundless optimism. As she travelled across Asia, AI tools like Adobe Sensei and Canva Pro helped Sofia automate her design process, significantly cutting down the time it took to complete client projects. The ability to deliver high-quality work faster meant more time for herself to explore new places.

However, as Sofia began to take on more clients, she found herself feeling overwhelmed. The AI tools made her more efficient, but they also increased the pressure to always be available and deliver work faster. Sofia experienced what many digital nomads encounter: a blurring of boundaries between work and personal life. The always-on nature of her work started taking a toll on her mental health.

To regain balance, Sofia turned to AI-powered wellness apps like Headspace and Calm, which offer guided meditations and mindfulness exercises. She also implemented AI-driven time management apps like RescueTime to ensure she carved out personal space. Sofia's journey is a reminder that while AI can elevate our professional lives, we must also be mindful of how it impacts our mental health.

Focus on Practical Application

The key to maintaining mental health while leveraging AI tools as a digital nomad is mindful implementation. Here are some ways you can harness AI for mental well-being:

1. AI for Mindfulness and Meditation

Apps like Headspace and Calm have integrated AI algorithms that tailor meditation practices and mindfulness exercises based on your stress levels, emotional states, and daily habits. These platforms can offer personalized suggestions to help digital nomads de-stress and maintain emotional balance while on the go.

Practical Tip: Set aside 10-15 minutes daily to engage with AI-powered meditation tools. Let the apps guide you through calming exercises, especially during times of high stress or workload.

2. AI for Work-Life Balance

Time-tracking tools such as Toggl and Clockify use AI to analyse your work habits, helping you identify when you need breaks. These tools offer suggestions to schedule downtime, ensuring you don't burn out from overworking —a common issue among digital nomads juggling multiple projects.

Practical Tip: Use AI time-management tools to allocate work hours and rest periods. Set reminders for regular breaks, and ensure you follow a structured workday even while working remotely.

3. AI for Productivity Without Overwhelm

While AI-driven productivity tools like Grammarly or Jasper AI can boost work efficiency, it's essential not to overload yourself with more work just because you can get things done faster. AI tools should help free up time, not add more to your plate.

Practical Tip: Set boundaries for your workload. Use AI tools to optimize your work, but be intentional about the number of tasks or projects you take on. Delegate more effectively and use the extra time for self-care and exploration.

Inspire Through Visionary Perspectives

As AI continues to evolve, the possibilities for enhancing mental well-being are expanding. Imagine AI tools that monitor your mental health in real-time, sending subtle reminders when you need to take a break or offering tailored advice for managing stress. These tools could analyse patterns in your behaviour, like when you're working long hours without breaks or when you've been sitting in front of a screen for too long.

In the future, AI might even provide "digital therapists," virtual counsellors that can provide emotional support based on real-time data. This type of personalized care could revolutionize mental health for digital nomads, especially those who might not have access to in-person therapy while traveling abroad.

Visionary Thought: What would your life look like if AI could act as both a productivity tool and a mental health coach? Imagine a world where your AI assistant not only manages your workload but also ensures you are emotionally and mentally balanced.

Balance Between Inspiration and Caution

While AI offers tremendous potential for improving mental health, it's crucial to recognize the potential downsides. Over-reliance on AI tools can create a sense of isolation, as digital nomads might find themselves interacting more with machines than with people. This detachment can exacerbate feelings of loneliness, a challenge that many nomads already face.

Additionally, the constant flow of information from AI tools —whether it's reminders, project updates, or productivity metrics—can lead to mental fatigue. The pressure to keep up with technology and stay ahead in a competitive remote work environment can add to stress.

Balanced Advice: Use AI as a supportive tool, but be cautious of overuse. Make time for human connections, whether through networking with fellow nomads or staying in touch with family and friends. Find a balance between AI-driven productivity and meaningful social interactions.

Highlight Global and Cultural Dimensions

AI is also changing how digital nomads interact with different cultures and communities, impacting their mental health in unexpected ways. In countries with strong digital nomad communities—such as Thailand, Portugal, and Mexico—AI-powered apps help nomads connect with locals and other travellers. Platforms like Meetup and Couchsurfing use AI to suggest events, meetups, and experiences tailored to your interests, helping nomads combat feelings of loneliness.

By facilitating connections across cultural boundaries, AI enables digital nomads to immerse themselves in local experiences while also maintaining their work schedules. This global cultural exchange can be both mentally stimulating and fulfilling.

Global Insight: Leverage AI tools to explore local culture and connect with others. Social interaction is a critical component of mental well-being, especially for digital nomads who often travel alone.

Motivate with Purpose and Fulfilment

For many digital nomads, the pursuit of this lifestyle is driven by a desire for personal growth, adventure, and fulfilment. AI can play a role in supporting these deeper goals. By automating mundane tasks, AI frees up time for nomads to pursue passion projects, build meaningful relationships, or engage in volunteer work. Instead of spending countless hours on administrative work, nomads can invest time in activities that bring them joy and purpose.

Inspirational Thought: Imagine how AI could free you to live a more fulfilling life. How would you use the extra time AI saves you to pursue your passions or build deeper connections with the world around you?

Conclusion: AI and Mental Health in the Nomadic Lifestyle

AI's impact on the mental health and well-being of digital nomads is complex and multifaceted. While it offers tools that can enhance productivity, manage stress, and even foster global connections, it also presents challenges that require thoughtful management. By using AI mindfully and balancing its advantages with personal boundaries, digital nomads can thrive both professionally and emotionally in the AI age.

As you continue your journey, remember that AI should serve as a tool to enhance your life, not overwhelm it. Use AI to optimize your work, but always make time for self-care, human connection, and activities that feed your soul.

CHAPTER 48:
DIGITAL NOMADS, AI, AND RELATIONSHIPS

How the Nomadic Lifestyle Coupled with AI Affects Personal Relationships and Friendships

In the age of digital nomadism, where work happens across borders, time zones, and oceans, personal relationships often face unique challenges. While the nomadic lifestyle promises freedom, adventure, and flexibility, it can also strain relationships, whether romantic, familial, or friendships. As technology—particularly AI—reshapes how digital nomads work and live, it also plays an increasingly significant role in maintaining and nurturing personal connections. This chapter explores how AI both enhances and complicates relationships for digital nomads, and offers strategies to build and sustain meaningful connections while living a life on the move.

Engage with Storytelling and Case Studies

Let's begin with Michael, a software developer from the United States who became a digital nomad in 2020. His dream was to travel the world, coding from beachside cafes, and using the flexibility of remote work to live life on his terms. But what Michael didn't anticipate was how difficult it would be to maintain close relationships with friends and family back home.

Initially, Michael relied on video calls to stay connected. Yet, with his erratic travel schedule and constantly changing time zones, keeping in touch became challenging. That's when he discovered AI-powered tools like Google Duplex and Calendly. These tools helped him automate and streamline communication by scheduling video calls and managing time differences. Additionally, AI-driven relationship-building apps like Replika offered him an outlet for conversation when he felt isolated.

Michael's story highlights a key theme for digital nomads: while AI can automate many aspects of communication and help bridge the gap created by distance, it's not a substitute for authentic human connection. Maintaining deep, meaningful relationships requires a proactive approach, balancing the use of AI tools with genuine effort and emotional investment.

Focus on Practical Application

Digital nomads can leverage AI to strengthen personal connections, even when they're miles away from their loved ones. Here are a few ways to do that:

1. AI for Scheduling and Time Zone Management
AI tools like Calendly and Google Assistant allow digital nomads to automate scheduling with family and friends across time zones. These tools help eliminate the guesswork of finding a mutually convenient time to connect, ensuring you can prioritize relationships despite your nomadic lifestyle.

Practical Tip: Set recurring video calls with loved ones, using AI to schedule them at regular intervals. Automation ensures you don't lose track of important conversations while moving from one destination to the next.

2. AI for Relationship Reminders

Tools like Rememory use AI to help you remember important dates—birthdays, anniversaries, or special moments in your friends' or partner's lives. It can even suggest ways to reconnect or plan surprises. For digital nomads, these small gestures can make a big difference in maintaining intimacy over long distances.

Practical Tip: Use an AI assistant to send reminders for birthdays and key milestones, and automate messages or gifts, making your loved ones feel valued, even when you're physically apart.

3. AI as an Emotional Support Tool

While no AI tool can replace real human interaction, apps like Replika provide conversational AI companions that help stave off loneliness and provide emotional support during times when face-to-face communication isn't possible. For some digital nomads who spend long periods alone in unfamiliar places, having an AI to talk to can offer temporary relief from isolation.

Practical Tip: Use AI companions sparingly for emotional support but be conscious of not allowing them to replace genuine human interaction. AI can offer a bridge in times of loneliness but should not become a replacement for real relationships.

Inspire Through Visionary Perspectives

As AI technology continues to advance, imagine a future where AI assistants could not only manage your calendar but also understand your emotional state and act as mediators in your relationships. These AI-driven assistants might help you recognize when a relationship is faltering and suggest ways to reconnect, offering insights based on communication patterns or mood analysis.

AI could also offer virtual relationship coaching, providing practical advice on how to handle conflicts or offering suggestions for long-distance romantic gestures. In this future, AI tools could act as a kind of relationship concierge, managing the logistics while leaving room for emotional depth and genuine connection.

Visionary Thought: What if AI could become your relationship advisor, ensuring that no matter how far you travel, your personal connections stay strong and healthy? Imagine an AI that offers personalized advice on how to deepen bonds with loved ones, based on data from your interactions.

Balance Between Inspiration and Caution

While AI offers exciting possibilities for maintaining and strengthening relationships, it's important to be cautious about its limitations. One risk is over-reliance on AI for communication, which can depersonalize relationships. While automating the logistics of connecting with others is helpful, it's crucial to remember that human relationships require emotional depth, time, and effort—things that AI cannot fully replicate.

Additionally, AI-driven apps that simulate companionship, like Replika, can create a false sense of connection. These tools, while useful for alleviating loneliness, should not replace the deep, meaningful relationships that humans need to thrive. A key challenge for digital nomads is to strike a balance between using AI for convenience and ensuring that their relationships remain authentic and emotionally fulfilling.

Balanced Advice: Use AI to enhance your relationships, not to replace real human connection. While AI can help with logistics and support, remember that true relationships thrive on vulnerability, honesty, and shared experiences.

Highlight Global and Cultural Dimensions

Digital nomads often forge friendships and relationships across different cultures and continents. AI tools have made cross-cultural relationships more accessible, offering translation services, cultural exchange platforms, and even AI-driven travel guides to help nomads better understand the places they visit.

For example, AI tools like Google Translate can help digital nomads overcome language barriers when forming friendships in foreign countries. Meanwhile, platforms like Couchsurfing and Meetup use AI algorithms to recommend local events and gatherings, enabling digital nomads to build connections with locals and other travellers alike.

Global Insight: Leverage AI not just for maintaining existing relationships, but also for fostering new cross-cultural friendships. By understanding and embracing different cultures, digital nomads can deepen their connections and enrich their global experience.

Motivate with Purpose and Fulfilment

Ultimately, digital nomads often pursue this lifestyle not just for the freedom it offers, but also for the fulfilment of living a life aligned with their passions and values. Relationships are a key part of this equation, and AI can play a role in helping nomads stay connected to loved ones, no matter where their journey takes them.

By using AI to optimize work and communication, digital nomads can carve out more time to nurture relationships, both old and new. AI allows them to balance the pursuit of career goals with the desire to build meaningful, lasting personal connections.

Inspirational Thought: Imagine how AI can help you maintain a lifestyle that nurtures both your professional ambitions and your personal relationships. With the right balance, you can live a fulfilling life without sacrificing your most important connections.

Conclusion: AI and Relationships in the Digital Nomad Lifestyle

The intersection of AI and digital nomadism presents both opportunities and challenges for personal relationships. AI tools have the potential to enhance communication, manage logistics, and even provide emotional support, but they should be used thoughtfully to ensure that relationships remain authentic and emotionally rich.

As a digital nomad, you have the unique opportunity to blend technology with meaningful connections. By leveraging AI wisely, you can sustain deep, fulfilling relationships even while embracing a lifestyle of global freedom. Remember, AI should enhance your life, not replace the human connections that matter most. Use it to free up time, manage your schedule, and stay connected to loved ones, but always make space for real, emotional interactions.

In the end, a balanced approach—where AI supports but doesn't dominate your relationships—will lead to a richer, more fulfilling experience as you navigate the nomadic lifestyle.

CHAPTER 49: FINANCIAL INDEPENDENCE WITH AI

How Digital Nomads Can Use AI to Achieve Financial Freedom

As the digital nomad lifestyle becomes increasingly mainstream, one of the most pressing goals for many nomads is achieving financial independence. Financial freedom allows nomads to live a lifestyle free of geographical constraints, and artificial intelligence (AI) is proving to be a powerful ally in reaching this goal. From automating routine tasks to optimizing investment strategies, AI opens up a world of opportunities for digital nomads to not only survive but thrive financially. This chapter delves into the various ways AI can empower nomads to achieve lasting financial independence while living a location-independent life.

Engage with Storytelling and Case Studies

Meet Alex, a copywriter who had been traveling through Latin America for over a year when he realized that his freelance work wasn't providing him with the financial stability he needed. Between project-based income and the unpredictable nature of freelance gigs, Alex found it difficult to plan for the future, let alone achieve financial freedom.

That's when he decided to leverage AI to automate parts of his business and enhance his financial planning. He began using Jasper AI to streamline content creation and QuickBooks AI to manage his freelance income and expenses more efficiently. With these AI tools in place, Alex reduced his manual workload by 40%, which freed up time for him to invest in more strategic projects. More importantly, he started using AI-powered investment platforms like Wealthfront, which allowed him to diversify his savings and take the first steps toward financial independence.

Within six months, Alex's workload was lighter, his financial portfolio was more diversified, and he was on a more secure financial path—all thanks to AI-driven solutions. His journey from struggling freelancer to financially independent nomad illustrates how AI can be a game-changer for digital nomads seeking financial freedom.

Focus on Practical Application

Financial independence for digital nomads often seems like a lofty goal, but AI offers practical tools to get there. From automating mundane tasks to enhancing investment strategies, here are some of the most effective ways digital nomads can leverage AI for financial success:

1. AI for Automating Freelance Work
   Many digital nomads rely on freelance gigs for income, but juggling multiple clients and projects can be overwhelming. AI tools like Jasper AI for content creation, Descript for audio and video editing, and Canva's AI-powered design tools allow nomads to automate and expedite repetitive tasks, freeing up time for higher-paying opportunities.

Practical Tip: Identify areas of your workflow that can be automated using AI. This could be drafting emails, editing content, or managing client interactions. Automation will allow you to focus on scaling your business rather than just maintaining it.

2. AI for Financial Management

One of the biggest challenges digital nomads face is managing inconsistent cash flow. AI-driven tools like QuickBooks and Wave use AI to track expenses, manage invoices, and predict future cash flow based on past financial behaviour. This allows digital nomads to better manage their income and plan for the future.

Practical Tip: Use AI financial tools to monitor your expenses, categorize transactions automatically, and generate financial reports. This will give you a clear overview of your financial situation, helping you make informed decisions on how to grow your income and savings.

3. AI for Investment Strategies

Achieving financial independence often involves investing wisely. AI-driven robo-advisors such as Wealthfront and Betterment help digital nomads create customized, diversified investment portfolios. These platforms use algorithms to assess risk tolerance, financial goals, and time horizons, allowing users to invest efficiently without needing a financial advisor.

Practical Tip: Begin by setting aside a small portion of your income to invest using AI-powered platforms. Let the algorithms handle portfolio management and adjustment, allowing your money to grow passively over time.

Inspire Through Visionary Perspectives

Imagine a future where your financial portfolio is managed entirely by AI, adjusting investments automatically based on your goals, market trends, and risk tolerance. AI assistants could notify you of new opportunities, whether it's a high-yield savings account in a country you've just arrived in, or a short-term rental investment in a fast-growing market.

As AI continues to evolve, it will likely offer even more advanced ways to automate income streams and optimize savings. In the future, digital nomads might rely on AI not just for managing investments, but for identifying emerging markets, tracking cryptocurrency trends, or even running fully AI-managed businesses.

Visionary Thought: What if your AI assistant could guide you to financial independence by creating a completely passive income stream from global investments? Envision a world where your AI analyses your spending habits, income potential, and future goals to design an optimized pathway toward financial freedom.

Balance Between Inspiration and Caution

While AI offers incredible potential for financial independence, it's important to approach it with a balanced perspective. Relying entirely on AI for financial decisions can carry risks. Automated systems may not always account for human factors such as emotional spending or economic uncertainties like pandemics. While AI is a powerful tool, it's not a substitute for careful planning and personal judgment.

For example, Alex, the digital nomad we introduced earlier, still checks in on his investments regularly. He uses AI to manage the day-to-day but doesn't blindly trust every algorithm without oversight. AI is a tool to enhance decision-making, not to replace it entirely.

Balanced Advice: Use AI to automate the repetitive, time-consuming aspects of your financial life, but stay informed and actively involved in significant financial decisions. A hybrid approach where AI handles routine tasks while you focus on larger strategic goals is the key to success.

Highlight Global and Cultural Dimensions

One of the most exciting aspects of AI for digital nomads is how it can facilitate financial independence across different cultural and economic contexts. In some countries, AI-powered platforms can help nomads tap into unique financial opportunities, such as local real estate investments, micro-lending platforms, or international savings accounts.

For example, in emerging markets like Southeast Asia, AI is helping small businesses and freelancers access global markets, levelling the playing field. Meanwhile, in Europe, nomads can leverage AI to secure favourable tax arrangements, manage offshore accounts, or participate in international e-commerce ventures.

Global Insight: As a global citizen, use AI not just to manage finances but to explore opportunities in different economies. Whether it's taking advantage of lower costs of living or finding tax-friendly jurisdictions, AI tools can provide the insights you need to grow your wealth globally.

Motivate with Purpose and Fulfilment

Financial independence isn't just about having more money —it's about having the freedom to live life on your own terms. For digital nomads, that often means pursuing a lifestyle of adventure, exploration, and purpose. AI allows nomads to optimize their finances so they can focus on what truly matters: traveling, experiencing new cultures, and working on passion projects that align with their values.

By automating repetitive tasks and streamlining financial management, AI gives nomads the opportunity to spend more time doing what they love, whether that's exploring a new city, learning a new skill, or building meaningful relationships.

Inspirational Thought: By leveraging AI, you're not just achieving financial independence—you're creating space in your life for purpose and fulfilment. With the right financial foundation, powered by AI, you can pursue your dreams without the constant worry of making ends meet.

Conclusion: Achieving Financial Independence with AI

In conclusion, AI is reshaping the path to financial independence for digital nomads, offering tools to automate freelance work, manage finances, and invest for the future. By embracing these technologies, nomads can focus on living a life of freedom, adventure, and purpose while ensuring that their financial foundation is secure.

With a strategic mix of AI-powered solutions and personal involvement, digital nomads can achieve lasting financial freedom, enabling them to live the life they've always dreamed of—on their own terms, anywhere in the world.

CHAPTER 50 AI-POWERED SELF-DEVELOPMENT FOR NOMADS: A PATH TO LIFELONG LEARNING

In an era where artificial intelligence (AI) is reshaping industries, careers, and the future of work, digital nomads find themselves at the intersection of a major transformation. As technology evolves, so must the skills and capabilities of those who embrace the nomadic lifestyle. One of the most compelling opportunities for nomads in the AI age is the ability to use these cutting-edge tools for self-development and continuous learning. In this chapter, we'll explore how digital nomads can leverage AI to accelerate their personal growth, upskill in real-time, and remain competitive in a rapidly changing world.

A Case Study: Mia's Journey of AI-Driven Growth

Mia, a 32-year-old freelance UX designer, has been a digital nomad for six years. While she loved the freedom and flexibility her lifestyle offered, she began to notice that her industry was shifting. With AI tools starting to automate design tasks, Mia realized she needed to enhance her skill set to stay relevant. Enter AI-powered learning platforms.

Mia discovered Coursera and Udemy, both of which now feature AI-driven personalization features that tailored her learning journey based on her career goals and previous experience. Instead of spending hours researching which courses to take, Mia's AI assistant suggested advanced design thinking, data analytics, and AI ethics courses. AI-generated learning pathways guided her step-by-step through the material, adjusting the pace and depth based on her quiz scores and engagement.

Thanks to these tools, Mia not only learned new skills but also gained insights into emerging trends in her field. Within months, she was offering AI-powered UX consulting services, capitalizing on her newfound knowledge. The integration of AI into her learning process allowed Mia to stay ahead of the curve, positioning herself as a leader in her industry.

How Digital Nomads Can Use AI for Self-Improvement

AI has the potential to revolutionize how digital nomads approach self-development, offering tools that are both highly efficient and customizable. Here's how you can use AI to elevate your personal and professional growth.

1. Personalized Learning Platforms: AI-powered platforms like LinkedIn Learning, Skillshare, and Coursera use algorithms to tailor course recommendations based on your current skills, career goals, and interests. These platforms assess your progress in real-time, providing you with feedback and additional resources, ensuring that your learning experience remains dynamic and personalized. Nomads can easily incorporate continuous learning into their daily routine, no matter where they are.

2. AI-Assisted Mentorship: AI can help bridge the gap between knowledge and application. Tools like MentorCruise

use AI to match you with industry experts and mentors based on your specific learning goals. Whether you're looking to break into a new field or refine a particular skill, AI-driven mentorship ensures that you're paired with the right person, optimizing your learning experience.

3. AI for Language Learning: For nomads living and working across borders, language is often a barrier. AI-powered platforms such as Duolingo and Babbel use machine learning to tailor lessons based on your performance, helping you learn new languages faster. These platforms make language acquisition engaging by adapting to your learning style, tracking your progress, and providing personalized content that keeps you motivated. For digital nomads, this means more seamless integration into new cultures and work environments.

4. AI-Driven Time Management and Productivity Tools: Self-improvement isn't just about learning new skills—it's also about optimizing how you manage your time. Tools like RescueTime and Toggl use AI to track your work habits, providing insights into how you spend your day and offering suggestions on how to improve productivity. These tools can identify inefficiencies in your workflow and suggest strategies for optimizing focus, allowing you to make the most of your work hours while still prioritizing self-development.

5. AI-Powered Well-Being Tools: Self-improvement extends beyond professional skills. For digital nomads, mental and physical well-being are crucial for maintaining a sustainable lifestyle. AI-driven apps like Headspace and Calm provide personalized meditation and mindfulness programs, adapting to your stress levels, mood, and daily routine. Meanwhile, fitness apps like Freeletics and MyFitnessPal offer customized workout and nutrition plans based on your goals, keeping you healthy while you travel.

Visionary Perspectives: The Future of AI-Enhanced Learning

As AI continues to evolve, the possibilities for self-development will expand in ways we can barely imagine. Imagine AI-powered tutors that not only teach you; new- skills; but also engage in real-time problem-solving alongside you. Virtual reality (VR) learning environments, enhanced by AI, could allow nomads to participate in immersive, hands-on experiences from anywhere in the world.

In the not-too-distant future, AI may be able to analyse your strengths, weaknesses, and career aspirations with unparalleled accuracy, offering fully customized learning pathways that dynamically evolve as you progress. Digital nomads will have access to a constant stream of learning opportunities, empowering them to adapt and thrive in the face of technological disruption.

Balancing Inspiration with Realism

While the potential of AI for self-development is undeniably exciting, it's important to approach this technology with both enthusiasm and caution. As AI becomes more integrated into learning and personal development, it's essential to be mindful of issues such as data privacy, algorithmic bias, and the potential over-reliance on technology. Digital nomads should use AI as a tool for empowerment, not as a crutch. Human intuition, creativity, and critical thinking remain irreplaceable assets in an AI-driven world.

Furthermore, AI should complement, not replace, the social and experiential aspects of learning. While AI-powered platforms are excellent for knowledge acquisition, digital nomads should still seek out opportunities to network, collaborate, and learn from diverse perspectives. The human element—whether through mentorship, peer learning, or immersive cultural experiences—will always be a critical component of self-development.

Final Thoughts: Lifelong Learning as a Digital Nomad's Superpower

In a world where change is constant and technology is rapidly evolving, the ability to learn, adapt, and grow is a digital nomad's greatest asset. AI offers unprecedented opportunities for personal and professional development, making lifelong learning more accessible, efficient, and enjoyable than ever before. By leveraging AI, digital nomads can not only stay competitive in the global marketplace but also lead more fulfilling, purpose-driven lives.

As you navigate your journey in the AI age, remember that self-improvement isn't just about staying relevant—it's about unlocking new potential, embracing challenges, and continually striving to be the best version of yourself. With AI as your ally, the possibilities for growth are limitless.

PART 11: AI AND THE FUTURE OF REMOTE WORK INFRASTRUCTURE

CHAPTER 51: AI AND REMOTE WORK INFRASTRUCTURE

How AI is Shaping the Future of Tools, Platforms, and Infrastructure for Remote Work

The rise of artificial intelligence (AI) has not only transformed industries but has also radically reshaped the infrastructure that powers remote work. For digital nomads, who rely on tools and platforms to seamlessly manage their businesses, AI is creating new opportunities to optimize productivity, streamline workflows, and maintain work-life balance. This chapter delves into how AI is influencing the digital infrastructure for remote work and how nomads can harness these innovations to thrive in the evolving landscape.

Engage with Storytelling and Case Studies

When Maya first became a digital nomad, she found herself juggling multiple platforms—managing projects, tracking client communications, and ensuring smooth collaboration with her remote team. The inefficiencies started adding up, and Maya realized she needed a solution that could integrate everything into a cohesive, easy-to-manage system.

That's when Maya discovered AI-powered platforms that

revolutionized her workflow. Using ClickUp AI for project management and Notion AI to help with content planning and communication, Maya automated her daily operations. Her AI-powered tools integrated seamlessly, allowing her to automate task assignments, set reminders for upcoming deadlines, and even generate ideas for new marketing strategies. Maya's transition to AI-driven infrastructure reduced the time she spent on manual tasks by 50%, giving her more freedom to focus on strategic growth and personal development.

Maya's experience illustrates how AI is shaping the remote work landscape, offering digital nomads more effective and integrated platforms that simplify operations and boost productivity.

Focus on Practical Application

AI is transforming the tools and platforms digital nomads rely on to manage remote work. Whether it's project management, communication, or file sharing, AI-driven platforms enhance efficiency while reducing the cognitive load of juggling multiple tasks. Here are some practical ways digital nomads can take advantage of these innovations:

1. AI-Powered Project Management Tools

Tools like Trello AI, ClickUp, and Monday.com use AI to manage tasks and streamline workflows. These platforms provide intelligent task prioritization, automatic deadline reminders, and AI-powered reporting to keep projects on track. Additionally, AI algorithms can analyse workload distribution and optimize task assignments, ensuring that team members work efficiently without burnout.

Practical Tip: Set up AI-powered notifications to remind you of key deadlines and automatically allocate tasks based on team strengths and availability. Let AI handle the logistics, while you focus on creative, strategic aspects of your work.

2. AI for Communication and Collaboration

For digital nomads, seamless communication is crucial. AI-powered communication tools such as Slack's AI assistant and Microsoft Teams AI features can provide smart summaries of meetings, flag important messages, and even recommend the best times for virtual meetings based on participant availability. These tools also use natural language processing (NLP) to organize and filter communication, ensuring you never miss an important update.

Practical Tip: Utilize AI to filter and prioritize your communications, ensuring that the most critical messages always rise to the top. This will reduce the clutter in your inbox and help you focus on tasks that matter most.

3. Cloud Storage and File Management with AI

AI-integrated cloud storage solutions like Google Drive AI and Dropbox AI not only offer file-sharing capabilities but also use AI to automatically tag, categorize, and organize your documents. These tools use machine learning to suggest relevant files based on your activity and help you quickly locate important resources.

Practical Tip: Enable AI-powered search in your cloud storage tools to instantly find relevant files without having to manually sift through folders. This can save you significant time, especially when you're working on the go.

Inspire Through Visionary Perspectives

Imagine a future where the infrastructure for remote work is completely automated, allowing digital nomads to focus entirely on creativity and innovation. AI-driven platforms could become your virtual assistants, autonomously managing client relationships, scheduling tasks, and even forecasting project timelines based on previous performance. In this future, digital nomads will be able to achieve an unprecedented level of productivity and freedom, as AI takes on the heavy lifting of daily tasks.

The potential for AI to continuously evolve infrastructure is enormous. Future iterations of AI could enhance platforms with predictive analytics, helping digital nomads anticipate market trends, manage global tax compliance, or even recommend emerging industries for new business ventures.

Visionary Thought: What would your life look like if AI could autonomously manage your entire workflow, freeing you to pursue your passions and creative projects? As AI infrastructure becomes more sophisticated, this reality is closer than you think.

Balance Between Inspiration and Caution

While AI-powered tools offer incredible benefits, they are not without challenges. Relying too heavily on AI can lead to over-automation, where human intuition and decision-making are sidelined. It's essential for digital nomads to strike a balance between allowing AI to handle routine tasks and staying actively involved in higher-level strategy and client relations.

For instance, while Maya benefited greatly from AI-powered project management, she still took time each week to personally review key tasks and make manual adjustments when necessary. This blend of human oversight with AI automation ensured that she maintained control over her business operations.

Balanced Advice: Use AI as a supplement to your workflow,

not a replacement for critical thinking. Ensure that you stay involved in essential business decisions, leveraging AI to enhance your capabilities rather than fully replace them.

Highlight Global and Cultural Dimensions

Digital nomads often work across borders, collaborating with teams in different countries and navigating various regulatory environments. AI can help simplify this by offering tools that adapt to the global nature of remote work. For example, Deel and Remote use AI to handle payroll and compliance for international teams, making it easier to manage employees or contractors from different countries.

Similarly, AI-powered translation tools such as DeepL and Google Translate AI allow for smoother communication across language barriers. These tools enable digital nomads to collaborate effectively with global clients, ensuring that cultural differences and languages are not a barrier to success.

Global Insight: Use AI to navigate complex global work environments. Whether it's handling multi-currency payroll or collaborating with international clients, AI tools can simplify the process, allowing you to focus on building global connections.

Motivate with Purpose and Fulfilment

AI-powered remote work infrastructure allows digital nomads to reclaim time and energy, focusing on the things that truly matter. By automating the logistics of remote work, nomads are free to pursue passion projects, immerse themselves in new cultures, or spend more time with loved ones—all without the constant stress of managing a growing business.

Whether you dream of exploring remote corners of the globe or diving deep into creative endeavours, AI provides the tools that make these aspirations achievable. As a digital nomad, leveraging AI doesn't just make your life more productive—it enhances the freedom that drew you to the nomadic lifestyle in the first place.

Inspirational Thought: By using AI to handle the operational side of your business, you can focus more on the journey—both professional and personal—that inspired your nomadic lifestyle.

Conclusion: The Future of AI-Driven Remote Work Infrastructure

In conclusion, AI is fundamentally reshaping the tools, platforms, and infrastructure that support remote work for digital nomads. By automating routine tasks, optimizing workflows, and providing global solutions, AI enables nomads to focus on higher-level creativity and strategic growth.

As AI continues to evolve, the infrastructure for remote work will become increasingly sophisticated, offering digital nomads the freedom to fully embrace the flexibility, independence, and adventure that comes with their unique lifestyle. Whether through AI-powered project management, smarter communication tools, or global payroll solutions, the future of digital nomadism is inextricably linked to the power of AI.

CHAPTER 52: AI-ENHANCED VIRTUAL OFFICES

How Digital Nomads Can Leverage AI to Create Dynamic Virtual Offices

As the world shifts toward a more distributed workforce, digital nomads are increasingly turning to artificial intelligence (AI) to build highly efficient and adaptive virtual offices. The concept of a virtual office goes far beyond email and video conferencing; it's about creating an ecosystem where business processes are automated, collaboration is seamless, and productivity is enhanced. With AI at the core, nomads can construct dynamic, responsive work environments that rival physical offices in effectiveness.

This chapter will explore how digital nomads can use AI to enhance their virtual office experience, improve collaboration, and achieve higher levels of productivity. We'll look at practical applications, visionary insights, and the global dimensions of this technological shift.

Engage with Storytelling and Case Studies

When Alex first began his journey as a digital nomad, managing a remote team felt overwhelming. Communication was disjointed, and finding ways to keep everyone on the same page was a constant struggle. Every task seemed to require several follow-ups, and managing documents across different platforms was chaotic.

Then Alex discovered how AI could streamline his virtual office. Using Slack's AI-powered assistant and Notion AI for team collaboration, his business transformed. The AI tools managed workflow integration tracked project progress, and automated document organization. By using Zoom's AI-powered transcription service and Otter.ai for meetings, he eliminated the need for lengthy minutes. AI seamlessly summarized meetings and flagged important actions for follow-up.

This automation not only helped Alex run his team smoothly but also freed up his time to focus on business strategy and creative projects. AI didn't just enhance Alex's virtual office; it redefined it, providing flexibility, speed, and structure to what was previously an unwieldy process.

Focus on Practical Application

For digital nomads, a virtual office isn't just a space for managing work remotely—it's a powerful hub of productivity, collaboration, and creativity. With AI-driven tools, you can automate many of the tasks that would typically slow down your workflow. Here's how you can build a dynamic virtual office using AI:

1. AI-Powered Communication Tools

Communication lies at the heart of a productive virtual office. Tools like Slack AI and Microsoft Teams AI allow you to manage conversations, prioritize important messages, and even summarize discussions for team members who missed the meeting. The natural language processing (NLP) capabilities of AI ensure that you can search conversations efficiently and retrieve critical information at any time.

Practical Tip: Use AI-powered bots within your communication platforms to automatically organize meetings, summarize discussions, and ensure that follow-ups are promptly assigned to the right team members.

2. Virtual Meeting Efficiency with AI

AI enhances virtual meetings by providing real-time transcription, action item tracking, and even sentiment analysis. Platforms like Zoom AI and Otter.ai offer automatic meeting summaries, reducing the need for extensive note-taking during calls.

Practical Tip: After each meeting, use AI tools to generate a concise action plan and share it with your team. This helps ensure accountability while saving time on manual meeting notes.

3. AI for Document Management and Collaboration

Managing documents and collaborating on projects is much more efficient with AI tools like Google Workspace AI and Dropbox AI. These tools automatically categorize and tag files, provide smart suggestions for relevant documents, and allow teams to collaborate seamlessly across time zones.

Practical Tip: Enable AI to sort and suggest documents based on your current tasks, minimizing time spent searching for relevant files and allowing for faster project completion.

Inspire Through Visionary Perspectives

Imagine a future where your virtual office operates as an intelligent entity that anticipates your needs, schedules tasks, and optimizes your work environment. AI won't just automate tasks; it will actively manage the flow of work in a virtual office.

In this future, AI assistants could track employee productivity, assess the mental well-being of team members, and even make recommendations on work-life balance improvements. Rather than simply managing workloads, these AI tools could help you forecast business trends, suggest new collaboration opportunities, and automate the creation of new workspaces on virtual platforms like Gather.town or Spatial.

Visionary Thought: What if your virtual office could automatically adapt to your workflow, removing the need for manual inputs and proactively identifying opportunities for growth? As AI evolves, digital nomads will gain even greater freedom and agility.

Balance Between Inspiration and Caution

While AI offers immense advantages, there are potential downsides to over-reliance on AI-powered virtual offices. Excessive automation can lead to reduced human interaction, which is vital for creativity and collaboration. Digital nomads must strike a balance between automation and personal engagement. Additionally, the more AI handles critical operations, the more vulnerable your business becomes to system failures or cybersecurity threats.

Take Alex's experience as an example. While AI tools improved productivity, he quickly realized that over-reliance on automation diminished team interaction. He adjusted by incorporating more human-centred check-ins, balancing the efficiency of AI with the necessity of personal connection.

Balanced Advice: Use AI to enhance your virtual office but maintain the human elements that foster creativity, trust, and teamwork. Balance automation with opportunities for organic interaction to keep your virtual workspace thriving.

Highlight Global and Cultural Dimensions

As digital nomads often collaborate across borders, AI tools provide the bridge that connects global teams. AI-powered translation services like DeepL and Google Translate AI make it easier to work with international clients and partners by breaking down language barriers. Additionally, AI tools can account for cultural nuances, helping ensure that communications are respectful and clear, regardless of the region.

Global payroll and compliance tools, such as Deel or Remote, use AI to manage international taxes, contracts, and compensation, ensuring digital nomads and their teams stay compliant with local regulations. These platforms allow nomads to build truly global teams without the logistical headaches that typically accompany international hiring.

Global Insight: Use AI tools to effortlessly manage communication, payroll, and compliance on a global scale. This will enable you to tap into talent across regions, fostering a more inclusive and diverse virtual office.

Motivate with Purpose and Fulfilment

By automating routine tasks and streamlining operations, AI helps digital nomads focus on what truly matters. Whether it's dedicating time to passion projects, traveling the world, or simply achieving a better work-life balance, the flexibility that AI provides allows nomads to align their work with their life goals.

Digital nomads are often drawn to this lifestyle not just for the freedom it offers but for the chance to pursue meaningful work while enjoying diverse experiences. With AI enhancing their virtual offices, nomads can dedicate more energy to their personal development, creativity, and community-building efforts.

Inspirational Thought: Embrace the potential of AI to help you create a life that prioritizes your passions, giving you the time and flexibility to truly thrive as a digital nomad.

Conclusion: Building the AI-Driven Virtual Office of the Future

AI is revolutionizing the way digital nomads create and manage their virtual offices. By automating repetitive tasks, improving communication, and enhancing collaboration, AI frees nomads from the operational burden, allowing them to focus on growth, creativity, and personal fulfilment.

The future of the virtual office is intelligent, adaptive, and global. As AI continues to evolve, digital nomads will enjoy an unprecedented level of flexibility and efficiency, making their work-life balance more attainable than ever before. Whether through smarter communication tools, AI-powered collaboration, or predictive business insights, digital nomads have the opportunity to redefine the workplace—and AI is leading the charge.

CHAPTER 53:
AI AND CLOUD COMPUTING FOR DIGITAL NOMADS

What Role Does Cloud Computing Play in Facilitating AI-Driven Remote Work?

As the world of work shifts towards a digital-first approach, digital nomads are leading the charge in leveraging emerging technologies like AI and cloud computing. The ability to work from anywhere and access powerful AI tools on demand is made possible largely by cloud computing. Whether you're a freelance graphic designer traveling across Asia or a tech consultant working with clients from around the world, the combination of AI and cloud computing has become the backbone of the modern nomadic lifestyle.

This chapter explores how digital nomads can use cloud computing to maximize the benefits of AI, streamline their workflows, and embrace the flexibility that comes with a borderless work environment. By diving into real-world examples, practical tips, and visionary perspectives, we'll show you how to unlock the potential of AI through cloud technologies.

Engage with Storytelling and Case Studies

Meet Emily, a content writer and digital nomad who has been traveling the world for over five years. Early on in her journey, she struggled with managing client projects while hopping between different countries and time zones. Constantly backing up files on external hard drives and relying on her laptop for everything limited her flexibility. Then, she discovered the power of cloud computing and AI-driven tools.

By moving her entire workflow onto platforms like Google Cloud and Microsoft Azure, Emily gained instant access to her files, no matter where she was or which device she was using. What used to take hours—researching for articles, drafting content, and communicating with clients—was now streamlined. AI-powered writing assistants like Jasper integrated seamlessly with the cloud, allowing her to generate high-quality content quickly, while Google Cloud AI helped her manage massive amounts of client data with ease.

This shift didn't just save time; it transformed the way Emily approached work. Her virtual office was no longer tied to any specific location or device. With the cloud and AI working in harmony, Emily found the freedom she sought as a digital nomad, all while scaling her business beyond what she thought was possible.

Focus on Practical Application

Cloud computing and AI aren't just buzzwords—they are essential tools that digital nomads can leverage to improve productivity and enhance their remote work experience. Here's how you can apply cloud computing to make the most out of AI in your virtual office:

1. AI-Driven Cloud Platforms

The integration of AI with cloud platforms such as Amazon Web Services (AWS), Google Cloud Platform (GCP), and Microsoft Azure enables you to scale your business effortlessly. These platforms offer powerful AI services, from natural language processing (NLP) to predictive analytics. You can automate repetitive tasks, process data faster, and even leverage machine learning algorithms without needing deep technical expertise.

Practical Tip: For content creators, use cloud-based AI tools like Jasper AI for writing, Canva AI for design, or Descript for editing podcasts and videos. These tools integrate directly into the cloud, ensuring your work is accessible and editable from any device.

2. Cloud-Based Collaboration

Collaboration tools such as Google Workspace, Slack, and Trello are powered by the cloud, enabling you to collaborate with team members across the globe in real time. Add AI to the mix, and you can automate workflow management, track project progress, and ensure everyone stays aligned—no matter where they are.

Practical Tip: Integrate AI-driven task managers like Monday.com with cloud storage solutions like Dropbox or Google Drive. This combination allows you to automatically organize files, update tasks, and ensure that the most recent versions of documents are always available.

3. Data Security and Accessibility

For digital nomads, data security and accessibility are paramount. Cloud computing ensures your data is encrypted, backed up, and accessible at any time. AI further enhances this by providing smart security solutions that detect potential threats, monitor your cloud activity, and offer real-time insights into data management.

Practical Tip: Use cloud-based AI tools like IBM Watson to monitor and manage data security across platforms. It will provide alerts on suspicious activity, enabling you to take preventive actions before any major breaches occur.

Inspire Through Visionary Perspectives

Imagine a future where your entire workspace exists in the cloud, powered by AI that anticipates your needs. Cloud-based AI could manage client relationships, forecast project deadlines, and automatically generate business strategies based on historical data and future trends. As AI continues to evolve, it's likely that cloud services will become even more intelligent and intuitive, enabling digital nomads to run businesses that practically manage themselves.

In this future, virtual offices will become more adaptive. Cloud platforms will not just store data—they will optimize workflows, enhance creativity, and offer real-time insights into business performance. Digital nomads could simply log in to their cloud environments and have AI-powered assistants organize their day, prioritize tasks, and even recommend breaks to enhance well-being.

Visionary Thought: How might your work life change if AI and cloud computing could take over all the logistical challenges of running a business, leaving you free to focus entirely on creative and strategic pursuits?

Balance Between Inspiration and Caution

While the benefits of AI and cloud computing are undeniable, it's important to approach this powerful combination with a degree of caution. Cloud security is a major consideration for digital nomads who rely on these platforms for storing sensitive data. It's crucial to invest in proper security protocols, including two-factor authentication, data encryption, and regular backups.

Another cautionary note is data dependency. As AI-driven cloud tools become more integral to daily operations, digital nomads need to be mindful of not becoming overly dependent on these technologies. Balancing automation with personal oversight will remain key in ensuring long-term success and adaptability.

Balanced Advice: Use AI-powered cloud tools to enhance your productivity, but maintain an active role in managing security, data governance, and decision-making.

Highlight Global and Cultural Dimensions

Cloud computing doesn't just connect your devices—it connects cultures. As a digital nomad, you're likely collaborating with people from all corners of the world. AI-powered cloud tools like DeepL Translate and Microsoft Azure's Cognitive Services provide real-time translations, making cross-cultural communication more seamless.

Additionally, cloud platforms allow you to adhere to regional data compliance laws, ensuring your work remains above board, no matter where you're conducting business. For example, platforms like AWS provide localized cloud infrastructures in multiple regions, allowing you to comply with local laws regarding data storage and transfer.

Global Insight: Use cloud-based AI tools to manage global compliance, enhance collaboration across borders, and ensure seamless communication, regardless of language barriers.

Motivate with Purpose and Fulfilment

The ultimate benefit of combining AI with cloud computing is the flexibility it provides. By automating mundane tasks and making your data accessible from anywhere, you can focus on what matters most—whether that's growing your business, exploring new cultures, or pursuing personal passions. Cloud computing helps you maintain that delicate balance between work and life, giving you the freedom to create a life filled with purpose and adventure.

Inspirational Thought: Cloud computing enables you to work smarter, not harder. By embracing AI and the cloud, you're not just optimizing your workflow—you're creating a more fulfilling, purpose-driven life.

Conclusion: The Future of AI and Cloud Computing for Nomads

AI and cloud computing are revolutionizing the digital nomad experience. By combining the limitless accessibility of the cloud with the power of AI, nomads can create dynamic virtual offices that are secure, efficient, and adaptable. Whether you're collaborating across continents or automating your business operations, this technology provides the tools you need to succeed in a rapidly evolving global landscape.

In the AI-driven, cloud-powered future, digital nomads will continue to thrive, breaking down barriers and building businesses that are as flexible and agile as the nomadic lifestyle itself.

CHAPTER 54: THE ROLE OF BLOCKCHAIN AND AI FOR DIGITAL NOMADS

How Will the Intersection of Blockchain and AI Impact Digital Nomads?

In the rapidly evolving landscape of technology, blockchain and AI are two of the most transformative forces shaping the future of work. While AI is reshaping how digital nomads approach their careers—automating tasks, enhancing creativity, and driving efficiency—blockchain offers a decentralized, secure, and transparent foundation for transactions, collaboration, and identity management. When these two technologies converge, they have the potential to revolutionize the lifestyle of digital nomads, creating new opportunities for work, payment, and global collaboration.

In this chapter, we explore how digital nomads can leverage the intersection of AI and blockchain to enhance their careers, manage their finances, and build secure, decentralized systems that allow them to thrive anywhere in the world.

Engage with Storytelling and Case Studies

Let's meet Alex, a freelance developer who has been living the digital nomad lifestyle for years, traveling from Bali to Lisbon while working for clients across the globe. Alex's primary concern was finding reliable ways to get paid without losing money to currency exchange fees and transaction delays. While traditional banking methods presented challenges for a global freelancer, blockchain and AI combined to provide Alex with the perfect solution.

By using blockchain-based smart contracts, Alex ensures secure and transparent agreements with clients. The contract automatically releases payment in cryptocurrency once the agreed-upon work is delivered and verified by an AI system that tracks the completion of tasks. This eliminates delays, disputes, and middlemen from the process. AI automates the administrative side of freelancing, from generating invoices to tracking hours worked, while blockchain ensures that every transaction is secure and recorded in an immutable ledger.

Through this innovative system, Alex no longer worries about delayed payments or hefty fees, allowing him to focus on his creative work. For Alex, the intersection of AI and blockchain has not only simplified his financial transactions but also given him greater freedom and confidence as a global digital nomad.

Focus on Practical Application

Digital nomads can harness the power of blockchain and AI in several practical ways. Whether it's managing payments, securing data, or enhancing collaboration, this intersection offers new tools for seamless, secure, and efficient workflows.

1. Smart Contracts for Secure Freelance Work

Blockchain-based smart contracts are self-executing contracts where the terms are directly written into code. These contracts automatically execute when the conditions are met, providing a reliable way for digital nomads to engage in work agreements without intermediaries. When integrated with AI, these contracts can track the progress of a project, ensuring that payments are released only when specific milestones are achieved.

Practical Tip: Use platforms like Ethereum or Polkadot to create smart contracts for freelance work. Pair these with AI tools like Toggl or Asana to automatically track your work hours and project progress, making your payment workflow seamless and transparent.

2. Decentralized Identity Verification

As digital nomads move from one country to another, managing personal identification, work permits, and visas can be complicated. Blockchain offers a decentralized solution for identity management, allowing digital nomads to create a digital identity that is secure, transparent, and universally recognized. With AI enhancing these platforms, digital nomads can securely store their work credentials, tax records, and other critical documents in one place, accessible anytime and from anywhere.

Practical Tip: Explore blockchain-based identity platforms like Civic or uPort, which allow you to create a secure, verifiable digital identity. These platforms can be integrated with AI for real-time verification, making it easier to manage visas, contracts, and credentials as you move between countries.

3. AI-Enhanced Cryptocurrency Management

Managing finances as a digital nomad can be complicated when dealing with multiple currencies and international transactions. With blockchain, cryptocurrencies offer a universal payment method that transcends borders. When combined with AI, managing cryptocurrency investments and payments becomes even easier. AI-powered tools can predict market trends, automatically convert currencies at optimal rates, and track your finances in real-time.

Practical Tip: Use AI-powered crypto platforms like Coinbase or Binance, which offer advanced trading and financial management tools. These platforms help digital nomads manage income streams, track investments, and automate payments without the need for traditional banks or payment processors.

Inspire Through Visionary Perspectives

Imagine a future where digital nomads don't need to rely on traditional banking systems or deal with cumbersome bureaucracy when moving between countries. Blockchain and AI together offer a future where digital nomads have total control over their work, identity, and finances—independent of borders or financial institutions.

In this future, a digital nomad could work on a project for a client in Japan while sitting in a café in Mexico. The smart contract on the blockchain would ensure that the client's payment is secured and automatically released once the AI system verifies the project's completion. The payment would be in cryptocurrency, instantly converted to the nomad's preferred currency using AI to track the best rates. Meanwhile, the nomad's digital identity, stored securely on the blockchain, would allow for seamless border crossings and work permits in any country.

Visionary Thought: Could blockchain and AI together create a global, borderless economy for digital nomads, where traditional financial and bureaucratic systems are replaced by decentralized, transparent, and efficient technologies?

Balance Between Inspiration and Caution

While blockchain and AI offer incredible possibilities, there are challenges to consider. Blockchain technology is still relatively new, and its mainstream adoption faces hurdles such as regulatory uncertainty and technical complexity. Additionally, the volatility of cryptocurrency markets means that digital nomads need to approach crypto payments with caution.

On the AI side, the risk of data privacy breaches or manipulation exists, especially when integrated with blockchain systems. Digital nomads need to stay informed about the latest security protocols to ensure that their data and financial assets remain protected.

Balanced Advice: Use blockchain and AI tools to enhance your work as a digital nomad, but ensure that you are aware of the risks involved. Stay updated on regulatory changes, employ strong security measures, and diversify your income streams to minimize potential volatility.

Highlight Global and Cultural Dimensions

The intersection of AI and blockchain is not just transforming the digital nomad lifestyle—it's also impacting cultures and economies around the world. Blockchain's decentralized nature allows people from different countries to collaborate seamlessly without the need for traditional financial or governmental intermediaries. AI, in turn, enhances these interactions by providing real-time translation tools, automating workflows, and offering predictive analytics that improve decision-making.

For example, in countries like Estonia, blockchain-based e-residency programs allow digital nomads to establish virtual businesses, pay taxes, and access government services without physically residing there. Meanwhile, in regions like Africa, blockchain and AI are being used to enable remote workers to receive payments in stable cryptocurrencies, bypassing the volatility of local currencies.

Global Insight: Look into blockchain and AI tools that are being developed in different parts of the world to optimize your work as a digital nomad. Whether it's e-residency in Estonia or decentralized payment platforms in Africa, there are global opportunities for digital nomads to leverage these technologies.

Motivate with Purpose and Fulfilment

At its core, the intersection of blockchain and AI is about more than just technology—it's about creating freedom, flexibility, and purpose. By embracing these innovations, digital nomads can take control of their work and finances, allowing them to focus on what truly matters—whether that's exploring new cultures, building meaningful connections, or making a positive impact on the world.

Inspirational Thought: Blockchain and AI offer digital nomads the opportunity to live a life untethered by traditional systems. By leveraging these technologies, you can create a work-life balance that aligns with your values, giving you the freedom to pursue your passions without compromise.

Conclusion: Embracing Blockchain and AI for the Future of Nomadic Work

The convergence of blockchain and AI is opening new doors for digital nomads, offering them unprecedented freedom and control over their work, finances, and personal identities. Whether through smart contracts, decentralized identity management, or AI-powered financial tools, digital nomads can harness these technologies to build a future that is more secure, flexible, and purpose-driven. By staying informed, embracing innovation, and navigating challenges with caution, digital nomads can thrive in a world where blockchain and AI define the future of work.

55. 5G, AI, and the Future of Connectivity

   - How will the combination of AI and 5G revolutionize how digital nomads work?

PART 12: AI-POWERED NETWORKING FOR DIGITAL NOMADS

CHAPTER 55: 5G, AI, AND THE FUTURE OF CONNECTIVITY

How Will the Combination of AI and 5G Revolutionize How Digital Nomads Work?

For digital nomads, connectivity is not a luxury; it's a necessity. A stable and fast internet connection can make the difference between a successful project and a missed deadline. As digital nomads move across borders and time zones, they rely heavily on tools that allow them to stay connected and productive. Enter the combination of AI and 5G—a powerful duo that is set to revolutionize the way digital nomads work, collaborate, and thrive across the globe.

In this chapter, we will explore how the deployment of 5G networks and advancements in AI are transforming connectivity, providing digital nomads with faster, more reliable, and smarter ways to work. From enhanced remote collaboration to seamless cloud access and real-time data analysis, this new era of connectivity is poised to reshape the digital nomad lifestyle in profound ways.

Engage with Storytelling and Case Studies

Meet Sarah, a freelance video editor who travels extensively while managing multiple international clients. For years, Sarah juggled slow Wi-Fi in remote locations, which hampered her ability to upload large video files or join video calls without buffering issues. She constantly faced connectivity challenges that disrupted her workflow, from hotel Wi-Fi limits to unstable mobile connections. Then came the rollout of 5G, and everything changed.

Using AI-powered tools combined with 5G's lightning-fast speed, Sarah could now edit videos in real-time, seamlessly syncing with cloud platforms to collaborate with clients across continents. The AI tools Sarah relied on, such as automated video editors, could process vast amounts of data in minutes, drastically reducing the time it took her to complete a project. She could sit at a café in Bali or a coworking space in Prague, working efficiently as if she were in a fully equipped office.

Sarah's story illustrates how AI and 5G together are not just about enhancing speed—they are about transforming how digital nomads can maximize productivity and eliminate previous barriers to remote work.

Focus on Practical Application

So, how can digital nomads make the most of the AI and 5G revolution? Let's break down the practical ways these technologies are shaping the future of work for nomads and what steps you can take to leverage these advancements.

1. Real-Time Collaboration Without Boundaries
    The low latency and ultra-high-speed connection of 5G enable seamless real-time collaboration with teams and clients globally. AI tools, from automated transcription services to real-time language translation, integrated with 5G, allow for virtual meetings that feel as if they're

happening face-to-face. Video conferencing, cloud-based project management, and content-sharing platforms will be more reliable, faster, and smoother, even in remote regions.

Practical Tip: Use AI-powered collaboration tools like Zoom with real-time language translation features, or Slack combined with AI automation bots that schedule, transcribe, and summarize conversations instantly during meetings, all powered by 5G's robust connectivity.

2. Cloud Computing at Supercharged Speeds
The combination of 5G and AI drastically improves access to cloud computing, a vital tool for digital nomads who need to access large files, collaborate with teams, or manage multiple workflows on the go. With 5G, uploading and downloading large datasets, video files, or graphics-heavy projects will happen in seconds. AI tools enhance this process by offering predictive analytics, automated file organization, and data synchronization, keeping digital nomads one step ahead of their work.

Practical Tip: For digital nomads working in data-heavy industries, platforms like Google Cloud or Amazon Web Services can now be accessed seamlessly on the go. Combine AI tools like Databricks for real-time data analysis to optimize workflow and deliver results faster.

3. AI-Powered Networking Solutions
5G networks, when paired with AI, can enhance the digital nomad's networking experience. AI-based virtual assistants can organize meetings, streamline project workflows, and provide reminders based on your location, calendar, and time zone. AI can analyse your working habits, predicting when and where you will need the best connection, and 5G ensures that you will always have access to high-speed internet, regardless of location.

Practical Tip: Use AI-powered assistants like Google

Assistant or Cortana in combination with 5G to manage your workflow, plan meetings across time zones, and ensure that your working hours are optimized for productivity. By leveraging location-based AI suggestions, you can maximize your connectivity for crucial deadlines.

Inspire Through Visionary Perspectives

Imagine a future where digital nomads have access to instant, AI-curated workspaces no matter where they are. In this future, 5G allows you to stream immersive, real-time AR (augmented reality) and VR (virtual reality) collaborative sessions with clients and coworkers, while AI optimizes these environments for productivity. Meetings could take place in virtual rooms where avatars and digital content interact seamlessly, transcending the traditional constraints of physical offices.

Envision 5G-connected smart cities where digital nomads have personalized AI-driven experiences at every turn. From knowing the best times to connect with clients in different time zones to suggesting the most suitable coworking spaces based on your work habits, AI will become a true partner in helping digital nomads thrive.

Visionary Thought: Could we see a world where physical offices become obsolete, replaced by AI-powered virtual offices that travel with you? Where your workspace adapts instantly to your location, time zone, and specific needs?

Balance Between Inspiration and Caution

While 5G and AI open up a world of possibilities, it's important to approach these advancements with balance and caution. One potential concern is data privacy. The widespread use of AI tools, coupled with 5G's far-reaching network, may make personal data more vulnerable to breaches. Additionally, 5G infrastructure is still under development in many regions, meaning that full, reliable access may take time to materialize in remote areas.

Balanced Advice: As you integrate AI and 5G into your workflow, be sure to use encrypted tools and stay informed about data protection protocols. Always choose trusted platforms with strong privacy policies and be aware of the limits of 5G in underdeveloped regions.

Highlight Global and Cultural Dimensions

5G and AI's impact is truly global. In regions like Europe, Asia, and North America, the race to deploy 5G has brought rapid advancements in connectivity, making these locations prime hubs for digital nomads seeking reliable infrastructure. Meanwhile, countries like South Korea and Japan are leading the way in AI integration with 5G, offering digital nomads unparalleled technological resources.

In developing countries, the rise of 5G has the potential to bridge the digital divide, providing nomads with better connectivity in areas that were previously underserved. As digital nomads venture into new markets, they will be able to contribute to local economies and gain access to new cultural experiences without sacrificing connectivity or productivity.

Global Insight: Look for emerging 5G hotspots and seek out countries that are early adopters of AI-powered services. These regions will offer you a competitive edge when it comes to connectivity, innovation, and collaboration.

Motivate with Purpose and Fulfilment

At its core, the combination of 5G and AI is about more than just enhanced connectivity—it's about unlocking new possibilities for personal growth, creativity, and meaningful work. By embracing these technologies, digital nomads can free themselves from the constraints of slow internet and time zones, opening the door to a life of seamless connection, exploration, and fulfilment.

Whether it's pursuing passion projects, learning new skills, or engaging with diverse cultures, AI and 5G empower digital nomads to lead purpose-driven lives without compromise. With the ability to work efficiently from anywhere, digital nomads can focus on what truly matters—whether that's building lasting relationships, contributing to meaningful causes, or exploring new corners of the world.

Conclusion: The 5G and AI Future Awaits Digital Nomads

As 5G networks roll out globally and AI continues to evolve, digital nomads will be at the forefront of this technological revolution. The enhanced speed, connectivity, and intelligence provided by these tools will fundamentally transform how we work, communicate, and live. By embracing these innovations, digital nomads can unlock unprecedented levels of productivity and creativity, empowering them to lead lives that transcend borders and limitations.

With 5G and AI in your toolkit, the future of digital nomadism is more connected, collaborative, and exciting than ever before.

CHAPTER 56: NETWORKING IN THE AI AGE

How Can Digital Nomads Use AI Tools to Build Meaningful Professional Networks?

For digital nomads, building a meaningful professional network can feel like a daunting task. Constantly on the move, working across time zones, and often relying on virtual communication, the traditional ways of networking may seem out of reach. However, the rise of artificial intelligence (AI) offers a new and exciting opportunity to revolutionize the way digital nomads connect with professionals around the globe.

In this chapter, we will explore how AI is reshaping the networking landscape for digital nomads and provide practical steps to leverage AI-powered tools to build lasting and impactful professional relationships. Whether you're a freelancer, entrepreneur, or remote worker, these insights will empower you to turn AI into a networking superpower.

Engage with Storytelling and Case Studies

Meet Miguel, a digital marketing consultant based in Medellín, Colombia, who works with clients across Europe, Asia, and the United States. A few years ago, networking was one of his biggest struggles. Attending in-person conferences was not an option due to his constant traveling, and virtual networking felt impersonal and ineffective. This challenge began to change when Miguel started using AI-powered networking tools to expand his professional connections.

Using an AI-driven platform called Shapr, which works like a professional version of Tinder, Miguel was able to connect with professionals from various industries by simply swiping through AI-suggested profiles based on his interests and goals. The AI algorithm not only introduced him to relevant professionals but also suggested conversation starters, helping to bridge the gap between casual connections and meaningful relationships. Within six months, Miguel had built a network that spanned three continents and resulted in new partnerships, collaborations, and clients.

Miguel's experience shows how AI can make networking more efficient, intuitive, and effective for digital nomads, transforming what was once a challenge into an opportunity for global growth.

Focus on Practical Application

For digital nomads looking to thrive in the AI age, here are practical ways you can leverage AI tools to enhance your networking and grow your professional community.

1. AI-Enhanced Networking Platforms
AI-powered platforms like Shapr or LinkedIn AI tools analyse your interests, industry, and professional goals to suggest meaningful connections. These tools take the guesswork out of finding relevant contacts by scanning vast networks and delivering highly targeted recommendations. AI algorithms

can even suggest mutual connections, shared interests, and potential collaboration opportunities.

Practical Tip: Make sure your professional profiles on platforms like LinkedIn are up to date, highlighting key skills and projects. AI thrives on data, so the more detailed your profile, the better the algorithm can match you with potential contacts.

2. Virtual Networking Events Powered by AI
With AI-driven event platforms like Brella or Hopin, digital nomads can attend virtual conferences, meetups, and workshops tailored to their interests. AI can help match you with the most relevant attendees and speakers based on your profile, suggesting who to connect with and facilitating introductions. These platforms often have built-in AI-powered meeting schedulers that ensure you get face time with the right people, even if they are halfway around the world.

Practical Tip: When attending virtual events, use AI-powered scheduling tools to arrange 1-on-1 meetings with attendees who share your professional goals. AI will do the heavy lifting of suggesting the best times and people to meet.

3. AI for Social Listening and Engagement
One of the best ways to grow your network is through active engagement on social media platforms. AI-powered tools like Hootsuite Insights or Brandwatch can help digital nomads identify trending conversations in their industry and participate in real-time. These tools analyse social media platforms to find discussions relevant to your expertise, enabling you to engage with potential connections by offering valuable insights and joining the conversation at the right moment.

Practical Tip: Use AI-driven social listening tools to track conversations in your field and engage with thought leaders.

AI will notify you of key discussions, giving you the opportunity to connect meaningfully with professionals who share your interests.

Inspire Through Visionary Perspectives

As AI continues to evolve, the future of networking for digital nomads holds exciting possibilities. Imagine AI that goes beyond simple introductions to act as a personalized networking assistant—an AI-powered agent that proactively scans global professional networks for opportunities that align with your long-term career goals. This AI would not only suggest connections but also arrange introductions, schedule meetings, and even provide real-time conversation tips based on your counterpart's interests.

Imagine attending a virtual conference where AI matches you with the ideal collaborators or mentors in real time. You could even enter a virtual space where AI curates and arranges small group discussions with like-minded professionals, ensuring that each interaction adds value to your network.

Visionary Thought: Could AI-driven virtual networking spaces become as immersive and valuable as attending a physical event? The future may see AI agents representing digital nomads in virtual rooms, fostering connections that happen automatically while you're focusing on your work.

Balance Between Inspiration and Caution

While AI-powered networking offers enormous potential, there are also challenges that digital nomads should keep in mind. One concern is that AI-based recommendations may rely too heavily on existing data, leading to a narrower pool of suggested connections. This could result in a "networking bubble," where nomads miss out on opportunities to connect with diverse professionals outside their immediate field.

Additionally, the reliance on AI can sometimes make interactions feel impersonal or transactional. Building deep, meaningful relationships still requires human connection, empathy, and follow-through—qualities that AI cannot yet fully replicate.

Balanced Advice: Use AI networking tools as a starting point, but don't let the technology replace genuine human connection. Be proactive in reaching out, personalizing your messages, and cultivating relationships over time.

Highlight Global and Cultural Dimensions

One of the greatest benefits of AI-powered networking for digital nomads is its ability to break down cultural and geographic barriers. AI tools can connect nomads with professionals from diverse regions and industries, fostering cross-cultural collaboration. In countries like Japan and China, AI is already enhancing professional networking by translating conversations in real-time, allowing digital nomads to engage with professionals in local languages without the need for extensive language skills.

By expanding your network globally, you also gain valuable cultural insights and the ability to tap into new markets, increasing your flexibility as a nomad. Whether you are working from a café in Berlin or a coworking space in Bangkok, AI tools ensure that you can connect with professionals around the world as seamlessly as if you were working in your home country.

Global Insight: Leverage AI-powered language translation tools to build cross-cultural relationships. Tools like Google

Translate and DeepL can help bridge language barriers, making global networking smoother than ever.

Motivate with Purpose and Fulfilment

At the heart of AI-powered networking lies the potential for digital nomads to build not just professional networks but also meaningful, purpose-driven connections. AI allows nomads to focus on building relationships that align with their personal values, passions, and long-term goals. By using AI to connect with professionals who share your vision and purpose, networking becomes less about transactional exchanges and more about collaboration, inspiration, and mutual growth.

Whether you're looking to find mentors, collaborators, or like-minded professionals who share your desire to make a positive impact, AI can help you curate a network that feels deeply personal and fulfilling. With the right tools, digital nomads can build networks that support not just their careers, but their sense of purpose and community.

Inspirational Reflection: How could AI help you build a network that aligns with your deeper sense of purpose? With AI tools, you can create meaningful connections that go beyond just work, enabling you to collaborate on projects that matter to you.

Conclusion: Building Your Network with AI

As digital nomads, your network is your most valuable asset. With the power of AI, you can grow your professional community more efficiently, purposefully, and globally than ever before. By leveraging AI-powered networking tools, you can connect with professionals who not only advance your career but also contribute to your journey as a nomad.

With AI as your networking ally, the world truly becomes your office, and your network becomes as global as your ambitions. Whether you're building new partnerships, collaborating across borders, or seeking like-minded professionals, AI offers the tools to make networking in the digital nomad era more meaningful and impactful than ever before.

CHAPTER 57: AI-POWERED MATCHMAKING FOR COLLABORATIONS

For digital nomads, building meaningful professional relationships is one of the most challenging but essential parts of success. Constantly traveling, working remotely, and interacting with people from diverse cultures makes traditional networking methods difficult. But in the AI age, the challenge of finding collaborators and co-founders no longer feels like a solitary task. With AI-driven platforms, digital nomads can now leverage cutting-edge technologies to build the professional relationships they need, no matter where they are in the world.

This chapter will dive deep into how AI platforms are revolutionizing the search for collaborators and co-founders. By showcasing real-life examples of digital nomads who have successfully leveraged these tools, this chapter will provide actionable insights and practical tips to help you expand your professional network, find the right partners, and create powerful collaborations.

Engage with Storytelling and Case Studies

Let's start with the story of Nathan, a digital marketing specialist who was based in Bali, Indonesia. Like many digital nomads, Nathan loved the freedom that came with his lifestyle, but he struggled to find the right people to collaborate with. Working on a large-scale marketing project for a client, he realized he needed a technical co-founder to help him build a product that could scale.

Nathan turned to an AI-powered matchmaking platform called CoFoundersLab. The platform's algorithms analysed his professional background, goals, and the specific skill set he was seeking in a co-founder. Within days, Nathan was matched with Anne, a software engineer from Berlin who was also a digital nomad, working out of coworking spaces across Europe. Anne's technical expertise perfectly complemented Nathan's marketing acumen, and after a few virtual meetings, they decided to collaborate on the project. The AI matchmaking platform didn't just introduce them; it helped them forge a partnership that led to launching a successful SaaS product within six months.

Nathan's journey illustrates how AI-powered matchmaking can bridge the gaps between nomads, helping them find the perfect collaborators and co-founders from all corners of the world. The obstacles of geographical distance and professional isolation are diminished as AI technologies reshape how digital nomads build meaningful business relationships.

Focus on Practical Application

AI-powered platforms can transform your search for collaborators into a structured and efficient process. Here are some practical ways to use AI tools to find the right people to work with, no matter where you are.

1. AI Matchmaking Platforms

Platforms like CoFoundersLab, AngelList Talent, and Shapr use advanced AI algorithms to match professionals based on skills, goals, and personal preferences. These platforms take into account your career ambitions, project needs, and preferred work style to suggest potential collaborators or co-founders. By eliminating much of the guesswork involved in finding the right person, these tools streamline the process of building your dream team.

Practical Tip: When setting up your profile on these platforms, be as detailed and transparent as possible about your goals and the type of collaborator you're looking for. The more data AI has to work with, the better it can match you with someone who truly complements your skills and aspirations.

2. AI-Enhanced Freelance Platforms

AI tools have also found their way into popular freelance platforms like Upwork and Fiverr. These platforms use machine learning algorithms to suggest collaborators based on past projects, ratings, and skills. Whether you're a digital nomad looking for a project partner or a specific skill set for a short-term collaboration, these platforms can quickly connect you with relevant professionals.

Practical Tip: When posting job descriptions or looking for partners on AI-driven freelance platforms, use clear keywords that describe the skills, tools, and project goals. This will help the AI algorithm refine the search and present you with highly relevant profiles.

3. AI for Virtual Networking Events

Another powerful way to find collaborators is through AI-enhanced virtual networking events. Platforms like Hopin and Brella use AI algorithms to match event attendees based on mutual interests and goals, facilitating personalized introductions. For digital nomads, these events offer the flexibility to connect with global professionals from the comfort of any location.

Practical Tip: Attend AI-enhanced networking events that align with your professional goals. Use the platform's AI recommendations to schedule 1-on-1 meetings with relevant participants, and come prepared with an idea or project in mind to maximize the value of each interaction.

Inspire Through Visionary Perspectives

Looking forward, AI's role in professional matchmaking will only become more advanced and intuitive. Imagine a future where AI can not only match you with collaborators based on your skills but also predict how well you'll work together. AI could analyse work habits, communication styles, and even cultural preferences to suggest collaborators who are not only skilled but also compatible with your work style.

Visionary Thought: In the future, could AI matchmaking platforms predict the success of collaborations based on past project data and personality analysis? Imagine AI-driven collaboration platforms that measure compatibility and provide ongoing feedback to optimize teamwork.

Balance Between Inspiration and Caution

While AI-powered matchmaking offers exciting opportunities for digital nomads, it's essential to approach these platforms with a balance of optimism and caution. Although AI can effectively match people based on data, it cannot fully capture the nuances of human connection. Building a strong collaboration still requires personal effort, communication, and trust. It's important to use AI as a starting point but not to rely on it entirely for building deep professional relationships.

Balanced Advice: Use AI to accelerate the discovery process and streamline connections, but invest time in nurturing those relationships. Even with the best AI match, strong partnerships are built on communication, empathy, and shared goals.

Highlight Global and Cultural Dimensions

AI-driven platforms are truly global in their reach, enabling digital nomads to connect with professionals from diverse backgrounds, industries, and regions. This multicultural perspective is particularly valuable in the AI age, where diverse teams often bring more innovative solutions to the table. For example, Nathan's collaboration with Anne involved navigating different time zones, work cultures, and communication styles, but the AI platform helped facilitate this global partnership.

AI also enables seamless cross-cultural collaborations by incorporating real-time translation tools. Platforms like DeepL and Google Translate are often integrated into AI matchmaking services, allowing nomads to work together even if they don't share a common language.

Global Insight: By embracing AI, digital nomads can tap into a truly global talent pool, collaborating with professionals from different regions and backgrounds to create projects that reflect a broader, more inclusive perspective.

Motivate with Purpose and Fulfilment

For digital nomads, finding collaborators is not just about business—it's about building relationships that align with a deeper purpose. AI tools allow you to filter potential partners not only by skills but also by shared values, missions, and long-term goals. Whether you want to collaborate on a project that promotes sustainability, helps small businesses, or advances a social cause, AI platforms can help you find like-minded professionals.

Inspirational Reflection: Consider using AI not just to find someone who can help you finish a project, but to find someone who shares your vision and passion for making a difference. When you align your work with your purpose, collaboration becomes more fulfilling and impactful.

Conclusion: Building Collaborative Success with AI

In the AI age, finding collaborators and co-founders no longer needs to feel like an uphill battle. AI-powered platforms have the potential to connect digital nomads with the right partners efficiently, intelligently, and globally. By leveraging these tools, you can build collaborations that transcend geographical boundaries, cultural differences, and time zones.

As you embrace AI-driven matchmaking platforms, you'll discover that the world becomes a smaller, more interconnected place, where the perfect collaborator is only a few clicks away. Whether you're building a startup, launching a creative project, or searching for like-minded professionals, AI is here to make the process faster, smarter, and more meaningful.

CHAPTER 58: AI-DRIVEN SOCIAL NETWORKS: ENHANCING THE NOMADIC LIFESTYLE

The digital nomad lifestyle has always been about blending freedom and work, but it comes with unique challenges—particularly in staying connected and building meaningful communities while on the move. In the age of AI, social media platforms have evolved, harnessing AI to create personalized, engaging, and efficient spaces for digital nomads. AI-driven social networks have reshaped how digital nomads connect, collaborate, and even find new opportunities, making them indispensable tools for thriving in this global, mobile lifestyle.

In this chapter, we will explore how AI is transforming social media and creating platforms that cater specifically to the needs of digital nomads. Through storytelling, practical applications, visionary insights, and cultural perspectives, you'll learn how to make the most of AI-powered social networks to elevate your career, expand your network, and enhance your lifestyle.

Engage with Storytelling and Case Studies

Consider the story of Mia, a content creator and travel blogger who spent most of her time hopping between cities in Europe and Asia. For years, Mia struggled to keep up with different time zones, feeling disconnected from potential clients and collaborators. Networking in person was nearly impossible, and Mia found herself feeling isolated in her professional journey.

But all that changed when she discovered Nomadlist, a social platform for digital nomads powered by AI. By using machine learning, the platform provided Mia with personalized recommendations of coworking spaces, digital nomad communities, and events in every city she visited. Nomadlist's AI-driven algorithm even suggested potential collaborators based on shared professional interests, geographic proximity, and mutual connections.

Soon, Mia was meeting fellow digital nomads everywhere she went, collaborating on joint projects, and expanding her audience. She no longer felt isolated; AI had transformed her social and professional network, making it effortless for her to maintain a sense of community and collaboration no matter where she was.

Focus on Practical Application

Social media platforms have become more than just spaces for sharing vacation photos—they are essential tools for networking, collaboration, and career growth. AI is playing a critical role in enhancing these platforms by delivering hyper-personalized experiences. Let's dive into how you can practically use AI-driven social media to your advantage as a digital nomad.

1. AI-Driven Connections on Professional Networks

Platforms like LinkedIn have integrated AI algorithms to enhance networking for digital nomads. By analysing your profile, activity, and interactions, LinkedIn's AI suggests new connections, relevant groups, and trending content tailored to your professional interests. The platform also provides job recommendations based on your skill set, location preferences, and connections, making it easier to discover remote work opportunities suited to your lifestyle.

Practical Tip: Keep your LinkedIn profile up-to-date with clear keywords related to your niche and skills. The more accurate your profile, the better the AI algorithms can recommend connections and opportunities that align with your goals.

2. AI-Powered Community Platforms

AI is helping digital nomads find like-minded communities, no matter where they are. Slack and Discord, for example, use AI to recommend niche communities based on your interests and career needs. Whether you're looking for a group of freelance writers, developers, or marketing experts, AI-powered features within these platforms streamline the search process and help you find your tribe faster.

Practical Tip: Join AI-powered communities that align with your professional and personal goals. Once inside, engage actively and let the platform's AI do the work of connecting you with relevant conversations and people.

3. AI-Enhanced Event Discovery

Platforms like Meetup and Eventbrite are incorporating AI to recommend events and gatherings tailored to your location, profession, and interests. For digital nomads, this feature is a game-changer—it allows you to discover coworking meetups, workshops, and networking events in cities you're traveling through, ensuring you never miss an opportunity to connect.

Practical Tip: Use the AI-powered event recommendations to find both virtual and in-person networking opportunities. These tools ensure that wherever you are, you can maintain and expand your professional network.

Inspire Through Visionary Perspectives

AI is evolving, and the future of AI-driven social networks holds immense possibilities for digital nomads. Imagine a world where social media platforms anticipate your needs before you even realize them—where AI algorithms analyse your communication style, project goals, and personal preferences to suggest not only collaborators but also mentorships, investment opportunities, and tailored skill-building courses.

The future of AI in social networking could involve virtual assistants that automatically schedule meetings with potential clients or collaborators, predict optimal times for you to post content based on your global audience, and even simulate personalized networking events within virtual reality spaces.

Visionary Thought: What if AI could predict trends in your industry and connect you with emerging leaders before those trends become mainstream? Envision AI-driven platforms that keep you ahead of the curve, positioning you as a thought leader in your field.

Balance Between Inspiration and Caution

AI-powered social networks offer a wealth of opportunities, but it's important to maintain a balanced approach. While AI can personalize and streamline connections, there's a human element that mustn't be overlooked. Building genuine relationships requires time, effort, and authenticity —qualities that even the most advanced algorithms cannot replicate.

Be mindful of over-relying on AI for social interactions. It's still essential to nurture relationships by following up, engaging meaningfully in conversations, and contributing value to your network. AI can facilitate introductions, but it's your responsibility to foster long-lasting connections.

Balanced Advice: Use AI as a tool to enhance your social networking experience, but always prioritize genuine human connections. Technology is there to support, not replace, meaningful relationships.

Highlight Global and Cultural Dimensions

AI-driven social networks are breaking down cultural and geographical barriers, allowing digital nomads to connect with professionals from all over the world. Platforms like Instagram and Twitter are using AI to suggest content and connections that reflect diverse cultural perspectives, helping digital nomads build global networks.

For instance, an AI algorithm on Instagram might suggest a local business influencer in Bali if it detects you're traveling there, while Twitter's AI could introduce you to a discussion on entrepreneurship trends in Africa based on your interests.

Global Insight: Embrace the diversity that AI-powered social platforms offer. By expanding your network beyond your immediate circles and cultures, you'll gain access to fresh perspectives, ideas, and opportunities.

Motivate with Purpose and Fulfilment

AI-driven social platforms offer more than just networking —they can help you find your purpose by connecting you with communities and causes that align with your values. Whether it's finding collaborators for a socially conscious project, building a startup that makes a difference, or simply connecting with others who share your passions, AI can help guide you toward more fulfilling, purpose-driven work.

Inspirational Reflection: Imagine using AI to connect not just for profit but for purpose. The right connections can transform your work into something that doesn't just support your lifestyle but contributes to something greater.

Use Accessible, Simple Language for Complex Topics

AI can be complex, but the way it's integrated into social networks is often intuitive. Social platforms do the heavy lifting behind the scenes, allowing you to interact with them seamlessly. AI works by learning from your preferences, interactions, and engagement patterns, and then recommending connections, content, and communities that fit your needs.

Friendly Explanation: Think of AI like a virtual matchmaker that introduces you to people, events, and conversations you didn't even know you needed. The more you interact, the better it gets at helping you connect.

Interactive and Engaging Content

Before you finish this chapter, consider exploring some AI-powered social networks. Reflect on your current social networking habits and identify ways AI could enhance your experience. Here's a quick exercise to try:

Interactive Exercise: Spend 15 minutes on LinkedIn or Instagram, paying attention to how AI algorithms suggest connections, content, and communities. How can these recommendations help you expand your network? Write down three new connections or communities you'd like to explore further.

Final Thoughts: AI as a Gateway to Connection

AI-driven social networks are more than just tools for expanding your professional reach—they are gateways to meaningful, global connections. For digital nomads, they offer the chance to stay connected, build communities, and find collaborators wherever the journey takes them. As AI continues to evolve, these platforms will only become more intuitive and essential, helping digital nomads not just survive, but thrive, in the AI age.

CHAPTER 59: BUILDING A PERSONAL BRAND WITH AI

In today's digital landscape, personal branding is more important than ever, especially for digital nomads who rely on their online presence to secure work, collaborations, and build relationships. But in a world where the digital landscape is crowded, how can you stand out while constantly on the move? Enter AI.

Artificial Intelligence has become a key tool in personal branding, helping individuals craft, maintain, and amplify their unique identities. From automating content creation to refining your social media presence and analysing engagement metrics, AI tools are transforming how digital nomads manage their personal brands. In this chapter, we'll explore how you can leverage AI to build a strong, authentic personal brand that resonates globally.

Engage with Storytelling and Case Studies

Let's start with the story of Leo, a graphic designer turned digital nomad. When Leo first started his journey, he quickly realized that freelancing in different time zones and marketing his work required more than talent—it required a compelling online presence. But Leo wasn't a marketer; he didn't know how to craft perfect social media posts, let alone analyse which ones were performing well.

One day, Leo discovered Canva Pro's AI-powered tools and Buffer's AI-powered scheduling features. He started using Canva's intuitive AI design assistant to create visually stunning graphics and social media banners for his portfolio. Then, Buffer's AI suggested optimal times for posting, giving him insights into which content was driving the most engagement. With just a few clicks, Leo was able to create a consistent, polished personal brand—one that not only attracted new clients but positioned him as an expert in his field.

Through AI, Leo was able to grow his social media following by 200% in just a few months. What would have taken hours of manual effort and analysis was now done efficiently, leaving Leo more time to focus on his creative work.

Focus on Practical Application

As a digital nomad, building a personal brand requires balancing multiple platforms and strategies while traveling. Here's how you can start integrating AI tools to streamline the process and elevate your brand.

1. AI for Content Creation
Creating content that reflects your brand's identity is crucial, but it can also be time-consuming. AI-powered tools like Jasper AI allow you to generate blog content, social media captions, and even website copy with a simple input of keywords or prompts. Jasper can produce relevant, SEO-optimized content in minutes, which you can customize to suit your tone and style.

Practical Tip: Use Jasper AI to generate drafts for your blog posts or social media updates. Then, refine the content manually to add your personal touch, ensuring the output stays authentic to your brand.

2. AI for Design and Visual Branding

Visuals play a significant role in personal branding, especially for digital nomads in creative industries. Platforms like Canva now offer AI-powered design suggestions, helping you create visually cohesive graphics that align with your brand's aesthetics. Whether you're creating logos, social media banners, or marketing materials, AI design assistants can significantly reduce the time and effort needed to develop professional-looking content.

Practical Tip: Use Canva's "Magic Resize" feature to automatically adjust your designs for different platforms (Instagram, LinkedIn, Twitter), ensuring that your visual branding stays consistent across all channels.

3. AI for Social Media Management

Maintaining a presence on multiple social media platforms can be overwhelming. AI-powered scheduling tools like Buffer or Hootsuite help digital nomads plan, schedule, and optimize their social media content based on audience behaviour. AI algorithms analyse engagement trends and recommend the best times to post, allowing you to maximize visibility while minimizing manual effort.

Practical Tip: Schedule your posts for the week ahead using Buffer's AI scheduling feature. Focus on creating high-quality, engaging content in one sitting, then let the platform post for you automatically.

Inspire Through Visionary Perspectives

Imagine a future where AI personal branding tools go beyond just automating content creation. What if your AI assistant could analyse industry trends in real-time, adjusting your branding strategy based on what's gaining traction? Picture an AI-driven platform that tailors your brand narrative on-the-fly, suggesting new markets to tap into or helping you build thought leadership within your niche.

This future isn't far off. As AI continues to advance, the personalization of branding will become even more precise, helping digital nomads adapt to changing trends effortlessly.

Visionary Thought: Imagine an AI assistant that not only creates content but continually evolves your brand based on real-time data and industry shifts. With AI, personal branding will be a dynamic, constantly evolving process, keeping you ahead of the curve.

Balance Between Inspiration and Caution

While AI offers incredible advantages in building a personal brand, it's important to maintain a sense of authenticity. AI can automate tasks, but it's still up to you to ensure that your voice, values, and personality shine through.

There's a risk of over-relying on AI-generated content, which can make your brand feel impersonal. The key is finding the right balance—letting AI handle the tedious tasks while you focus on the creative and human elements that make your brand unique.

Balanced Advice: Use AI to enhance your workflow, not replace your creativity. AI can offer suggestions, but the essence of your brand should always come from you.

Highlight Global and Cultural Dimensions

As a global citizen, your personal brand needs to resonate across different cultures and regions. AI tools like Grammarly not only improve your writing but can adapt your content for different linguistic and cultural contexts. For digital nomads working in diverse markets, this level of cultural adaptability is crucial in building a globally appealing brand.

Global Insight: Use AI tools to tailor your content for different audiences. Grammarly, for example, can help you switch between British and American English, while AI-driven platforms like Linguix can offer insights into local linguistic preferences, ensuring your brand resonates globally.

Motivate with Purpose and Fulfilment

Building a personal brand isn't just about self-promotion —it's about aligning your professional identity with your passions and purpose. AI tools can help you achieve your professional goals, but more importantly, they free up your time to focus on what truly matters to you. Whether that's working on passion projects, spending time with family, or traveling the world, AI allows you to craft a brand that aligns with a fulfilling, purpose-driven life.

Inspirational Reflection: Imagine using AI not just to build a career, but to create a brand that reflects your deeper values. With the right tools, you can carve out time for personal fulfilment while still advancing your professional goals.

Use Accessible, Simple Language for Complex Topics

Building a personal brand with AI may sound complex, but the tools are designed to simplify the process. AI platforms work behind the scenes, analysing data and suggesting optimizations, so you can focus on the creative aspects. Think of AI as your personal branding assistant—handling the technical details, while you focus on creating authentic, engaging content.

Friendly Explanation: AI is like having a personal assistant that helps you look your best online. It analyses what works and makes suggestions, so you can focus on creating content that truly represents who you are.

Interactive and Engaging Content

As you finish this chapter, take a moment to reflect on your current personal branding efforts. Here's a quick exercise to help you integrate AI tools into your process:

Interactive Exercise: Choose one AI tool from this chapter, such as Jasper or Canva. Spend 15 minutes exploring its features and create one piece of content for your personal brand—whether that's a blog post, social media graphic, or portfolio update. How did the AI tool simplify the process? Reflect on how you can use this tool to streamline your branding efforts in the future.

Final Thoughts: The Future of Personal Branding with AI

AI tools are revolutionizing how digital nomads build and maintain personal brands, making the process more efficient, strategic, and impactful. From content creation to visual design and social media management, AI allows you to craft a brand that is not only professional but personal, reflecting your unique values and goals.

As you continue your journey as a digital nomad, embrace AI's potential to streamline your branding efforts. Let it handle the technical side while you focus on being creative, authentic, and purposeful. The world is your platform—use AI to make your mark.

CHAPTER 60: AI AND PROFESSIONAL DEVELOPMENT FOR NOMADS

In the rapidly changing work landscape of the 21st century, professional development is no longer confined to a physical office or traditional career paths. For digital nomads, continuous growth and skill development are essential to thrive in an unpredictable global economy. AI is now playing a transformative role in how professionals, particularly those who embrace the nomadic lifestyle, can learn, grow, and evolve in their careers. From personalized learning platforms to AI-driven mentoring and skill assessments, AI offers unique opportunities for digital nomads to keep pace with their industries while traveling the world.

Engage with Storytelling and Case Studies

Let's start with the story of Alex, a freelance web developer who travelled across Europe while managing projects for various clients. Although Alex was well-versed in coding, he wanted to expand his skill set to include AI and machine learning but had no idea how to structure his learning journey with his unpredictable schedule. Alex discovered

Coursera and Udacity, platforms that offer AI-powered personalized learning paths. By analysing his existing skills and interests, the AI suggested specific courses that would enhance his knowledge and tailor his learning schedule based on his availability.

With AI-generated progress reports and suggestions for improvement, Alex was able to balance work, travel, and learning seamlessly. Over time, Alex built proficiency in AI, which he then integrated into his freelance offerings, enabling him to secure higher-paying clients. AI not only empowered Alex to enhance his skills but also allowed him to expand his professional opportunities while maintaining his nomadic lifestyle.

Focus on Practical Application

AI is revolutionizing how digital nomads engage in professional development by offering practical, accessible, and flexible tools that align with their transient lifestyles. Below are some ways you can integrate AI into your professional growth strategy.

1. AI for Personalized Learning
Platforms like Coursera and Udacity use AI to provide personalized learning experiences, creating tailored learning paths based on your goals, existing skills, and areas of interest. Whether you want to learn a new programming language, develop marketing strategies, or dive into AI itself, these platforms can adapt to your pace and availability.

Practical Tip: Use AI-powered learning platforms to create a flexible schedule that works around your lifestyle. Set goals within the platform and let AI guide you to relevant courses, certifications, or even suggest learning formats—be it videos, articles, or hands-on projects.

2. AI for Skill Assessment

Knowing which skills you need to develop is key to staying relevant in a competitive, digital-first economy. AI tools like Skillsoft's Percipio or LinkedIn Learning offer assessments that evaluate your current abilities and suggest areas of improvement. These assessments, driven by AI, are dynamic and continuously adapt as you complete courses or apply new skills.

Practical Tip: Regularly assess your skills using AI-powered platforms. These tools can help you identify gaps in your expertise and suggest which new competencies you should acquire to remain competitive in your industry.

3. AI for Career Growth

AI-driven career development tools like MentorCruise pair digital nomads with mentors who can offer industry-specific advice. AI helps match mentees with mentors based on goals, learning preferences, and industry trends, providing a more personalized and impactful mentorship experience. This can be particularly useful for digital nomads seeking guidance in unfamiliar markets or industries.

Practical Tip: Join a mentorship platform that uses AI to connect you with professionals who align with your career goals. Use the AI to navigate your interactions, ensuring that you focus on actionable advice and skill development.

Inspire Through Visionary Perspectives

Imagine a future where AI doesn't just suggest learning paths but can predict industry trends and identify emerging skills needed to stay ahead of the curve. AI could act as a real-time career coach, alerting you to changes in your field and recommending new areas to explore before the competition catches up. For digital nomads, AI could one day create virtual co-learning spaces where professionals from different parts of the world collaborate, learn, and grow together, regardless of location.

The future of professional development is one of limitless possibilities, where AI can tailor not just the learning experience but anticipate the shifts in industry demands, helping digital nomads stay agile and adaptable.

Visionary Thought: Imagine a world where AI serves as your personal career strategist, continuously updating your development plan based on industry trends and global opportunities. For digital nomads, this will redefine what it means to be a lifelong learner.

Balance Between Inspiration and Caution

While AI can certainly enhance professional development, it's important to approach it with a balanced mindset. The convenience and efficiency AI brings can sometimes overshadow the human element needed for genuine learning and growth. Relying too heavily on AI might result in a more mechanical approach to career growth, one that misses the nuances of personal passion and creativity.

The key is to use AI as a tool, not a replacement for critical thinking, creativity, and personal motivation. AI can guide and suggest, but your passion and curiosity should still drive your professional development.

Balanced Advice: Let AI be your guide, but remember that your curiosity, ambition, and human connections are equally important in your journey to professional growth. AI is a tool to amplify your potential, not a substitute for your creativity and decision-making.

Highlight Global and Cultural Dimensions

As a digital nomad, your career growth is inherently global. AI platforms like Duolingo not only help with language acquisition but provide a cultural context to facilitate communication across borders. Similarly, AI-powered global job platforms like Turing connect digital nomads with opportunities in diverse markets, making cultural and professional adaptability essential.

Global Insight: Use AI tools that facilitate cross-cultural learning, such as language acquisition and global job search platforms. These tools allow you to integrate seamlessly into new markets while expanding your professional opportunities globally.

Motivate with Purpose and Fulfilment

For digital nomads, professional development is not just about climbing the corporate ladder or securing higher-paying clients—it's about achieving a life of purpose and balance. AI enables nomads to align their work with their personal values by offering flexible, personalized growth paths that fit into their lives. Whether it's learning new skills to contribute to a meaningful cause or gaining expertise to pursue passion projects, AI helps you grow in ways that align with your purpose.

Inspirational Reflection: Professional development through AI allows you to pursue not just career success, but fulfilment. By continuously learning and growing, you can build a career that aligns with your values and passions while living a flexible, purpose-driven life.

Use Accessible, Simple Language for Complex Topics

AI-driven professional development might sound complicated, but it's simpler than you think. These tools are designed to make learning and growth more efficient, accessible, and personalized. AI takes the guesswork out of what to learn next and how to learn it, leaving you to focus on what you do best—growing, evolving, and thriving in your career.

Friendly Explanation: AI is like having a personal career coach that suggests what skills you need next, helps you find the right resources, and keeps you on track—all while understanding your personal schedule and goals.

Interactive and Engaging Content

Now that you understand how AI can revolutionize your professional development, here's a quick exercise to put these insights into practice:

Interactive Exercise: Take 20 minutes to explore an AI-powered learning platform like Coursera or Udacity. Identify a course or learning path that aligns with your current career goals. How does the AI personalize your learning journey? Reflect on how this platform could fit into your digital nomadic lifestyle.

Final Thoughts: The Future of Professional Development with AI

AI is empowering digital nomads to continue growing professionally, no matter where they are. By leveraging AI's ability to personalize learning, assess skills, and connect nomads with mentors and global opportunities, you can ensure that your professional growth never stalls. Embrace AI as a tool to enhance your skills, expand your opportunities, and align your career path with your purpose, passions, and values. The future of work is dynamic, and with AI, you can stay ahead of the curve while maintaining the freedom and flexibility that define the digital nomad lifestyle.

PART 13: ADVANCED AI TOOLS FOR DIGITAL NOMADS

CHAPTER 61: AI-POWERED DESIGN TOOLS FOR DIGITAL NOMADS

The rise of AI-powered design tools has transformed how digital nomads work, offering new ways to approach creativity, productivity, and the business of design. Whether you're a freelance graphic designer, a content creator, or a marketer looking to enhance your visual storytelling, AI is reshaping the tools of the trade. For digital nomads, these innovations allow for streamlined workflows, greater flexibility, and the ability to produce high-quality designs from anywhere in the world. In this chapter, we'll explore some of the most innovative AI-powered design tools and how you can leverage them to enhance your creativity, productivity, and profitability.

Engage with Storytelling and Case Studies

Meet Emma, a digital nomad and freelance web designer who travels between Bali and Portugal. Emma's business took off when she began using AI-powered design tools to optimize her workflow. She started with Canva, a user-friendly platform that employs AI to help with layout suggestions, colour schemes, and even content creation. Instead of spending hours manually selecting design elements, Emma used Canva's AI-assisted templates to quickly produce professional-level designs.

What used to take Emma several hours now only took minutes. She also integrated Jasper AI into her content creation process to develop engaging copy that matched the designs she created. By using AI tools to automate 70% of her workflow, Emma was able to take on more clients, increasing her income while still maintaining her nomadic lifestyle. Emma's success is a testament to how AI-powered design tools can unlock both creativity and efficiency for digital nomads.

Focus on Practical Application

AI design tools can streamline your workflow, save time, and enhance your creative output. Here's how you can start using them in your design work.

1. Canva – AI for Easy, Professional Design
One of the most widely used platforms by digital nomads, Canva provides AI-driven suggestions for design layouts, colour palettes, and font combinations, making it easier than ever to create visually appealing content. Whether you're designing social media graphics, presentations, or marketing materials, Canva's AI enhances the creative process, giving you time to focus on more strategic tasks.

Practical Tip: Use Canva's AI-powered "Magic Resize" feature to automatically adjust designs for different platforms. This is particularly useful for social media campaigns where you need consistent branding across multiple channels.

2. Jasper AI – AI-Assisted Content for Design
Pairing Jasper AI with your design tools allows you to

generate high-quality written content that complements your visuals. Jasper is an AI content generator that can create blog posts, social media captions, email copy, and even headlines in seconds. Integrating Jasper with design tools allows you to create cohesive designs and copy without needing to switch between multiple platforms.

Practical Tip: Use Jasper's AI to generate copy for infographics, promotional materials, or websites directly within your design platform. The seamless integration between text and visuals can elevate your overall design project.

3. Figma – AI-Powered Collaboration for UX/UI Designers

If you're working on web or mobile app designs, Figma is a robust tool that integrates AI features like design auto-completion, smart layout recommendations, and collaboration tools. Figma's AI capabilities allow you to anticipate user needs, generating responsive designs and layouts that adapt to different screen sizes automatically.

Practical Tip: Take advantage of Figma's real-time collaboration tools and AI-powered layout suggestions to create responsive designs that adapt fluidly to any device. This allows you to work faster and more efficiently, especially when working remotely with a team.

Inspire Through Visionary Perspectives

Imagine a future where AI-driven design platforms become so intuitive that they can predict design trends before they happen. AI could scan millions of design inputs globally, offering you insights on emerging styles, colour preferences, and layout trends specific to different regions or industries. The AI would then help digital nomads stay ahead of the curve, offering custom design suggestions based on market demands and cultural preferences.

Visionary Thought: In the near future, AI could anticipate design needs before you even start working on a project. It could analyse market trends and customer behaviour to predict the most effective visuals for specific audiences, enabling you to create highly personalized and impactful designs effortlessly.

Balance Between Inspiration and Caution

While AI-powered design tools open up incredible possibilities, it's essential to remember that creativity remains uniquely human. AI can streamline tasks, offer suggestions, and automate repetitive processes, but it cannot replicate the creative spark that comes from personal experience, cultural understanding, and emotional intuition.

As a digital nomad, your experiences across different countries and cultures feed into your creativity. While AI tools can enhance your process, they should never replace your unique vision. Balancing the use of AI with your creative intuition is key to maintaining originality in your work.

Balanced Advice: Leverage AI to automate and enhance your workflow but stay true to your creative instincts. Use AI as an assistant, not a replacement for your creativity and expertise.

Highlight Global and Cultural Dimensions

Digital nomads frequently work with clients from diverse cultural backgrounds. AI-powered design tools, like Crello and Fotor, help by offering templates and design elements that cater to various cultural preferences. These platforms use AI to suggest culturally appropriate imagery, fonts, and colour schemes based on the project's target audience, enabling you to produce culturally sensitive and globally resonant designs.

Global Insight: Use AI design tools that offer multicultural design templates and suggestions. This allows you to create work that resonates with international clients and adapts to various cultural contexts without extensive research.

Motivate with Purpose and Fulfilment

For many digital nomads, design is more than just a job—it's a way to express creativity, communicate ideas, and make an impact. AI empowers you to spend less time on the tedious parts of design and more time on what really matters: creating meaningful work that aligns with your values and passions.

Whether you're working on a social cause, creating art, or building a brand, AI can help you maximize the time you have to focus on your passion projects, enabling you to lead a more fulfilling and balanced life.

Inspirational Reflection: By integrating AI tools into your workflow, you're not just optimizing your work process—you're giving yourself more time to focus on the creative projects that matter most to you. AI frees you to pursue purpose-driven work, whether that means contributing to social causes or developing personal passion projects.

Use Accessible, Simple Language for Complex Topics

AI might sound complex, but using these tools is surprisingly simple. Many platforms are designed for non-technical users, meaning you don't need to be a programmer to integrate AI into your design workflow. Most AI-powered design tools have intuitive interfaces that offer suggestions and recommendations without requiring deep technical knowledge.

Friendly Explanation: Think of AI-powered design tools as a creative assistant that works alongside you, offering suggestions, automating repetitive tasks, and freeing up your time for the more strategic and creative parts of your work.

Interactive and Engaging Content

Before you move on, here's a quick exercise to help you get hands-on with AI-powered design tools.

Interactive Exercise: Spend 20 minutes exploring Canva or Figma. Use one of their AI-driven features, such as automated layout suggestions or Magic Resize. Create a design for your next social media post or marketing campaign. Reflect on how much time the AI saved you and how it influenced your design process.

Final Thoughts: AI-Powered Design for the Future of Work

AI-powered design tools are revolutionizing how digital nomads work, offering streamlined workflows, more efficient processes, and the ability to produce high-quality designs from anywhere in the world. By integrating AI tools into your design practice, you can enhance your creativity, increase your productivity, and create designs that resonate across cultures. Embrace AI as a partner in your design journey, allowing it to take care of the routine tasks while you focus on what truly matters: creating, innovating, and thriving as a digital nomad.

CHAPTER 62: AI FOR AUTOMATING REPETITIVE TASKS

For digital nomads, efficiency is key. When you're constantly on the move, managing a business from a beachfront café or a co-working space in a foreign city, the last thing you want is to be bogged down by repetitive administrative tasks. Thankfully, artificial intelligence (AI) has stepped in to take care of much of that busywork, freeing up your time for more creative and fulfilling pursuits. This chapter explores how AI can help digital nomads automate routine tasks, giving you more control over your time and helping you thrive in the AI age.

Engage with Storytelling and Case Studies

Let's start with the story of Jake, a digital nomad who runs an online consulting business while traveling across South America. Early in his career, Jake found himself drowning in administrative tasks—answering emails, scheduling meetings, and invoicing clients. These repetitive tasks ate up hours of his day, leaving him with little time to focus on growing his business or enjoying the nomadic lifestyle that had initially drawn him in.

That's when Jake discovered the power of AI. Using

tools like Zapier and Calendly, Jake automated many of his routine processes. With Zapier, he set up workflows that automatically logged client inquiries, generated email responses, and even transferred data between platforms like Google Sheets and his project management tool. Meanwhile, Calendly eliminated the back-and-forth scheduling hassle, allowing clients to book consultations based on his availability. These AI tools gave Jake back precious hours each day, which he used to focus on expanding his business and immersing himself in local cultures.

Today, Jake spends more time strategizing for his clients and exploring new destinations—confident that AI is handling the small stuff. His story is a testament to how AI-powered automation can transform a digital nomad's workflow, reducing stress and increasing productivity.

Focus on Practical Application

Automation is one of the most practical and accessible uses of AI for digital nomads. Here's how you can harness the power of AI to streamline repetitive tasks and reclaim your time.

1. Zapier – Automate Your Workflow
Zapier is a tool designed to connect different apps and automate workflows between them. For example, if you receive an inquiry via a web form, Zapier can automatically generate an email response, add the client's information to a CRM, and create a task in your project management tool. By automating these steps, you eliminate the need for manual input and minimize the risk of errors.

Practical Tip: Use Zapier to create "Zaps" that automate processes across platforms like Gmail, Google Drive, Slack, and Trello. For instance, when you receive a new client email, Zapier can trigger an automated workflow that logs the client's details in a Google Sheet and sends them an onboarding document.

2. Calendly – Automate Scheduling

Scheduling meetings can be a hassle, especially when dealing with clients across different time zones. Calendly solves this by automating the entire scheduling process. Simply set your availability, and clients can book meetings at times that work for both of you. Calendly integrates with Google Calendar and Zoom, so meetings are automatically scheduled and linked to your video conferencing software.

Practical Tip: Set up Calendly to manage your client consultations, coaching sessions, or even personal appointments. With automatic scheduling, you can eliminate email ping-pong and ensure that your calendar stays organized without any manual input.

3. Grammarly – Automate Editing

If you're a content creator or writer, Grammarly is an AI-powered tool that can streamline the editing process by automatically checking your grammar, spelling, and tone. Instead of spending hours proofreading your work, Grammarly quickly analyses your text and provides real-time suggestions, helping you produce polished content in less time.

Practical Tip: Use Grammarly to proofread blog posts, client emails, social media content, and other written communications. It can be particularly useful when you're working on tight deadlines, ensuring that your content is error-free without extensive manual review.

Inspire Through Visionary Perspectives

Now, imagine a future where AI takes on an even more

advanced role in automating the repetitive tasks of digital nomads. Picture an AI assistant that not only automates your current workflows but also anticipates your needs. This AI could predict which clients might need follow-ups, draft customized email responses based on previous interactions, and even negotiate contracts on your behalf. With more advanced machine learning capabilities, the AI assistant would evolve alongside your business, becoming smarter and more efficient the longer you use it.

Visionary Thought: The future of AI automation goes beyond simply handling routine tasks—it could evolve into a personal business manager that anticipates your needs, offering suggestions and completing complex tasks with minimal oversight, freeing you to focus solely on growth and creativity.

Balance Between Inspiration and Caution

While AI-powered automation can dramatically enhance productivity, it's important to maintain a balance between automation and human interaction. Over-automation can lead to a depersonalized experience for clients, which might be detrimental to your business in the long run. For example, while automated emails are useful, personalizing responses for high-value clients or important communications is still crucial. Likewise, relying too heavily on AI without understanding the processes it handles could leave you vulnerable if the technology fails or experiences glitches.

Balanced Advice: Use AI automation to streamline your workflow, but stay engaged with the tasks that matter most to your business. Always review automated processes to ensure they're functioning correctly, and don't lose the human touch in your client interactions.

Highlight Global and Cultural Dimensions

Automation can be especially helpful for digital nomads working across multiple time zones and cultural contexts. AI scheduling tools like Calendly make it easier to coordinate meetings with clients across the globe, while translation tools like DeepL can help automate and streamline multilingual communication. AI tools that are culturally adaptable can assist in bridging cultural gaps by providing translation, localization, and contextually appropriate suggestions for communication.

Global Insight: Use AI tools that can adapt to different time zones, languages, and cultural contexts. These tools help ensure that your communications are effective, no matter where you or your clients are located.

Motivate with Purpose and Fulfilment

For many digital nomads, the goal is not just to be efficient but to have more time for meaningful work and personal fulfilment. By automating repetitive tasks with AI, you can focus on what truly matters—whether it's pursuing passion projects, spending more time with family, or exploring new destinations. Automation doesn't just optimize your business; it enhances your life by giving you more freedom and flexibility.

Inspirational Reflection: Think about how much more fulfilling your work-life balance could be if AI took care of your administrative tasks. Imagine having the time to dedicate to creative projects, learning new skills, or immersing yourself in new cultures—all because AI has given you back the most valuable resource of all: time.

Use Accessible, Simple Language for Complex Topics

AI might seem complicated, but using AI-powered automation tools is surprisingly straightforward. Most platforms, like Zapier or Grammarly, are designed with user-friendly interfaces that require little to no technical knowledge. Setting up automated workflows often involves simple drag-and-drop functionality, and AI tools typically come with detailed guides to help you get started.

Friendly Explanation: Think of AI automation as having a virtual assistant that takes care of the small but important tasks in your business. You don't need to know how to code or understand complex algorithms—these tools are designed to be intuitive and accessible to everyone.

Interactive and Engaging Content

Before moving on, take 10 minutes to explore Zapier. Create a simple workflow, or "Zap," that automates a process you often do manually—like logging client emails or scheduling social media posts. Reflect on how much time this automation could save you in the long run and what you might do with that extra time.

Final Thoughts: Automate for Freedom and Success

Automation isn't just about saving time—it's about freeing yourself to pursue what matters most. By integrating AI-powered automation tools into your workflow, you can enhance your productivity, reduce stress, and focus on the things that bring you joy and fulfilment. For digital nomads, AI is the key to thriving in a fast-paced, ever-changing work environment, providing the freedom and flexibility you need to succeed in the AI age.

CHAPTER 63: AI FOR VIDEO PRODUCTION AND EDITING

Video content has quickly become one of the most powerful forms of communication in the digital age. Whether it's sharing experiences on social media, creating promotional content for a business, or developing an engaging vlog series, digital nomads are increasingly turning to video to connect with audiences worldwide. However, the traditional process of video production and editing can be time-consuming and complex, which isn't ideal when you're constantly on the move.

This is where AI comes in. With the rise of AI-powered tools, video production has become more streamlined, accessible, and efficient—allowing digital nomads to produce high-quality content from anywhere in the world. This chapter will explore how AI is transforming video production for digital nomads, highlighting tools and practical strategies that help save time and deliver professional results.

Engage with Storytelling and Case Studies

Let's begin with the story of Sam, a digital nomad and vlogger who travels through Europe while documenting his journey on YouTube. For Sam, video production was initially a major challenge. He had no formal background in editing, and the process of cutting hours of footage, adding transitions, and colour-correcting clips took up an enormous amount of time. It left him stressed, unable to focus on his travels, and frequently behind on his content schedule.

Sam's workflow dramatically changed when he discovered AI-powered video editing tools like Lumen5 and Pictory. These platforms allowed him to upload raw footage and have the AI automatically create videos using advanced algorithms to cut, trim, and add captions. With Lumen5, Sam could simply input his blog content, and the tool would generate a video script, suggest relevant visuals, and even create engaging animations. What used to take days, now took mere hours, and the quality of the videos improved with each edit.

Today, Sam produces more content with greater ease and continues his travels without worrying about falling behind on his editing. His journey is a prime example of how AI-driven tools have empowered digital nomads to focus more on their adventures and storytelling, while still maintaining a polished, professional online presence.

Focus on Practical Application

If you're a digital nomad looking to up your video production game, AI tools can be a game changer. Here's how you can integrate AI into your video creation workflow to save time, reduce complexity, and achieve professional results.

1. Lumen5 – From Blog to Video
Lumen5 is designed for content creators who want to transform text into video content. If you're a digital nomad who runs a blog or creates social media content, this tool can turn your written words into engaging video content. The

AI in Lumen5 analyses your text, selects key sentences, and pairs them with appropriate images and video clips, creating a ready-made video in minutes.

Practical Tip: Use Lumen5 to repurpose your blog posts into short, visually appealing videos for platforms like YouTube, Instagram, or Facebook. This is especially useful when you want to engage with audiences who prefer visual content but don't have the time to read lengthy posts.

2. Pictory – Automated Video Summarization
Pictory offers another innovative way to streamline video editing. This tool uses AI to summarize lengthy videos, automatically pulling out key moments and creating highlight reels. Whether you're documenting your travels or creating business-related content, Pictory can reduce hours of footage into concise, engaging clips, ready for sharing on social media or other platforms.

Practical Tip: After recording long vlogs or interviews, let Pictory summarize your video. This feature saves you time by identifying the most engaging parts of your content and cutting away unnecessary footage.

3. Descript – Video and Podcast Editing Simplified
If you create both video and podcast content, Descript is a must-have tool. Descript's AI-driven transcription feature allows you to edit your content as easily as editing text. You can cut out mistakes or add in clips simply by deleting or inserting sentences in the transcription, and the video/audio will be edited automatically.

Practical Tip: Use Descript to quickly edit out filler words, pauses, or mistakes from your podcasts or videos. This tool also makes it easy to add captions, improve audio quality, and streamline the overall editing process.

Inspire Through Visionary Perspectives

Looking ahead, the future of video production with AI is even more exciting. Imagine a world where AI not only edits your video content but also suggests new creative directions. For example, future AI systems could recommend camera angles, lighting adjustments, and even provide real-time editing suggestions while you're filming. AI could also help you produce fully automated live streams, optimizing the experience for viewers across various platforms.

Visionary Thought: Picture AI acting as your virtual film assistant, automating the technical aspects of video production while allowing you to focus purely on the storytelling. As AI continues to advance, it will empower digital nomads to create cinematic-quality content with minimal equipment and effort, all while on the go.

Balance Between Inspiration and Caution

While AI video production tools are incredibly useful, they shouldn't completely replace the human touch. Relying too heavily on AI can sometimes lead to generic results that lack the creative flair or personal connection that viewers crave. It's essential to find a balance between automation and personal input. AI can handle the technicalities, but your vision, creativity, and personal style should guide the final product.

Balanced Advice: Use AI tools to automate repetitive tasks like trimming clips, adding captions, or syncing audio, but ensure that your unique voice and creative direction remain at the forefront of your content.

Highlight Global and Cultural Dimensions

AI-powered video tools are particularly helpful for digital nomads working across diverse cultural landscapes. Tools like Google's Auto Translate can automatically add translated captions to videos, allowing you to reach a global audience. Additionally, AI-driven localization tools ensure that your content resonates with viewers from different regions by adapting the tone, visuals, and message to suit cultural preferences.

Global Insight: Leverage AI-powered translation and localization tools to create videos that appeal to audiences in different parts of the world. This is especially valuable for digital nomads who want to build a global brand and connect with diverse audiences.

Motivate with Purpose and Fulfilment

Ultimately, AI's role in video production is about freeing you from the mundane aspects of editing so that you can focus on what truly matters—telling your story. Whether it's capturing the beauty of a new city, sharing your expertise, or documenting your entrepreneurial journey, AI tools allow you to create more, with less time spent on the technical side. This gives you the freedom to engage more deeply with your travels, passions, and audience.

Inspirational Reflection: Imagine the stories you could tell and the experiences you could share if AI took care of the heavy lifting in video production. With the time saved, you could dedicate more energy to meaningful projects, deepening your connections with your audience and making a greater impact.

Use Accessible, Simple Language for Complex Topics

AI-powered video production might sound complex, but these tools are designed to be user-friendly and accessible. Most platforms offer intuitive drag-and-drop interfaces, requiring no advanced technical skills. With a few clicks, AI will handle the editing, transitions, and even suggest creative elements, allowing you to focus on creating content without worrying about the technical side.

Friendly Explanation: Think of AI tools like a personal video editor working behind the scenes to turn your raw footage into polished content. You don't need to be a video editing expert—just upload your clips, and let AI handle the rest.

Interactive and Engaging Content

Take a few moments to explore Lumen5 or Pictory. Upload some text or raw video footage and let the AI transform it into a polished video. Reflect on how much time you saved and think about the creative possibilities AI can open up in your content creation process.

Final Thoughts: AI for Creative Freedom

AI is revolutionizing video production for digital nomads, making it easier than ever to create professional content while traveling. By integrating these tools into your workflow, you can streamline the production process, allowing you to focus on your passion, creativity, and exploration. AI offers digital nomads the gift of time—time to explore new places, dive deeper into storytelling, and live more fully in the moment.

With AI by your side, you'll not only create stunning videos but also have the freedom to enjoy the lifestyle that drew you to digital nomadism in the first place.

CHAPTER 64: AI IN PODCASTING AND AUDIO CONTENT

In recent years, podcasting and audio content have become essential tools for digital nomads seeking to share their stories, build businesses, and connect with global audiences. However, creating high-quality audio content often requires time, effort, and specialized equipment—luxuries that many digital nomads do not have while constantly on the move. This is where artificial intelligence (AI) steps in, revolutionizing how podcasts and audio content are created, edited, and shared.

AI tools are making the process of podcasting simpler and more efficient, allowing digital nomads to produce professional-quality content without needing to spend hours on editing or mastering audio. Whether you're recording podcasts in a bustling city, narrating an audiobook from a beach, or conducting interviews remotely, AI is transforming the landscape of audio content creation.

Engage with Storytelling and Case Studies

Meet David, a digital nomad based in Portugal, who runs a successful travel podcast. David's journey into podcasting began as a hobby, sharing his experiences of living and working in different countries. But as his audience grew, so did the demands on his time. Each episode required hours of editing, sound optimization, and transcription—a daunting task for someone who was constantly on the move.

Frustrated with the time-consuming process, David turned to AI-powered tools like Descript and Auphonic. Descript's innovative editing platform allowed David to edit his podcast simply by editing the text transcript—cutting sections, rearranging audio, and making tweaks in minutes. Auphonic, on the other hand, handled audio levelling and noise reduction, ensuring his recordings sounded crisp and professional, regardless of where they were recorded.

With these AI tools, David could now create, edit, and publish episodes in a fraction of the time. What was once a tedious process had become streamlined and efficient, allowing him to focus on creating engaging content for his listeners. David's podcast has since grown into a major platform for digital nomads, thanks to the power of AI.

Focus on Practical Application

For digital nomads eager to dive into the world of audio content, AI tools offer a range of practical benefits. Whether you're starting a podcast, creating audiobooks, or producing interview series, these tools can help you save time, reduce complexity, and improve the quality of your content.

1. Descript: AI-Powered Editing and Transcription
Descript is an all-in-one tool that makes podcasting easy. By converting your audio into a text transcript, Descript allows you to edit your podcast by simply cutting or moving text. It also offers features like Overdub, which can generate new spoken words in your own voice, making it ideal for quick edits.

Practical Tip: Use Descript to transcribe your audio files automatically and edit them as you would a text document. This not only speeds up your workflow but also reduces the technical knowledge required to create professional audio.

2. Auphonic: Audio Levelling and Noise Reduction

Recording podcasts on the go often means dealing with imperfect conditions—background noise, uneven audio levels, or inconsistent sound quality. Auphonic uses AI to optimize your recordings, levelling the audio, removing background noise, and ensuring your content sounds professional no matter where it's recorded.

Practical Tip: Upload your podcast or audio files to Auphonic before publishing to ensure the best sound quality. This tool takes care of audio engineering tasks that would otherwise require specialized knowledge.

3. Sonix: Accurate Transcription and Repurposing

Sonix is an AI-powered transcription tool that makes it easy to convert your podcast into written content. Whether you're creating show notes, blog posts, or SEO-optimized transcripts, Sonix provides quick and accurate transcriptions that can be repurposed across different platforms.

Practical Tip: Transcribe your podcast episodes using Sonix to create show notes or blog content. This allows you to extend the life of your audio content and reach more people by offering written versions.

Inspire Through Visionary Perspectives

AI's impact on podcasting is just the beginning. As AI technology advances, the future of audio content creation could see even more sophisticated applications. Imagine AI tools that can analyse audience engagement in real-time, adjusting your content on the fly or even suggesting topics that resonate with your listeners.

Beyond editing, AI could help digital nomads produce fully automated podcast episodes, complete with voice synthesis, real-time sound effects, and AI-generated conversations. Platforms like Riverside.fm are already making it easier for podcasters to collaborate remotely, enabling high-quality recording from different corners of the world.

Visionary Perspective: Imagine a world where digital nomads could host live podcasts with AI handling everything from sound engineering to audience interaction. The possibilities for creativity, reach, and engagement are limitless.

Balance Between Inspiration and Caution

While AI offers exciting opportunities for podcasting, it's important to acknowledge the limitations and potential challenges. AI tools, though powerful, are not a replacement for human creativity and authenticity. Your unique voice, style, and perspective are what make your content stand out.

Balanced Advice: Leverage AI to handle the technical aspects of audio production, but always remember that the heart of your podcast is your connection with your audience. AI can enhance your workflow, but it's your authenticity and passion that keep listeners coming back.

Highlight Global and Cultural Dimensions

Podcasting is a medium with global reach, and AI makes it easier to cater to diverse audiences. Tools like Google AutoML Translation allow you to automatically translate your podcast transcripts into multiple languages, making your content accessible to a global audience. This is particularly useful for digital nomads who are building international brands.

Global Insight: If your podcast covers topics like travel or culture, consider using AI translation tools to make your content available in the languages of the regions you cover. This will broaden your audience and enhance your connection with global listeners.

Motivate with Purpose and Fulfilment

For many digital nomads, podcasting is not just a way to share knowledge—it's a way to connect with others, inspire change, and fulfil a deeper sense of purpose. AI tools enable you to focus on your message and storytelling by automating the tedious aspects of content production.

Inspirational Reflection: With AI taking care of the technical details, you have more time to focus on the passion that drives your content. Whether you're educating, entertaining, or inspiring your listeners, AI allows you to spend less time on the 'how' and more time on the 'why.'

Use Accessible, Simple Language for Complex Topics

AI technology can sound intimidating, but many tools are designed with simplicity in mind. Descript, Auphonic, and other AI-powered platforms offer intuitive interfaces, allowing anyone to create professional-quality audio without advanced technical skills.

Friendly Explanation: Think of AI as your creative assistant —one that handles the heavy lifting of podcasting so you can focus on sharing your story. These tools are designed to be easy to use, even for beginners.

Interactive and Engaging Content

Before moving on to the next chapter, take a moment to experiment with Descript or Auphonic. Try editing a short audio clip, applying noise reduction, or using AI transcription. Reflect on how these tools might streamline your workflow and elevate the quality of your content.

Conclusion

AI is transforming the way digital nomads create and share audio content. From simplifying the editing process to enhancing sound quality, AI-powered tools empower content creators to focus on what truly matters—telling stories, sharing experiences, and building connections. With AI handling the technical aspects, digital nomads can embrace the freedom to travel, create, and inspire, all while producing high-quality content that resonates with a global audience.

CHAPTER 65: AI AND THE RISE OF THE DIGITAL NOMAD

As the sun set over Bali's iconic rice terraces, Liam sat at a small café, sipping his favourite local coffee. He wasn't on vacation—he was at work, drafting the final details of a marketing campaign for a client based in London. What would have been a taxing process just a few years ago now took Liam only a fraction of the time. Thanks to AI-powered tools, 70% of his workload was automated, leaving him more time to explore new cultures, focus on creative tasks, and truly live the digital nomad dream. Liam's story is one of many that showcase the intersection of AI and the modern digital nomad lifestyle, where advanced technology is transforming careers and enabling individuals to thrive across the globe.

For digital nomads like Liam, AI is more than just a set of tools—it's an enabler of freedom, creativity, and efficiency. In this chapter, we will explore how AI is reshaping the careers of digital nomads, diving into real-life stories, practical applications, and the broader impact AI has on this ever-growing movement. Whether you're a freelancer, a remote worker, or an entrepreneur, AI has the potential to revolutionize the way you live and work, making the digital nomad lifestyle more accessible and sustainable than ever before.

The AI-Powered Nomad: A Day in the Life

Consider Sarah, a freelance graphic designer who roams between Thailand, Vietnam, and Indonesia while managing a global clientele. Before AI, Sarah spent hours on manual design tasks, from sketching layouts to colour correction. But now, with AI-driven design platforms like Canva, she automates much of her workflow. Canva's AI suggestions save her hours by recommending design improvements, adjusting colours, and even creating entire templates based on her brief.

Sarah also uses Jasper AI for writing product descriptions and social media captions, allowing her to deliver more content in less time. This isn't about replacing her creativity; instead, it frees up her time to focus on higher-level tasks— like brainstorming new concepts or traveling to the next city on her list. AI tools have become her co-pilot, accelerating her work, enhancing her creativity, and enabling her to take on more clients without sacrificing her nomadic lifestyle.

These stories illustrate a common theme among AI-enabled digital nomads: the ability to do more with less effort. By integrating AI into their work, they streamline mundane tasks, optimize time, and unlock new opportunities for personal and professional growth.

Practical Applications: How You Can Use AI to Thrive

While Sarah and Liam have already incorporated AI into their workflows, you might be wondering how you can do the same. The good news is, AI tools are becoming increasingly accessible and user-friendly, even if you aren't a tech expert. Here are a few practical ways to integrate AI into your digital nomad journey:

- Content Creation: Whether you're a writer, marketer, or content strategist, tools like Jasper AI and Writesonic can help you generate blog ideas, product descriptions, and even long-form articles. Pair these tools with Grammarly to refine your drafts with AI-enhanced editing suggestions.

- Design and Visuals: For graphic designers or social media managers, platforms like Canva and Adobe Sensei allow you to automate repetitive design tasks and create visually appealing content in minutes.

- Project Management: Staying on top of tasks while traveling can be a challenge. AI-powered project management tools like Trello with automation features or Asana help you keep track of deadlines, assignments, and client communication, ensuring you never miss a beat.

- Client Outreach and Networking: Tools like HubSpot's AI-powered CRM system enable you to manage relationships with clients, automate follow-up emails, and track leads—all while you're sipping a coconut on a beach.

By incorporating these tools into your workflow, you can free up valuable time, reduce stress, and focus on what truly matters: the experiences that define your nomadic journey.

The Future of Work: AI as a Partner, Not a Threat

One common fear surrounding AI is the potential for job displacement. But for digital nomads, AI is more of an enabler than a competitor. The key lies in adopting a mindset of continuous learning and adaptation. While AI will inevitably take over certain repetitive tasks, it also opens doors to new opportunities in fields like AI consulting, content automation, data analysis, and more.

As AI continues to evolve, it's important to remember that human creativity, critical thinking, and emotional intelligence will remain irreplaceable. AI may handle the nuts and bolts of routine tasks, but it's your ability to think creatively, solve complex problems, and adapt to new environments that will set you apart in an AI-driven world. The future of work isn't about being replaced by machines— it's about partnering with AI to amplify your potential and achieve more.

Imagine a future where your AI assistant handles every mundane task, from organizing meetings to drafting reports. You'll be free to focus on your passion projects, travel to new destinations, and immerse yourself in cultural experiences without the weight of administrative tasks holding you back. This vision of the future is already becoming a reality for many digital nomads, and it's only the beginning.

Navigating Challenges: Balance, Privacy, and Control

While the benefits of AI are vast, it's important to approach this technology with a balance of optimism and caution. One concern for digital nomads is maintaining a healthy work-life balance when AI allows for constant productivity. The risk of burnout is real, especially when you can automate more tasks and take on additional work. To counter this, set boundaries for work hours and build time for exploration and relaxation into your schedule.

Another challenge lies in data privacy. With AI tools collecting vast amounts of data, it's critical to ensure that your personal information and that of your clients are protected. Always use reputable AI platforms with strong data security measures and familiarize yourself with privacy policies before sharing sensitive information.

A Global Perspective: AI's Impact Across Cultures

As a digital nomad, you'll find that AI adoption varies from country to country, creating unique opportunities in different regions. For instance, in Estonia, AI is integral to their government's e-residency program, making it easier for nomads to register businesses and operate remotely. In India, AI is transforming small businesses, enabling them to reach a global market with minimal resources. These examples highlight how AI is levelling the playing field, allowing digital nomads to work seamlessly across borders and cultures.

Embracing AI for a Purpose-Driven Life

Ultimately, the goal of adopting AI as a digital nomad isn't just to optimize your work—it's to enable a more purpose-driven life. By freeing up time, AI allows you to focus on what truly matters: experiencing new cultures, building meaningful relationships, and pursuing passion projects that align with your values.

AI isn't just reshaping the digital nomad landscape—it's empowering you to live a life of adventure, fulfilment, and impact. The future of work is here, and it's time to embrace it.

PART 14: AI AND EDUCATION FOR DIGITAL NOMADS

CHAPTER 66: AI FOR SELF-LEARNING: EMPOWERING DIGITAL NOMADS TO MASTER NEW SKILLS

As the sun rose over a quiet village in the south of Spain, Rachel sat on her patio, a cup of coffee in hand, preparing for her daily routine. But instead of scrolling through social media or diving into her work, she opened her laptop to an AI-powered learning platform. Within minutes, she was engrossed in a personalized course on machine learning, a skill she had always been curious about but never had the time to pursue—until now. The beauty of Rachel's story lies not just in her quest for knowledge but in how AI is enabling digital nomads like her to learn faster, smarter, and more effectively.

This chapter will explore how digital nomads can harness the power of AI for self-learning, using real-life examples, practical applications, and a glimpse into the future of learning. The nomadic lifestyle often comes with the challenge of balancing work, travel, and personal growth, but AI is revolutionizing how we learn, making education accessible, personalized, and convenient.

Rachel's Journey: From Curiosity to Mastery

Rachel's story mirrors the experiences of countless digital nomads who are leveraging AI-driven learning platforms to upskill and adapt in a fast-changing world. Living in Spain while freelancing as a graphic designer, she felt the need to stay ahead of industry trends, particularly with the rise of AI in design. She enrolled in courses on Coursera and Udemy, but the game changer for her was EdX's AI-powered adaptive learning platform. This platform tailored the learning experience to her pace, skill level, and schedule.

AI algorithms analysed her performance in real-time, adjusting the difficulty of the lessons based on her understanding. When she struggled with complex concepts, the platform automatically provided extra resources, practice exercises, and video tutorials. And when she excelled, it moved her forward at a faster pace, ensuring she never felt held back or overwhelmed. Rachel's once-daunting goal of mastering machine learning became achievable, and she found herself able to balance her learning with work and travel effortlessly.

For digital nomads, AI-powered learning tools aren't just about acquiring new skills—they're about maximizing efficiency. They offer a way to stay competitive in a rapidly evolving job market without sacrificing the flexibility and freedom that comes with the nomadic lifestyle.

Practical Applications: How You Can Use AI for Self-Learning

AI is transforming education by making learning more personalized and flexible. Here are several AI-powered tools and platforms that can help you, as a digital nomad, thrive in your learning journey:

- Duolingo: If you're traveling through non-English-speaking countries, Duolingo's AI-driven language learning platform is a must. The app uses machine learning to adapt lessons based on your language proficiency and pace, allowing you to learn new languages faster and more effectively. Whether it's mastering basic conversation or diving into complex grammar, Duolingo adjusts to your learning style in real-time.

- Coursera and Udemy: These platforms offer a wide variety of AI-enhanced courses. Coursera, in particular, uses AI to recommend courses tailored to your career goals and personal interests. Many of the courses are structured with interactive elements powered by AI, such as personalized quizzes, adaptive learning paths, and peer-based feedback loops.

- Khan Academy: Known for its AI-powered tools to support personalized learning, Khan Academy adjusts to the learner's pace and understanding, making it easier for digital nomads to engage in subjects ranging from mathematics to economics without feeling lost.

- LinkedIn Learning: As part of the LinkedIn ecosystem, this platform uses AI to recommend courses based on your professional profile, helping you upskill in areas relevant to your industry. The integration with LinkedIn means that the skills you acquire are automatically reflected in your profile, making you more attractive to potential clients or employers.

By integrating these AI tools into your learning routine, you'll be able to stay ahead of trends, develop new skills, and improve your existing talents, all while maintaining the flexibility of the digital nomad lifestyle.

A Visionary Look at the Future of AI-Powered Learning

Imagine a future where your AI assistant not only schedules your learning sessions but also curates your entire education based on your goals, preferences, and career trajectory. In this vision, AI would track your performance across various subjects, suggesting new learning opportunities before you even realize you need them. The lessons themselves would be crafted in real-time, adjusted to your learning speed and style.

You wouldn't just be a passive recipient of knowledge— you'd actively co-create your learning experience with the AI, tailoring it to match your goals as you evolve. Whether you want to learn a new programming language, dive into advanced design techniques, or even pick up a hobby like photography, AI will guide you through a hyper-personalized educational journey.

This future isn't far off. With AI already transforming platforms like Google's AI-driven learning initiatives and IBM's AI-enhanced training programs, the future of self-learning is one where knowledge adapts to the learner—not the other way around.

Navigating Challenges: AI Overload and Maintaining Focus

While AI can undoubtedly enhance your learning experience, it's essential to approach it with a balance of enthusiasm and caution. One of the challenges digital nomads face is AI overload—the overwhelming number of tools, apps, and platforms available can make it hard to stay focused. It's easy to fall into the trap of downloading too many apps or enrolling in too many courses, only to feel burned out and less productive.

The key is to start small. Focus on mastering one AI-powered tool or platform at a time. Set realistic learning goals and be mindful of your progress. Avoid the temptation to rush through lessons just because AI allows you to move faster. Learning, after all, is not just about speed—it's about depth, understanding, and long-term retention.

Moreover, it's essential to maintain a balance between work, learning, and leisure. While AI makes it easier to learn on the go, the nomadic lifestyle thrives on experiencing the world. Don't let your learning goals overshadow the incredible cultural experiences waiting outside your door. Use AI to enhance your knowledge, but make sure it fits within a broader, purpose-driven life.

Global Learning in a Connected World

In a world where digital nomads work across borders and cultures, the ability to learn on the go is invaluable. AI is creating opportunities for global citizens to access education wherever they are. In countries like Singapore, AI is integrated into lifelong learning programs, helping individuals stay relevant in a competitive job market. In Nigeria, AI-powered mobile learning platforms are providing education to communities that lack traditional schooling infrastructure.

As digital nomads, we are uniquely positioned to take advantage of these global trends. By leveraging AI, we can continually upskill ourselves, expanding our opportunities while contributing to local communities through shared knowledge.

AI and a Purpose-Driven Learning Experience

At its core, AI for self-learning is about more than just acquiring skills—it's about building a meaningful life. Digital nomads aren't just seeking new career opportunities; they're also seeking personal growth, fulfilment, and purpose. By embracing AI-powered learning, you're not just becoming a more efficient worker—you're expanding your horizons, learning new ways to contribute to the world, and empowering yourself to live a life of greater impact.

Whether it's through mastering a new skill, learning a

language, or diving into a completely new field, AI makes learning accessible, adaptable, and fun. As you continue on your nomadic journey, remember that the world is your classroom—and with AI as your guide, there's no limit to what you can achieve.

CHAPTER 67: AI-POWERED ONLINE LEARNING: TRANSFORMING EDUCATION FOR DIGITAL NOMADS

As the turquoise waters of the Mediterranean lapped against the shores of Crete, James sat at a café with his laptop, diving into an advanced course on digital marketing. What once required hours of in-person classes and a strict schedule was now just a few clicks away. James wasn't enrolled in a traditional school or university. Instead, he had turned to an AI-powered online learning platform to master the latest marketing strategies and techniques, all while continuing his journey as a digital nomad. With personalized content tailored to his learning speed and skill level, James was advancing faster than ever before—without ever setting foot in a classroom.

This chapter explores the remarkable transformation that AI has brought to the world of online education, especially for digital nomads. As remote workers who thrive on flexibility, digital nomads are finding in AI the perfect companion for continued education. Whether it's acquiring new professional skills, learning a language, or pursuing personal interests, AI-powered platforms are reshaping how, when, and where learning happens. This shift is empowering nomads to thrive in an increasingly competitive global market.

James' Story: Learning at His Own Pace

James had been a freelance graphic designer for years, but when the pandemic hit, demand for his services dipped, and he realized it was time to pivot. With an interest in digital marketing, James knew he needed to upskill quickly. But he didn't have the time—or desire—to enrol in a full-time university program.

That's when he discovered Coursera, a platform offering AI-powered, on-demand courses. With AI algorithms analysing his performance, the system tailored the course material to his strengths and weaknesses. If he struggled with a concept, additional resources and tutorials would appear, ensuring he grasped the material before moving on. When he mastered a lesson quickly, the platform adapted, fast-tracking him through sections that didn't need as much attention. In this way, AI turned what could have been a daunting experience into an engaging, personalized learning journey.

This AI-driven adaptability is a key feature that makes online learning particularly appealing for digital nomads. It's not just about convenience—AI enables a personalized learning experience, accelerating progress and ensuring mastery at a pace that fits each individual's unique needs and circumstances.

How AI is Shaping the Future of Online Learning

The integration of AI into online learning platforms has made education more accessible, flexible, and engaging than ever before. Here's how AI is revolutionizing online education for digital nomads:

1. Personalized Learning Paths

AI-powered platforms, like EdX and LinkedIn Learning, use machine learning algorithms to tailor learning experiences to individual users. By tracking user engagement and performance, these platforms adjust the difficulty of content, suggest additional resources, and even provide real-time feedback. This personalized approach ensures that learners stay motivated and progress efficiently, making it easier for digital nomads to fit learning into their busy, ever-changing schedules.

2. Adaptive Learning

AI can analyse patterns in how students learn and provide dynamic feedback. For example, platforms like Khan Academy use AI to offer adaptive learning experiences. If a learner struggles with a particular topic, AI algorithms will provide additional exercises, explanations, and resources to help improve understanding. This type of customized support ensures that no learner gets left behind, even when traveling from one city or country to the next.

3. Natural Language Processing (NLP) and Translation Tools

For digital nomads navigating diverse cultures and languages, AI-powered translation tools like Google Translate and DeepL can break down language barriers. In the context of online learning, this means that courses offered in different languages can be more accessible, with automatic translations for course materials, captions, and even interactions with international peers.

4. AI Tutors and Mentors

Imagine having access to a virtual tutor available 24/7. With AI, this is already a reality. Platforms like Socratic by Google use AI to provide instant answers to student queries and guide learners through complex topics. These AI-driven tutors are designed to offer the same personalized assistance as a traditional mentor, making learning more interactive and effective, no matter where you are in the world.

5. Automated Assessments and Certifications

For digital nomads looking to validate their skills or transition into new fields, AI-powered platforms offer instant assessments and certifications. For example, Udacity's Nanodegree programs use AI to evaluate projects and provide feedback, helping learners improve in real time. Once a course is completed, these platforms also offer certifications that can be added to professional profiles like LinkedIn, increasing the nomad's marketability and credibility.

Practical Tips: How Digital Nomads Can Leverage AI-Powered Education

Whether you're looking to change careers, advance in your current field, or simply learn something new, here are practical ways to incorporate AI-powered education into your digital nomad lifestyle:

1. Start Small with Microlearning: Platforms like Udemy and Skillshare offer short, digestible lessons that can be completed in under an hour. AI algorithms curate these microlearning sessions to your interests and skill level, making it easy to learn on the go without committing to long courses.

2. Track Your Progress with AI Tools: Many platforms, including LinkedIn Learning, use AI to track your progress and recommend the next steps in your learning journey. Set weekly goals and use these personalized recommendations to stay motivated and focused.

3. Join Global Learning Communities: AI-powered platforms

often connect you with global learners who share your interests. By joining study groups or forums, you can build a network of like-minded individuals while gaining diverse perspectives from learners around the world.

4. Apply Your Skills in Real Time: Use AI-enhanced tools like Grammarly and Canva to apply what you've learned immediately. This helps solidify new skills, especially for digital nomads working in fields like writing, marketing, or design.

The Visionary Future of AI-Powered Learning

Imagine a world where learning becomes fully integrated into your daily life—where AI tracks your goals, automatically curates lessons, and schedules learning sessions that fit seamlessly into your lifestyle. This vision isn't far from reality. With the rapid advancement of AI, the future of online learning will likely be even more immersive and tailored.

AI will enable hyper-personalized learning environments, offering real-time feedback, virtual collaboration spaces, and customized learning paths that evolve with you. As digital nomads, this means you'll be able to learn anything, anywhere, at any time—empowered by AI to continually grow and adapt.

Balancing Learning with Work and Travel

While AI makes education more accessible, it's important to balance learning with the freedom that comes with the digital nomad lifestyle. Too often, nomads fall into the trap of overloading their schedules with courses and certifications. Remember to pace yourself, focusing on quality over quantity. Make sure you leave time for the experiences that drew you to this lifestyle in the first place —exploring new cultures, meeting new people, and finding inspiration in the world around you.

A Purpose-Driven Approach to Learning

At its core, AI-powered learning isn't just about acquiring new skills—it's about personal growth and purpose-driven education. Whether you're learning a language to better connect with the locals in a foreign country, or mastering new skills to build a business that aligns with your values, AI is an enabler. By incorporating AI into your learning journey, you can align your education with your passion, creating a life of both professional success and personal fulfilment.

The opportunities are endless. Embrace AI-powered learning and watch as it transforms your journey as a digital nomad—not just in your career, but in the deeper purpose of your life.

CHAPTER 68: AI-DRIVEN CERTIFICATIONS FOR DIGITAL NOMADS: STAYING COMPETITIVE IN A RAPIDLY EVOLVING LANDSCAPE

As Emma packed up her belongings in her co-working space in Chiang Mai, Thailand, she couldn't help but feel excited. She had just completed a course in AI-driven content automation from Coursera and earned a certification that would boost her credibility with future clients. In the world of freelancing and remote work, Emma understood the importance of staying ahead. AI was revolutionizing her field of digital marketing, and the certification she'd earned was more than just a badge of knowledge—it was a testament to her adaptability in a fast-changing work landscape. Emma's story is one of many, highlighting how digital nomads are leveraging AI certifications to stay competitive, maintain relevance, and unlock new opportunities in the global marketplace.

In this chapter, we'll explore how AI-driven certifications can help digital nomads thrive. These certifications are not just for tech-savvy professionals—they are designed to equip remote workers across various industries with skills that are increasingly in demand. From digital marketing to content creation, project management, and beyond, certifications in AI-powered tools can open up new doors and ensure long-term career success.

Emma's Journey: From Freelancer to AI Expert

Emma's freelance career as a digital marketer had always been a comfortable one. She managed campaigns, crafted social media strategies, and wrote content for clients across the globe. But in recent years, she noticed a shift: clients were beginning to ask about AI-powered marketing solutions, and competitors were embracing automation. Realizing that she needed to evolve, Emma started researching online certifications that would teach her how to harness AI in her workflow.

She enrolled in an AI certification program on Udemy that specialized in marketing automation. The course taught her how to use tools like Jasper AI for content creation, HubSpot's AI-driven CRM for customer relationship management, and Google's AI-powered ad tools for targeted marketing. Upon completing the certification, Emma felt more confident in offering AI-integrated services to her clients, ultimately winning more contracts and scaling her freelance business. Now, instead of manually handling content creation and scheduling, she uses AI to automate these tasks, giving her more time to focus on strategy and client relationships.

Emma's story reflects a key trend in the digital nomad world: staying relevant requires more than just being adaptable—

it requires actively seeking new knowledge and integrating AI tools into your work. With AI certifications, nomads like Emma are building skills that not only future-proof their careers but also increase their value in an ever-competitive market.

Why AI Certifications Matter for Digital Nomads

For digital nomads, the appeal of AI certifications is clear: they offer flexibility, relevance, and recognition. As nomads often move between different projects and clients, certifications serve as a tangible way to demonstrate their expertise and differentiate themselves in a global marketplace. Here are the key reasons why AI certifications are crucial for today's digital nomads:

1. Adaptability in a Changing Job Market: AI is disrupting industries across the board—from marketing and design to finance and healthcare. Earning AI certifications ensures that nomads are well-prepared to navigate these changes and continue offering valuable services that meet modern client needs.

2. Enhanced Credibility: Certifications from trusted platforms like Coursera, Udacity, and LinkedIn Learning provide a formal recognition of a nomad's skills. For clients, these certifications serve as proof of a freelancer's expertise in AI-powered tools, increasing the likelihood of landing projects that require advanced tech skills.

3. Increased Earning Potential: As demand for AI-savvy professionals rises, digital nomads with certifications can command higher rates. Whether it's using AI in content creation, automation in digital marketing, or machine learning in data analysis, these new skills make nomads more competitive and valuable in the global gig economy.

Top AI Certifications for Digital Nomads

If you're a digital nomad looking to dive into AI and stay competitive, here are some top AI-driven certifications that can elevate your career:

1. Google AI for Everyone (Coursera): This beginner-friendly course introduces the basics of AI and machine learning. It's perfect for digital nomads who want a foundational understanding of AI concepts and how they can apply them in various industries like marketing, customer service, and content creation.

2. AI in Digital Marketing (Udemy): Tailored for marketers, this course focuses on using AI-driven tools to optimize campaigns, target the right audiences, and automate marketing efforts. You'll learn how to integrate AI into platforms like Google Ads, Facebook, and content automation tools like Jasper AI.

3. Data Science and AI Certification (LinkedIn Learning): Ideal for digital nomads working with data, this certification teaches you how to use machine learning to analyse trends, make predictions, and drive business decisions. The certification covers popular tools like Python, TensorFlow, and Jupyter Notebooks.

4. AI for Creative Professionals (Udacity): Focused on the creative industries, this course is perfect for digital nomads in design, photography, and content production. You'll learn how to integrate AI tools like Adobe Sensei and Canva's AI tools into your workflow, automating tasks while enhancing your creativity.

5. AI Product Management (Coursera): If you're working in product development or tech, this course will teach you how to design and manage AI products. This certification is valuable for digital nomads who work with startups, tech companies, or clients building AI-driven platforms.

Practical Tips: How to Get the Most Out of Your AI Certification

1. Choose a Certification Aligned with Your Career Goals: Before jumping into a course, take the time to identify which AI tools and skills will most benefit your line of work. Whether you're in marketing, design, project management, or another field, choose a certification that will directly improve your ability to serve clients or employers.

2. Apply What You Learn Immediately: One of the biggest advantages of AI certifications is their practical application. As you progress through the course, start integrating the tools and techniques into your current projects. If you're learning about AI-driven content creation, try using a tool like Jasper AI to craft your next blog post or social media campaign.

3. Leverage Your Certification on Platforms Like LinkedIn: Once you've completed your certification, don't hesitate to showcase it on your LinkedIn profile or other professional platforms. Certifications act as badges of expertise and will help you stand out to potential clients or employers. You can also join online communities related to your certification, offering networking opportunities with other professionals in your field.

4. Stay Updated: AI is constantly evolving, and certifications are not a one-and-done task. Stay proactive in seeking new certifications or continuing education courses that keep you updated with the latest trends and tools in AI.

Looking Ahead: AI as a Lifelong Learning Tool

As AI continues to evolve, the need for digital nomads to stay adaptable and competitive will only grow. In the future, AI certifications could become a standard part of every professional's toolkit, serving not only as a way to learn new skills but also as a path to discovering new career opportunities. Imagine a future where AI-driven platforms continuously suggest the most relevant certifications and learning paths based on your career trajectory, keeping you ahead of the curve in real-time.

Digital nomads who embrace this learning journey will not only future-proof their careers but will also find that AI opens up new creative possibilities. The key is to view AI not as a threat but as a tool that amplifies your potential. As you explore AI certifications, remember that each new skill you acquire brings you one step closer to mastering the future of work, no matter where in the world you happen to be.

By earning certifications in AI, you're not just staying competitive—you're becoming a leader in your field. The world of digital nomadism is evolving, and AI is guiding the way forward. Embrace it, and thrive.

CHAPTER 69:
AI TUTORS
AND MENTORS:
PERSONALIZED
LEARNING FOR
DIGITAL NOMADS

As Maya strolled through the bustling streets of Medellín, Colombia, her mind wasn't on the vibrant food stalls or the music filling the air. Instead, she was thinking about a concept in data science that had stumped her earlier in the day. But Maya wasn't worried. She knew that later that evening, in the quiet of her Airbnb, her AI tutor would guide her through the problem. No rigid schedules, no commuting to a classroom. Just a tailored, one-on-one learning experience powered by artificial intelligence—available to her wherever she was in the world. For Maya, as for many other digital nomads, AI-driven tutoring had become an invaluable part of her lifestyle, offering her the flexibility, personalization, and expertise she needed to thrive.

This chapter will explore how AI tutors and mentors are transforming the way digital nomads learn and develop new skills. These advanced tools are revolutionizing education, providing personalized support for everything from coding to language learning, career development, and creative skills. The power of AI means digital nomads can now access tailored, on-demand mentorship that adjusts to their unique learning styles, schedules, and goals.

Maya's Story: Unlocking the Power of Personalized Tutoring

Maya's journey as a digital nomad began as a freelance web developer, but she quickly realized that the tech industry was changing faster than ever. New programming languages, frameworks, and data science concepts seemed to emerge overnight. Maya knew she needed to keep up, but the traditional classroom setting wasn't an option for her constantly changing locations and unpredictable work schedule.

That's when she discovered Socratic by Google, an AI-powered tutoring tool that could answer her questions and explain complex coding concepts in real-time. What made Socratic special wasn't just its ability to provide answers—it was its ability to adapt. If Maya didn't grasp a concept, the AI would break it down further, offering alternative explanations, video tutorials, and practical examples. In essence, it was like having a personal tutor in her pocket.

For Maya, the most remarkable aspect of AI tutoring was its flexibility. She didn't have to rearrange her travel plans or work schedule around a class timetable. Whether she was sitting in a café in Colombia or hiking through the mountains of Nepal, her AI tutor was ready whenever she was. This convenience empowered Maya to stay at the cutting edge of her field without sacrificing her nomadic lifestyle.

AI Tutors and Mentors: How They Work

AI-driven tutoring platforms leverage machine learning,

natural language processing, and data analytics to offer a highly personalized educational experience. Here's how they're helping digital nomads learn more effectively:

1. Instant Problem-Solving: Like Maya's experience with Socratic, AI tutoring platforms can provide immediate answers to questions. Whether you're struggling with coding, grammar, or math, AI tutors analyse your query and offer solutions in real-time. For digital nomads who can't attend in-person classes or schedule regular meetings with human tutors, this feature is invaluable.

2. Adaptive Learning: AI tutors use machine learning algorithms to track a learner's progress. If you're excelling, the AI will challenge you with more advanced material. If you're struggling, it will provide more foundational resources, slowing down to ensure you grasp each concept fully. This type of adaptive learning ensures that you're always progressing at a pace that suits your abilities.

3. Tailored Mentorship: Beyond tutoring, some platforms also offer AI-driven mentorship for skill development. For instance, tools like LinkedIn Learning use AI to recommend career development courses based on your job profile, skillset, and professional goals. It's like having a virtual mentor constantly guiding you toward your next career move.

Practical Applications: How Digital Nomads Can Use AI Mentorship

Here are a few practical ways you can leverage AI-driven tutoring and mentorship as a digital nomad:

- For Learning New Skills: Platforms like Khan Academy use AI to provide personalized learning paths in subjects like mathematics, history, and economics. The platform adapts to your learning speed and offers detailed feedback, ensuring you truly understand the material before moving on. It's perfect for nomads who need flexibility and structure.

- For Language Learning: Language barriers can be a challenge for digital nomads traveling to new countries. AI-powered tools like Duolingo and Babbel are designed to teach languages in an engaging and adaptive way. These platforms adjust lessons to your language proficiency, provide real-time feedback on pronunciation, and use gamified techniques to keep you motivated.

- For Coding and Technical Skills: If you're in tech, tools like Codecademy and Udacity provide AI-driven support to help you learn programming languages, web development, and data science. These platforms track your coding habits, offering tips and additional resources if you hit a roadblock.

- For Career Development: LinkedIn Learning uses AI to offer tailored career advice and skill-building opportunities. It analyses your job history and recommends courses that can enhance your professional profile. This is particularly useful for digital nomads who want to stay competitive in an evolving market.

A Visionary Look: The Future of AI-Driven Learning for Nomads

The future of AI-driven tutoring and mentorship is bright. Imagine an AI system that not only helps you solve problems in real-time but also learns about your long-term goals and adjusts your learning path accordingly. For example, if you're a digital nomad interested in becoming a software developer, the AI tutor might suggest a mix of coding courses, real-world projects, and soft skills training, continuously refining your learning experience based on your progress.

As AI continues to evolve, we can expect more immersive and personalized learning environments. AI tutors may soon integrate with augmented reality (AR), allowing nomads to practice skills like coding, design, or even language in a virtual environment that mimics real-world scenarios. Imagine learning Spanish while virtually walking through the streets of Barcelona, interacting with locals via AI-generated simulations.

Balancing AI Tutoring with Real-World Experience

While AI tutors offer a wealth of knowledge and personalized instruction, it's important to remember that they should complement, not replace, real-world learning experiences. For digital nomads, the beauty of their lifestyle lies in their ability to immerse themselves in different cultures, meet new people, and explore diverse perspectives. Use AI tutoring as a tool to build technical skills and knowledge, but don't forget to engage with the world around you. After all, true growth happens when learning is combined with experience.

Challenges and Caution: Privacy and Balance

With the rapid development of AI-driven tutoring, there are some important challenges to consider. Privacy is a key concern—many AI platforms collect vast amounts of personal data to tailor learning experiences. As a digital nomad, it's essential to research the privacy policies of the tools you use, ensuring that your data is handled responsibly.

Moreover, maintaining balance is crucial. With AI-driven platforms offering 24/7 access to learning, it can be easy to fall into the trap of overworking. Set boundaries for when and how much you engage with your AI tutor, ensuring that you have time to enjoy the freedom that comes with the nomadic lifestyle.

Conclusion: AI as Your Personal Mentor

AI tutors and mentors are reshaping the future of education

for digital nomads, offering personalized and flexible learning experiences that can be accessed from anywhere in the world. Whether you're diving into new skills, mastering a language, or advancing your career, AI-driven platforms are ready to guide you every step of the way. By embracing these tools, digital nomads can stay competitive, continuously grow, and find fulfilment in both their personal and professional lives.

Imagine a world where your education is as flexible and dynamic as your lifestyle—a world where you have a personal mentor in your pocket, ready to help you unlock your next opportunity. That future is here, and it's powered by AI.

CHAPTER 70: AI AND UPSKILLING IN REAL-TIME: LEARNING AND APPLYING NEW SKILLS ON THE GO

As the sun rose over Lisbon's historic streets, Diego was already a few hours into his workday, juggling client emails, project management, and freelance writing tasks. But this wasn't just any ordinary workday for Diego—he was also learning a new skill in real time. While collaborating with a startup on a marketing project, Diego encountered the need for basic coding knowledge to automate some of his marketing workflows. Instead of pausing his work to enrol in a lengthy course, Diego turned to AI-powered tools to upskill himself on the spot. Within hours, he was using platforms like Codecademy and GitHub Copilot to write simple code and automate his processes—all without missing a deadline. Diego's experience highlights one of the most powerful aspects of AI in the digital nomad lifestyle: the ability to learn and apply new skills in real-time, without disrupting the flow of work or travel.

In this chapter, we will explore how AI enables digital nomads to learn, adapt, and upskill on the go. We'll dive into real-life case studies like Diego's, offer practical applications for integrating AI into your learning process, and provide a visionary look at how AI will continue to reshape how nomads stay competitive and grow in their careers.

Diego's Story: Learning as You Work

When Diego received a request from his client to automate portions of their marketing workflow, he realized he needed coding skills—specifically in Python. However, Diego's work as a marketing consultant meant he couldn't afford to step away from his projects to dedicate weeks to a coding bootcamp. Enter AI.

Using Codecademy's interactive Python course, Diego was able to receive personalized learning experiences in bite-sized lessons. The AI in the platform adapted to his learning style, providing extra resources when needed and skipping over topics he quickly mastered. Alongside this, GitHub Copilot, an AI-driven code-completion tool, helped Diego write efficient code without having to be a coding expert.

What would have once been a daunting learning curve became manageable and even enjoyable. Diego was able to seamlessly upskill and immediately apply what he learned, boosting his confidence and productivity in real-time. His story illustrates the power of AI to offer just-in-time learning, tailored to the unique needs of each learner—a key advantage for nomads who live and work in fast-paced, ever-changing environments.

Practical Applications: How You Can Use AI to Upskill in Real-Time

AI-powered platforms are designed to provide on-demand, adaptive learning that fits into the busy lifestyle of digital nomads. Here are some practical ways you can integrate AI into your workflow to learn and apply new skills:

1. Real-Time Coding Assistance: If you're venturing into the tech world, tools like GitHub Copilot or Tabnine use machine learning to help you write code faster and with fewer errors. These platforms suggest code snippets, catch bugs, and provide recommendations as you type—perfect for those who need to learn coding on the job without taking formal lessons.

2. Content Creation and Optimization: For digital nomads involved in writing, marketing, or content strategy, Jasper AI and Grammarly offer real-time writing suggestions that improve both speed and quality. You can use Jasper to generate ideas, outlines, or entire drafts, while Grammarly provides AI-enhanced suggestions to improve readability, grammar, and tone—helping you upskill in content writing without the need for formal training.

3. Design with AI: For creative professionals, Canva's AI-powered design suggestions are a game-changer. Whether you're designing graphics for a blog or creating marketing materials, AI can help optimize layouts, suggest colour schemes, and offer design templates, helping you upskill in design in real-time.

4. Learning New Languages: Nomads frequently travel across borders and work with global clients, making language skills essential. AI-driven platforms like Duolingo and Babbel provide adaptive learning paths that help you master new languages. These platforms adjust the difficulty based on your proficiency and offer gamified lessons, allowing you to apply your new language skills immediately in conversations.

By integrating these AI tools into your daily workflow, you can upskill as you go—whether it's learning to code, improving your writing, or mastering a new language. The beauty of AI in upskilling is that it doesn't require a full commitment of time or resources; instead, it blends learning with productivity, allowing you to apply new skills in real-time.

The Future of Real-Time Upskilling: AI as a Constant Learning Companion

Imagine a future where AI knows your career trajectory better than you do. As you work, the AI monitors your tasks, identifies areas where you could improve, and offers real-time learning suggestions based on what you're doing in the moment. If you're building a website, the AI might suggest a tutorial on advanced CSS. If you're managing a project, it might recommend a quick course on leadership or time management.

This hyper-personalized learning experience is becoming more possible with advancements in AI-driven platforms like Coursera, Udacity, and LinkedIn Learning. These platforms are increasingly incorporating AI to suggest learning paths tailored to each user's current skills, career goals, and job requirements. For digital nomads, this means learning is no longer a separate task—it becomes an integrated part of daily work life, continuously evolving alongside you.

Imagine AI-powered tools like Skillshare that automatically curate lessons based on the tasks you perform throughout the day. For instance, if you spend part of your morning working on social media marketing, your AI assistant could recommend the latest strategies in content marketing or suggest improvements to your ad copy. You'd be learning and implementing new techniques in real-time, without needing to carve out extra hours for study.

Balancing Upskilling with Nomadic Freedom

While AI makes it easier than ever to upskill on the go, it's important to maintain balance. The digital nomad lifestyle is about more than just productivity—it's about experiencing new cultures, building relationships, and finding inspiration in the world around you. Be mindful of how much time you dedicate to upskilling, and make sure you're still leaving room for the adventures that drew you to this lifestyle in the first place.

Consider setting boundaries for when you engage in active learning. For instance, dedicate the first hour of your workday to upskilling with AI-powered platforms, and then switch gears to focus on your projects. This way, you can make meaningful progress without overwhelming yourself or sacrificing the freedom that comes with being a digital nomad.

Inspiring Purpose: Learning with Impact

Ultimately, the power of AI in real-time upskilling lies not just in the practical skills you acquire but in the sense of purpose it brings to your journey. Upskilling allows you to contribute more meaningfully to your clients, your community, and the world. For example, by learning new technologies or languages, you can better collaborate with diverse teams, make an impact in global markets, or even dedicate time to causes you care about.

AI empowers digital nomads to live purpose-driven lives by making learning a continuous, accessible process. It turns each day into an opportunity for growth, allowing you to expand your horizons and contribute in ways you never thought possible. Whether it's mastering a new tool, improving your communication skills, or gaining technical expertise, AI is the key to unlocking your full potential as a digital nomad.

Conclusion: Embrace Real-Time Upskilling

The digital nomad lifestyle offers unparalleled freedom, but it also demands constant growth and adaptation. With AI by your side, upskilling no longer has to be a burden—it can be a seamless, enjoyable part of your daily routine. By embracing real-time learning powered by AI, you're not just staying relevant in a fast-paced world—you're building a career and life filled with opportunity, creativity, and purpose.

As you continue your journey, remember that learning is no longer confined to classrooms or scheduled study hours. With AI, the world is your classroom, and every moment is a chance to grow. Embrace this new way of learning, and let AI guide you toward the next stage of your nomadic adventure.

PART 15: THE IMPACT OF AI ON GLOBAL WORKPLACES

CHAPTER 71: REMOTE TEAMS IN AN AI WORLD: THE FUTURE OF DISTRIBUTED WORKFORCES

As Carlos opened his laptop from his temporary home in Mexico City, his first task wasn't to check emails or schedule meetings—it was to review a performance report generated by AI. The software had analysed the productivity of his remote team, identifying patterns and bottlenecks that Carlos hadn't even considered. His team, spread across four continents, was thriving in this new era of AI-enhanced remote work. Thanks to AI-powered tools, Carlos could now manage his team with unparalleled efficiency, allowing them to collaborate seamlessly across time zones, languages, and cultures. Carlos' experience is a prime example of how AI is reshaping the way companies manage remote and distributed teams in today's fast-paced, globalized work environment.

In this chapter, we will explore how AI is transforming remote team management, improving communication, collaboration, and productivity across borders. By engaging with real-world examples, we'll dive into the practical applications of AI in distributed workforces and provide a visionary look at the future of work as AI continues to evolve. Whether you're managing a small freelance team or a large, fully remote organization, AI offers tools and strategies that can help you navigate the complexities of a global workforce.

Carlos' Story: AI as a Manager's Best Friend

Carlos, a project manager for a software development company, had been managing a distributed team for several years, but the challenges were mounting. Coordinating across time zones, managing workload distribution, and ensuring team cohesion were constant struggles. It wasn't until his company adopted AI-powered project management tools that things began to change.

Carlos implemented Monday.com, a platform that uses AI to automate workflows, allocate resources, and optimize team communication. With AI-driven insights, the platform analysed task completion rates, identified bottlenecks, and even suggested improvements for more efficient collaboration. Carlos' team saw an immediate boost in productivity. His developers, located in India, Spain, and Canada, began collaborating more smoothly, thanks to automated task reminders and a dynamic project timeline that adjusted in real time based on team activity.

The biggest revelation came when the AI suggested changing the timing of team meetings to accommodate natural productivity peaks across different time zones. What was once a challenge in coordinating asynchronous work now became a seamless process of collaboration. Carlos no longer had to micromanage; instead, he trusted the AI to guide him and his team through the complexities of remote work.

Practical Applications: AI Tools for Managing Remote Teams

AI tools offer a wealth of solutions to streamline the management of remote and distributed teams. Here's how you can use AI to improve communication, productivity, and collaboration within your team:

1. Automated Task Management: Tools like Trello and Asana use AI to prioritize tasks based on deadlines, project progress, and team availability. These platforms ensure that nothing slips through the cracks, automatically assigning tasks and sending reminders to keep team members on track.

2. Real-Time Collaboration: AI-driven platforms like Slack and Microsoft Teams are now equipped with AI-powered bots that automate meeting scheduling, track project updates, and provide real-time translations for global teams. These tools foster a collaborative environment, making it easier for remote workers to stay connected, regardless of their location.

3. AI-Enhanced Performance Reviews: AI tools like Lattice and Leapsome help managers conduct data-driven performance evaluations. These platforms analyse productivity trends, employee feedback, and project outcomes, offering actionable insights on team performance and areas for improvement.

4. AI-Driven Communication: Grammarly and Linguix are not just for writers; they help team members communicate more effectively by improving clarity and tone. These tools ensure that emails, reports, and messages are professional, clear, and free of misunderstandings—crucial for teams working across different cultures and languages.

Inspiring Vision: The Future of Remote Work in an AI-Driven World

Imagine a future where AI doesn't just support team management—it actively predicts and enhances team performance. AI will soon be able to analyse vast amounts of data across different teams, identifying patterns of collaboration and conflict before they escalate. For example, an AI platform could notice that a particular team member works best with minimal interruptions and recommend that their tasks be batch-scheduled, freeing them up for deep work. Or, AI might predict which employees are at risk of burnout based on workload and suggest distributing tasks more evenly across the team.

Moreover, as AI becomes more advanced, it will bridge cultural gaps in global teams by automatically translating not just language but also context, making cross-cultural communication smoother and more nuanced. Virtual reality (VR) environments powered by AI could even simulate in-person meetings, allowing team members to connect on a more personal level despite physical distance.

Balancing AI with Human Leadership

While AI offers powerful tools for managing remote teams, it's important to remember that technology is not a replacement for human leadership. Managers must continue to cultivate empathy, adaptability, and creativity—skills that AI cannot replicate. The role of AI should be to enhance human leadership, not replace it. For instance, while AI can offer insights into team productivity, it's up to the manager to provide the emotional support and vision that keep teams motivated and engaged.

As a manager, balance the use of AI tools with regular check-ins that focus on team well-being, career development, and personal growth. AI can help automate tasks, but it's human connection that fosters trust, loyalty, and a positive team culture. AI is there to handle the data, but leadership comes from building relationships and understanding the unique strengths and challenges of each team member.

Global and Cultural Dimensions of AI-Powered Teams

One of the greatest benefits of AI in managing remote teams is its ability to bridge the gap between different cultures. With teams working across time zones and borders, cultural misunderstandings can easily arise. However, AI tools are making it easier for distributed teams to work together smoothly. For example, Google Translate and DeepL allow team members to communicate in real time, breaking down language barriers. AI can also analyse cultural differences in communication styles, helping teams navigate different expectations around feedback, decision-making, and collaboration.

In Japan, where hierarchical decision-making is common, AI can help teams adapt their workflows to respect these cultural norms, while in more decentralized cultures like Sweden, AI can foster greater autonomy and collaborative decision-making. These tools offer a global perspective that not only makes remote work more inclusive but also helps teams leverage the diversity of thought and experience that comes from working with people around the world.

Inspiring Purpose: Leading with Impact in an AI-Enhanced World

At the core of managing remote teams in an AI-driven world is the need to focus on purpose-driven leadership. Digital nomads and remote workers are not just looking for jobs— they are seeking opportunities that align with their values and passions. By leveraging AI, managers can not only streamline operations but also create a work environment that empowers their teams to focus on what matters most: meaningful, impactful work.

AI frees up time and mental energy by automating repetitive tasks, allowing remote workers to concentrate on creative problem-solving, strategy, and personal development. For managers, this means encouraging your team to use the tools at their disposal to work smarter, not harder—enabling them to pursue their passions both in and out of work.

Conclusion: The Future of Remote Work is AI-Driven and Human-Centred

AI is revolutionizing the way companies manage remote and distributed teams, making it easier to communicate, collaborate, and innovate across borders. With AI-powered tools at our disposal, we can optimize workflows, enhance communication, and even predict team dynamics, leading to more productive and harmonious work environments.

However, as AI continues to evolve, it's critical that we maintain the human touch in leadership. Technology should serve as a tool to enhance our abilities as leaders, not replace them. By embracing AI while focusing on empathy, purpose, and cultural inclusivity, we can build remote teams that are not only efficient but also deeply connected and motivated to make a positive impact.

The future of work is here—and it's powered by AI, driven by human connection, and enriched by global collaboration.

CHAPTER 72: AI AND CROSS-CULTURAL TEAM COLLABORATION

The digital nomad lifestyle thrives on global connections. Nomads travel the world, living in different cultures and collaborating with teams from all corners of the globe. Yet, with the rise of remote work, one challenge consistently arises—how can people from different cultural backgrounds collaborate effectively, particularly when working remotely? The answer lies in artificial intelligence (AI).

AI tools are now revolutionizing the way digital nomads interact and collaborate with cross-cultural teams. Whether breaking down language barriers, facilitating real-time communication, or providing cultural insights, AI is transforming how teams work across borders. In this chapter, we'll explore how AI is enhancing cross-cultural collaboration, backed by real-world examples, practical applications, and a visionary look at the future.

Engage with Storytelling and Case Studies

Meet Laura, a digital nomad who calls no country her permanent home. Laura is a UX designer who frequently collaborates with teams in different time zones—developers in India, project managers in Germany, and clients from the U.S. At first, managing communication between such diverse teams seemed daunting. Differences in language, cultural expectations, and working styles led to misunderstandings that slowed down projects and affected team dynamics.

However, things changed when Laura adopted AI-powered collaboration tools. Google Translate became her lifeline for quick communication, allowing her to bridge language gaps in real-time. Tools like Grammarly helped ensure her emails were clear and culturally neutral, avoiding miscommunication. Additionally, Time Zone Ninja assisted in scheduling meetings that worked for everyone.

With AI facilitating seamless communication, Laura's workflow improved drastically. The misunderstandings decreased, deadlines were met, and the team began to gel as a cohesive unit, despite being spread across continents. AI made it possible for Laura to thrive in cross-cultural teams, making her remote work experience not just productive but deeply rewarding.

Focus on Practical Application

For digital nomads who work with global teams, AI offers a host of tools designed to improve collaboration across cultural and linguistic divides. Here's how you can use AI to overcome common cross-cultural challenges:

1. Language Translation and Communication
Language is often the biggest hurdle in cross-cultural collaboration. Thankfully, AI tools like Google Translate, DeepL, and Microsoft Translator offer real-time language translation for emails, chats, and even video meetings. While these tools aren't perfect, they significantly reduce

language barriers, allowing teams to communicate clearly and efficiently.

Practical Tip: Use Google Translate or DeepL for instant translations of text, but ensure the message is reviewed by a native speaker for cultural nuances when appropriate. For ongoing conversations, consider using translation tools integrated directly into your chat platforms, like Microsoft Teams or Slack.

2. Time Zone Management
Working with teams across multiple time zones can be a logistical nightmare. AI-powered scheduling tools like World Time Buddy and Time Zone Ninja automatically calculate the best meeting times for all participants based on their time zones. This saves digital nomads the headache of manually coordinating meeting times and ensures everyone can participate during their most productive hours.

Practical Tip: Sync your calendar with a tool like World Time Buddy to effortlessly schedule meetings without worrying about clashing time zones. Use this in combination with AI assistants like Clara or x.ai, which can automatically manage meeting arrangements on your behalf.

3. Cultural Insights and Awareness
Beyond language, understanding cultural nuances is crucial to successful collaboration. AI tools like GLOBIS and CultureWizard offer digital nomads insights into different cultural norms, from business etiquette to communication styles. These tools help teams avoid cultural missteps, fostering smoother interactions.

Practical Tip: Before engaging with a new international team, consult AI-driven cultural insight platforms like GLOBIS to gain an understanding of the local business culture, communication preferences, and key values. This can help you build stronger, more respectful relationships from the start.

Inspire Through Visionary Perspectives

As AI continues to evolve, it's exciting to imagine how cross-cultural collaboration will develop in the future. Picture AI tools that not only translate languages but also interpret tone and context with accuracy. Imagine virtual collaboration spaces that adjust in real-time to accommodate different cultural preferences—whether it's how meetings are structured or how feedback is given.

One promising development is real-time AI emotion detection. By analysing facial expressions, voice tone, and text sentiment, AI could alert team members if their message is being received positively or negatively, even across cultural lines. This could transform how digital nomads communicate, ensuring cultural sensitivities are respected.

Visionary Perspective: As AI improves, it will likely become a key enabler of global collaboration, helping teams overcome linguistic and cultural barriers while working more harmoniously. With AI guiding team interactions, cross-cultural misunderstandings may soon be a thing of the past.

Balance Between Inspiration and Caution

While AI offers groundbreaking solutions for cross-cultural collaboration, it's important to remain mindful of its limitations. Translation tools, for example, are still prone to errors, particularly when dealing with idioms or complex cultural concepts. Relying solely on AI can lead to miscommunication if not balanced with human judgment.

Balanced Advice: Use AI tools to enhance, not replace, human understanding. Always have a backup plan for more sensitive communications—such as hiring a human translator or consultant when entering unfamiliar cultural territory. Recognize that AI is a tool to assist but not a replacement for genuine interpersonal understanding.

Highlight Global and Cultural Dimensions

AI's impact on cross-cultural collaboration is especially profound in regions where language diversity is high, such as Southeast Asia or Africa. In countries like India, where businesses operate in multiple languages, AI-powered translation and communication tools have transformed the ability of local teams to work seamlessly with international partners.

In Estonia, the government's e-Residency program has leveraged AI to support international entrepreneurs and digital nomads in establishing businesses without needing to be physically present. These initiatives highlight how AI is helping diverse regions participate in the global economy, creating new opportunities for digital nomads to collaborate across borders.

Global Insight: Digital nomads should look to countries like Estonia, India, and Singapore, which are integrating AI into their infrastructure to facilitate global business. These regions offer a glimpse into the future of AI-driven collaboration across borders.

Motivate with Purpose and Fulfilment

At its core, cross-cultural collaboration isn't just about productivity—it's about connection. For many digital nomads, working with people from diverse backgrounds is one of the most fulfilling aspects of the lifestyle. AI can help you communicate and collaborate more effectively, but the relationships you build through your work will always be the most valuable part.

Inspirational Reflection: Embrace AI as a way to enhance your ability to connect with people across the globe. With AI breaking down barriers, you can focus more on building meaningful relationships that transcend cultural differences and foster mutual respect and understanding.

Use Accessible, Simple Language for Complex Topics

When discussing AI tools, it's easy to get lost in technical jargon. However, the best AI solutions are often the simplest. AI tools like Google Translate or World Time Buddy don't require advanced technical knowledge to use. Their straightforward interfaces allow digital nomads to integrate AI into their work with ease.

Friendly Explanation: Think of AI tools as practical aids that help smooth out the complexities of working in a global context. These tools are designed to make your life easier, not harder, so don't be intimidated by the technology.

Interactive and Engaging Content

Before diving into the next chapter, take a moment to explore how AI can improve your cross-cultural collaboration. Try using Google Translate or DeepL for a real-time conversation with a colleague in another language. Reflect on how AI has enhanced your communication and what challenges it has helped you overcome.

Conclusion

AI is reshaping the way digital nomads collaborate across cultures. By breaking down language barriers, managing time zones, and providing cultural insights, AI enables global teams to work together with unprecedented ease. However, while AI enhances collaboration, the relationships you build through meaningful, respectful interactions remain irreplaceable. As AI continues to evolve, the future of cross-cultural teamwork is full of promise, offering digital nomads endless opportunities to connect, create, and succeed in the global workplace.

CHAPTER 73: MANAGING REMOTE TEAMS WITH AI

Managing remote teams has always been a unique challenge, but with the rise of digital nomadism and the evolution of artificial intelligence (AI), it's becoming more efficient, streamlined, and even inspiring. The digital nomad lifestyle embraces flexibility, autonomy, and global collaboration, but coordinating a remote team across different time zones, cultures, and working styles can quickly become overwhelming. AI is stepping in as the game-changer, offering powerful tools that help digital nomads manage teams with greater precision, empathy, and insight.

This chapter dives into how AI-powered tools are reshaping remote team management and provides practical applications to help digital nomads thrive in this evolving landscape. Through real-life examples, visionary perspectives, and actionable tips, you'll gain insight into the future of AI-driven leadership in a digital world.

Engage with Storytelling and Case Studies

Meet Alejandro, a digital nomad leading a remote software development team spread across four continents. Before AI, managing the team was an ongoing struggle.

Different time zones made scheduling meetings a constant headache, communication breakdowns led to delays, and tracking productivity was nearly impossible without micromanaging.

That all changed when Alejandro integrated Trello and Monday.com, two AI-powered project management tools, into his workflow. These platforms used AI to automate tasks like project updates, deadlines, and task delegation. Alejandro no longer needed to send reminders manually, as the AI could do it based on team progress. The tools also provided detailed analytics on team performance, allowing him to offer targeted feedback and support where needed.

Most importantly, Alejandro integrated Krisp, an AI-powered noise cancellation app, to ensure clear communication during meetings. This became essential, especially when team members joined calls from bustling cafes or noisy coworking spaces—a reality for many digital nomads. With AI helping Alejandro manage his remote team, productivity soared, team cohesion improved, and he had more time to focus on strategic growth.

Focus on Practical Application

For digital nomads managing remote teams, AI offers invaluable tools that streamline operations and foster better team dynamics. Below are key AI-driven solutions to enhance your leadership and management of remote teams:

1. Automating Task Management
Tools like Trello, Asana, and Monday.com offer AI-driven task management features that automate repetitive tasks such as setting deadlines, assigning projects, and sending progress updates. AI tracks team progress in real-time, provides reminders, and offers suggestions for optimizing

workflows.

Practical Tip: Use Monday.com's AI-powered features to automatically assign tasks based on team members' workload and past performance. This helps balance the workload and ensures that no one is overwhelmed while still meeting deadlines.

2. Enhancing Communication

AI has revolutionized team communication. Tools like Slack and Microsoft Teams now offer AI-powered chatbots that assist with managing conversations, answering common questions, and even translating messages in real-time for teams that work across different languages. Zoom and Google Meet also offer AI-driven transcription and recording services, making meetings more accessible and organized.

Practical Tip: Integrate AI chatbots like Slackbot into your team's communication channels to automate routine questions, set reminders, and even schedule meetings. This reduces manual communication, freeing up time for more strategic conversations.

3. Improving Productivity and Motivation

AI is not just about automation; it also helps motivate and guide your team's performance. Tools like Hubstaff or Time Doctor offer AI-driven insights into productivity patterns, helping managers identify when team members are most productive and where support might be needed. AI also tracks engagement and suggests ways to improve morale, such as encouraging breaks during periods of high stress.

Practical Tip: Use Time Doctor to analyse team productivity trends and adjust project timelines accordingly. If the tool identifies burnout risks, consider reorganizing tasks or promoting wellness initiatives to keep your team motivated and healthy.

Inspire Through Visionary Perspectives

The future of managing remote teams is filled with potential as AI becomes even more integrated into daily workflows. Imagine AI assistants that not only automate tasks but also predict potential issues within teams. For example, AI could analyse communication patterns to identify potential conflicts before they escalate, recommending proactive steps for resolution.

Visionary Perspective: Envision AI tools that assess emotional tone in team communication, offering managers insights into team well-being. AI could suggest tailored management strategies, from scheduling mental health check-ins to recommending training programs for skill development, enabling a more empathetic and human-centric approach to remote leadership.

Balance Between Inspiration and Caution

While AI offers significant benefits in managing remote teams, it's crucial to remain mindful of the challenges. Relying too heavily on AI-driven productivity metrics, for instance, can reduce the human connection that's essential for a cohesive team. Additionally, concerns about privacy and the ethical use of AI in tracking employees' behaviour are valid and should be addressed transparently with your team.

Balanced Advice: Use AI as a tool to complement, not replace, human intuition and leadership. Ensure that your team knows how AI is being used, especially when it comes to tracking productivity or performance. Transparency fosters trust and ensures AI enhances rather than erodes team morale.

Highlight Global and Cultural Dimensions

Managing a remote team often involves navigating cultural differences. AI is playing a pivotal role in bridging cultural gaps. For instance, tools like Grammarly and DeepL help refine communication by removing language barriers and suggesting culturally neutral phrasing. Moreover, AI-powered platforms like CultureAmp offer insights into global team dynamics, helping managers better understand how cultural backgrounds influence work styles.

Global Insight: Digital nomads working with global teams should consider AI tools like GLOBIS that offer cultural insights. These tools provide tips on communication etiquette, meeting styles, and leadership practices that resonate with different cultures, helping you foster stronger international team collaboration.

Motivate with Purpose and Fulfilment

One of the greatest challenges in managing remote teams is maintaining a sense of purpose and connection. AI helps alleviate this by facilitating more personalized communication, offering feedback that aligns with individual team members' strengths, and providing insights into what motivates them.

Inspirational Reflection: Use AI to empower your team, but remember that motivation is deeply human. AI can help identify trends and recommend strategies, but it's the personal connections you build with your team members that will ultimately lead to long-term success and fulfilment.

Use Accessible, Simple Language for Complex Topics

AI tools can seem intimidating, especially for those unfamiliar with technology. However, many AI-powered platforms are user-friendly and designed to be intuitive. Tools like Zapier allow you to create simple workflows without needing coding expertise, helping automate tasks in just a few clicks.

Friendly Explanation: Think of AI as a personal assistant. It handles repetitive tasks so you can focus on leading, strategizing, and building relationships. No coding experience is necessary—just a willingness to explore and experiment with different tools to find what works best for you and your team.

Interactive and Engaging Content

Before diving into the next chapter, take some time to explore AI tools for managing remote teams. Try using Trello or Monday.com to automate your project management, or experiment with Slack's AI chatbot for improved communication. Reflect on how these tools could transform the way you lead your team and note any challenges you face along the way.

Conclusion

Managing remote teams in the AI age offers incredible opportunities for digital nomads. By leveraging AI-powered tools for task automation, communication, and productivity insights, leaders can foster more efficient, cohesive, and motivated teams. However, while AI can streamline many aspects of management, it's essential to maintain a balance between automation and human connection. By embracing the possibilities of AI while leading with empathy and transparency, you'll not only thrive in managing remote teams but also inspire and elevate your team to reach new heights.

CHAPTER 74: AI AND WORKPLACE DIVERSITY

How AI Supports Diversity and Inclusion Initiatives for Global Digital Nomads

As the digital nomad lifestyle continues to rise in popularity, there is a growing awareness of the importance of diversity and inclusion (D&I) within global workforces. Remote work, while freeing us from geographical constraints, can sometimes expose us to new challenges: from language barriers to cultural misunderstandings. Digital nomads come from all corners of the world, representing different nationalities, ethnicities, genders, abilities, and perspectives. How do you ensure that these diverse voices are heard and valued? The answer is increasingly found in the capabilities of artificial intelligence (AI).

In this chapter, we'll explore how AI is playing a vital role in driving diversity and inclusion for digital nomads, enhancing workplace culture, and fostering innovation through a global lens. Through real-world examples, practical applications, and visionary thinking, you will discover how AI can help you manage D&I within your remote teams and create a more inclusive digital nomad ecosystem.

Engage with Storytelling and Case Studies

Maria, a Brazilian digital nomad, faced significant challenges when working for a global tech startup based in the U.S. While the company prided itself on diversity, Maria often found herself excluded from critical conversations due to language barriers and cultural differences. She felt that her unique insights, shaped by her experiences in South America, weren't being valued or understood. Her frustration was compounded by frequent miscommunications in team meetings and collaboration tools.

That all changed when the company adopted Microsoft Teams' AI-powered translation and sentiment analysis features. With automatic real-time translation of messages and video calls, Maria was now able to participate more actively. Moreover, AI-driven sentiment analysis flagged instances where certain voices, including Maria's, weren't being heard as much during meetings, prompting managers to proactively involve quieter team members in discussions. This AI-driven initiative helped Maria feel more connected and valued, and her contributions to the team's projects significantly increased.

Focus on Practical Application

AI offers numerous ways to support diversity and inclusion within the global digital nomad community. From automated translation tools to unbiased recruitment algorithms, here are several key AI-powered strategies that digital nomads and organizations can adopt to promote a more inclusive work environment:

1. Real-Time Language Translation and Cultural Sensitivity

Digital nomads often work with clients and team members across multiple languages and cultures. AI-powered tools like Google Translate, Microsoft Teams, and DeepL have revolutionized communication by providing real-time translations for both text and speech. However, more advanced AI tools are going beyond translation to include cultural sensitivity. These tools suggest contextually appropriate phrases and tone, ensuring that your message is understood correctly across cultures.

Practical Tip: Use Microsoft Teams' real-time transcription and translation feature in global meetings to ensure everyone can participate regardless of language. Additionally, AI-powered tools like Lilt help businesses ensure that cultural nuances are respected in written communication.

2. Bias Reduction in Recruitment and Hiring

One of the most significant challenges in promoting workplace diversity is overcoming unconscious bias during recruitment. AI-powered platforms like Pymetrics and HireVue are designed to remove bias from the hiring process by assessing candidates based on skills and potential rather than cultural background or personal characteristics. These tools can evaluate soft skills, language proficiency, and leadership potential, ensuring that you attract a more diverse and capable talent pool.

Practical Tip: Implement AI-based hiring tools such as HireVue, which uses video interviews analysed by AI to assess candidates' communication skills, problem-solving ability, and more—without being influenced by their gender, ethnicity, or appearance.

3. Enhancing Accessibility for Remote Workers

Diversity also includes individuals with disabilities. AI

is significantly improving the accessibility of remote workspaces for digital nomads with visual, auditory, or cognitive impairments. Tools like Otter.ai provide real-time captions for video calls, while Be My Eyes and Aira offer AI-powered support for visually impaired workers. AI tools can read documents aloud, interpret visual content, and help individuals navigate digital environments.

Practical Tip: Use tools like Otter.ai or Google's Live Caption feature in meetings to provide captions for team members with hearing impairments. Encourage the use of AI-powered screen readers like JAWS or NVDA to create an accessible work environment for those with visual impairments.

Inspire Through Visionary Perspectives

Imagine a future where AI doesn't just assist in D&I efforts —it actively champions them. In this future, AI could be capable of analysing team dynamics in real-time and offering suggestions for improving inclusivity. It might notice if certain voices aren't being heard or if team conversations tend to overlook certain perspectives. Based on these observations, the AI could suggest ways to engage those individuals or introduce new perspectives that would enhance the team's creativity and productivity.

Visionary Perspective: AI could act as an inclusivity advisor, scanning team communications to identify patterns of exclusion or bias and suggesting immediate corrective actions. For example, an AI assistant could recommend rotating leadership roles in meetings to ensure more diverse voices are heard, or flag instances of cultural insensitivity and offer suggestions for respectful dialogue.

Balance Between Inspiration and Caution

While AI is a powerful tool for promoting diversity and inclusion, it's important to approach its use with caution. Algorithms can unintentionally perpetuate bias if they're not carefully designed or regularly audited. AI systems learn from historical data, and if that data is biased, the AI will reflect those biases. Therefore, it's essential to combine AI's capabilities with human oversight to ensure that it remains a force for good.

Balanced Advice: Regularly audit AI tools for bias. AI alone isn't a solution to workplace diversity—humans must take responsibility for setting ethical guidelines and ensuring that AI operates fairly. Encourage open conversations within your team about AI's role in D&I and be transparent about how these tools are being used.

Highlight Global and Cultural Dimensions

Diversity and inclusion aren't limited to nationality or ethnicity—they also encompass the vast cultural differences that exist between regions. AI-powered tools are enabling digital nomads to navigate these cultural differences with more ease. For instance, platforms like CultureAmp provide insights into how cultural factors may influence workplace dynamics, helping managers foster more inclusive global teams.

Global Insight: Use AI tools like Glint or CultureAmp to gather feedback from team members on how culturally inclusive they feel the workplace is. AI can identify patterns of cultural misunderstanding and provide actionable steps for creating a more inclusive environment.

Motivate with Purpose and Fulfilment

Diversity and inclusion are more than just policies—they are the foundation for a purpose-driven work environment. By embracing AI to support D&I initiatives, digital nomads can create a workspace where all team members feel valued, respected, and motivated. Inclusivity drives creativity, innovation, and personal fulfilment, making it a cornerstone of thriving digital nomad communities.

Inspirational Reflection: Consider AI as a tool for unlocking your team's full potential. By embracing AI to support diversity, you are not only building a more inclusive workforce but also empowering individuals to bring their unique perspectives and talents to the table—leading to more innovative and fulfilling outcomes for all.

Use Accessible, Simple Language for Complex Topics

AI's role in diversity and inclusion doesn't have to be complex. Think of AI as an ally in making sure that everyone has a seat at the table. It removes barriers—whether those barriers are linguistic, cultural, or even unconscious biases in hiring.

Friendly Explanation: AI acts like a translator, a facilitator, and a guide in promoting diversity and inclusion. It helps ensure that voices from all corners of the world are heard, respected, and empowered. And it does this seamlessly, enabling teams to focus on what truly matters—collaboration and innovation.

Interactive and Engaging Content

Before you move on to the next chapter, take a few moments to reflect on how AI can enhance diversity and inclusion in your work life. Consider the AI tools discussed here and experiment with one that seems relevant to your work. Ask yourself: How can this tool help you bridge gaps in communication, understanding, or representation within your global team?

Conclusion

AI is transforming how we think about diversity and inclusion in the workplace, particularly for digital nomads. From facilitating real-time translations to offering bias-free hiring solutions, AI is opening doors for a more inclusive and equitable future. However, it's essential to approach AI as a tool that supports human-led initiatives and requires ongoing oversight to prevent bias. By embracing these tools and using them thoughtfully, digital nomads can create diverse, dynamic, and purpose-driven teams that thrive in today's globalized world.

CHAPTER 75: AI FOR MONITORING AND EVALUATING EMPLOYEE PERFORMANCE

How AI Is Changing the Way Companies Monitor and Evaluate Remote Workers and What It Means for Digital Nomads

In the world of remote work, one of the greatest challenges companies face is ensuring productivity and efficiency when employees are scattered across the globe. For digital nomads, this presents a unique opportunity—and a unique challenge. As a digital nomad, you're free from the constraints of the traditional office, but at the same time, you're part of a growing workforce that companies increasingly monitor and evaluate through artificial intelligence (AI). How does AI change the dynamics of performance monitoring? And more importantly, what does this mean for digital nomads?

In this chapter, we will explore how AI-powered tools are being used to monitor and evaluate employee performance in remote work environments. We'll discuss the advantages of AI in this field, the potential downsides, and how you, as a digital nomad, can make the most of these technologies to showcase your skills and efficiency. By incorporating real-life stories and actionable advice, we will highlight the transformative potential of AI while offering a balanced view of the implications it brings to the workforce.

Engage with Storytelling and Case Studies

Let's start with the story of Alex, a digital nomad who works as a project manager for a tech startup. Based in Bali but managing a team located in Europe and North America, Alex faced a dilemma. Despite delivering results, he struggled with the perception of being "disconnected" because he wasn't physically present in any office. When his company adopted an AI-powered productivity and performance tool, the game changed for Alex. The tool tracked work patterns, provided insights into team dynamics, and even recommended improvements based on data from hundreds of projects.

For the first time, Alex's true productivity was visible to everyone. The AI system logged his contributions, noted his communication with the team, and even measured the efficiency of his project timelines. As a result, Alex's performance was recognized not just for the work output, but for his ability to manage a global team efficiently. This transparency built trust and credibility, and Alex was promoted within six months.

Focus on Practical Application

AI has revolutionized the way companies monitor and evaluate performance, especially for remote workers and digital nomads. Here are some key AI tools and methods currently in use, along with practical tips on how you can leverage them to your advantage:

1. AI-Powered Task Management and Productivity Tools

AI tools like Trello, Asana, and Monday.com offer much more than task management. They use AI algorithms to track deadlines, monitor work patterns, and analyse productivity trends. These tools can highlight inefficiencies in workflows and suggest optimizations, all while offering real-time data on performance.

Practical Tip: Use AI-powered tools like RescueTime to monitor your productivity and ensure that you're on top of your tasks. These platforms can provide insights into your work habits, helping you identify the best times to focus and be more productive.

2. Performance Analytics and Feedback Tools

Companies increasingly rely on AI systems like Sapience or Veriato to track time spent on tasks, communication patterns, and overall engagement. These systems evaluate performance based on metrics such as response times, project progress, and collaboration levels. For digital nomads, this means that your work is being evaluated based on data rather than office presence, allowing you to focus on delivering high-quality results.

Practical Tip: Track your own performance data using these tools, and use the insights they provide to enhance your work. This could include improving response times, staying ahead of deadlines, or contributing more to team collaboration.

3. AI in Communication and Collaboration

Platforms like Slack and Microsoft Teams are already leveraging AI to analyse communication patterns. AI can measure engagement, detect gaps in collaboration, and even suggest improvements for team interactions. For remote workers, AI ensures that communication bottlenecks are identified and resolved quickly.

Practical Tip: Pay attention to AI insights that come from collaboration tools. If your communication is flagged as sporadic, take proactive steps to improve your visibility and engagement in team discussions.

Inspire Through Visionary Perspectives

The future of AI in performance evaluation is exciting and full of potential. Imagine a world where AI can evaluate soft skills like leadership, empathy, and creativity—skills traditionally hard to quantify. AI could also evolve to provide real-time feedback on your work, offering suggestions on how to improve your communication, manage tasks better, or optimize your work schedule based on peak performance times.

Visionary Perspective: Envision AI as your personal mentor, constantly giving you feedback not only on the quality of your work but on how you engage with others and contribute to team success. The more you embrace these tools, the more you can grow in your role and stand out in your career as a digital nomad.

Balance Between Inspiration and Caution

While AI offers incredible potential to help digital nomads showcase their performance, there are legitimate concerns about privacy and over-monitoring. AI tools that track time spent on specific websites, monitor keystrokes, or evaluate every email you send can feel invasive. The key is finding the balance between using AI for growth and ensuring it doesn't infringe on personal privacy or contribute to burnout.

Balanced Advice: Advocate for transparency in AI monitoring practices. Ensure that your employer clearly communicates what is being tracked and how it will be used. While AI can highlight areas for improvement, it's crucial to set boundaries to maintain work-life balance, particularly as a digital nomad.

Highlight Global and Cultural Dimensions

Digital nomads come from all corners of the world, and AI has the potential to remove biases from performance evaluations across different cultures. A worker from Asia might have different communication styles than someone from Europe, and AI can help bridge these gaps by evaluating everyone based on objective performance data rather than cultural differences.

Global Insight: Use AI tools to understand cultural nuances in team interactions. Tools like Slack can provide data on communication patterns, while AI-powered collaboration platforms can help ensure that cultural differences do not lead to misunderstandings or misjudged performance.

Motivate with Purpose and Fulfilment

AI in performance monitoring is not just about keeping track of tasks—it's about helping you grow in your career. Digital nomads can use AI to demonstrate their value to employers without being confined to traditional office metrics like "face time" or office hours. By embracing AI, you can show that productivity is about results, not location.

Inspirational Reflection: Think of AI as a tool that allows you to work smarter, not harder. It's a way to showcase your strengths as a digital nomad and make sure your performance is visible to those who matter. With AI, you can take ownership of your career growth and show the world what you're capable of—no matter where you are.

Use Accessible, Simple Language for Complex Topics

AI monitoring might sound complicated, but it's really just a smart assistant keeping track of how you're doing and offering ways to improve. It helps you stay organized, meet deadlines, and communicate more effectively with your team.

Friendly Explanation: Imagine having an assistant who keeps tabs on your work, gently reminding you when a deadline is approaching or offering tips on how to be more productive. That's essentially what AI monitoring tools do— they help you perform at your best.

Interactive and Engaging Content

Before you finish this chapter, take a moment to reflect on your current work habits. Are there areas where you feel you could improve? What tools are you using to track your performance? Spend a few minutes exploring an AI-powered tool like RescueTime or Monday.com. Set up a simple task-tracking system and see how AI can help streamline your workflow.

Conclusion

AI-powered tools for monitoring and evaluating performance are reshaping how companies manage their remote workers and digital nomads. By offering real-time feedback, tracking productivity, and providing insights into communication patterns, AI allows digital nomads to showcase their true value—based on results, not location. However, it's essential to maintain a balance between leveraging AI for growth and protecting your privacy. By embracing AI in performance evaluation, digital nomads can take control of their career trajectory and excel in an increasingly AI-driven world.

PART 16: AI-POWERED ENTREPRENEURSHIP FOR NOMADS

CHAPTER 76: STARTING AN AI-BASED BUSINESS AS A DIGITAL NOMAD

How Digital Nomads Can Create AI-Driven Startups

In today's rapidly changing work landscape, AI is not only a tool for remote workers and digital nomads, but it's also a powerful engine for entrepreneurship. Digital nomads, with their global perspectives and flexible lifestyles, are uniquely positioned to create AI-driven businesses that can thrive in an increasingly interconnected world. But what does it take to launch an AI-based startup while maintaining the freedom of the nomadic lifestyle?

This chapter will dive into the practicalities of starting an AI-powered business as a digital nomad, the opportunities AI offers in various industries, and the tools that make it possible to run an efficient and scalable business from anywhere in the world. Through storytelling and case studies, you'll gain insights into how others have successfully launched AI-driven businesses and the strategies they've used to overcome obstacles along the way.

Engage with Storytelling and Case Studies

Let's begin with the story of Mark, a digital nomad who was traveling through Central America while working as a freelance software developer. Mark had always been interested in AI but wasn't sure how to turn that interest into a scalable business. During a co-working session in Costa Rica, he met a fellow nomad who was struggling with customer support for her e-commerce business. This sparked an idea.

Mark used his AI skills to create an AI-driven chatbot that could handle customer inquiries and automate basic support functions. What started as a small project for one client turned into a full-fledged business when he realized that many small online businesses faced similar challenges. Using AI to solve real problems for global e-commerce stores, Mark's business quickly scaled. Today, Mark runs an AI-powered customer support business with clients in five countries—all while continuing to explore the world.

Mark's story demonstrates the immense potential AI offers for creating a sustainable, location-independent business. By identifying a common problem and applying AI technology to solve it, he was able to build a scalable business that supports his nomadic lifestyle.

Focus on Practical Application

If you're a digital nomad looking to start an AI-based business, here are some actionable steps to help you get started:

1. Identify a Problem AI Can Solve

Successful AI startups begin with a clear problem that AI can address. Whether it's streamlining business operations, improving customer experiences, or automating repetitive tasks, AI excels in making processes more efficient. Start by identifying a pain point within an industry you're familiar with. For example, AI can be applied in industries like e-commerce (AI-driven chatbots), healthcare (AI for diagnostic tools), and education (AI-powered learning platforms).

Practical Tip: Use your unique position as a global nomad to tap into different markets and identify problems that may not be visible from a single location. Attend local meetups, engage with local entrepreneurs, and observe global business trends.

2. Choose the Right AI Tools

The beauty of starting an AI-driven business today is that many of the tools you need are readily available and accessible. You don't need to build everything from scratch. Platforms like Google Cloud AI, Amazon Web Services (AWS), and IBM Watson offer powerful AI tools and APIs that you can integrate into your business.

Practical Tip: Start with free or low-cost AI tools to prototype your solution. Many platforms offer generous free tiers for startups, so you can experiment without a significant financial commitment. For example, OpenAI's GPT-3 can be used for natural language processing tasks, and TensorFlow is a great tool for developing machine learning models.

3. Build a Minimal Viable Product (MVP)

As a digital nomad, one of the best ways to test the viability of your AI startup is to build an MVP—a simple version of your product that solves the core problem without all the bells and whistles. An MVP allows you to test your concept with real users and gather feedback, enabling you to iterate and improve the product over time.

Practical Tip: Use platforms like Upwork or Fiverr to hire talent for parts of the project that are outside your skill set.

As a nomad, you can build a virtual team of freelancers from around the world to help you bring your AI solution to life.

Inspire Through Visionary Perspectives

The future of AI-powered businesses is vast and filled with opportunity. As AI technology continues to evolve, the barriers to entry for starting a tech business are lowering. Imagine a world where AI handles everything from mundane administrative tasks to complex decision-making processes. What could your life as a digital nomad look like when AI runs most of your business operations?

Visionary Perspective: AI enables entrepreneurs to scale their businesses rapidly and efficiently. The key is thinking beyond current technologies and imagining how AI can be integrated into new industries and markets. The next great AI startup could come from a digital nomad working in a beachside café in Bali or a remote village in Thailand. With AI, the world is your office, and the opportunities are limitless.

Balance Between Inspiration and Caution

While AI offers a promising pathway for starting a scalable business, there are also challenges. One of the biggest concerns for digital nomads is the potential for job displacement caused by AI automation. As AI replaces certain job functions, some traditional roles may diminish, but this also creates space for new opportunities in AI-related fields.

Balanced Advice: Focus on building AI solutions that enhance human potential rather than replace it. Use AI to complement human creativity and problem-solving, creating tools that improve the way people work rather than taking away opportunities. By positioning your AI-driven startup as a tool for empowerment, you'll be able to navigate the balance between automation and job creation.

Highlight Global and Cultural Dimensions

Digital nomads are global citizens, and AI businesses founded by nomads are uniquely positioned to operate across borders. This global perspective is an advantage when building AI startups because you can tap into diverse markets and cater to the specific needs of different cultures. AI can also help bridge cultural gaps, providing solutions that are scalable across multiple regions.

Global Insight: For example, AI-powered translation tools like DeepL or Google Translate can help businesses operate in multiple languages, allowing you to serve clients in various countries without language barriers. As a digital nomad, you can use your global experience to tailor your AI product to diverse markets and cultures.

Motivate with Purpose and Fulfilment

One of the most fulfilling aspects of starting an AI-driven business as a digital nomad is the ability to pursue a life of purpose while maintaining financial independence. With AI taking over repetitive tasks and optimizing operations, you have more time to focus on what matters most—whether it's exploring new cultures, pursuing passion projects, or contributing to causes that inspire you.

Inspirational Reflection: By harnessing the power of AI, you can design a business that aligns with your values and allows you to live a life of freedom and purpose. The key is not just to create a profitable business, but to use AI as a tool to improve both your work and your life.

Use Accessible, Simple Language for Complex Topics

AI can seem like a complex topic, but it doesn't have to be intimidating. Starting an AI-driven business is like hiring a smart assistant to handle tasks that would normally require hours of work. Think of AI as a tool that can help you scale your efforts, making it easier to manage multiple aspects of your business without being tied down to one location.

Conclusion: Take Action

Starting an AI-based business as a digital nomad is an exciting and achievable goal. By identifying a problem, leveraging AI tools, and building a minimal viable product, you can create a business that scales across borders while maintaining the freedom to work from anywhere in the world. With the power of AI, the possibilities are endless. All it takes is an idea and the willingness to embrace the future of technology. Now, it's your turn—what AI-driven solution will you build to shape the future of digital nomadism?

CHAPTER 77: AI AND E-COMMERCE FOR NOMADS

How AI is Transforming E-Commerce Opportunities for Digital Nomads

In the ever-evolving world of e-commerce, AI is more than just a trend—it's a game changer. As digital nomads, the freedom to build and scale businesses from anywhere in the world has been amplified by the power of AI. Whether you're a solopreneur selling handmade crafts or an entrepreneur running a global dropshipping empire, AI is reshaping the way e-commerce businesses operate, providing more opportunities than ever before. This chapter will explore how digital nomads are leveraging AI to create successful e-commerce businesses, streamline operations, and thrive in a competitive marketplace.

Engage with Storytelling and Case Studies

Meet Lisa, a digital nomad who travels between Mexico, Bali, and Portugal. After leaving her corporate marketing job, she decided to launch her own e-commerce store selling eco-friendly skincare products. But with minimal experience in running a business and a saturated market, she needed an edge to grow her brand while maintaining her nomadic lifestyle.

Lisa discovered the power of AI tools designed for e-commerce. She started using Shopify's AI-driven product recommendations to offer personalized suggestions to her customers based on their browsing behaviour. This not only improved the customer experience but also increased sales by 30% within a few months. Additionally, Lisa used AI-powered inventory management systems to automate reordering stock and ensure she never ran out of her best-selling products.

But the real turning point came when Lisa adopted AI-driven marketing tools like Jasper AI to generate content for her website and social media channels. This allowed her to engage with customers without spending hours drafting posts or email campaigns. Now, Lisa runs a thriving e-commerce business from anywhere in the world, all thanks to AI.

Lisa's story is just one example of how AI has transformed the e-commerce landscape for digital nomads. The integration of AI allows nomads to automate tasks, scale their businesses, and maintain the flexibility they crave while growing a global brand.

Focus on Practical Application

If you're a digital nomad considering entering the e-commerce space, here are the ways AI can help you streamline operations and grow your business:

1. Personalized Shopping Experiences

AI-powered tools can analyse customer behaviour, helping e-commerce stores provide personalized product recommendations. Platforms like Shopify and BigCommerce have integrated AI features that analyse browsing data, purchase history, and preferences to offer tailored suggestions, driving conversions.

Practical Tip: Leverage AI-driven recommendation engines to create a more personalized shopping experience for your customers. The better your store can anticipate customer needs, the higher your chances of increasing sales and retaining loyal clients.

2. Inventory Management Automation

AI can also help automate one of the most tedious aspects of e-commerce—inventory management. AI-powered systems can predict demand based on trends, past sales, and seasonal patterns, ensuring you always have the right amount of stock. This reduces human error, saves time, and ensures you avoid costly stockouts or overstocking.

Practical Tip: Use AI tools like TradeGecko or Skubana to streamline your inventory management and automatically reorder products when supplies run low.

3. AI-Driven Customer Support

As a digital nomad, you may not always be available to respond to customer inquiries, especially if you're traveling across time zones. AI chatbots can fill this gap, offering instant customer support. Chatbots like Tidio or Zendesk use AI to provide real-time responses to common customer questions, improving the overall customer experience and boosting retention.

Practical Tip: Implement an AI chatbot on your website to handle frequently asked questions and support tickets. This ensures 24/7 support, even while you're on a plane or enjoying time offline.

Inspire Through Visionary Perspectives

The future of AI in e-commerce is filled with possibilities, especially for digital nomads. Imagine a world where AI-powered virtual shopping assistants guide your customers through the buying process, or where machine learning predicts market trends with unparalleled accuracy, allowing you to adapt your business strategy on the fly.

Visionary Perspective: As AI continues to evolve, the role of the entrepreneur will shift from managing day-to-day tasks to focusing on innovation and strategy. In the near future, AI may even help digital nomads create fully autonomous businesses—operations that run smoothly with minimal human input, giving you even more time to pursue your passions and explore the world. The key is to stay ahead of the curve, continuously learning and adopting the latest AI advancements.

Balance Between Inspiration and Caution

While AI brings a wealth of opportunities to e-commerce, it also presents challenges that digital nomads must be prepared to navigate. The rise of AI in customer interactions, for example, can sometimes depersonalize the shopping experience if not used carefully. Moreover, as AI tools become more sophisticated, competition in the e-commerce space will intensify.

Balanced Advice: Focus on using AI as a tool to enhance, not replace, the human touch in your business. For example, while AI chatbots are great for initial interactions, always provide an option for customers to reach a real person if needed. Stay mindful of how AI affects your business strategy and make sure it aligns with your values of creating meaningful customer relationships.

Highlight Global and Cultural Dimensions

One of the greatest advantages of being a digital nomad in the AI age is the ability to operate a truly global business. AI tools like DeepL for translation or Google's Natural Language Processing (NLP) for cross-cultural communication can help you break down language barriers and tap into international markets with ease.

Global Insight: With AI handling translation and localization, your e-commerce store can cater to customers in different regions, from Southeast Asia to South America. This opens up vast opportunities for growth, allowing you to build a brand that resonates across cultures.

Motivate with Purpose and Fulfilment

Building an AI-powered e-commerce business as a digital nomad isn't just about financial freedom—it's about creating a life that aligns with your values and aspirations. AI allows you to automate the mundane aspects of running a business, giving you the freedom to focus on what truly matters: whether it's exploring new destinations, working on creative projects, or dedicating time to social causes that inspire you.

Inspirational Reflection: By integrating AI into your business, you can achieve the perfect balance between work and lifestyle. AI allows you to scale without losing the freedom to live life on your own terms. It's a powerful tool for unlocking both professional success and personal fulfilment.

Use Accessible, Simple Language for Complex Topics

AI may seem daunting, but it's just another tool in your entrepreneurial toolkit. Think of AI as your personal assistant, capable of automating repetitive tasks and analysing vast amounts of data to help you make informed decisions. It's not magic—it's technology that simplifies your business and makes it more efficient.

Interactive and Engaging Content

Here's a quick exercise: Spend 15 minutes exploring AI-driven e-commerce tools like Shopify's Kit, which helps you create and manage Facebook ads using AI. After you've tested it, reflect on how it could improve your marketing efforts. What tasks could you automate to save time, and how could AI help you reach a wider audience?

Conclusion: Take Action

AI is revolutionizing e-commerce for digital nomads, offering powerful tools to scale businesses, improve customer experiences, and operate across borders. By embracing AI, you can streamline operations, automate tasks, and focus on growing a brand that aligns with your lifestyle. Now is the time to take advantage of the AI revolution in e-commerce and create a business that not only supports your nomadic life but also thrives in the global marketplace. What will you build with the power of AI?

CHAPTER 78: AI FOR MARKETING YOUR BUSINESS

What AI Tools Are Essential for Digital Nomad Entrepreneurs to Market Their Businesses?

As a digital nomad entrepreneur, marketing is the lifeblood of your business. However, balancing effective marketing with the demands of travel, project management, and personal life can be daunting. Fortunately, artificial intelligence (AI) offers a host of tools designed to make marketing more efficient, targeted, and scalable. This chapter dives into the essential AI-powered marketing tools that digital nomads are using to automate, optimize, and grow their businesses while enjoying the freedom of a nomadic lifestyle.

Engage with Storytelling and Case Studies

Let's meet Tom, a digital nomad who's been running an online coaching business while hopping from one destination to another. Tom had a great business model, but his marketing efforts were sporadic due to time zone differences, shifting client needs, and the inconsistency that comes with frequent travel. After struggling to keep up with content creation, social media engagement, and lead generation, Tom discovered AI-powered marketing tools.

He started using Jasper AI to generate blog posts, social media captions, and email content. This tool allowed him to produce high-quality content in a fraction of the time it used to take. Meanwhile, Tom also implemented Hootsuite's AI-driven social media scheduler, which enabled him to manage multiple platforms and schedule posts in advance. He even experimented with Phrasee, an AI tool that optimizes email subject lines, improving his open rates by 20%.

Tom's transformation wasn't just about automation. The AI tools he employed gave him back hours of his week and allowed him to focus on what mattered most: providing exceptional coaching services and exploring new destinations. With AI handling much of the marketing grunt work, Tom's revenue increased by 40% in just six months— all while he jetted from Europe to Southeast Asia.

Tom's story highlights how AI has become a valuable partner for digital nomads who want to scale their marketing efforts without sacrificing their freedom. Through strategic use of AI, nomads can unlock new levels of efficiency, creativity, and business growth.

Focus on Practical Application

If you're a digital nomad entrepreneur, here are some AI tools and techniques that can elevate your marketing strategy:

1. Content Creation with AI Writing Tools

One of the most time-consuming tasks for any entrepreneur is content creation. Whether it's blog posts, social media updates, or email newsletters, keeping your audience engaged requires a steady flow of fresh, relevant content. AI-powered tools like Jasper AI and Copy.ai are designed to assist with generating high-quality content quickly.

Practical Tip: Use these tools to brainstorm blog post ideas, write introductory paragraphs, or generate catchy social media captions. They can also help repurpose existing content, making it easier to post regularly without starting from scratch every time.

2. Automating Social Media with AI

Managing multiple social media accounts can be overwhelming, especially when you're on the move. AI-powered social media platforms like Hootsuite and Buffer allow you to schedule posts in advance, manage customer interactions, and analyse performance metrics in real time.

Practical Tip: Schedule your social media content at the beginning of each month using AI-driven platforms. This will give you the freedom to focus on traveling and other business activities without worrying about posting daily.

3. AI-Powered SEO Optimization

To attract organic traffic, optimizing your website for search engines is crucial. Tools like SurferSEO and MarketMuse use AI to analyse your website content and suggest improvements that can boost your ranking on Google. These tools can help with keyword research, content optimization, and competitive analysis.

Practical Tip: Use AI-powered SEO tools to audit your site and identify areas for improvement. Many of these platforms can automatically recommend keywords and even rewrite sections of your content for better ranking.

Inspire Through Visionary Perspectives

AI's potential in marketing is far-reaching, and the future is filled with exciting possibilities. Imagine a world where your marketing efforts are fully automated, with AI algorithms running A/B tests, segmenting your audiences, and delivering personalized experiences to your customers across all channels.

Visionary Perspective: In the near future, AI could make marketing more predictive. For example, machine learning algorithms might identify patterns in consumer behaviour and predict which products or services are most likely to sell in specific regions. Imagine an AI tool that understands your audience better than you do and can automatically adjust your marketing messages based on real-time data. The opportunities are endless, and digital nomads who embrace AI early on will have a competitive edge.

Balance Between Inspiration and Caution

While AI-powered marketing tools are incredibly powerful, it's important to balance automation with authenticity. There's a risk that relying too much on AI could make your marketing feel impersonal, detaching you from your audience.

Balanced Advice: Use AI to handle repetitive tasks, but ensure that your brand voice remains human and relatable. Incorporate your personal experiences and values into your marketing content. This will help you build genuine connections with your audience and avoid the pitfalls of over-automation.

Highlight Global and Cultural Dimensions

As a digital nomad, you're operating in a global marketplace. AI tools can help you localize your marketing campaigns for different regions and cultures. For instance, platforms like Unbabel use AI to provide real-time translations and localization services, making it easier for you to communicate with customers in multiple languages.

Global Insight: Leveraging AI to localize content for international markets is an untapped opportunity for many digital nomads. Tailoring your marketing efforts to resonate with local audiences can greatly expand your reach, allowing you to grow your business across continents with minimal effort.

Motivate with Purpose and Fulfilment

Marketing isn't just about generating leads and making sales —it's about connecting with your audience in meaningful ways. AI allows you to automate mundane tasks so you can focus on creating a brand that aligns with your purpose. Whether you're passionate about sustainability, travel, or personal development, AI frees up time to focus on what truly matters.

Inspirational Reflection: By integrating AI into your marketing strategy, you're not just optimizing your business —you're creating more space for personal fulfilment. With the help of AI, you can engage your audience, share your passions, and build a purpose-driven business that aligns with your values.

Use Accessible, Simple Language for Complex Topics

AI may sound technical, but it's just a tool that can make your life easier. Think of AI as an assistant that takes care of the busy work, like scheduling posts or analysing data, so you can focus on the creative and strategic aspects of your business.

Simple Analogy: Imagine AI as a co-pilot on your entrepreneurial journey. While you're steering the ship, AI is in the background, helping you navigate by adjusting the sails and ensuring you stay on course. It's not replacing you—it's enhancing what you do.

Interactive and Engaging Content

Before you finish this chapter, take a moment to explore one of the AI marketing tools mentioned. Spend 15 minutes on Jasper AI or Hootsuite, and experiment with automating a marketing task. Reflect on how it changed your workflow: Did it save you time? Did it help you think of new content ideas?

Final Style Summary

AI is revolutionizing the way digital nomads market their businesses, offering tools that save time, optimize content, and personalize interactions. By integrating AI into your marketing strategy, you can free up time to focus on growing your business while exploring the world. The future of marketing is bright, and by harnessing the power of AI, you'll be well-positioned to thrive in the competitive global marketplace.

With the right blend of technology, strategy, and personal touch, you can take your digital nomad business to new heights. Let AI handle the heavy lifting while you focus on building the life and business of your dreams. What marketing potential will you unlock with AI?

CHAPTER 79: SCALING A GLOBAL BUSINESS WITH AI

How Can AI Help Nomad Entrepreneurs Scale Their Operations Globally?

As the digital nomad lifestyle continues to flourish, more entrepreneurs are realizing the incredible potential of leveraging artificial intelligence (AI) to scale their businesses across borders. With AI, the barriers of time zones, language, and logistical complexity are no longer obstacles, but opportunities. In this chapter, we will explore how AI empowers nomad entrepreneurs to scale globally, touching on real-life success stories, practical applications, and the visionary possibilities that AI brings to the table.

Engage with Storytelling and Case Studies

Meet Maya, a digital nomad who runs a thriving e-commerce business selling handmade, eco-friendly products sourced from around the world. While based in Bali, Maya's business initially catered to local markets in Southeast Asia. However, Maya dreamed of expanding her operations globally, reaching markets in Europe, North America, and beyond. The challenge? She needed to scale her marketing, customer service, and logistics—without hiring a massive team or losing the freedom to travel.

Enter AI.

Maya began using Shopify's AI-powered analytics to understand her customers' preferences in different regions. This allowed her to create targeted marketing campaigns that resonated with her international audiences. She also integrated AI-powered chatbots, like Tidio, to handle customer service queries in multiple languages. This gave Maya the ability to support her global clientele without being glued to her phone or laptop.

What really set Maya's business apart, however, was the integration of AI-driven supply chain management tools. These tools analysed global shipping patterns, predicting the most efficient routes and times for delivery. Maya was able to minimize delays, optimize shipping costs, and manage inventory seamlessly—even while backpacking through South America.

With AI at the core of her operations, Maya expanded her e-commerce business to over 30 countries in just two years, all while maintaining her digital nomad lifestyle. AI didn't just automate tasks—it gave Maya the freedom to scale her business on her terms.

Focus on Practical Application

If you're looking to scale your business as a digital nomad, here's how AI can become your most valuable ally:

1. AI-Powered Customer Support

Providing timely and personalized customer support is crucial when scaling internationally. With AI, digital nomads can deploy chatbots like Tidio or Zendesk that handle queries 24/7 in multiple languages. These AI tools can process common customer inquiries, recommend products, or troubleshoot issues, providing fast and effective support without you needing to be constantly online.

Practical Tip: Start by integrating an AI chatbot to manage customer interactions. These bots learn from customer behaviour over time, becoming more efficient at resolving issues without human intervention.

2. Global Marketing with AI

Marketing across borders requires an understanding of local preferences, behaviours, and trends. AI tools like Google Analytics and HubSpot offer deep insights into audience behaviour across different countries. By using AI for market analysis, you can tailor your advertising and content strategies to resonate with global customers.

Practical Tip: Leverage AI-driven tools to segment your audience based on geography, behaviour, and preferences. This way, you can create targeted marketing campaigns that speak to the unique needs of each market.

3. Scaling Operations with AI Supply Chain Management

AI-driven logistics platforms like ClearMetal or ShipHawk offer predictive analytics that can optimize your supply chain. Whether it's forecasting demand, managing inventory, or selecting the most efficient shipping routes, AI ensures you stay ahead of logistical challenges as you scale internationally.

Practical Tip: Use AI to predict demand fluctuations across different regions. This allows you to plan inventory more accurately, reduce waste, and optimize shipping costs.

Inspire Through Visionary Perspectives

The potential for AI in scaling global businesses is limitless.

Imagine a future where AI not only manages customer service, marketing, and logistics but also adapts to regional economic trends in real-time. AI could potentially anticipate market shifts, allowing digital nomads to adjust strategies before competitors even realize changes are happening.

Visionary Perspective: Consider an AI platform that not only manages operations but continuously learns and adapts to global market conditions. Such an AI could analyse economic forecasts, predict product demand in emerging markets, and provide insights on where to launch your next marketing campaign—making scaling globally almost effortless.

Balance Between Inspiration and Caution

AI presents incredible opportunities, but it's important to approach this powerful tool with both inspiration and caution. Automating too many aspects of your business can lead to a loss of personal touch—something that's crucial for building relationships with international customers.

Balanced Advice: Use AI to scale repetitive or data-driven tasks but maintain a personal connection with your audience. While AI can handle customer inquiries or social media posts, personal touches, such as handwritten thank-you notes or personalized video messages, will set your brand apart in a world increasingly dominated by automation.

Highlight Global and Cultural Dimensions

Scaling a business globally also requires understanding and respecting different cultures. AI can support this by offering localized content and customer service. For example, AI-driven platforms like Unbabel provide translation services that can help you communicate with customers in their native languages, while tools like Phrasee can adapt your marketing content to match local cultural nuances.

Global Insight: Use AI tools to localize your messaging. The way you market a product in Spain may differ from how you promote it in Japan. By utilizing AI for real-time translations and regional insights, you'll avoid cultural missteps and build trust with global customers.

Motivate with Purpose and Fulfilment

Scaling a global business isn't just about profit. For digital nomads, it's often tied to a larger purpose—whether that's creating a sustainable business, supporting local communities, or championing a cause. AI frees you from the daily grind, enabling you to focus on the bigger picture of why you started your business in the first place.

Inspirational Reflection: By leveraging AI, you're not only growing your business but also creating more time to pursue meaningful work. Whether it's engaging in passion projects or using your business to impact the world positively, AI gives you the freedom to scale with purpose.

Use Accessible, Simple Language for Complex Topics

AI might sound like a complex, technical concept, but think of it as your business assistant—always there, always learning, and always optimizing. It's like having a team member who never sleeps, is highly efficient, and constantly improves your operations.

Simple Analogy: Imagine AI as a virtual operations manager who oversees your marketing, logistics, and customer service, ensuring everything runs smoothly while you focus on your creative and strategic goals.

Interactive and Engaging Content

Before you move on to the next chapter, consider trying one of the AI tools mentioned here. Spend time exploring how AI-driven logistics platforms or customer support chatbots could simplify and scale your business. Reflect: How can these tools free up more time for you to focus on strategy and growth?

Final Style Summary

AI provides an unparalleled opportunity for digital nomads to scale their businesses globally while maintaining the freedom to travel and explore. By using AI for customer service, marketing, logistics, and beyond, you can manage complex operations effortlessly, reaching customers in new regions and markets.

With AI, the world truly becomes your office. As you embrace these tools, you're not just building a business—you're creating a scalable, impactful enterprise that can thrive anywhere. What's your next step in harnessing the power of AI to grow your global business?

The future of scaling globally with AI is already here. Now is the time to embrace this technology and leverage it to turn your entrepreneurial dreams into reality. What global opportunities will AI open for you?

CHAPTER 80: AI AND FINANCIAL MANAGEMENT FOR NOMAD ENTREPRENEURS

How Digital Nomads Can Use AI to Manage Finances and Optimize Their Businesses

As a digital nomad entrepreneur, one of the key challenges you face is managing your finances while constantly on the move. Whether you're working from a café in Lisbon or a beach in Bali, maintaining control over your financial health is essential. Fortunately, AI has revolutionized financial management for digital nomads, providing tools that streamline everything from invoicing to tax optimization. In this chapter, we'll dive into how AI can help digital nomads manage their finances efficiently and optimize their businesses for long-term success.

Engage with Storytelling and Case Studies

Let's start with a real-world example. Alex, a digital nomad from Australia, runs a freelance consulting business while traveling across Europe. Like many nomad entrepreneurs, he found managing his income, taxes, and expenses a constant headache. Invoicing clients in different currencies, tracking expenses, and ensuring he had enough cash flow to support his travels added unnecessary stress to his otherwise dream lifestyle.

Then Alex discovered QuickBooks AI-powered financial management software. The platform automatically tracked his income, categorized his expenses, and even generated reports to help him understand his spending habits. Using AI-driven algorithms, QuickBooks also provided Alex with insights into his tax liabilities in each country he worked in, helping him plan ahead and avoid unpleasant surprises during tax season.

What used to take Alex hours of manual work was now automated and simplified by AI. With the help of AI, Alex optimized his finances, allowing him to focus on growing his business rather than worrying about paperwork.

Focus on Practical Application

So, how can you integrate AI into your financial management as a digital nomad entrepreneur? Here are some practical ways AI can help optimize your finances and business operations:

1. AI-Powered Invoicing and Payments

One of the most time-consuming aspects of running a nomadic business is invoicing and managing payments. AI-powered tools like FreshBooks and QuickBooks can automate this process, generating and sending invoices, tracking payment statuses, and even following up on overdue payments. You can invoice in multiple currencies and accept payments from clients around the world with ease.

Practical Tip: Use AI invoicing software that syncs with your bank accounts and provides real-time insights into your cash flow. This way, you can ensure that payments are on track without manual intervention.

2. Expense Tracking and Categorization

Managing your expenses while traveling can be overwhelming. AI tools like Expensify automate expense tracking, allowing you to snap photos of receipts on the go. The AI will categorize them for you, saving you from manually entering expenses and ensuring you're ready come tax time.

Practical Tip: Set up automatic categorization rules for common expenses, like meals, transportation, and accommodation. This will ensure all your costs are tracked without needing constant attention.

3. Tax Optimization with AI

As a digital nomad working in multiple countries, tax planning can be a complex task. AI tax software like Taxfyle or TurboTax AI offers tailored solutions that calculate your taxes based on the jurisdictions you work in. These tools also help you identify deductions and credits, ensuring you don't overpay.

Practical Tip: Use AI-driven tax software that tracks your location and income to give you insights into your tax obligations in real-time. This helps avoid underpayment or penalties, and keeps your financials in order.

4. AI for Budgeting and Cash Flow Forecasting

Predicting cash flow as a freelancer or entrepreneur is often tricky, but AI makes this easier. Tools like Fathom and Float provide real-time budgeting and cash flow forecasting by analysing your income, expenses, and trends over time.

These AI tools allow you to make informed decisions about your finances, ensuring that you never run into liquidity issues while scaling your business.

Practical Tip: Regularly check your AI-powered budgeting tool to ensure your business is on track financially. These forecasts can help you decide when to invest, hire new talent, or save for the future.

Inspire Through Visionary Perspectives

The future of AI-powered financial management holds even more promise for digital nomads. Imagine a system where AI not only tracks your finances but also makes real-time investment recommendations based on market trends, or even automatically adjusts your budget based on fluctuating currency rates.

Visionary Perspective: In the near future, AI could provide personalized financial planning, suggesting investment opportunities while you travel. AI algorithms could optimize your savings in high-yield accounts or even suggest cost-effective travel routes based on your financial goals.

Balance Between Inspiration and Caution

While AI offers incredible opportunities to automate and optimize financial management, it's essential to maintain a balanced approach. Over-reliance on AI without understanding your finances can lead to mistakes, especially when software updates or errors occur.

Balanced Advice: Use AI to handle routine and time-consuming tasks like invoicing, budgeting, and tax preparation, but keep an eye on the bigger picture. Regularly review your financial reports to ensure everything is on track and align AI recommendations with your long-term goals.

Highlight Global and Cultural Dimensions

For nomad entrepreneurs who work across borders, the complexity of managing finances multiplies. Different countries have different tax laws, currencies, and banking systems. AI tools, such as Wise for cross-border payments or Xero for international accounting, help bridge these gaps. AI can assist with currency conversion, ensure compliance with local tax laws, and provide clarity on your global financial position.

Global Insight: Using AI tools that specialize in international transactions, like Wise, can help you avoid high conversion fees and navigate complex tax laws in various countries.

Motivate with Purpose and Fulfilment

By embracing AI for financial management, you're not just streamlining your business operations—you're freeing up time to focus on what matters most. Whether it's pursuing your passion, growing your business, or spending more time exploring new cultures, AI allows you to lead a more fulfilling life as a digital nomad.

Inspirational Reflection: By offloading the time-consuming aspects of financial management to AI, you have more bandwidth to focus on achieving your personal and professional goals. Whether that's launching new projects or simply enjoying your nomadic lifestyle, AI ensures that you remain financially stable and secure.

Use Accessible, Simple Language for Complex Topics

AI in financial management might sound intimidating, but it's really just like having a virtual accountant. Think of AI as your financial assistant, automating routine tasks, offering recommendations, and keeping everything organized while you focus on growing your business.

Simple Analogy: Imagine AI as a smart personal accountant, who tracks all your expenses, predicts future financial needs, and files your taxes—all while you sip your coffee on a sunny terrace in Italy.

Interactive and Engaging Content

Before you move on to the next chapter, try using an AI financial tool like QuickBooks or Expensify. Spend a few minutes entering your recent expenses and observe how the tool automatically organizes and categorizes your data. Reflect: How did AI improve your financial workflow, and how could this automation free up more of your time?

Final Style Summary

AI offers an unparalleled opportunity for digital nomads to streamline financial management and focus on their business's growth. By integrating AI tools for invoicing, expense tracking, tax optimization, and cash flow forecasting, you can manage your finances effortlessly— even from a remote island. AI isn't just about automating tasks; it's about giving you the freedom to thrive, no matter where you are in the world.

As you embrace AI in your financial management, you'll find that the complexities of running a global business become more manageable, allowing you to live the nomadic life you've always dreamed of. The future of financial freedom as a digital nomad is already here—are you ready to embrace it?

PART 17: AI AND THE EVOLUTION OF CREATIVITY FOR NOMADS

CHAPTER 81: AI AS A CREATIVE PARTNER

How Digital Nomads Can Work with AI as Creative Collaborators in Content Creation

The rise of AI has transformed not only the way digital nomads work but also how they create. As a digital nomad, you may find yourself balancing multiple creative tasks —whether that's developing content for clients, creating marketing materials for your own business, or pursuing passion projects. Fortunately, AI has become a powerful creative partner, enabling you to unlock new levels of productivity, creativity, and efficiency. This chapter explores how digital nomads can work with AI as collaborators in content creation and thrive in this dynamic landscape.

Engage with Storytelling and Case Studies

Take the case of Amanda, a travel blogger and digital nomad who spends her time exploring remote destinations across the globe. With a growing audience on Instagram and YouTube, Amanda was finding it increasingly difficult to create fresh, engaging content on a daily basis while maintaining her freelance work as a copywriter. She turned to AI to lighten the creative load.

Amanda discovered Jasper AI, an AI writing tool that helped her generate blog posts and social media content in a fraction of the time it used to take. Using Jasper, she could input basic prompts, and the AI would produce well-structured drafts based on her style preferences. Instead of spending hours researching and drafting posts, she now had a strong foundation to build on, giving her more time to focus on photography and video content.

With the help of Lumen5, an AI-powered video creation tool, Amanda transformed her blog content into visually appealing videos for her YouTube channel, further expanding her reach. AI didn't replace her creative voice—it amplified it, allowing her to do more with less time. Her followers began to notice a consistent flow of high-quality content, and her business thrived as a result.

Focus on Practical Application

So, how can you, as a digital nomad, harness AI to boost your creative endeavours? Here are some practical ways AI can serve as a creative partner in content creation:

1. AI-Powered Writing Assistants

AI writing tools like Jasper AI and Copy.ai can generate blog posts, product descriptions, marketing copy, and even creative stories. These tools use natural language processing to understand your input and produce high-quality drafts that you can then refine.

Practical Tip: Use AI writing assistants to create content outlines or first drafts. They can help you overcome writer's block by offering creative suggestions, helping you maintain a consistent flow of content.

2. Visual Content Creation with AI

Tools like Canva Pro and Designify use AI to help you design eye-catching graphics, logos, and marketing materials. Whether you're creating Instagram posts,

YouTube thumbnails, or business presentations, AI-powered design tools offer customizable templates and suggestions that streamline your creative workflow.

Practical Tip: Leverage AI design tools to maintain a consistent visual style across your platforms. With the ability to automatically apply brand colours, fonts, and design elements, AI allows you to produce professional-quality visuals without needing expert design skills.

3. AI for Video Editing and Production

AI tools like Lumen5 and Magisto can turn text-based content into dynamic videos with minimal effort. By analysing the structure of your content, these platforms select relevant visuals, apply transitions, and add music or voiceovers, creating engaging videos in minutes.

Practical Tip: Use AI video creation platforms to repurpose your blog posts or written content into short, shareable videos for platforms like YouTube, Instagram, or TikTok. This not only expands your reach but also saves you time on manual editing.

4. AI for Image Editing and Enhancement

When working remotely, finding time to perfect your visual content can be challenging. AI-powered image editing tools like Luminar AI and Photoshop's AI features can enhance your photos automatically, applying filters, correcting lighting, and removing unwanted elements.

Practical Tip: Let AI handle the technical side of photo editing so you can focus on capturing authentic, creative moments. With features like sky replacement, portrait enhancement, and automatic adjustments, AI tools make photo editing easier and faster.

Inspire Through Visionary Perspectives

Looking ahead, the relationship between digital nomads and AI will only grow more dynamic and collaborative. Imagine a future where AI tools evolve into full-fledged creative collaborators—able to suggest new content ideas, develop sophisticated marketing strategies, or even create personalized artwork and animations on demand. Rather than seeing AI as a threat to creativity, nomads can view it as a tool to amplify their creative potential.

Visionary Perspective: AI could soon become the ultimate creative partner, offering real-time collaboration on projects, suggesting ways to improve content, and even generating personalized designs based on your audience's preferences. Imagine the possibilities when AI understands your style so well that it can assist with branding, storyboarding, and content development—all while you focus on strategy and growth.

Balance Between Inspiration and Caution

While AI offers exciting creative possibilities, it's essential to recognize its limitations. AI is powerful, but it's not perfect. The creative process still requires human oversight, and AI-generated content should be reviewed, refined, and personalized to maintain authenticity. Using AI as a tool rather than a crutch is key.

Balanced Advice: Always ensure that AI-generated content aligns with your brand's voice and values. AI can generate the foundation for your work, but it's up to you to inject the personality, emotion, and storytelling that resonate with your audience.

Highlight Global and Cultural Dimensions

As digital nomads work across borders and cultures, AI can be a valuable ally in ensuring content is culturally relevant and resonates with diverse audiences. For instance, AI-powered translation tools like DeepL allow you to create content in multiple languages, while AI sentiment analysis can help gauge how content might be perceived by different cultural groups.

Global Insight: Use AI to localize your content and ensure its relevant to your target audience, no matter where they're based. AI-driven analytics can also help you tailor your content strategy for different cultural preferences, ensuring that your brand connects with global audiences.

Motivate with Purpose and Fulfilment

By working with AI as a creative collaborator, you're not just streamlining your workflow—you're freeing up time to focus on what matters most. Whether it's exploring new destinations, deepening your creative projects, or finding more time to relax, AI can help you create a more balanced and fulfilling digital nomad lifestyle.

Inspirational Reflection: The more time you save with AI, the more freedom you have to pursue your creative passions or explore new cultures. Rather than seeing AI as a shortcut, think of it as a way to enhance your creativity and make space for the experiences that matter to you.

Use Accessible, Simple Language for Complex Topics

AI in content creation might sound complex, but it's simply a helpful assistant that can automate repetitive tasks. Think of it as a creative co-pilot that handles the technical details, allowing you to focus on what you love: creating.

Simple Analogy: AI is like having a creative partner who's always there to help brainstorm ideas, refine your drafts, and enhance your visuals—leaving you free to focus on your big-picture vision.

Interactive and Engaging Content

Before you move on to the next chapter, take 15 minutes to explore an AI-powered creative tool like Jasper AI or Canva Pro. Experiment with creating content using AI-generated prompts or templates, and reflect on how these tools can enhance your creative process. How did AI change the way you approach content creation?

Final Style Summary

AI is reshaping content creation for digital nomads, transforming them from solitary creators into collaborators with powerful tools that enhance creativity. By embracing AI as a creative partner, you can unlock new levels of productivity, develop innovative content, and maintain a balanced lifestyle while traveling the world.

Whether you're generating blog posts, editing videos, or designing graphics, AI can streamline your creative process, leaving you with more time to explore, grow your business, and pursue your passions. AI isn't a replacement for creativity—it's a catalyst for unlocking your full potential as a digital nomad.

Are you ready to collaborate with AI to elevate your creative work? The possibilities are endless.

CHAPTER 82: AI-GENERATED ART AND ITS IMPACT ON DIGITAL NOMADS

How AI-Generated Art is Transforming Creative Work for Digital Nomads

The digital nomad lifestyle thrives on creativity, flexibility, and innovation. As more nomads embrace technology, a fascinating frontier has emerged: AI-generated art. Once the domain of highly trained designers and artists, the creative process is now being transformed by AI tools that make art more accessible, customizable, and scalable. This chapter will explore how digital nomads are leveraging AI-generated art to enhance their creative work, save time, and push the boundaries of visual storytelling.

Engage with Storytelling and Case Studies

Let's begin with the story of Leo, a graphic designer and digital nomad who found himself overwhelmed by the sheer volume of creative requests from clients. Traveling through the vibrant streets of Medellín, Colombia, Leo realized he needed help streamlining his design process without sacrificing quality. Enter Deep Dream Generator, an AI tool that creates dreamlike digital art from simple inputs.

Leo started experimenting with Deep Dream Generator and found that it could transform his hand-drawn sketches into high-quality, AI-enhanced artworks. He no longer needed to spend hours polishing his designs manually. By integrating AI into his workflow, Leo could focus on creative direction while the AI took care of repetitive tasks like refining textures and adjusting colour palettes.

Soon, Leo's designs evolved into more complex pieces. He started combining Runway ML, another AI art tool, with traditional graphic design software. With Runway ML, Leo generated unique visual styles, rapidly prototyping logos, posters, and other assets for his clients. Thanks to AI, he not only increased his creative output but also found the time to explore his passion for photography, using AI-generated filters and enhancements on his travel photos.

Leo's business blossomed, and the feedback from his clients was overwhelmingly positive. By embracing AI-generated art, he had unlocked new levels of creativity and efficiency. Leo's story exemplifies how AI can serve as an artistic collaborator, not a replacement, allowing digital nomads to thrive in today's fast-paced creative economy.

Focus on Practical Application

For digital nomads, time and mobility are crucial. AI-generated art offers a solution to create visually stunning work without the need for extensive design skills or hours spent in front of a computer. Here are some practical applications of AI-generated art that nomads can incorporate into their workflows:

1. Creating Custom Art for Branding and Marketing

AI art platforms like Artbreeder allow you to generate custom artwork by blending multiple styles and elements. Whether you're creating social media graphics, website banners, or business logos, AI can accelerate the design process.

Practical Tip: Use AI tools to quickly prototype designs for personal branding. For instance, by inputting various elements into Artbreeder, you can generate unique logo designs and colour schemes in minutes, then refine them using traditional software like Adobe Illustrator.

2. Scaling Artistic Output with Automation

AI-generated art tools like DALL·E or Midjourney can produce detailed artwork based on textual descriptions. This is particularly useful for digital nomads who need high-quality visuals for multiple platforms, but don't have the time or expertise to design everything from scratch.

Practical Tip: Try using these tools for blog illustrations, YouTube thumbnails, or even book covers. With a simple text prompt (e.g., "a serene beach with abstract shapes in the sky"), AI can generate multiple variations for you to choose from, enabling you to scale your visual content efficiently.

3. Enhancing Photography with AI Filters

For nomads who are photographers or content creators, AI-powered photo editing tools like Luminar AI and Prisma can enhance your images with artistic filters or automatic adjustments. This allows you to create visually striking content for social media without needing a professional editing team.

Practical Tip: Apply AI-generated filters to your travel photos to create consistent aesthetics for your Instagram feed or portfolio. AI can quickly adjust lighting, colours, and details to match your unique brand style.

Inspire Through Visionary Perspectives

The possibilities of AI-generated art extend far beyond just speeding up the creative process—they open up entirely new artistic avenues. Imagine a future where digital nomads can collaborate with AI to create personalized artworks for clients around the globe, in real-time, as they explore the world. AI will be able to capture the essence of different cultures, places, and people, blending those elements into unique artistic expressions.

Visionary Perspective: What if AI-generated art could adapt to your environment, creating visuals based on the city you're working from? Imagine generating artwork inspired by the bustling streets of Tokyo, the tranquil beaches of Bali, or the rugged landscapes of Patagonia, all through the lens of AI. The future of AI-generated art is not just faster—it's smarter, more culturally aware, and deeply personal.

Balance Between Inspiration and Caution

While AI-generated art offers incredible benefits, it's essential to recognize its limitations. AI may excel at generating art quickly, but it lacks the human intuition and emotional depth that often defines great art. As a digital nomad, you must maintain a balance between leveraging AI for efficiency and preserving the authenticity of your creative vision.

Balanced Advice: Use AI as a tool to enhance your creativity, but don't rely on it to define your artistic voice. Remember that AI-generated art can sometimes feel generic or overly polished, so always review and customize the final product to reflect your unique style and message.

Highlight Global and Cultural Dimensions

AI-generated art has the potential to democratize creativity across cultures. Digital nomads often work in diverse environments, and AI can help bridge cultural gaps by generating art that resonates with different audiences. Tools like Google's AutoDraw or Runway ML allow creators from various backgrounds to contribute their artistic styles, blending global influences into a single piece of art.

Global Insight: Nomads working in different countries can use AI to create culturally relevant artwork that speaks to local audiences. By inputting regional themes, symbols, and aesthetics into AI tools, digital nomads can produce art that is both globally appealing and locally meaningful.

Motivate with Purpose and Fulfilment

The beauty of AI-generated art is that it frees digital nomads from the more tedious aspects of design work, allowing them to focus on projects that bring purpose and fulfilment. Whether you're a graphic designer creating marketing materials or a photographer looking to enhance your images, AI can serve as a powerful partner in your creative journey.

Inspirational Reflection: By using AI as a creative collaborator, you're not just saving time—you're expanding your creative horizons. With the ability to quickly generate high-quality visuals, you can spend more time on the projects that inspire you, whether that's exploring new destinations or diving deeper into your artistic passions.

Use Accessible, Simple Language for Complex Topics

While AI-generated art might sound intimidating, it's really just another tool in your creative toolbox. Think of it as having a personal assistant who can handle the technical details of design, so you can focus on the creative big picture.

Simple Analogy: Imagine AI as a co-pilot who helps you navigate the creative process. You provide the direction, and AI helps bring your ideas to life more quickly and efficiently.

Interactive and Engaging Content

Before moving on, experiment with an AI art tool like Deep Dream Generator or Runway ML. Create a simple piece of artwork using the tool, and reflect on how the process influenced your creative approach. Did AI help you visualize new ideas? Did it change the way you think about design?

Final Style Summary

AI-generated art is transforming the creative process for digital nomads, allowing them to scale their artistic output, experiment with new ideas, and create visually stunning content—all while on the move. By embracing AI as a creative partner, nomads can elevate their work, spend less time on repetitive tasks, and focus more on exploring the world and pursuing their passions.

With AI as an artistic collaborator, the boundaries of creativity are expanding. Whether you're enhancing your travel photography, designing brand logos, or creating digital art for clients, AI can help you bring your vision to life— faster, smarter, and more creatively than ever before.

Now, it's time to unleash your creativity. How will

you incorporate AI-generated art into your digital nomad journey?

CHAPTER 83: AI FOR WRITING AND STORYTELLING

How AI Tools Like GPT Are Revolutionizing Writing for Digital Nomads

In the world of digital nomads, writing and storytelling are essential skills. Whether it's creating compelling blog posts, producing social media content, or crafting long-form narratives, the ability to communicate effectively through the written word is vital. Yet, as digital nomads juggle various projects, clients, and their wanderlust-driven lifestyles, many struggle with time constraints and maintaining creative momentum. Enter AI tools like GPT (Generative Pre-trained Transformer), which are reshaping the landscape of writing and storytelling for nomads. These AI-driven writing assistants have the potential to elevate productivity, streamline the writing process, and open new creative possibilities.

Engage with Storytelling and Case Studies

Let's start with the story of Emma, a freelance travel blogger and digital nomad who splits her time between Bali and Lisbon. Emma often faced writer's block while trying to document her adventures and share insights with her growing audience. The pressure to consistently produce high-quality content became overwhelming. That's when Emma discovered GPT-3, an AI writing assistant capable of generating text based on simple prompts.

At first, Emma was hesitant to rely on AI, fearing it might dilute her authentic voice. But after experimenting with it, she realized that GPT-3 was not a replacement for her creativity but a powerful tool to enhance it. By inputting her ideas and key points, she could generate full paragraphs of engaging content, which she then edited to align with her style. AI wasn't writing for her; it was sparking new ideas and helping her overcome creative roadblocks.

One notable moment came when Emma used GPT-3 to generate story ideas for a blog series on sustainable travel. The AI suggested unique angles she hadn't considered, such as "exploring how AI can help reduce carbon footprints for digital nomads." Inspired by this, Emma wrote a piece that went viral, expanding her readership significantly. By leveraging AI, she was able to stay consistent with her content output, increase engagement, and ultimately grow her business—all while maintaining her voice and vision.

Focus on Practical Application

AI tools like GPT are designed to assist writers in various stages of their creative process. Whether you're a digital nomad working on blog posts, social media updates, or even e-books, AI can be a game-changer. Here's how you can practically incorporate AI-driven writing tools into your work:

1. Generating Content Ideas
AI tools like Jasper AI or Writesonic can help you brainstorm topics and develop content outlines. Simply input a few keywords, and the AI will generate a list of potential topics

or headlines. This is particularly useful for bloggers, content creators, and digital marketers who need to produce content regularly but may struggle with ideation.

Practical Tip: Use GPT-powered tools to create a content calendar. If you're writing about travel, input keywords like "sustainable travel," "remote work destinations," or "AI for digital nomads." The AI will generate topics you can expand upon throughout the year.

2. Overcoming Writer's Block
One of the biggest challenges for writers is the dreaded writer's block. AI can provide a jumpstart by generating introductory paragraphs or even entire sections based on your brief prompts.

Practical Tip: Stuck on an introduction? Ask GPT to generate a few variations. You'll likely find a starting point you can build upon, saving you time and frustration.

3. Editing and Refining Content
Tools like Grammarly and ProWritingAid are AI-driven editors that help you refine your drafts, improving grammar, style, and tone. These tools can instantly catch errors and suggest more concise wording, ensuring your writing is polished and professional.

Practical Tip: After writing a first draft, run it through AI editors to clean up your work. This way, you can focus on higher-level edits, such as content flow and narrative structure, without getting bogged down by grammar issues.

Inspire Through Visionary Perspectives

AI is not just a writing tool; it's shaping the future of storytelling. Imagine a world where AI collaborates with digital nomads to co-create narratives—where an AI tool can analyse your personal style, understand your voice, and suggest plotlines or character developments that align with your creative vision.

Visionary Perspective: In the near future, AI could become a co-author, assisting in complex projects like novels, documentaries, or even interactive storytelling. For digital nomads, this opens up exciting opportunities for experimentation. You could combine travel experiences with AI-generated stories, creating unique narratives that blend human experience with machine creativity.

Imagine crafting a travel memoir where AI fills in descriptive passages or historical context, leaving you to focus on your personal reflections. With AI as a creative partner, the possibilities for storytelling are limitless.

Balance Between Inspiration and Caution

While AI tools like GPT are incredibly useful, it's essential to approach them with caution. AI can generate content quickly, but it lacks the nuance and emotional depth that human writers bring to their work. Digital nomads who rely too heavily on AI-generated content risk losing their authentic voice.

Balanced Advice: Use AI as a collaborator, not a crutch. It's there to help you overcome writer's block, brainstorm ideas, or clean up grammar, but it shouldn't replace your unique perspective and creativity. Always edit AI-generated content thoroughly to ensure it aligns with your vision and message.

Highlight Global and Cultural Dimensions

AI's ability to process vast amounts of information makes it a valuable tool for digital nomads working across cultures. For example, AI can help you localize content for different audiences, providing culturally relevant language, references, and tone adjustments.

Global Insight: If you're writing content for a global audience, AI tools like DeepL can help you translate text accurately, while GPT can suggest ways to adapt your writing to fit local customs and values. This makes it easier for nomads to create content that resonates across different regions, enhancing their global reach.

Motivate with Purpose and Fulfilment

Ultimately, AI tools free digital nomads from the mundane aspects of writing, allowing them to focus on what matters most: telling stories that inspire, inform, and connect. By automating tasks like grammar checks, content generation, and ideation, AI empowers nomads to spend more time exploring new places and creating meaningful work.

Inspirational Reflection: By embracing AI in your writing process, you're not just improving efficiency— you're giving yourself the freedom to pursue deeper, more fulfilling creative projects. Whether it's sharing your travel experiences, creating content for social impact, or documenting your personal growth, AI can help you focus on what truly inspires you.

Use Accessible, Simple Language for Complex Topics

Writing with AI doesn't have to be intimidating. Think of AI like a virtual assistant that helps you manage the technical aspects of writing, leaving you free to explore your creative side.

Simple Analogy: Imagine AI as your editor—one that works

at lightning speed and never tires. You provide the direction and ideas, and AI helps bring them to life by handling the repetitive tasks of writing, editing, and brainstorming.

Interactive and Engaging Content

Before moving on, take 15 minutes to explore a writing AI tool like Jasper or Writesonic. Use it to generate ideas for your next blog post or creative project. Reflect on how the AI suggestions influenced your thought process. Did it spark new ideas? Did it help you overcome a creative hurdle?

Final Style Summary

AI is reshaping the way digital nomads approach writing and storytelling. By incorporating AI tools into their workflows, nomads can unlock new levels of creativity, streamline the writing process, and overcome common obstacles like writer's block. These tools don't just save time; they enhance creativity, enabling nomads to focus on producing meaningful and impactful content.

As AI continues to evolve, it will offer even more possibilities for collaboration and creative expression. Whether you're a travel blogger, a social media strategist, or a novelist, AI can become a trusted partner in your creative journey. How will you integrate AI into your storytelling process?

The future of writing is here, and it's time to embrace it.

CHAPTER 84: AI AND PHOTOGRAPHY FOR NOMADS

How Digital Nomads Can Use AI to Enhance Their Photography While Traveling

In the life of a digital nomad, capturing the essence of your travels is crucial. Whether you're a blogger, a freelance photographer, or simply someone who enjoys documenting your journeys, photography is an essential tool for telling stories and sharing experiences. With the rise of AI technology, photography has undergone a revolution, offering digital nomads a range of innovative tools to enhance their images, streamline their editing process, and even automate tasks that once required hours of manual work.

In this chapter, we'll explore how AI is transforming photography for digital nomads, offering practical tips on how to leverage these tools to elevate your craft and make your travel photos stand out.

Engage with Storytelling and Case Studies

Meet Alex, a freelance photographer and digital nomad who has been traveling through South America for the last two years. Alex was always passionate about photography, but keeping up with editing and managing a large portfolio while constantly on the move was overwhelming. Spending hours in Lightroom or Photoshop after long days of shooting landscapes and cityscapes left him feeling burnt out.

Everything changed when Alex discovered AI-powered editing tools like Luminar AI and Topaz Labs. These tools offered intelligent automation that transformed his workflow. Luminar AI, for instance, uses machine learning to analyse photos and automatically enhance them. Whether it's adjusting the lighting, improving skin tones in portraits, or highlighting the vibrancy of landscapes, AI tools enabled Alex to quickly edit large batches of photos with professional results.

What once took Alex several hours to perfect, now took mere minutes. For instance, during his time in Patagonia, Alex shot hundreds of photos capturing the rugged beauty of the mountains. Using Luminar AI, he was able to enhance the dramatic clouds and light over the peaks with just a few clicks, giving his images a cinematic feel. This efficiency freed up his time to explore more and focus on creative composition during his shoots. Alex's photography business boomed because he was able to deliver higher-quality images to clients faster.

Focus on Practical Application

AI in photography goes far beyond just editing—there are a host of AI-driven tools available to help digital nomads take their photography to the next level. Below are some key tools and techniques to integrate AI into your photography practice:

1. AI-Powered Editing Tools
AI-driven editing tools like Luminar AI and Skylum analyse

photos and make intelligent suggestions on how to improve them. These tools can automatically enhance contrast, adjust colour balance, and even replace skies in landscape photos, creating stunning, professional-looking images.

Practical Tip: After a day of shooting, import your photos into an AI-powered tool and use its automatic enhancement features to quickly polish your images. This is especially useful if you're short on time and need to meet client deadlines while traveling.

2. AI for Noise Reduction and Image Sharpening
Low-light photography or fast-moving subjects can lead to noise and blur, which were traditionally difficult to fix. AI tools like Topaz Denoise AI and Sharpen AI can remove noise from photos and sharpen them with impressive precision.

Practical Tip: Use AI noise reduction tools when shooting in challenging environments, like nighttime cityscapes or wildlife photography. These tools allow you to recover details that would otherwise be lost, ensuring your images remain sharp and clear.

3. AI-Based Object Recognition and Sorting
When managing thousands of travel photos, sorting and categorizing images can be a daunting task. AI tools like Google Photos and Adobe Sensei use object recognition to automatically tag, categorize, and organize your photos based on location, objects, or even facial recognition.

Practical Tip: Set up your photo library with AI-driven tools that sort images by subject, location, or event. This makes it easier to retrieve photos for specific projects or share with clients.

Inspire Through Visionary Perspectives

Imagine a future where AI not only helps you edit photos but collaborates with you in real-time during the creative process. AI could suggest ideal angles for a shot, analyse lighting conditions, or even create composite images from multiple photos while you're still in the field.

Visionary Perspective: In the near future, AI may become your personal photography assistant. AI-driven cameras already exist that help with autofocus, facial recognition, and exposure adjustments. As this technology advances, it's possible AI could take on a more collaborative role in photography, offering real-time feedback to improve your composition and creativity. This means that as a digital nomad, you'll be able to push the boundaries of what's creatively possible, whether you're shooting from a mountaintop or in a bustling city.

Balance Between Inspiration and Caution

While AI tools provide unprecedented convenience and power, it's essential to strike a balance between using AI and maintaining your creative vision. AI-driven edits may be fast, but they can also feel formulaic if overused. The key is to view AI as a partner in your creative process, not a replacement for your eye as a photographer.

Balanced Advice: Use AI to enhance your photos, but always apply your unique style and vision. Don't rely solely on AI-generated adjustments—review and tweak them to make sure they align with the mood and story you're trying to convey in your images.

Highlight Global and Cultural Dimensions

For digital nomads, AI tools also provide the flexibility to tailor photography for diverse cultures and global audiences. AI-powered localization tools can help photographers create culturally relevant imagery by adjusting colour tones, atmospheres, and even subject matter to suit specific regions or traditions.

Global Insight: If you're working on a project in a country with unique cultural aesthetics, AI tools can assist you in aligning your images with local preferences. For instance, you might shoot a vibrant festival in India or capture the serenity of the Japanese countryside—AI tools can help emphasize the specific colours and elements that resonate with those cultures.

Motivate with Purpose and Fulfilment

AI tools do more than speed up workflow; they allow digital nomads to spend less time on tedious tasks and more time living in the moment. By freeing up time from editing and organizing, you can focus on what really matters: capturing the essence of your journey and telling stories that matter.

Inspirational Reflection: By embracing AI in your photography practice, you're not only enhancing your work but also gaining the freedom to explore deeper creative projects. Whether it's documenting the beauty of the natural world or telling the stories of people you meet along the way, AI enables you to focus on your passion for photography while still maintaining a successful career as a digital nomad.

Use Accessible, Simple Language for Complex Topics

Think of AI as your photography co-pilot. It's there to handle the repetitive or technical tasks, giving you the space to focus on the art of photography.

Simple Analogy: Imagine AI as the automatic focus on your camera—it doesn't take the picture for you, but it makes sure the shot is crisp and clear, allowing you to focus on capturing the perfect moment.

Interactive and Engaging Content

Before you move on to your next photography adventure, spend 15 minutes experimenting with an AI-powered tool like Luminar AI or Topaz Sharpen AI. Import one of your travel photos, and let the AI make suggestions for improvements. Compare the AI-enhanced version with your original. What did you like? What would you change?

Final Style Summary

AI has transformed the way digital nomads approach photography. From editing tools that save hours of work to intelligent sorting systems that streamline image management, AI is becoming an invaluable partner for traveling photographers. By embracing these tools, you can elevate your photography while maintaining the freedom to explore and create on your terms.

The future of photography is here, and it's powered by AI. How will you harness this technology to tell your stories?

CHAPTER 85: AI FOR MUSIC CREATION

How AI is Transforming Music for Digital Nomads

As digital nomads, many of us travel the world, seeking inspiration for our creative endeavours. For those working in the fields of music and sound design, AI is revolutionizing how we compose, produce, and distribute our art. The convergence of AI with music creation opens up unprecedented possibilities, allowing artists to create tracks more efficiently while still exploring their creative expression.

In this chapter, we'll explore how AI tools are reshaping the music industry for digital nomads and how you can leverage these technologies to fuel your creativity, streamline your workflow, and even collaborate across the globe.

Engage with Storytelling and Case Studies

Take the story of Javier, a digital nomad and electronic music producer traveling through Europe. Armed with nothing more than his laptop, MIDI keyboard, and a pair of headphones, Javier would compose tracks in different cities—Vienna, Lisbon, Berlin—each city adding its unique flavour to his sound. But as his workload increased, Javier found himself spending hours refining small details, from balancing the EQ to layering harmonies. He began feeling overwhelmed and uninspired.

That all changed when he discovered AIVA, an AI-powered tool designed to assist with music composition. By analysing existing compositions, AIVA was able to help Javier create harmonic progressions and melodies based on his creative direction. The AI tool allowed him to build complex arrangements in minutes instead of hours, giving him more time to experiment with soundscapes and textures. He found a perfect blend between human creativity and AI efficiency, and the result was a unique sound that quickly gained popularity on streaming platforms.

For digital nomads like Javier, AI tools serve as collaborators, providing support in generating new ideas, enhancing productivity, and allowing greater focus on the creative aspects of music.

Focus on Practical Application

There are numerous AI-driven tools available to help digital nomads working in music creation, from composing melodies to mastering tracks. Here are some key AI-powered tools and their practical applications:

1. AI-Powered Music Composition
Tools like AIVA (Artificial Intelligence Virtual Artist) and Amper Music help artists compose entire tracks. These platforms allow you to specify musical genres, instruments, and moods, and the AI generates music that aligns with your input. While it may sound too good to be true, these tools are widely used in the media industry to create soundtracks for commercials, films, and games.

Practical Tip: Use AI-powered composition tools to generate the foundation of your tracks. Afterward, you can add your personal touch, experimenting with melodies or tweaking chord progressions to fit your vision.

2. AI for Mixing and Mastering

Platforms like Landr and eMastered use AI algorithms to automate the mixing and mastering process. These tools analyse your track and apply a set of adjustments to give it a professional sound, saving you the time and effort of manually balancing audio levels and adding effects.

Practical Tip: After composing and arranging your track, use AI-driven mastering tools to polish your final product. This is especially useful if you need to quickly finish a demo or deliver tracks to clients while traveling.

3. AI-Assisted Sound Design

For those into experimental sound design, tools like Endlesss and Soundraw allow you to create unique soundscapes and effects. Whether you're a film composer or an electronic music producer, AI can assist in generating ambient sound textures, atmospheric effects, or novel instrument sounds that add depth to your projects.

Practical Tip: Use AI-driven sound design tools to push the boundaries of your music, creating original and unusual sound textures that can differentiate your work in a crowded market.

Inspire Through Visionary Perspectives

Imagine a future where AI doesn't just assist with music creation but collaborates in real time with musicians. As AI learns your musical preferences, it could suggest harmonies, rhythms, or effects in the moment, giving you a "second pair of ears" while producing.

Visionary Perspective: In the near future, AI could become your creative partner, anticipating your musical choices and working alongside you to co-create. This dynamic collaboration could lead to completely new genres of music, blending human intuition with machine precision. You'll be able to travel anywhere in the world and have an intelligent assistant with you at all times—expanding what's possible for both independent musicians and larger productions alike.

Balance Between Inspiration and Caution

While AI offers exciting potential for music creation, it's essential to strike a balance between AI-generated components and your own creative input. AI can provide the foundation or enhancement, but the soul of the music will always come from the human touch.

Balanced Advice: Allow AI tools to handle repetitive tasks, such as harmonizing or mastering, but always review the final output. Your unique musical style and artistic vision should guide the process. AI is a powerful tool, but it's not a substitute for your creativity.

Highlight Global and Cultural Dimensions

For digital nomads working in music, AI tools enable a broader reach into global and cross-cultural markets. AI can analyse various musical styles from different regions, helping you create music that resonates with diverse audiences.

Global Insight: Imagine creating a fusion track blending traditional Indian music with modern electronic beats. AI can help you incorporate regional rhythms, scales, and instruments that may be unfamiliar, allowing you to produce authentic cross-cultural compositions while on the go.

Motivate with Purpose and Fulfilment

Using AI to enhance your music creation isn't just about efficiency—it's about freeing up time to focus on the deeper aspects of your craft. As a digital nomad, your creative journey is closely tied to your travels, and AI allows you to document those experiences through sound while maintaining professional output.

Inspirational Reflection: By incorporating AI into your music workflow, you're creating space for what truly matters— exploring your creativity. AI will handle the technical details, so you can spend more time experimenting with new sounds, telling stories through your music, and connecting with global audiences.

Use Accessible, Simple Language for Complex Topics

Think of AI in music creation like an intelligent collaborator who helps simplify your workflow. It's not replacing your creativity, but enhancing your ability to produce music faster and more efficiently.

Simple Analogy: If music production is like cooking, then AI is the sous-chef that preps the ingredients and ensures your kitchen runs smoothly, allowing you to focus on creating the perfect dish.

Interactive and Engaging Content

Before moving to the next chapter, try using an AI-powered tool like Amper Music or Landr to enhance your own music projects. Spend 20 minutes experimenting with how AI can assist you in composing or mastering a track. Reflect on how the AI's output compares to your manual process—what did you like, and what would you modify?

Final Style Summary

AI is transforming the way digital nomads approach music creation. From composition to mastering, AI tools are reshaping how we produce and distribute music, offering greater efficiency without sacrificing creativity. For digital nomads, this means spending more time traveling and less time bogged down in repetitive tasks, while still producing high-quality music.

The future of music creation is an exciting frontier where AI becomes a creative partner, opening new pathways for collaboration, experimentation, and global reach. How will you use AI to take your music to the next level?

PART 18: REGIONAL PERSPECTIVES ON AI AND NOMADISM

CHAPTER 86:
AI IN ASIA:
OPPORTUNITIES
FOR DIGITAL
NOMADS

How AI is Evolving in Asia and What it Means for Digital Nomads

As AI continues to revolutionize the global work landscape, Asia is quickly emerging as a powerful hub for innovation, research, and application in the AI industry. From bustling tech ecosystems in cities like Singapore, Seoul, and Tokyo, to emerging AI-driven startups in countries like India and Vietnam, Asia presents a dynamic environment for digital nomads seeking opportunities in AI-driven industries. But how is AI evolving in Asia, and what does it mean for digital nomads working across the continent?

In this chapter, we will explore the current landscape of AI across Asia, focusing on how digital nomads can leverage these advancements to enhance their careers, explore new opportunities, and thrive in a region at the forefront of technological change.

Engage with Storytelling and Case Studies

Take the story of Linda, a freelance marketer and digital nomad based in Bali, Indonesia. She found herself intrigued by the rise of AI in Southeast Asia and how startups were integrating AI into their operations. While traveling through Singapore, Linda attended an AI-focused tech conference where she met a team developing AI-driven customer engagement software. Excited about the potential of AI in her line of work, Linda began using AI tools like HubSpot's predictive analytics and Conversica's AI sales assistants to automate lead generation, analyse customer behaviour, and enhance her marketing strategies.

By incorporating these AI tools into her freelance marketing services, Linda was able to scale her business and attract larger international clients. With AI handling the routine tasks, she now focuses on crafting more personalized marketing campaigns, growing her client base, and living the digital nomad lifestyle across Asia, from co-working spaces in Bangkok to beach-side cafes in the Philippines.

Linda's story highlights how digital nomads can benefit from the rapid growth of AI in Asia. The region offers not only cutting-edge technologies but also a supportive community of innovators, developers, and startups eager to collaborate.

Focus on Practical Application

AI is reshaping the way digital nomads work in Asia, offering practical solutions to optimize productivity, expand services, and collaborate with local and global teams. Below are some key AI-powered tools and platforms that digital nomads can use to thrive in Asia's evolving AI landscape:

1. AI-Powered Marketing Tools

For freelancers in marketing, Asia offers a vast pool of AI-driven tools to automate tasks like social media scheduling, audience analysis, and content creation. Platforms like Jasper AI and Adext AI help nomads create high-quality content, while tools like Hootsuite's AI-powered analytics optimize social media strategies for better engagement and conversion.

Practical Tip: Use AI-driven marketing platforms to automate repetitive tasks and focus on more strategic elements like campaign creativity and personalized messaging for clients.

2. AI for Business Process Automation

For digital nomads running e-commerce or other small businesses, AI-powered platforms such as Alibaba Cloud offer tools for inventory management, customer support chatbots, and even supply chain optimization. These tools streamline operations, allowing entrepreneurs to focus on expanding their market reach.

Practical Tip: Integrate AI-driven business management tools to reduce manual effort in managing your online store, freeing up time for scaling your business and exploring new markets in Asia.

3. AI-Powered Translation and Communication

One of the challenges digital nomads face when working across multiple countries in Asia is language barriers. AI-powered tools like Google Translate, DeepL, and iFlytek's voice translation services allow nomads to communicate effectively with clients, collaborators, and locals. These tools are essential for navigating both business and everyday life across diverse linguistic landscapes.

Practical Tip: Use AI-powered translation apps to work seamlessly with clients in multiple languages, allowing you to expand your business across countries like Japan, Korea, and China without language constraints.

Inspire Through Visionary Perspectives

The future of AI in Asia is promising, with innovations across industries from healthcare to education, and digital nomads have the chance to be part of this transformative movement. Asia's focus on smart cities, automation, and advanced AI research opens up endless opportunities for digital nomads to collaborate with startups and research institutions, or even create AI-driven businesses of their own.

Visionary Perspective: Imagine a future where digital nomads co-create AI solutions with local entrepreneurs, solving region-specific problems like smart urban development, agricultural automation, or AI-driven financial inclusion. In this rapidly evolving region, the possibilities for AI-enabled entrepreneurship are limitless.

Balance Between Inspiration and Caution

While the opportunities are vast, digital nomads should approach the evolving AI landscape in Asia with a balanced perspective. The rise of AI does bring challenges, such as the need to continuously upskill in AI-related technologies and adapt to changing job markets. Furthermore, privacy regulations and data security concerns differ across countries, and it's important to stay informed about local policies.

Balanced Advice: Stay proactive in learning new AI-related skills. Platforms like Coursera and Udemy offer AI and machine learning courses specifically tailored for freelancers and entrepreneurs. Additionally, ensure you comply with data privacy laws in the region, such as the Personal Data Protection Act (PDPA) in Singapore or China's cybersecurity regulations.

Highlight Global and Cultural Dimensions

Asia is incredibly diverse, and the way AI is being adopted varies significantly across different regions. In India, AI is being used to revolutionize small businesses and bring digital tools to traditionally underserved markets, while in China, AI is deeply embedded in industries like e-commerce and logistics. Singapore is known for its smart city initiatives, and Japan leads the way in AI for robotics.

Global Insight: As a digital nomad in Asia, you can tap into these different ecosystems by understanding the unique needs and applications of AI in each country. Whether you're a freelancer in Vietnam helping local businesses embrace AI tools or a consultant in Malaysia working with global clients, the diverse applications of AI across Asia present limitless possibilities.

Motivate with Purpose and Fulfilment

For many digital nomads, the pursuit of freedom and purpose drives their lifestyle. The integration of AI into their work not only boosts productivity but also aligns with their broader goals of meaningful work and global exploration. AI enables digital nomads to focus on what matters most— creativity, passion projects, and meaningful impact.

Inspirational Reflection: By leveraging AI, digital nomads can create more time for the things they truly care about, whether it's developing a personal passion project, exploring new cultures, or contributing to meaningful causes like digital literacy or environmental sustainability in the communities they visit.

Use Accessible, Simple Language for Complex Topics

AI might seem like a complex and intimidating topic, but at its core, it's a tool designed to make life easier. Think of AI as an assistant that helps you manage and simplify routine tasks—whether it's translating documents, analysing market trends, or automating business processes. The technology exists to free up your time for higher-level, creative work.

Interactive and Engaging Content

Before you move on to the next chapter, explore one AI tool mentioned in this chapter, such as HubSpot or Alibaba Cloud, and reflect on how it could enhance your work. Spend 15 minutes exploring its features, and consider how integrating such tools could improve your productivity while you continue your journey as a digital nomad in Asia.

Final Style Summary

As AI continues to evolve across Asia, digital nomads are in a prime position to leverage this technological revolution. From marketing automation to language translation, AI offers new ways to optimize workflows and expand global reach. By understanding the diverse applications of AI in different Asian markets, digital nomads can unlock vast opportunities for professional growth and personal fulfilment.

The key to thriving in this rapidly changing landscape is

staying curious, adaptable, and proactive. AI is here to assist you, freeing you to pursue your passions while contributing to the dynamic innovation happening across the region.

CHAPTER 87: AI IN EUROPE: A REMOTE WORK POWERHOUSE

As the early morning light filtered through the tall windows of a co-working space in Tallinn, Estonia, Rachel prepared for another productive day. She wasn't worried about time zones or collaborating with her remote team members in Germany, France, and Italy. With the help of AI-powered tools, her workday was seamlessly automated, from language translation to task delegation. In fact, Estonia had quickly become her favourite hub for digital nomads, with its e-residency program and AI-enhanced infrastructure making remote work smoother than ever. Europe, with its progressive policies and tech-forward cities, was rapidly becoming the AI-powered remote work powerhouse of the world.

This chapter will explore how AI is transforming the landscape for digital nomads in Europe, showcasing how innovative policies, tech adoption, and AI tools are fostering an ideal environment for remote workers. We'll share case studies of nomads thriving in European cities and offer practical insights into the AI-driven systems that are making Europe a global leader in the remote work revolution.

Rachel's Story: Estonia and the e-Residency Revolution

Rachel, a freelance digital marketer, had always loved traveling across Europe, but she struggled with the complexities of running her freelance business across borders. Setting up business accounts, managing invoices, and navigating the tax systems of multiple countries felt like a full-time job on its own. That's when she discovered Estonia's e-residency program, a groundbreaking initiative designed for digital nomads and entrepreneurs who wanted to run their businesses without being tied to a physical location.

With the help of Estonia's AI-powered e-government tools, Rachel was able to set up her business in just a few hours. AI handled the bureaucracy: automating the registration, ensuring legal compliance, and providing her with seamless access to digital banking. She was also able to manage her taxes and invoices with AI-driven platforms that minimized paperwork and automatically updated her financial records in real time.

Now, instead of worrying about administrative tasks, Rachel could focus on her clients and creative work, knowing that AI was taking care of the backend logistics. Her productivity skyrocketed, and she found more time to enjoy the cultural diversity of Europe.

How AI is Reshaping the Digital Nomad Landscape in Europe

Europe has long been a hub for remote work, but AI is supercharging the continent's ability to attract and retain digital nomads. From progressive digital policies to AI-driven services, Europe is creating a future where working remotely is not only possible but thriving. Here are some of the key ways AI is transforming Europe into a remote work powerhouse:

1. AI-Driven Bureaucracy and e-Government Services

Countries like Estonia and Lithuania are leading the charge with AI-powered e-government services designed for digital nomads. Estonia's e-residency program is a perfect example. By integrating AI into its administrative processes, Estonia has made it possible for anyone, anywhere in the world, to run a business in Europe entirely online. AI automates everything from business registration to tax filing, significantly reducing the time and hassle it takes to manage a cross-border enterprise.

This AI-driven approach allows digital nomads to focus on their work rather than get bogged down by complicated bureaucracy—a common challenge in traditional business environments.

2. Multilingual Collaboration with AI-Powered Tools

With Europe being a patchwork of countries, languages, and cultures, communication can often be a barrier for remote teams. However, AI-powered language tools like DeepL and Google Translate are transforming cross-cultural collaboration. These platforms provide real-time translation for emails, documents, and even voice communication, making it easier than ever for digital nomads and their teams to work together seamlessly across borders.

For example, a marketing team with members in Spain, Poland, and Sweden can communicate without needing to worry about language differences. AI tools automatically translate project documents and messages, allowing each team member to contribute in their native language, saving time and fostering more inclusive collaboration.

3. AI-Enhanced Productivity Tools

Europe's embrace of AI-enhanced productivity platforms has made it easier for digital nomads to manage their workloads effectively. Tools like Trello and Notion leverage AI to automate task assignments, prioritize deadlines, and track progress. These platforms integrate seamlessly with popular co-working spaces across Europe, where digital nomads can access high-speed internet and smart work environments optimized by AI.

For instance, CoWomen in Berlin and Talent Garden in Milan are designed to facilitate AI-powered collaboration, offering digital nomads access to AI-enhanced brainstorming software, automated task management, and personalized workspaces based on productivity patterns. These tools allow nomads to stay on top of their tasks while moving from one European city to the next.

Visionary Perspectives: AI's Future in Europe's Digital Nomad Scene

As AI technology continues to evolve, we can expect Europe to become even more attractive for digital nomads. Imagine a future where AI-powered immigration systems enable nomads to move seamlessly between European countries with real-time visa updates and tax adjustments tailored to their location. AI could also offer predictive analytics that guide nomads to the best cities based on their work habits, lifestyle preferences, and network connections, creating a customized nomadic experience tailored to personal and professional growth.

AI might also evolve to help nomads discover hidden opportunities—like finding untapped freelance markets or networking with key industry figures based on predictive insights about job trends and industry shifts. With AI's ability to analyse vast amounts of data in real-time, digital nomads could be notified of emerging opportunities before they happen, positioning themselves as early movers in exciting new industries.

Practical Tips: Leveraging AI to Thrive as a Digital Nomad in

Europe

Here are some practical ways to harness the power of AI while living and working across Europe:

- Simplify Business Operations: Use AI-driven e-government tools like Estonia's e-residency to manage your business remotely with ease. Platforms like Xolo can handle invoicing, taxes, and compliance, all powered by AI, making it simpler for you to focus on your core work.

- Collaborate Across Borders: For multilingual teams, tools like DeepL and Grammarly can assist with translating documents and refining communication, making it easier to work with clients and collaborators from different language backgrounds.

- Boost Productivity with AI-Powered Workspaces: Take advantage of co-working spaces that offer AI-enhanced productivity tools. Whether you're in Lisbon, Berlin, or Amsterdam, you can find spaces that integrate AI into the work environment to help manage tasks, track projects, and optimize your workflow.

Balancing Inspiration and Caution: The Challenges of AI-Powered Nomadism in Europe

While Europe is quickly becoming a hub for AI-enhanced remote work, it's essential to approach the opportunities with a balanced perspective. As AI becomes increasingly integrated into the digital nomad lifestyle, there are also concerns about data privacy and job displacement. European countries are known for their strong data privacy regulations (such as GDPR), but nomads must remain vigilant about how their personal and business data are used by AI-driven platforms.

Additionally, as AI continues to automate tasks, some nomads may find themselves competing in an increasingly automated freelance market. The key is to adapt by continually upskilling and learning how to work alongside AI, rather than being replaced by it.

Motivate with Purpose: Thriving Beyond the Work

At the heart of being a digital nomad in Europe isn't just the ease of work—it's the lifestyle. AI empowers nomads to automate mundane tasks, freeing up more time to explore Europe's rich history, culture, and diversity. Whether you're wandering through Parisian art galleries, biking along Amsterdam's canals, or hiking the Alps, AI helps you spend less time on administrative tasks and more time living.

For digital nomads like Rachel, AI is not just a tool for efficiency—it's a gateway to a more purposeful life. By automating the administrative complexities of her work, Rachel found more time to volunteer with local non-profits in Estonia and immerse herself in the cultural richness of her surroundings. With AI as a partner, nomads can strike the perfect balance between work and personal fulfilment, living more meaningfully across borders.

Conclusion: Europe's AI-Powered Future for Digital Nomads

Europe is rapidly becoming the ultimate destination for digital nomads, thanks to its AI-driven infrastructure, progressive policies, and thriving co-working culture. Whether through streamlined bureaucracy, real-time language translation, or AI-enhanced productivity tools, the continent is leading the way in making remote work not only possible but enjoyable.

As AI continues to evolve, the opportunities for digital nomads in Europe will only expand, creating a future where work is seamlessly integrated with personal growth, exploration, and purpose. The time to embrace AI as a digital nomad in Europe is now.

CHAPTER 88: AI IN AFRICA: A GROWING FRONTIER FOR DIGITAL NOMADS

As the sun set over the bustling streets of Lagos, Nigeria, Lila sat on a rooftop café, laptop open, finalizing a project for her client in London. What was once a challenge —working from an African city known for its dynamic energy but inconsistent infrastructure—was now a smooth, tech-empowered experience. Thanks to AI-driven tools that streamlined her work, from content creation to remote team collaboration, Lila thrived as a digital nomad. Africa, often viewed through a lens of challenges, was becoming a vibrant new frontier for digital nomads, and AI was playing a pivotal role in this transformation.

This chapter will dive into how AI is reshaping the digital nomad ecosystem across Africa, spotlighting how innovative tech is creating opportunities in regions once considered off-limits for remote workers. We'll share real-life stories of digital nomads thriving in African cities, practical applications of AI tools, and a visionary look at how Africa is poised to be a leader in the digital nomad space, powered by AI.

Lila's Story: Thriving in Lagos with AI

Lila, a content strategist and freelance writer, never expected Lagos to be the ideal destination for her digital nomad lifestyle. Known for its traffic, energy, and creative chaos, Lagos was a far cry from the tranquil co-working spaces she had experienced in Europe and Southeast Asia. However, after visiting Nigeria for a short-term project, she quickly realized the potential the city held—especially with AI powering many of her daily tasks.

Using AI platforms like Jasper AI for content generation and Trello's AI-powered project management tools, Lila was able to keep up with her clients worldwide without missing a beat. When the local internet connectivity was slow, she turned to AI-enhanced network optimization tools that boosted her productivity.

Perhaps most transformative was AI-driven translation tools like DeepL. Working with clients in both French-speaking and English-speaking African countries became seamless. AI handled real-time language translation, ensuring clear communication regardless of the regional languages she encountered. Lila's experience reflects the broader trend of AI creating possibilities in places where infrastructure challenges would have once hindered digital nomads from setting up base.

AI's Impact on the African Digital Nomad Landscape

Africa's diversity of cultures, languages, and economies has historically presented both incredible opportunities and significant challenges. Yet, with the rapid rise of AI, digital nomads are discovering that the continent is becoming more connected, efficient, and innovative—making it a compelling destination for remote work. Here's how AI is transforming the digital nomad landscape across Africa:

1. AI-Enhanced Connectivity

While internet infrastructure in some parts of Africa has historically been unreliable, AI is helping bridge this gap. Tools like Google's AI-powered network management systems are optimizing bandwidth and providing faster, more stable internet connections. Digital nomads working in cities like Accra, Nairobi, or Cape Town are now leveraging AI to ensure they can work from virtually anywhere, even during periods of network instability. AI-powered tools that detect and optimize internet performance in real-time ensure smoother video calls, faster downloads, and more reliable access to cloud services.

2. Language Translation for Multilingual Communication

Africa is home to over 2,000 languages, making communication across borders complex. For digital nomads working across various African countries or with local businesses, AI-powered translation tools like DeepL and Google Translate are essential. These tools allow seamless communication in multiple languages, whether it's conducting a client call in French from Dakar or reading a business proposal in Swahili from Nairobi. AI is breaking down language barriers and fostering cross-border collaborations in a way that was previously unimaginable.

3. AI-Powered Business Services

Africa's entrepreneurial spirit is thriving, and many digital nomads are collaborating with startups or running their own businesses in the region. Platforms like Xero and QuickBooks, enhanced with AI-driven features, are simplifying accounting, tax filing, and expense tracking for remote entrepreneurs. In countries like Kenya and South Africa, where fintech is booming, digital nomads can also access AI-enhanced banking services like M-Pesa for mobile payments, streamlining financial transactions across borders.

Furthermore, AI is helping to automate customer service for businesses, allowing nomads to manage global clients with chatbots and AI-powered customer support that operates around the clock.

A Vision for AI and Digital Nomadism in Africa's Future

As AI continues to advance, Africa is emerging as a frontier with massive potential for remote work. In the near future, AI could transform the way nomads select their destinations within Africa. AI-driven platforms might analyse data across regions—such as cost of living, political stability, and infrastructure improvements—to recommend ideal work locations for digital nomads. A real-time AI-powered dashboard could help nomads make informed decisions about where to live and work, whether in bustling hubs like Lagos and Nairobi or emerging destinations like Kigali and Dakar.

Moreover, AI could play a pivotal role in sustainability efforts. Digital nomads passionate about social and environmental impact might use AI tools to collaborate with local African organizations, leveraging data-driven insights to contribute to projects in areas like conservation, renewable energy, and healthcare development.

The vision of AI-powered remote work in Africa is not just one of economic efficiency—it's also about creating purpose-driven opportunities for global citizens to collaborate with local innovators and drive positive change on the continent.

Practical Applications: Leveraging AI as a Digital Nomad in Africa

Here are a few key ways to integrate AI tools into your daily workflow while living and working as a digital nomad in Africa:

- Boost Productivity with AI: Platforms like Jasper AI for content creation and Grammarly for editing can save hours of manual work, allowing you to produce high-quality deliverables quickly.

- Use AI for Financial Management: Whether running a small business or managing personal finances, tools like Xero and Wave leverage AI to automate invoicing, track expenses, and simplify tax filing, even in countries with complex tax systems.

- Access Real-Time Translations: For nomads working across multiple countries, tools like DeepL provide real-time translation for emails, documents, and conversations, ensuring you stay connected with local clients and partners regardless of language barriers.

Balancing Inspiration with Realism: Challenges of AI in Africa

While the potential of AI in Africa is exciting, it's important to approach the opportunities with a balanced perspective. Access to reliable internet remains inconsistent in some regions, and while AI can help optimize connectivity, it cannot fully compensate for underdeveloped infrastructure. Digital nomads should carefully research the connectivity and resources available in their desired locations and consider using AI-powered satellite internet options where necessary.

Moreover, while AI is expanding opportunities, it's crucial to remain mindful of ethical considerations, such as data privacy and the role of AI in job displacement. Africa's emerging economies rely on many traditional sectors, and as AI continues to automate processes, it's essential to balance innovation with inclusive development strategies that benefit local workers and communities.

Motivate with Purpose: Leveraging AI for Social Impact

At the heart of digital nomadism in Africa is the opportunity to create meaningful connections and make an impact. AI can be a tool not just for optimizing work, but for collaborating with local communities, contributing to social projects, and driving innovation on the continent. Many digital nomads find purpose in working alongside African startups or non-profits, using AI-driven solutions to tackle challenges like access to education, healthcare, and environmental sustainability.

By embracing AI, digital nomads in Africa can work more efficiently while contributing to the growth and development of the communities around them, all while living a lifestyle rich with adventure and cultural discovery.

Conclusion: Africa and AI—a New Era for Digital Nomads

Africa is quickly becoming an exciting frontier for digital nomads, and AI is at the heart of this transformation. From enhancing connectivity and simplifying cross-border communication to powering business operations and creating new opportunities for social impact, AI is empowering digital nomads to thrive across Africa's diverse and dynamic landscapes.

As AI continues to evolve, digital nomads who embrace this growing frontier will find themselves at the cutting edge of remote work—able to live, work, and make an impact in one of the most exciting and rapidly changing regions in the world.

CHAPTER 89: AI IN LATIN AMERICA: GROWTH AND CHALLENGES FOR DIGITAL NOMADS

Sitting at a café in Medellín, Colombia, Carlos opened his laptop and was ready for another day of work. The city, once infamous for its turbulent past, had emerged as a top destination for digital nomads, with its vibrant culture, affordable living, and growing tech ecosystem. For Carlos, a freelance web developer from Argentina, the ability to work remotely from one of Latin America's rising tech hubs was a dream come true. What made his life easier, however, was the integration of AI-powered tools that streamlined his workflow, allowing him to collaborate with clients across the globe. As Carlos plugged into his digital workspace, he reflected on how AI had empowered his career as a digital nomad, giving him the flexibility and efficiency to thrive.

Latin America, with its diverse landscapes, affordable cost of living, and expanding tech infrastructure, is becoming a hotspot for digital nomads. However, it's the rise of artificial intelligence (AI) that is truly shaping the future of remote work in the region. From productivity tools to AI-driven business platforms, this chapter will explore how AI is influencing the growth of digital nomadism in Latin America, highlighting both the opportunities and challenges.

Carlos' Story: AI-Powered Productivity in Medellín

Carlos had always been drawn to Medellín for its mild climate and entrepreneurial energy. After working remotely for several years, he realized that AI could be his secret weapon for balancing multiple clients across time zones. Using tools like Grammarly to perfect his client communications and Jasper AI for drafting content, Carlos found that he could automate much of his work while focusing on the creative aspects of his projects.

What made the biggest difference, however, was how AI helped him collaborate with his clients back in the U.S. and Europe. Using Notion AI and Slack's AI features, Carlos could manage tasks, set deadlines, and communicate in real time, all while having his AI assistant handle the minor details. His workday became smoother, allowing him more time to enjoy Medellín's rich cultural life.

Carlos' story is not unique. Across Latin America, AI is empowering digital nomads to balance work and travel, making destinations like Colombia, Mexico, and Brazil attractive bases for the global workforce.

The Role of AI in the Growth of Digital Nomadism in Latin America

Latin America has long been an appealing destination for digital nomads, offering vibrant cultures, affordable living, and favourable climates. But it's the rise of AI tools and tech ecosystems in the region that are propelling it into the next frontier of remote work. Here's how AI is driving the growth of digital nomadism in Latin America:

1. AI-Enhanced Workspaces and Infrastructure

Cities like Buenos Aires, Mexico City, and São Paulo are developing into tech hubs, and with this growth comes improved infrastructure for remote work. AI-powered co-working spaces like WeWork are already common in these cities, offering digital nomads smart environments where AI adjusts lighting, temperature, and even workspace availability based on user patterns.

In addition, AI platforms are enabling better remote collaboration. Tools like Monday.com or Asana use machine learning algorithms to optimize project management and workflow efficiency. Nomads like Carlos can seamlessly juggle multiple projects, even when they're thousands of miles from their clients. For those hopping between cities in Latin America, AI-enhanced platforms ensure they can maintain their productivity, no matter where they set up their laptop.

2. AI-Driven Language Translation

With 20 countries in Latin America speaking predominantly Spanish or Portuguese, language barriers can be a challenge for non-native speakers. However, AI-powered translation tools like DeepL and Google Translate are making it easier for digital nomads to work across borders and languages. Whether you're negotiating a business deal with a local client in Mexico City or collaborating on a project with a team in Brazil, AI-driven language translation is bridging communication gaps.

These tools also help nomads participate in local communities more effectively, whether they're ordering food at a café in Bogotá or attending a business networking event in Buenos Aires. AI ensures that language is no longer a limiting factor for nomads eager to immerse themselves in the region.

3. AI in Fintech and Business Services

Latin America's rapidly growing fintech sector is another example of how AI is impacting the rise of digital nomadism. Fintech platforms powered by AI, such as Nubank in Brazil and MercadoPago in Argentina, are simplifying how nomads manage their finances across borders. These platforms offer seamless financial transactions, from paying freelancers to managing personal expenses, making it easier for nomads to work remotely without the hassle of complex banking systems.

Moreover, AI-powered business tools like Xero and QuickBooks are automating invoicing, tax filing, and bookkeeping for freelancers, ensuring compliance with local regulations while reducing administrative burdens. As a result, digital nomads can focus on growing their businesses rather than getting lost in paperwork.

Visionary Perspectives: Latin America as a Remote Work Hub

Looking ahead, AI could play an even more transformative role in making Latin America a remote work powerhouse. Imagine AI-driven platforms that recommend ideal cities for nomads based on real-time data about cost of living, internet speeds, and safety. AI could help digital nomads discover lesser-known gems, such as Cartagena in Colombia or Puerto Escondido in Mexico, which offer ideal conditions for work and travel but are still off the radar for most global nomads.

Furthermore, as AI continues to evolve, Latin American cities may start offering AI-enhanced government services designed for digital nomads. Governments could use AI to streamline visa applications, automate business registrations, and provide tax incentives tailored to remote workers, making the region even more attractive for nomads worldwide.

Practical Applications: How Digital Nomads Can Leverage AI in Latin America

Here are some practical ways that digital nomads can use AI tools to enhance their productivity and lifestyle while living and working across Latin America:

- AI-Powered Content Creation: Use tools like Jasper AI or Copy.ai to automate blog posts, marketing copy, and even social media content. This allows nomads to create high-quality content without spending hours on manual writing.

- Automate Project Management: Leverage AI-driven platforms like Trello or Monday.com to manage projects across time zones and clients. These tools help streamline tasks, assign deadlines, and track progress without needing to micromanage.

- Improve Communication: Tools like Grammarly and DeepL can refine your written communication in both English and Spanish, ensuring that you communicate professionally with clients and local collaborators.

- Financial Management with AI: Simplify your financial life by using AI-powered apps like Wave or QuickBooks to track expenses, invoice clients, and manage taxes in multiple currencies and jurisdictions.

Balancing Inspiration and Caution: The Challenges of AI in Latin America

While AI is creating exciting opportunities for digital nomads in Latin America, there are still challenges to navigate. Some regions may have inconsistent internet infrastructure, which can limit the full potential of AI-powered tools. Nomads should be prepared to invest in tools like Starlink, which provides satellite internet, to maintain reliable connectivity in more remote areas.

Additionally, as AI continues to automate various aspects of work, concerns around job displacement are valid. While digital nomads benefit from AI, there is a growing need for upskilling among local workforces. It's crucial for nomads to contribute positively to the communities they work in by supporting local innovation and ensuring that technology benefits everyone, not just those with access to advanced tools.

Conclusion: AI in Latin America—Opportunities and Challenges

Latin America is at the cusp of a digital transformation, and AI is playing a critical role in making the region an attractive destination for digital nomads. From AI-enhanced productivity tools to seamless language translation and fintech innovations, the region is becoming more accessible and tech-driven. However, as with any emerging technology, there are challenges to overcome—namely, ensuring that infrastructure keeps pace and that the benefits of AI are shared inclusively.

For digital nomads, the opportunities in Latin America are immense. By embracing AI and navigating the region's growth with intention, they can create a lifestyle that balances work, adventure, and cultural enrichment in one of the most dynamic and exciting parts of the world.

CHAPTER 90: AI IN NORTH AMERICA: THE HUB OF INNOVATION FOR DIGITAL NOMADS

As she settled into her favourite co-working space in Austin, Texas, Emily opened her laptop, greeted by the familiar hum of productivity. The workspace around her buzzed with a blend of creatives, tech developers, and entrepreneurs—all thriving in one of North America's most innovative cities for digital nomads. What set Emily's day apart, however, wasn't just the dynamic environment—it was her use of AI tools that streamlined her workflow, from automating mundane tasks to analysing client data in seconds. As a freelance UX designer, Emily knew that North America, with its AI-driven innovation, was leading the charge in reshaping the future of remote work.

North America—home to Silicon Valley, New York, and Toronto—is at the heart of the AI revolution. Digital nomads, drawn by the region's cutting-edge technologies and world-class infrastructure, are leveraging AI to enhance their work efficiency and lifestyle. In this chapter, we'll explore how AI is propelling North America to the forefront of the digital nomad movement. Through real-life case studies, practical applications, and visionary insights, we'll see how AI is enabling digital nomads to thrive in a rapidly evolving work landscape.

Emily's Story: A Day in the Life of an AI-Powered Nomad in Austin

Emily had been a digital nomad for five years, hopping between cities in Europe, Southeast Asia, and now North America. When she first arrived in Austin, she was drawn to the city's blend of innovation and creativity. But what made her transition seamless was the array of AI-powered tools she integrated into her daily workflow.

For Emily, Grammarly's AI-enhanced editing became a game-changer, ensuring that her UX documentation was polished and error-free before delivering it to clients. She also used Notion's AI features to manage her projects, allowing her to automate task lists, set reminders, and even draft outlines for her client presentations.

What really stood out, however, was how AI optimized her creative work. Using Jasper AI, Emily could generate ideas for design concepts based on minimal inputs, helping her brainstorm faster and more efficiently. As she navigated the competitive UX design market, these tools gave her a clear advantage—allowing her to focus on the creative elements while the AI handled the administrative and repetitive tasks.

Emily's story mirrors the experiences of thousands of digital nomads who are thriving across North America. Whether in Austin, San Francisco, or Toronto, AI-powered tools are transforming the way they work, communicate, and collaborate with clients globally.

AI and Innovation: How North America is Shaping the Future of Digital Nomadism

North America has long been recognized as a global hub for innovation. The region's leadership in AI development is now playing a critical role in the digital nomad ecosystem. From Silicon Valley's tech giants to Toronto's thriving AI research scene, North America is at the forefront of developing tools that cater to the needs of a global remote workforce.

1. AI-Powered Collaboration and Productivity Tools

One of the biggest draws of North America for digital nomads is the availability of AI-driven collaboration platforms that make remote work seamless. Tools like Trello, Monday.com, and Asana are widely used in the U.S. and Canada, leveraging machine learning to automate task management, track project progress, and optimize workflow. These platforms offer real-time collaboration, allowing teams to stay connected across time zones and continents. For digital nomads like Emily, who juggle multiple clients, AI-driven task management ensures that nothing slips through the cracks, no matter how fast-paced the work gets.

2. AI and the Gig Economy

North America is home to a thriving gig economy, driven in part by platforms like Upwork and Fiverr. These platforms are now using AI to match freelancers with clients more effectively. Machine learning algorithms analyse skills, project history, and client feedback to ensure that digital nomads are connected with the most relevant opportunities.

For instance, AI-driven talent matching can predict which projects are most likely to align with a freelancer's skills and interests, streamlining the job search process. This means less time spent applying for gigs and more time focusing on meaningful, creative work. For digital nomads operating in competitive fields, these AI-powered platforms are essential tools for staying ahead in the market.

3. Smart Co-Working Spaces

Across North America, co-working spaces are becoming smarter, thanks to AI. In cities like New York, Vancouver, and San Francisco, AI-enhanced co-working spaces are designed to optimize productivity and connectivity. These workspaces leverage AI to manage everything from desk availability to lighting and temperature control. For digital nomads, this means working in an environment that adapts to their needs, creating a seamless blend of comfort and efficiency.

In addition, AI-driven networking events are becoming more common. For example, platforms like Meetup are using machine learning to recommend events and professional connections based on the nomad's interests, location, and industry. This allows nomads to build networks more strategically, fostering collaboration and potential business partnerships.

Visionary Perspectives: The Future of AI for Digital Nomads in North America

As AI continues to evolve, the opportunities for digital nomads in North America are expanding. Imagine a future where AI assistants anticipate the needs of remote workers, managing their schedules, optimizing their workflows, and even automating entire projects. These AI tools will not just support work—they will predict and adapt to it, allowing digital nomads to maximize their creativity and productivity.

For instance, AI could soon create real-time work-life balance recommendations, analysing a nomad's productivity levels and suggesting breaks, mindfulness activities, or even the best time to relocate to a new city based on work and personal goals. This future of AI-powered personalization will empower digital nomads to achieve their professional objectives without sacrificing their well-being.

Practical Applications: Leveraging AI for Success in North America

If you're a digital nomad in North America or considering a move, here are some practical ways you can integrate AI into your workflow to thrive:

- Automate Routine Tasks: Use platforms like Zapier to automate repetitive tasks such as sending invoices, scheduling meetings, and even posting social media content. By automating these tasks, you can focus more on your creative and strategic work.

- Enhance Communication: Use AI-driven communication tools like Grammarly and Loom to ensure clarity in emails and client presentations. These tools can help refine language and tone, making sure your message is professional and polished.

- Manage Projects with AI: Platforms like Monday.com and Trello offer AI-powered features that help manage complex projects. These tools can prioritize tasks, track deadlines, and even predict potential roadblocks, allowing you to stay on top of your projects.

Balancing Innovation with Responsibility: Challenges in the AI Era

While North America leads in AI innovation, it's essential to remain aware of the challenges. Job displacement is a growing concern, as AI continues to automate more roles. For digital nomads, the key is to focus on skills that complement AI, such as creative problem-solving, strategic thinking, and emotional intelligence.

Additionally, issues around data privacy and algorithmic

bias require careful consideration. As AI becomes more integrated into daily work, digital nomads must remain proactive about understanding how their data is being used and advocating for ethical AI development.

Inspiring Purpose: The Role of AI in Achieving a Balanced, Fulfilling Lifestyle

For many digital nomads, the goal is not just to work remotely but to lead a life that balances professional success with personal fulfilment. AI offers the tools to achieve that balance, by freeing up time for meaningful pursuits —whether that's traveling, learning new skills, or building relationships. By embracing AI, digital nomads can not only optimize their work but also design a lifestyle that is rich with purpose and creativity.

For Emily, working in Austin's AI-enhanced co-working spaces has given her more time to engage in passion projects, collaborate with like-minded professionals, and explore the city's vibrant culture. By letting AI handle the mundane, she can focus on what truly matters—her personal and professional growth.

Conclusion: North America's AI-Driven Future for Digital Nomads

As the AI revolution continues to unfold, North America remains at the forefront of innovation, offering digital nomads the tools and infrastructure they need to thrive. From AI-powered productivity tools to smart co-working spaces, the region is leading the way in creating a remote work ecosystem that is efficient, flexible, and future-focused.

For digital nomads, the opportunities are endless. By embracing AI, you can not only streamline your work but also enhance your lifestyle, achieving a perfect balance between professional success and personal fulfilment. The future of work is here—and North America is where it's happening.

PART 19: PREPARING FOR THE FUTURE AS A DIGITAL NOMAD

CHAPTER 91: FUTURE-PROOFING YOUR CAREER WITH AI

As the sun rose over Bali, Marcus reflected on how AI had transformed his journey as a digital nomad. When he first started freelancing as a web developer, his greatest concerns were staying ahead of industry trends and continuously upskilling. However, with the rapid advancement of artificial intelligence, Marcus realized that his approach to staying competitive in the market had to evolve. Like many digital nomads, Marcus had to find new ways to adapt, learn, and thrive in an AI-driven economy. The tools that once seemed futuristic were now essential for maintaining relevance in a rapidly changing world.

This chapter delves into the strategies digital nomads like Marcus are using to future-proof their careers in an AI-powered world. By sharing real-life case studies, practical advice, and visionary insights, this chapter will provide readers with the tools and mindset they need to stay relevant, adaptable, and competitive in the AI-driven economy.

Marcus' Story: Adapting to the AI Evolution

Marcus' career as a digital nomad started in the early 2010s. Back then, the biggest challenge was finding stable remote work. Fast forward to the present, and Marcus faces a different set of challenges—AI is automating many of the tasks he once spent hours perfecting, from coding to project management. Initially, Marcus felt overwhelmed by the thought that AI might make his skills obsolete, but he soon realized that AI could be a powerful ally if used strategically.

Marcus began incorporating AI into his workflow, using tools like GitHub Copilot to help automate parts of his coding process. Instead of seeing AI as a threat, Marcus embraced it as a tool for enhancing his creativity and productivity. Now, with AI handling routine tasks, he focuses on more complex projects that require strategic thinking, problem-solving, and innovation. By continuously learning and adapting, Marcus is not only surviving but thriving in the AI age.

Embracing AI as a Tool for Growth

The key to future-proofing your career as a digital nomad is not resisting AI, but learning to work alongside it. AI is rapidly transforming industries across the globe, and the digital nomad lifestyle is no exception. Here are some strategies to ensure your career remains adaptable and relevant in an AI-driven economy:

1. Leverage AI for Upskilling

One of the greatest advantages of AI is its ability to provide real-time feedback and learning opportunities. Platforms like Coursera and Udacity use AI to personalize learning experiences, recommending courses and resources tailored to your skill gaps and career goals. Digital nomads can use these platforms to stay ahead of trends in their industry, learning AI-related skills like data analysis, machine learning, and automation.

For example, Marcus enrolled in an AI for Developers course on Coursera, where AI-powered recommendations guided him through a learning path that focused on areas where his skills were weakest. As a result, he quickly mastered AI-powered tools like TensorFlow, which allowed him to take on more complex projects and clients.

2. AI-Powered Productivity Tools

Productivity is critical for digital nomads, and AI is redefining how efficiently we work. By using AI-enhanced tools, you can automate mundane tasks and free up time for higher-level work. Tools like Grammarly for writing, Jasper AI for content creation, and Trello's AI-powered project management features are designed to help digital nomads save time and increase output.

By integrating these AI-driven tools into his workflow, Marcus was able to spend more time on creative problem-solving and innovation—skills that remain in high demand even in an AI-dominated economy. The lesson here is clear: to stay relevant, digital nomads must use AI not just to replace tasks, but to elevate their work and differentiate themselves from others.

3. Focus on Uniquely Human Skills

As AI automates routine tasks, the skills that remain valuable are those that are uniquely human—critical thinking, creativity, empathy, and leadership. These skills are much harder for AI to replicate, and they are essential for digital nomads working across industries. While AI can generate code or automate workflows, it cannot replace the human ability to navigate complex problems, build relationships, or lead teams.

For Marcus, this meant focusing on client relationships and strategic consulting. By positioning himself as a problem-solver and thought leader, he ensured that his clients valued his insights and creativity—skills that AI could not replace.

Visionary Perspectives: AI and the Future of Work

As AI technology continues to evolve, digital nomads must think beyond the immediate applications and consider how AI will shape the future of work. The roles of the future may not even exist yet, but by staying adaptable, curious, and forward-thinking, digital nomads can carve out new opportunities that leverage both human and AI capabilities.

Imagine a future where AI serves as a personal career coach, continuously monitoring the job market, analysing skill gaps, and recommending upskilling opportunities in real-time. AI could help nomads identify emerging industries or sectors where their skills are in high demand, ensuring they stay ahead of the curve.

Moreover, AI could analyse global trends and suggest optimal locations for digital nomads to base themselves, based on factors such as cost of living, industry growth, and cultural fit. By harnessing AI's predictive analytics, digital nomads can make strategic decisions that align with both their professional and personal goals.

Practical Steps for Future-Proofing Your Career

Here are some actionable steps you can take to ensure your career remains future-proof in the AI age:

- Invest in Continuous Learning: Use AI-powered platforms like Udemy, LinkedIn Learning, and DataCamp to acquire new skills. Focus on learning AI-related competencies, such as automation, data analytics, and machine learning, which are becoming essential in today's workforce.

- Embrace AI in Your Workflow: Identify areas where AI can enhance your productivity. Whether it's using Notion for project management, Zapier for automating tasks, or Jasper AI for content creation, these tools will give you a competitive edge by saving time and boosting efficiency.

- Develop Emotional Intelligence: While AI excels at logic and automation, it cannot replicate emotional intelligence, empathy, and leadership. Focus on developing these human skills, which will remain irreplaceable in any work environment.

- Stay Adaptable: The future of work is constantly evolving. Embrace a mindset of flexibility and adaptability, allowing you to pivot as needed. Keep an eye on emerging industries and be willing to explore new sectors where AI is opening doors to innovation.

Balancing Inspiration with Caution: The Challenges of AI

While the opportunities with AI are vast, it's essential to approach them with a balanced mindset. Job displacement is a real concern as automation becomes more prevalent. However, rather than seeing AI as a threat, digital nomads must see it as an opportunity to reinvent themselves and find roles where human creativity and insight are valued.

At the same time, issues of data privacy and AI ethics are becoming more important. As you integrate AI into your work, it's crucial to understand how your data is being used and to advocate for ethical AI development that benefits everyone, not just large corporations.

Motivate with Purpose: Using AI to Achieve a Balanced Life

For digital nomads, AI is not just a tool for career growth —it's also a way to achieve a more balanced, fulfilling lifestyle. By automating routine tasks and leveraging AI for productivity, you can free up more time to pursue passion projects, travel, and spend time with loved ones.

For Marcus, embracing AI allowed him to focus on what truly mattered—working on projects that inspired him, while maintaining the freedom to explore new places and build meaningful relationships. AI became not just a career tool but a lifestyle enabler.

Conclusion: Thriving in the AI-Driven Economy

Future-proofing your career in an AI-driven world requires a proactive approach. By embracing continuous learning, leveraging AI for productivity, and focusing on uniquely human skills, digital nomads can thrive in the evolving work landscape. The key is to remain adaptable, curious, and forward-thinking, ensuring that you not only stay relevant but also find new ways to grow and innovate in the AI age.

CHAPTER 92: AI AND SUSTAINABILITY FOR DIGITAL NOMADS

As Chloe sat at a café in Copenhagen, working on her sustainability consulting business, she reflected on how her digital nomad lifestyle had transformed over the years. When she first began her career, traveling while working remotely meant constant flights, disposable products, and often, a lack of focus on environmental impact. But now, with AI-driven tools at her disposal, Chloe was able to live and work more sustainably. From optimizing her travel routes to reducing her business's carbon footprint, AI was helping her align her work and lifestyle with her passion for sustainability.

In a world increasingly concerned with climate change and environmental degradation, digital nomads are in a unique position to drive sustainability efforts. However, the constant movement and international nature of their lifestyle present challenges. AI is emerging as a powerful solution, helping digital nomads adopt eco-friendly practices in both their work and personal lives. This chapter explores how AI is being leveraged by digital nomads like Chloe to promote sustainability, reduce environmental impact, and contribute to a greener planet.

Chloe's Journey: AI and Sustainable Consulting

Chloe, a digital nomad who specialized in sustainability consulting, faced a dilemma early in her career. She loved her work, but the travel and energy consumption required to run her business left her feeling like she was contributing to the very problems she sought to solve. Her turning point came when she discovered AI-powered tools that allowed her to transform both her business and lifestyle.

Using platforms like Trello's AI-powered project management system, Chloe was able to reduce the time spent on administrative tasks, cutting down on unnecessary meetings and client trips. Instead, she shifted to virtual consultations powered by Zoom's AI-enhanced video conferencing, which optimizes bandwidth to reduce energy use. When she did need to travel, Chloe used Skyscanner's AI-based carbon tracker, helping her choose flights with the lowest carbon footprints.

With AI driving much of her workflow, Chloe became more efficient and was able to significantly reduce her environmental impact. She even began offering workshops to other digital nomads on how to use AI to create more sustainable businesses. Chloe's story is an inspiring example of how AI can help digital nomads not only achieve business success but also promote sustainability in a meaningful way.

AI-Powered Sustainability Solutions for Digital Nomads

AI technology offers countless ways for digital nomads to integrate sustainability into their work and daily lives. From optimizing travel plans to reducing energy consumption, AI-powered solutions provide practical and impactful methods for digital nomads to live more consciously.

1. AI for Reducing Carbon Footprint

One of the most effective ways AI is helping digital nomads promote sustainability is by reducing carbon footprints, particularly when it comes to travel. Travel is often a necessity for digital nomads, but it is also one of the largest contributors to their environmental impact. However, tools like Google Flights' carbon emission tracking feature and Skyscanner's carbon impact tracker help travellers choose more eco-friendly routes and airlines.

Digital nomads can also use AI-driven tools like GoClimate to calculate their carbon emissions from flights and other activities. The platform offers recommendations for carbon offset programs, allowing nomads to contribute to projects that help neutralize their environmental impact.

2. Optimizing Energy Use with AI

AI-powered platforms are making it easier for digital nomads to reduce energy consumption in their daily routines. Tools like Nest and Tado, which use AI to learn users' behaviour, optimize heating and cooling systems in remote workspaces or rented accommodations, reducing unnecessary energy use. Nomads who work in shared office spaces can also rely on smart buildings that use AI to control lighting, temperature, and resource use, ensuring minimal waste.

For those living and working out of co-working spaces, platforms like WeWork use AI to regulate energy consumption based on the number of occupants in the building. This not only makes the workspace more comfortable but also reduces overall environmental impact.

3. Sustainable Workflows with AI Automation

Digital nomads often juggle multiple tasks and clients across different time zones. With AI-powered tools, they can automate much of their workflow, reducing the need for excessive travel or time-consuming activities. Zapier, an automation tool that connects apps and services, allows digital nomads to automate everything from sending invoices to setting up client calls, minimizing unnecessary use of resources.

In Chloe's case, she used Notion AI to manage her sustainability projects and client communications in one place. This allowed her to reduce the need for face-to-face meetings and streamline her operations, cutting down on the energy and time spent on logistics. These efficiencies also reduced her reliance on paper and other physical resources, making her consulting business more sustainable.

Visionary Perspectives: AI and the Future of Sustainable Nomadism

Looking ahead, AI has the potential to revolutionize how digital nomads contribute to global sustainability efforts. Imagine AI systems that could provide real-time sustainability insights based on a nomad's location and behaviour. For example, AI could suggest local eco-friendly accommodations, recommend carbon-neutral transport options, or even calculate the environmental impact of an entire trip.

AI could also help nomads find sustainable co-working spaces or connect them with local communities focused on green initiatives. This would allow digital nomads to integrate their work with local efforts, creating a global network of environmentally conscious professionals driving meaningful change.

AI might also assist digital nomads in reducing waste through AI-powered supply chain monitoring. For example, AI could analyse the supply chain of the digital tools or services they use, identifying opportunities to switch to greener alternatives and reduce environmental harm.

Practical Tips: How to Use AI for a Sustainable Nomad

Lifestyle

If you're a digital nomad looking to promote sustainability in your work and life, here are some practical ways AI can help you achieve your goals:

- Choose Low-Carbon Travel: Use AI-powered tools like Google Flights and Skyscanner to choose flights and travel options with the lowest carbon impact. Consider using carbon offset platforms like GoClimate to neutralize emissions.

- Optimize Your Workspace: Whether working from a co-working space or a home office, use AI-driven energy management systems like Nest or Tado to reduce energy consumption by optimizing heating and cooling systems.

- Automate Sustainable Workflows: Use tools like Zapier and Notion AI to automate repetitive tasks and reduce your need for physical resources. AI can help you streamline operations and reduce your environmental impact through efficiency.

- Engage in AI-Powered Offsetting: Platforms like Pachama use AI to identify credible carbon offset projects, allowing you to contribute to reforestation, conservation, or renewable energy initiatives that align with your sustainability goals.

Balancing Inspiration and Caution: Challenges and Ethical Considerations

While AI offers exciting opportunities for digital nomads to live and work more sustainably, it's important to consider the potential challenges. Data privacy and ethical AI development remain critical concerns as AI systems become more integrated into daily life. Digital nomads should take care to ensure that the tools they use adhere to ethical standards, promoting transparency and responsible use of technology.

Additionally, AI alone cannot solve all environmental challenges. Digital nomads must pair AI-powered sustainability efforts with conscious choices about consumption, waste reduction, and supporting sustainable industries.

Motivate with Purpose: AI as a Tool for a Greener Future

For digital nomads, AI is more than just a tool for efficiency—it's a way to live a life aligned with purpose. By using AI to make more sustainable choices, digital nomads can contribute to global efforts to combat climate change and environmental degradation. The goal is not just to reduce one's carbon footprint, but to create a lifestyle that prioritizes sustainability at every level.

Chloe's journey is a testament to how AI can empower individuals to live more sustainably while still thriving professionally. Her ability to balance her love of travel, work, and environmental impact serves as an inspiration to digital nomads around the world.

Conclusion: AI and the Sustainable Nomad Movement

As digital nomads, we are in a unique position to leverage technology and innovation to create positive change. AI offers unprecedented opportunities to reduce our environmental impact, making it possible to work and live sustainably no matter where we are in the world. By integrating AI-powered sustainability solutions into our workflows and lifestyles, we can contribute to a more sustainable future—one that supports both our careers and the planet.

The future is green, and with AI on our side, the path to sustainability is clearer than ever.

CHAPTER 93: ADAPTING TO AI-DRIVEN INDUSTRIES

As Maya sat overlooking the coast of Portugal, she marvelled at the journey she had taken as a digital nomad. Five years ago, she had been working as a freelance marketing consultant, helping small businesses build their online presence. Today, she was at the cutting edge of a different world—using AI tools to optimize digital marketing strategies, predict customer behaviour, and automate content creation. Maya's career had shifted dramatically as AI transformed the marketing industry, but her adaptability had allowed her not just to survive but to thrive.

This chapter explores how digital nomads like Maya are adapting to industries increasingly shaped by artificial intelligence. From healthcare to finance, AI is revolutionizing traditional business models and creating new opportunities for those ready to embrace the change. We will dive into the key industries being disrupted by AI, share real-life case studies of digital nomads succeeding in these fields, and offer practical strategies for staying ahead in an AI-driven world.

Maya's Story: Thriving in AI-Powered Marketing

Maya's journey into AI began when she noticed that many of her clients were shifting towards automation in their marketing strategies. Campaigns that once required hours of manual analysis could now be executed in minutes, thanks to AI tools like HubSpot and Marketo. Initially intimidated by the technology, Maya decided to upskill by taking online courses in AI-driven marketing tools and data analytics. Soon, she was integrating tools like Jasper AI for automated content generation and Hootsuite AI for predictive social media management into her client workflows. These tools didn't just make her more efficient; they allowed her to offer more value to her clients by delivering personalized marketing strategies at scale.

Today, Maya's business has grown exponentially. She now works with international clients, helping them harness AI for customer segmentation, email marketing, and campaign optimization. By adapting to AI-driven technologies, Maya has positioned herself at the forefront of the marketing industry, offering insights and expertise that keep her clients competitive in a fast-changing landscape.

AI-Driven Industries: Where Nomads Can Thrive

As AI continues to reshape global industries, it's crucial for digital nomads to understand where the most significant opportunities lie. The key is not just to be aware of how AI is impacting different sectors but to actively seek out ways to integrate AI into your career. Here are some of the industries that are most affected by AI, along with practical tips on how digital nomads can thrive within them.

1. Marketing and Advertising

As Maya's story demonstrates, marketing is one of the industries most affected by AI. AI-powered tools for customer behaviour analysis, content creation, and campaign automation have revolutionized the way marketing works. Digital nomads in this field can take advantage of platforms like Google Analytics, which now uses machine learning to offer insights into customer behaviour and predict trends. Tools like Jasper AI can generate blog posts, social media content, and ad copy based on minimal input, saving time and increasing productivity.

For digital nomads working in marketing, the key is to become fluent in AI-driven tools and platforms. By offering clients services that integrate AI—such as predictive analytics, personalized content strategies, and AI-enhanced SEO—you can stay ahead of the curve and command higher rates.

2. Healthcare and Telemedicine

Healthcare is experiencing a significant transformation due to AI. AI-driven diagnostics, personalized medicine, and telehealth platforms are making healthcare more accessible and efficient. Digital nomads working in healthcare can leverage AI-powered tools like IBM Watson Health, which helps analyse patient data and recommend treatment plans, or Tempus, an AI platform that provides precision medicine insights.

Telemedicine has also opened up new possibilities for healthcare professionals to offer services remotely. AI-enhanced telehealth platforms are being used to diagnose patients, manage treatment plans, and streamline communication between doctors and patients. Digital nomads with a background in healthcare can offer their services to clients around the world by utilizing these AI-powered platforms, allowing them to practice medicine remotely and with greater accuracy.

3. Finance and FinTech

The finance industry is undergoing a major transformation due to AI-powered technologies that streamline processes like fraud detection, risk management, and trading algorithms. Platforms like Kensho and AlphaSense provide financial insights using machine learning, helping analysts make more informed decisions. AI tools are also being used to manage portfolios, optimize trades, and offer personalized investment advice.

For digital nomads working in finance, staying ahead means mastering AI tools like Robo-Advisors, which automate investment management, and using machine learning to analyse market trends. FinTech startups are also expanding globally, offering nomads opportunities to consult on AI-powered finance solutions, develop algorithms, or manage digital assets.

4. Education and E-Learning

AI is transforming the education industry by making learning more personalized and accessible. Platforms like Coursera, Udemy, and Duolingo use AI to create customized learning paths for users, while tools like Grammarly provide real-time feedback on writing. AI-driven chatbots and virtual tutors are helping educators provide real-time assistance to students across the globe.

For digital nomads interested in education, offering AI-enhanced services like personalized tutoring, online course creation, or curriculum development can be highly lucrative. By staying informed about the latest AI tools for education and e-learning, nomads can create and deliver educational experiences that are tailored to each learner's needs, regardless of location.

5. Creative Industries: Art, Music, and Design

While the creative industries were once thought to be immune to automation, AI is now making its mark in art, music, and design. AI-powered design tools like Canva and Adobe Sensei are helping creatives streamline workflows and generate new ideas. In the music industry, AI-driven platforms like Amper Music and Aiva can compose original tracks based on input parameters, offering new opportunities for musicians to experiment with sound.

Digital nomads in creative fields can use AI to boost their output, experiment with new forms of expression, and even collaborate with AI to generate novel ideas. The combination of human creativity and AI's computational power opens up endless possibilities for innovation in these fields.

Visionary Perspectives: The Future of AI-Driven Work

As AI continues to evolve, it will not only transform existing industries but also give rise to entirely new ones. Digital nomads who are adaptable, curious, and forward-thinking will be best positioned to take advantage of these changes. Imagine a future where AI assistants not only help manage your daily work but also predict the skills you'll need for future projects, offering real-time learning suggestions and automating tasks that require creativity and strategy.

Moreover, as industries continue to merge with AI, new cross-disciplinary opportunities will arise. Digital nomads with a blend of skills—like marketing and AI programming or healthcare and data analysis—will have a unique advantage in the job market. AI is reshaping the boundaries of work, and those willing to explore these intersections will be the pioneers of tomorrow.

Practical Steps for Thriving in AI-Driven Industries

If you're looking to future-proof your career as a digital nomad, here are some steps to take:

- Invest in AI Skills: Start by learning the basics of AI through platforms like Coursera, Udemy, or LinkedIn Learning. Focus on areas that align with your industry, such as AI for marketing, finance, or healthcare.

- Stay Curious and Experiment: Don't be afraid to experiment with new AI tools. Try out AI-enhanced design platforms, predictive analytics software, or machine learning algorithms relevant to your work.

- Blend Disciplines: As AI reshapes industries, it's important to cultivate a diverse skill set. Combine your current expertise with AI knowledge, opening up new opportunities for interdisciplinary work.

- Network in AI-Driven Communities: Join AI-focused communities, attend conferences, or participate in online forums where professionals discuss AI's impact on various industries. This will help you stay informed about the latest trends and opportunities.

Balancing Inspiration and Caution

While AI presents incredible opportunities, it's important to acknowledge the challenges that come with it. Job displacement is a real concern as automation becomes more prevalent. However, rather than viewing AI as a threat, digital nomads should see it as an opportunity to upskill, adapt, and offer services that complement AI's capabilities.

Additionally, issues around data privacy and ethical AI use will continue to grow in importance. As industries become more reliant on AI, digital nomads must ensure that they are using ethical AI tools and protecting the privacy of their clients and users.

Conclusion: A New Era of Opportunity

AI is more than just a tool for enhancing efficiency— it's opening the door to entirely new possibilities across industries. For digital nomads, this means an unprecedented opportunity to work in innovative fields, create new services, and adapt to the demands of a rapidly evolving job market.

By staying curious, continuously learning, and embracing AI as a partner, digital nomads can thrive in an AI-driven economy and carve out their own niche in the future of work.

CHAPTER 94: PREPARING FOR AI DISRUPTION: A DIGITAL NOMAD'S GUIDE

As Elena zipped through the busy streets of Mexico City on her way to a co-working space, she couldn't help but think about how much her career had changed in the last few years. A freelance translator by trade, she had built her business on her ability to work with multiple languages. But AI tools like Google Translate and DeepL had gradually encroached on her niche. Instead of panicking, Elena took it as a sign to adapt. She began learning how to integrate AI translation tools into her work, offering services that involved both human oversight and machine translation. This hybrid approach allowed her to stay competitive in a rapidly shifting market, and she even began advising other translators on how to future-proof their careers.

Elena's story is one of resilience and adaptability—two traits that are essential for digital nomads navigating the disruptions caused by AI. As industries evolve and jobs transform, it's crucial for digital nomads to be proactive about the changes that lie ahead. This chapter will explore practical strategies for preparing for AI-driven disruptions, highlighting real-world examples of nomads like Elena who have successfully adapted to these shifts.

Understanding the Scope of AI Disruption

AI is reshaping industries at an unprecedented pace, and its impact is being felt across a wide range of fields, from finance to healthcare to the creative arts. For digital nomads, this presents both challenges and opportunities. While automation and AI-powered tools may replace certain tasks, they also open up new possibilities for innovation, efficiency, and growth.

AI disruption isn't something that happens overnight— it's a gradual process. The key is to stay ahead of the curve by being informed, adaptable, and proactive. Digital nomads, who are already skilled at navigating change and uncertainty, are in a prime position to leverage these technologies rather than be displaced by them.

Case Study: Elena's Adaptation to AI in Translation

Elena's journey is a perfect example of how digital nomads can prepare for AI disruptions in their industries. When she first noticed the rise of AI translation tools, she could have viewed them as direct competition. Instead, she saw an opportunity to expand her services. She began offering AI-assisted translation services, where she used AI tools to handle the bulk of the translation work but added a layer of human expertise for cultural nuances and context. This allowed her to take on more clients and focus on higher-value tasks, such as providing linguistic consultation or managing multilingual projects.

Elena's proactive approach enabled her to not only survive in an AI-disrupted industry but also thrive by embracing AI as an enhancement to her work. The lesson here is that

AI doesn't necessarily mean the end of traditional jobs—it often means a transformation of those roles, with new opportunities for growth and specialization.

Practical Steps to Prepare for AI Disruption

If you're a digital nomad, the question isn't whether AI will affect your industry—it's how and when. Here are some practical steps you can take to prepare for AI-driven disruptions in your field:

1. Stay Informed About Industry Trends

The first step in preparing for AI disruption is to stay informed. This means keeping up with the latest advancements in AI technologies and understanding how they're impacting your industry. Subscribe to relevant blogs, attend webinars, or participate in online communities that discuss the intersection of AI and your field.

For example, if you work in marketing, AI tools like Jasper AI and HubSpot are already making significant strides in automating content creation and customer segmentation. Understanding these tools and how they work will allow you to offer value-added services that go beyond what AI can do on its own.

2. Invest in Continuous Learning

One of the best ways to future-proof your career is to invest in continuous learning. As AI continues to evolve, new skills will be in demand. Whether it's learning to code, understanding machine learning algorithms, or mastering AI-driven platforms specific to your industry, upskilling is essential.

Platforms like Coursera and Udemy offer AI-focused courses in everything from data analysis to automation tools. For digital nomads, the ability to learn on the go is a major advantage. By dedicating time to learning new skills, you'll be better equipped to adapt to the changing landscape.

3. Embrace AI as a Tool, Not a Threat

As Elena's story illustrates, AI doesn't have to be a threat—it can be a powerful tool that enhances your work. Instead of viewing AI as competition, look for ways to integrate it into your workflow. This could mean using AI-powered tools to automate repetitive tasks, freeing you up to focus on higher-level work.

For example, if you're a freelance writer, tools like Grammarly and Jasper AI can help you speed up the editing process and generate content ideas. If you're in graphic design, AI platforms like Adobe Sensei can assist in creating templates and layouts, allowing you to focus on creative direction.

4. Diversify Your Skill Set

AI disruptions often affect specific tasks within industries, but they rarely eliminate entire professions. One way to prepare for these disruptions is to diversify your skill set. For instance, if you're a content creator, learning how to integrate AI tools for content optimization can expand the services you offer.

Diversification also allows you to pivot more easily if AI significantly disrupts one area of your work. For example, a digital nomad who works in social media management could also learn SEO, analytics, and digital advertising, creating a more comprehensive service offering.

5. Network with AI-Forward Communities

As AI continues to transform industries, networking with like-minded professionals is more important than ever. Join AI-forward communities, attend virtual conferences, and participate in online forums where AI developments are discussed. Being part of these communities will keep you informed about new trends and help you build connections with others who are navigating similar challenges.

Communities like AI for Good or Women in AI offer resources, networking opportunities, and support for those working in AI-driven industries. By connecting with others, you'll gain insights into how different fields are evolving and be better equipped to adapt to those changes.

Visionary Perspectives: The Future of AI-Driven Work

The future of work is evolving rapidly, with AI at the forefront of this transformation. As digital nomads, the ability to adapt, learn, and evolve is crucial for staying relevant. AI will continue to change how industries operate, but it will also create new opportunities for those willing to embrace it.

Imagine a world where AI acts as an assistant, handling mundane tasks and allowing you to focus on creative and strategic work. AI might not replace your job, but it could reshape it in ways that give you more freedom and flexibility. The key is to stay open to these changes, continuously learn, and remain adaptable.

Balancing Inspiration with Caution

While AI offers exciting opportunities, it's also important to approach these advancements with caution. Job displacement is a real concern, particularly for tasks that can be easily automated. However, by focusing on skills that AI cannot replicate—such as emotional intelligence, creativity, and complex problem-solving—you can position yourself in roles that remain essential in an AI-driven world.

Privacy and ethics are also critical considerations. As digital nomads, you'll need to be mindful of how AI tools handle data and ensure that you're using platforms that prioritize transparency and ethical practices.

Conclusion: Embrace AI, Don't Fear It

The world is moving toward a future where AI plays an integral role in nearly every industry. For digital nomads, this presents a unique opportunity to embrace change, adapt quickly, and stay ahead of the curve. By investing in continuous learning, diversifying your skill set, and leveraging AI as a tool rather than a threat, you can prepare for the disruptions ahead and ensure your place in an AI-powered world.

Elena's journey shows that adaptability and a willingness to embrace technology are the keys to thriving in a rapidly changing landscape. As digital nomads, you have the flexibility to navigate these changes with creativity and resilience, turning AI-driven disruptions into opportunities for growth and innovation.

CHAPTER 95: AI, LONGEVITY, AND WORK-LIFE BALANCE

As Amanda travelled through the picturesque landscapes of Bali, she marvelled at how much her digital nomad lifestyle had evolved. A few years ago, balancing her work as a freelance copywriter with her passion for travel seemed overwhelming. Long hours, the stress of constant deadlines, and the pressure to stay ahead in a competitive field had taken a toll on her well-being. But today, things were different. Thanks to AI tools like Jasper AI and Grammarly, Amanda had not only streamlined her work processes but also carved out time to recharge, explore, and enjoy a richer, more balanced lifestyle.

Amanda's story is one of many digital nomads who have successfully harnessed the power of AI to enhance both their professional longevity and work-life balance. While the digital nomad lifestyle offers unparalleled freedom, it can also lead to burnout if not managed properly. This chapter will explore how AI can serve as a powerful ally in helping nomads maintain longevity in their careers, all while avoiding the dreaded burnout that so many remote workers face.

The Strain of Constant Mobility

The life of a digital nomad comes with a unique set of

challenges. The freedom to work from anywhere in the world can sometimes feel like a double-edged sword. On one hand, it allows individuals to immerse themselves in new cultures, meet diverse people, and live life on their own terms. On the other hand, the lack of routine, time zone differences, and the pressure to maintain a steady income can lead to fatigue, mental exhaustion, and ultimately burnout.

AI technology is stepping in to offer solutions that not only improve productivity but also protect mental health by allowing nomads to work smarter, not harder. By automating repetitive tasks, optimizing time management, and facilitating better decision-making, AI can help digital nomads reclaim time for what matters most—whether that's pursuing personal passions, nurturing relationships, or simply resting.

Case Study: Amanda's Use of AI to Boost Work-Life Balance

Amanda's transformation is a shining example of how AI can enhance both productivity and well-being. As a content creator, she often found herself drowning in a sea of deadlines, revisions, and client requests. She would work late into the night, struggling to maintain her creative edge while meeting client demands.

Once Amanda integrated AI into her daily workflow, everything changed. Tools like Jasper AI helped her draft content faster by suggesting ideas and frameworks, while Grammarly ensured her writing was polished with minimal effort on her part. Instead of spending hours on repetitive tasks, Amanda now focuses on creative strategy and client relationship building. With AI handling much of the operational grind, she has significantly reduced her working hours, leaving more time for personal pursuits like yoga, exploring new destinations, and meeting fellow travellers.

By leveraging AI, Amanda not only maintained her career

but elevated it, positioning herself as a strategic consultant rather than a mere content producer. Her mental clarity and reduced stress levels have allowed her to remain energized, creative, and committed to her lifestyle as a digital nomad.

How AI Can Support Longevity in a Digital Nomad Career

AI can play a vital role in helping digital nomads sustain their careers over the long term. Here's how:

1. Automating Time-Consuming Tasks

Many digital nomads struggle with tasks that drain their time and energy. Whether it's scheduling social media posts, editing content, managing client emails, or processing invoices, these repetitive tasks can add up, leaving less time for high-impact work.

AI-powered tools like Buffer for social media scheduling, Grammarly for content editing, and Xero for automating finances help streamline daily tasks, allowing digital nomads to focus on what they do best. By automating the mundane, nomads can avoid burnout while increasing efficiency.

2. Optimizing Time Management

Time management can be tricky for digital nomads, especially when juggling multiple projects across different time zones. AI tools like Toggl and RescueTime use data to analyse how time is spent, providing actionable insights on how to allocate it more effectively. These tools help nomads identify time-wasting activities and optimize their schedules for peak productivity.

By using AI to create a more structured workday, digital nomads can achieve better work-life balance, ensuring they have ample time for both work and play.

3. Enhancing Decision-Making

One of the most underrated benefits of AI is its ability to support decision-making. AI tools like Trello and Asana, powered by intelligent algorithms, help nomads organize their projects, prioritize tasks, and allocate resources efficiently. This reduces the mental strain of managing complex workflows, allowing digital nomads to focus on strategic tasks that drive growth.

By relieving nomads from the burden of making constant, small decisions, AI enhances mental clarity and reduces decision fatigue—a common cause of burnout.

Inspire Through Visionary Perspectives

The future of work for digital nomads holds exciting possibilities as AI continues to evolve. Imagine a world where AI tools anticipate your work patterns, learn your preferences, and adjust your workload accordingly. AI could act as your personal assistant, taking over administrative tasks, managing your calendar, and even suggesting times to take breaks based on your energy levels. The balance between work and personal life could become so seamless that burnout becomes a thing of the past.

We are already seeing early signs of this. Tools like Clockwise, an AI-driven calendar assistant, are designed to protect focused work time while ensuring sufficient breaks throughout the day. This foresight into managing workloads could fundamentally change the way digital nomads approach their careers, leading to sustainable long-term success.

Balance Between Inspiration and Caution

While AI offers remarkable opportunities for enhancing work-life balance, it's important to acknowledge potential downsides. Over-reliance on automation could result in a loss of creativity and human touch in certain fields. Digital nomads should aim to strike a balance by using AI as a tool to assist, not replace, their unique human contributions.

Moreover, mental health and well-being should remain a priority, even with AI assistance. It's essential to maintain boundaries and not allow the convenience of 24/7 work capabilities to blur the line between work and personal life. AI should be used to create space for rest and recharge, not to extend working hours.

Motivating with Purpose and Fulfilment

AI offers digital nomads the opportunity to rethink how they approach work. By reducing the burden of menial tasks, it frees up time to pursue more fulfilling endeavours, whether that's expanding a business, exploring new cultures, or investing in personal growth. The flexibility that AI brings allows nomads to focus on passion projects, humanitarian causes, or simply spend more time in nature—fostering a deep sense of purpose beyond just work.

Conclusion: Embrace AI for Long-Term Success

Incorporating AI into your career as a digital nomad isn't just about increasing productivity—it's about creating a lifestyle that supports longevity and well-being. By automating repetitive tasks, optimizing time management, and providing valuable insights, AI can help you maintain balance, stay energized, and focus on what truly matters.

Just as Amanda's story illustrates, AI can be a game-changer for digital nomads who want to thrive without sacrificing their health and happiness. As you embrace these tools, you'll find yourself not only more productive but more fulfilled, with the energy and clarity to continue your journey for years to come.

PART 20: THE ENDGAME FOR AI AND DIGITAL NOMADS

CHAPTER 96: AI AND UNIVERSAL BASIC INCOME – A NEW PARADIGM FOR DIGITAL NOMADS

As Carlos sat on the balcony of his apartment in Lisbon, enjoying the Atlantic breeze, he reflected on how much his life had changed. Only a year ago, he had been juggling multiple freelance projects, working long hours to make ends meet, and constantly worrying about where his next pay check would come from. Today, thanks to a combination of AI-driven productivity tools and a new initiative that provided a universal basic income (UBI) to all residents of his country, Carlos's life as a digital nomad had reached new heights of balance, creativity, and freedom.

Carlos's story is a glimpse into the future of work, where artificial intelligence and universal basic income (UBI) are reshaping the lifestyle of digital nomads. In a world where AI continues to automate routine tasks, UBI presents an intriguing opportunity for nomads to achieve financial security, pursue passion projects, and explore a more balanced way of life. This chapter will delve into how these two transformative forces—AI and UBI—are intersecting and impacting the nomadic workforce.

The Promise of Universal Basic Income

Universal Basic Income is a concept in which every citizen receives a regular, unconditional sum of money from the government, regardless of their employment status. The idea is simple: provide people with a financial safety net to cover basic needs, such as housing, food, and healthcare. Proponents argue that UBI could address the growing economic inequality exacerbated by automation and AI-driven job displacement.

For digital nomads, UBI holds the promise of stability in an uncertain world. Many nomads work freelance or contract jobs, which come with inconsistent pay and no guarantees. UBI could offer a foundation of financial security, allowing nomads to focus on building sustainable businesses, exploring creative endeavours, or traveling the world without the constant pressure to secure new clients or gigs.

Case Study: Carlos's Journey with AI and UBI

Carlos was a software developer who had always dreamed of becoming a full-time digital nomad. However, he hesitated for years due to the financial instability of freelance work. In his previous job, he felt trapped by the need for a steady pay check to cover his basic expenses.

When his country introduced UBI, everything changed. With a monthly stipend covering his essential costs, Carlos took the leap into digital nomadism, leveraging AI tools to streamline his freelance work. He used GitHub Copilot, an AI-powered coding assistant, to speed up his programming tasks. What once took him hours to write by hand, Copilot could generate in a fraction of the time, freeing Carlos to focus on more creative coding challenges.

With UBI covering his living expenses and AI boosting his productivity, Carlos had the freedom to take on passion projects he'd never had time for before. He started contributing to open-source projects, launching a blog to teach others about AI programming, and even began learning new languages as he travelled through Europe. UBI and AI transformed Carlos's life by allowing him to pursue work that brought him joy rather than simply taking on gigs to survive.

AI and UBI: A New Era of Work-Life Balance

The combination of AI and UBI represents a shift in the digital nomad experience from one of survival to one of thriving. AI tools enhance productivity by automating repetitive tasks, enabling nomads to complete more work in less time. Meanwhile, UBI provides a financial cushion that alleviates the constant pressure of chasing income. Together, these two forces enable digital nomads to focus on higher-value activities that fuel personal growth, creativity, and fulfilment.

In the past, digital nomads often faced the challenge of balancing work and life. The allure of traveling the world while working remotely was tempered by the reality of long hours, unstable income, and the pressure to maintain a steady flow of clients. AI and UBI could address these challenges by:

- Reducing financial anxiety: UBI provides a baseline income, which alleviates the stress of financial insecurity. This allows digital nomads to take on projects that align with their passions rather than just those that pay the bills.
- Fostering creativity: With AI tools taking care of mundane tasks, digital nomads can focus on creative and strategic work. Whether it's building a new product, starting a side business, or contributing to a cause they care about, AI frees

up time for what truly matters.

- Supporting continuous learning: AI-powered learning platforms, like Coursera and Udemy, offer personalized, self-paced courses that digital nomads can access from anywhere. Combined with the financial freedom provided by UBI, nomads can continually upskill, staying competitive in the fast-changing job market.

Practical Application: How to Leverage AI and UBI for a Better Life

For digital nomads, the integration of AI and UBI could create a more balanced, purpose-driven life. Here are some actionable ways to thrive in this new paradigm:

1. Automate the Routine: Use AI tools like Jasper AI for content creation, Grammarly for editing, and Toggl for time management to reduce the time spent on routine tasks. This allows you to focus on higher-value activities that contribute to your long-term goals.

2. Embrace Financial Freedom: If you have access to UBI or a similar safety net, consider how you can use that financial stability to explore new ventures. With basic expenses covered, take the opportunity to launch a passion project, learn new skills, or travel to new destinations.

3. Prioritize Work-Life Balance: Leverage the combination of AI and UBI to create a schedule that prioritizes your well-being. Build in time for rest, exploration, and hobbies. Use AI to optimize your work hours, and remember that UBI can give you the financial flexibility to take a break when needed.

4. Explore Creative Ventures: With more time on your hands, now is the perfect moment to dive into creative pursuits. Whether it's starting a podcast, writing a book, or learning a new art form, use AI to enhance your creative processes and UBI to remove the financial barrier to pursuing those

passions.

Visionary Perspectives: The Future of Work for Digital Nomads

Looking ahead, the intersection of AI and UBI could redefine what it means to be a digital nomad. Imagine a future where AI assistants handle 80% of your administrative tasks, while UBI ensures that no matter where you are in the world, your basic needs are met. This shift could open up endless possibilities for nomads to pursue passion projects, engage in social impact work, or even start their own businesses without the fear of financial instability.

AI's role in shaping the future of work goes beyond just productivity—it's about giving people the freedom to create, innovate, and live with purpose. As AI continues to evolve, it will unlock new ways for digital nomads to maximize their time and resources, allowing them to lead richer, more fulfilling lives.

Conclusion: A Purpose-Driven Future with AI and UBI

The combination of AI and universal basic income offers digital nomads a unique opportunity to thrive in ways previously unimaginable. By automating routine tasks, enhancing productivity, and providing financial security, these two forces empower nomads to focus on what truly matters. Whether it's pursuing creative passions, exploring the world, or giving back to communities, AI and UBI provide the foundation for a life that is not only sustainable but also deeply fulfilling.

As the world continues to change, digital nomads who embrace AI and UBI will find themselves at the forefront of a new era of work—one defined not by survival but by the pursuit of purpose, passion, and personal growth.

CHAPTER 97: WILL AI REDEFINE THE NOMADIC DREAM?

As Diego packed his laptop into his backpack and prepared to leave his temporary office—a cozy café in Buenos Aires —he reflected on how profoundly AI had transformed his life as a digital nomad. It wasn't just about automating tasks or using smart tools to streamline his work; AI had fundamentally redefined what it meant to live a location-independent lifestyle. With AI-powered platforms helping him find clients, automate repetitive work, and even organize his travel logistics, Diego found himself with more time to explore the world and pursue his passions.

Diego's journey, like that of many digital nomads, highlights a deeper shift in the digital nomad movement: AI is not just changing how nomads work—it's reshaping the very nature of what it means to be a nomad. In this chapter, we'll explore how AI might redefine the nomadic dream, making it more accessible, sustainable, and purpose-driven than ever before.

AI-Powered Workflows: Beyond Efficiency

For many digital nomads, the dream of working remotely while traveling the world often comes with the reality of juggling multiple freelance jobs, meeting deadlines, and managing clients across different time zones. But AI is changing that equation. Tools like Jasper AI for content generation, Canva's AI-powered design templates, and GitHub Copilot for coding are allowing nomads to automate much of their routine work, reducing the time spent on tedious tasks.

Take the story of Sophia, a freelance writer who travels full-time. AI tools have completely transformed how she approaches her work. With Jasper AI, Sophia can generate outlines, blog posts, and even SEO-optimized content in a fraction of the time it used to take her. Once she has a draft, she refines it with Grammarly, which suggests style improvements, grammar corrections, and tone adjustments. The result? Sophia now spends 50% less time on writing and editing, allowing her more time to explore new places, take on passion projects, and pursue deeper personal fulfilment.

But beyond productivity gains, AI is creating new opportunities for nomads to move up the value chain. Instead of being bogged down by repetitive work, AI frees nomads to focus on more strategic, creative, and relationship-driven aspects of their work. By leveraging AI as a partner, digital nomads are able to offer clients higher-value services like creative strategy, innovation consulting, or data-driven insights.

Practical Application: How AI Can Amplify Your Nomadic Career

The integration of AI into the digital nomad lifestyle is not just a theoretical concept—it's a practical revolution that can be applied today. Here are actionable steps to make the most of AI in your career:

1. Automate Client Communication: Use AI chatbots or virtual assistants like ManyChat or Tidio to handle basic inquiries, schedule meetings, and provide updates to clients in real-time, no matter where you are in the world.

2. Content Creation on Autopilot: Writers, designers, and marketers can use tools like Copy.ai, Descript, or Lumen5 to generate ideas, draft copy, and create engaging multimedia content quickly and efficiently.

3. AI-Powered Market Research: Platforms like Crimson Hexagon or Quid can sift through vast amounts of data to provide insights about industry trends, consumer sentiment, or competitive analysis—allowing nomads to stay ahead of the curve and offer clients valuable insights.

4. Remote Collaboration Made Seamless: Tools like Notion AI or Miro powered by AI allow teams to collaborate asynchronously, using smart assistants to automate workflow creation, task assignments, and project updates— perfect for nomads managing global teams.

5. AI for Personal Development: Leverage AI-powered learning platforms such as Coursera or LinkedIn Learning, which provide tailored courses to help you develop new skills and stay competitive. With AI-curated learning paths, you can focus on gaining expertise in areas where your career is most likely to thrive in the AI age.

A New Vision for Nomadic Freedom

Traditionally, the digital nomad dream revolved around freedom—freedom from the 9-to-5 grind, freedom from location constraints, and freedom to live life on one's own terms. But AI is expanding this vision in unexpected ways.

Imagine a world where AI handles all mundane work, from email sorting to appointment scheduling, leaving you free to pursue your most creative and fulfilling activities. Digital nomads like Zoe, a visual artist who travels throughout Southeast Asia, are already living this reality. Using RunwayML, an AI-powered creative tool, Zoe experiments with generative art, pushing the boundaries of her work in ways she never thought possible.

What's even more exciting is that AI opens up opportunities for nomads to not only optimize their work-life balance but to create entirely new career paths. As AI automates more jobs, roles like AI trainers, digital curators, and creative strategists will become increasingly vital. Nomads who embrace continuous learning and upskilling will find themselves positioned at the forefront of these emerging industries.

A Balanced Perspective: The Challenges of AI for Nomads

While AI brings incredible opportunities, it's essential to address the potential challenges it introduces. One concern is that AI might lead to increased job displacement, particularly for those who rely on routine or administrative freelance work. While AI has the potential to take over these lower-value tasks, it's crucial for nomads to proactively learn new skills and adapt to AI advancements.

Carlos, a digital marketer, faced this reality head-on when AI tools began to replace some of the basic marketing services he offered. Rather than resist the change, he embraced the opportunity to upskill. He took courses on data science and AI-driven marketing strategies, which allowed him to offer more advanced and valuable services to his clients. By staying ahead of AI developments, Carlos transformed what could have been a challenge into a competitive advantage.

The key lesson? AI will undoubtedly continue to disrupt industries, but those who embrace lifelong learning and adapt to new technologies will thrive. As digital nomads, staying agile is the secret to longevity in the AI age.

Inspiring the Future: The AI-Powered Nomad Dream

Looking to the future, AI may even reshape the digital nomad dream itself. Imagine a future where AI-powered virtual workspaces make it possible to collaborate seamlessly across time zones, cultures, and even languages. Virtual assistants might anticipate our work needs before we do, managing everything from booking travel to predicting market shifts.

In this AI-powered future, the definition of "freedom" will expand to include not just the ability to work from anywhere, but the opportunity to craft a life of purpose, passion, and constant reinvention. With AI handling the routine, digital nomads will be free to pursue endeavours that inspire and fulfil them—whether that means building businesses, contributing to social impact projects, or embarking on creative adventures.

Conclusion: Crafting a Purpose-Driven Nomadic Life with AI

AI is set to redefine what it means to be a digital nomad, offering opportunities for deeper freedom, creativity, and purpose. By embracing AI as a partner rather than a competitor, digital nomads can elevate their work and personal lives to new heights. Whether through automating tasks, exploring new creative avenues, or staying ahead of industry trends, AI empowers nomads to craft a life not just of mobility but of meaning.

As the AI revolution unfolds, digital nomads will be among the first to experience the full potential of this new era. The question isn't whether AI will redefine the nomadic dream— but how boldly we will embrace the future it offers.

CHAPTER 98: THE ROLE OF GOVERNMENTS IN AN AI-NOMAD WORLD

As digital nomadism continues to grow in popularity and artificial intelligence (AI) reshapes industries worldwide, a new question has emerged: How are governments adapting to this shift? The intersection of AI and the digital nomad lifestyle has brought about opportunities, challenges, and the need for policy adaptations. Governments, once focused solely on traditional workforce policies, are now beginning to explore what it means to support a future where more people work remotely, often moving across borders while leveraging AI tools for unprecedented productivity and flexibility.

In this chapter, we will explore how governments are preparing for this AI-powered, borderless workforce. Through real-life examples, practical policy changes, and visionary perspectives, we'll dive into what the future may hold for digital nomads and how the role of governments is evolving in this new era.

A Story of Change: Estonia's E-Residency

In 2014, Estonia became one of the first countries to truly embrace the digital revolution by introducing the e-Residency program, an initiative that allowed entrepreneurs and freelancers from around the world to establish and run an EU-based business without needing to reside in Estonia. This visionary move has since attracted thousands of digital nomads seeking legal, financial, and business infrastructure without the burden of geographical limitations.

Take the story of Emily, a freelance graphic designer from the United States. Emily had always dreamed of working remotely and traveling across Europe, but she was concerned about the logistics of taxes, business registration, and dealing with clients in various countries. After discovering Estonia's e-Residency program, she quickly set up her business within the EU, allowing her to operate as a digital nomad with a legitimate, tax-efficient structure. This flexibility allowed her to focus on scaling her business rather than getting bogged down in legal complexities.

Governments like Estonia's are pioneering initiatives that remove obstacles for digital nomads, recognizing the potential for economic and cultural growth by attracting talent from all over the world. As more countries look to tap into the global workforce, we are witnessing an increase in policy frameworks designed to support nomads and digital entrepreneurs.

Practical Application: How Governments Are Adapting to the AI-Nomad Shift

Countries are realizing the potential economic benefits of supporting digital nomads and the AI-driven future of work. Here's how some governments are taking proactive steps to accommodate this shift:

1. Digital Nomad Visas: Governments like those of Croatia,

Portugal, and Dubai have introduced digital nomad visas. These visas allow remote workers to stay in the country for an extended period while contributing to the local economy without competing for local jobs. This provides digital nomads with a legal framework for living and working remotely, while governments gain from increased tourism, housing rentals, and business taxes.

2. Tax Incentives and Simplification: Countries such as Georgia and Bermuda have introduced simplified tax structures for digital nomads. This includes tax exemptions or lower rates for remote workers who live in the country but are employed elsewhere. These initiatives attract global talent while creating an appealing environment for entrepreneurs and freelancers to thrive.

3. Remote Work Hubs: Governments in countries like Spain and Bali are investing in infrastructure by building remote work hubs in cities and rural areas alike. These hubs offer coworking spaces, high-speed internet, and community-driven initiatives to foster collaboration among remote workers. As a result, local economies benefit from the influx of skilled professionals, and digital nomads enjoy the convenience and connection of community workspaces.

4. E-Residency Programs: Beyond Estonia, countries like Lithuania and Portugal are beginning to explore the possibility of e-residency programs, allowing remote workers to establish businesses without physically residing in the country. This innovation reduces bureaucratic challenges and opens up new opportunities for freelancers and entrepreneurs to engage in international business.

Inspire Through Visionary Perspectives: The Global Implications of AI and Nomadism

The rise of AI, paired with an increasingly mobile workforce, could lead to a future where borders become less significant for the way we work and live. The prospect of governments around the world embracing the AI-driven nomadic lifestyle opens the door to a new age of freedom and opportunity.

Imagine a future where digital nomads have the legal and logistical support to travel freely between nations while maintaining stable employment through AI-powered platforms. In this future, nomads are not just workers—they are global citizens contributing to diverse economies, creating cultural exchange, and generating innovation across borders.

This new age could see a rise in global digital citizenship, where traditional passports are supplemented by digital identities recognized across borders. With AI assisting in real-time translation, tax filing, and remote business management, nomads could seamlessly operate across countries without the friction of outdated legal structures.

Balancing the Benefits and Challenges: What Governments Must Consider

While the advantages of embracing digital nomads and AI are vast, there are also challenges governments must address. One concern is regulation and taxation. How should governments ensure that nomads contribute to local economies without creating tax loopholes or unfair advantages over residents? Countries like Portugal have begun addressing this by offering balanced tax structures for digital nomads, ensuring they contribute to the local economy without overburdening them with administrative red tape.

There are also concerns about social cohesion. As digital nomads move between countries, they often do not integrate into local communities in the same way that traditional residents do. Governments must ensure that this transient population is contributing positively to society, perhaps by encouraging community engagement through local collaborations, mentorship programs, or volunteering opportunities.

Finally, data privacy is a key issue in the AI-driven world. Digital nomads often rely on various AI tools for their work, many of which collect and analyse personal data. Governments must create robust data protection frameworks to safeguard this sensitive information while encouraging innovation in AI and remote work.

Motivate with Purpose and Fulfilment: Governments as Catalysts for a New Era

As digital nomads thrive in an AI-powered world, governments have the unique opportunity to become catalysts for a new kind of global mobility. By creating policies that support remote work and AI integration, governments can empower their citizens—and those of the world—to pursue lives rich with purpose, creativity, and adventure.

At its core, the digital nomad lifestyle is about more than just work; it's about freedom, exploration, and fulfilment. By partnering with governments that understand and embrace this ethos, nomads can create careers and lives that align with their deepest values. AI offers the tools, and forward-thinking governments provide the framework for a borderless, fulfilling future.

Conclusion: Shaping a New Global Workforce

The convergence of AI and digital nomadism is leading to profound changes in how we work, live, and engage with the world. Governments that adapt to this shift and embrace the possibilities of a borderless, AI-driven workforce will be at the forefront of this new era. Whether through e-residency programs, digital nomad visas, or remote work hubs, these nations are not only supporting a new generation of workers but also unlocking the potential of a truly global, mobile, and interconnected economy.

By understanding the needs of this evolving workforce and crafting policies that align with a digital, AI-powered future, governments have the power to shape a new global workforce—one that thrives on freedom, innovation, and possibility.

CHAPTER 99:
NOMADS AND
THE FUTURE OF
AI ETHICS

In the evolving landscape of digital nomadism, artificial intelligence (AI) is more than just a tool for increased productivity—it's a driving force that's transforming the very nature of how we work, live, and interact with the world. With this transformation comes a crucial question: what ethical responsibilities do digital nomads have as early adopters and influencers of AI technologies? As AI continues to shape industries and society, nomads are uniquely positioned to play a pivotal role in ensuring these technologies evolve in ways that are ethical, inclusive, and aligned with the values of a global community.

In this chapter, we will explore the role digital nomads can play in shaping AI ethics, offering practical insights, case studies, and visionary perspectives on how the future of work can maintain its human core amidst rapid technological change.

Storytelling: Sophia's Journey as an Ethical AI Advocate

Sophia had been a digital nomad for over five years, splitting her time between Bali and Lisbon. As a freelance UX designer, she used AI-driven tools to streamline her workflow, creating stunning digital experiences for her clients in record time. But as her reliance on AI grew, so did her concerns about the ethical implications of these technologies.

During one project, Sophia discovered that the AI software her team was using to optimize customer data was biased, skewing its recommendations based on flawed algorithms. Disturbed by the potential harm this could cause to marginalized users, Sophia took action. She not only informed her client about the issue but also began advocating for ethical AI practices within the digital nomad community.

Sophia's story is just one of many examples of how digital nomads, who are at the forefront of AI adoption, have a responsibility to address the ethical challenges that come with these tools. As global citizens working across borders and cultures, nomads are in a unique position to influence the development and deployment of AI systems in ways that prioritize fairness, transparency, and inclusivity.

Practical Application: How Nomads Can Lead in AI Ethics

As digital nomads leverage AI to increase efficiency, creativity, and freedom in their work, they must also be aware of the ethical dimensions involved. Here are some practical ways nomads can contribute to a more ethical AI ecosystem:

1. Choose Ethical AI Tools: Not all AI tools are created equal. Digital nomads should prioritize using AI software that is transparent about how its algorithms function, especially when it comes to data collection and privacy. Tools like DuckDuckGo for private browsing and Brave for ad-blocking are examples of platforms that prioritize user privacy over data exploitation.

2. Advocate for Algorithmic Transparency: One of the most pressing ethical concerns in AI is the opacity of algorithms. Nomads can push for transparency by asking companies to disclose how their AI systems make decisions, particularly in sensitive areas like hiring, lending, or personalized advertising. Transparency helps mitigate the risks of bias and unfair treatment.

3. Engage in Continuous Learning: AI is a rapidly evolving field, and its ethical implications are constantly shifting. Digital nomads should stay informed about the latest developments in AI ethics by engaging in online courses, attending webinars, or joining professional networks that focus on AI responsibility. Platforms like Coursera and Udemy offer courses on AI ethics that provide valuable insights into how nomads can navigate this complex landscape.

4. Foster Inclusive AI Practices: Digital nomads often work across diverse cultures, and this global perspective makes them ideal advocates for inclusive AI practices. When developing or using AI tools, nomads should ensure that these systems are designed to accommodate people from all walks of life, including those from underrepresented or marginalized communities. This can involve providing feedback on AI tools that fail to consider cultural differences or challenging AI solutions that perpetuate harmful stereotypes.

5. Support Open Source and Decentralized AI: One way to democratize AI and make it more ethical is by supporting open-source and decentralized AI platforms. These systems allow for greater scrutiny and collective governance, ensuring that AI development is not dominated by a few powerful tech giants. Digital nomads can contribute to these projects, either by sharing their expertise or simply by

choosing to use open-source AI tools over proprietary, closed systems.

Visionary Perspectives: The Future of AI Ethics and Nomadism

Imagine a world where digital nomads are not only users of AI but also active participants in shaping its ethical boundaries. In this future, nomads leverage AI to address global challenges like climate change, economic inequality, and social justice, using their diverse, cross-cultural perspectives to ensure that AI tools are used for the greater good.

As AI becomes more integrated into our daily lives, the need for ethical oversight will grow. Digital nomads, with their global perspective and ability to work across borders, could form the backbone of a decentralized AI ethics council. This council would be composed of nomads, technologists, and ethicists from around the world, providing guidance on how AI tools should be developed and deployed in ways that respect human rights, privacy, and equality.

Nomads might also collaborate with local governments, NGOs, and tech companies to develop policies that protect vulnerable populations from AI's potential harms while ensuring that the benefits of these technologies are distributed equitably. This global coalition could act as a bridge between technologists and policymakers, ensuring that ethical considerations are baked into AI systems from the outset.

Balance Between Inspiration and Caution

While the potential for AI to revolutionize the digital nomad lifestyle is exciting, it's essential to balance this optimism with caution. AI tools can empower nomads to work more efficiently, but they also come with risks—privacy invasions, data misuse, and algorithmic bias being chief among them.

By being proactive in shaping the ethical use of AI, digital nomads can help ensure that these tools are not only powerful but also fair and respectful of human dignity. Rather than waiting for governments or corporations to regulate AI, nomads can take a grassroots approach, influencing the conversation from the ground up.

Global and Cultural Dimensions: AI Ethics Across Borders

Digital nomads have the advantage of living and working in different cultures, and this exposure provides valuable insight into how AI affects people in diverse ways. For instance, AI tools designed for Western markets may not translate well to other cultural contexts, leading to unintended biases or exclusions.

Nomads working in countries like India or Brazil, where tech infrastructure and societal norms differ significantly from those in Silicon Valley, can bring these disparities to light. By advocating for culturally inclusive AI development, nomads can ensure that AI serves a truly global population, rather than reinforcing existing power dynamics.

Motivate with Purpose: Ethical AI as a Path to Fulfilment

For many digital nomads, the pursuit of purpose and fulfilment is as important as financial success. By engaging with AI ethics, nomads can align their work with a broader mission—ensuring that the tools they use and the systems they contribute to benefit society as a whole.

Ethical AI isn't just about avoiding harm; it's about using AI to create a better, more just world. Whether it's ensuring that AI tools are accessible to all or advocating for transparent data practices, nomads have the power to shape the future of AI in ways that promote equity, sustainability, and human well-being.

Conclusion: Shaping the Future of AI Ethics

Digital nomads are more than just users of AI—they are early adopters and influencers in how these technologies will shape the future. By taking an active role in promoting ethical AI practices, nomads can ensure that the AI revolution benefits everyone, not just a privileged few. In doing so, they help create a future where technology serves humanity, rather than the other way around.

CHAPTER 100: THRIVING IN THE AI AGE: A DIGITAL NOMAD'S VISION FOR THE FUTURE

As we look to the future, the convergence of artificial intelligence (AI) and the digital nomad lifestyle promises to redefine how we work, live, and connect with the world. The rapid evolution of AI is enabling digital nomads to thrive in ways previously unimaginable, unlocking new levels of freedom, creativity, and global opportunities. But with this promise comes the need for adaptability, foresight, and a willingness to embrace the complexities of a world where AI shapes not only our careers but also our everyday lives.

In this final chapter, we'll explore what this convergence could look like in the coming decades, drawing on real-life stories, practical applications, and visionary perspectives that illustrate how digital nomads can navigate and shape this AI-driven future.

Storytelling: Lisa's Life in 2035

Lisa, a digital nomad since 2025, is living a life that many could only dream of just a decade earlier. She calls no single place home, working from the sun-drenched beaches of Mexico one month and the bustling streets of Tokyo the next. What enables this fluid, borderless existence? AI.

In 2035, AI is seamlessly integrated into every aspect of her work and life. Lisa's client meetings are handled by an AI scheduling assistant that works across multiple time zones. AI-driven tools automate most of her content creation, freeing her to focus on the creative aspects of her work as a freelance marketing consultant. Even her housing and travel plans are optimized by AI platforms that analyse flight trends, local housing markets, and visa regulations to ensure she's always in the right place at the right time.

The most striking aspect of Lisa's life is how stress-free it has become. What used to be logistical headaches—like managing finances across multiple countries or staying on top of projects—are now effortlessly handled by AI-powered systems. She can focus her energy on growth, exploration, and personal fulfilment. This future, where AI is a supportive companion rather than a looming threat, is what digital nomads today should be preparing for.

Practical Application: How to Harness AI for a Future-Ready Nomadic Life

AI's role in shaping the future of digital nomadism is already clear, and as we look ahead, it will only become more integral. Here's how digital nomads today can begin to harness AI to thrive in this evolving landscape:

1. AI-Enhanced Productivity: To stay competitive, digital nomads can use AI tools to streamline their workflows. Platforms like Jasper AI for content generation or Descript for video editing allow nomads to produce high-quality work faster, reducing the time spent on repetitive tasks. The key is to use AI not as a replacement for your skills but as a complement, helping you focus on high-value, creative

aspects of your work.

2. AI in Personalization and Client Management: Personalization will be a key differentiator in the future. AI-driven customer relationship management (CRM) tools can analyse client preferences, communication patterns, and project histories to tailor your services more precisely. HubSpot's AI features already help businesses identify client needs, making it easier for freelancers to deliver exactly what their clients want, improving retention and satisfaction.

3. Data-Driven Decision Making: AI-powered data analysis tools can help nomads make better decisions in real-time, whether that's choosing the best location for remote work based on health, internet speeds, or cost of living, or analysing market trends to pivot into new opportunities. Tools like Nomad List and SafetyWing already provide data-driven insights for nomads, but as AI grows, these platforms will become even more predictive and personalized.

4. AI in Personal Finances: As digital nomads live across multiple countries, managing taxes, currency conversions, and investments becomes a challenge. AI-driven financial management platforms like Revolut and Wise allow nomads to streamline these processes by automating conversions, analysing spending patterns, and suggesting the most tax-efficient ways to manage income globally. The future will see AI tools become even more proactive, offering real-time tax optimization or cross-border investment advice.

Visionary Perspectives: Imagining the AI-Nomad Future

As we push forward into the AI age, the future for digital nomads looks incredibly bright. The fusion of AI and remote work will open up opportunities that go beyond simply making work more efficient—it will fundamentally redefine what work and life look like for global citizens.

Imagine a world where every aspect of work is optimized by AI. From content creation to project management, every tool you use will not only assist you but will learn from your preferences, improving over time and offering tailored solutions that enhance your productivity. AI assistants may evolve into full-fledged collaborators, offering creative input based on vast data sets and helping digital nomads scale their businesses faster than ever before.

But AI's impact won't stop at work. It will transform how nomads interact with the world, from AI-powered travel companions that suggest personalized itineraries based on your interests, to tools that can translate languages in real-time, making the world more accessible to those who roam.

Balance Between Inspiration and Caution

However, this exciting future also requires caution. As AI becomes more advanced, digital nomads will need to stay vigilant about ethical implications. AI-driven decisions— whether in hiring, content creation, or customer relations —could introduce biases that harm certain groups. Nomads who adopt AI early on have a responsibility to advocate for transparent, fair, and ethical AI systems that work for everyone, not just the privileged few.

Moreover, AI will also disrupt industries, and some jobs may become obsolete. But instead of fearing these changes, digital nomads can thrive by continuously upskilling and staying adaptable. Whether that means learning how to program AI tools, becoming proficient in data science, or leveraging AI to enter entirely new markets, nomads who commit to lifelong learning will always find opportunities in an AI-driven economy.

Global Dimensions: AI's Role in Different Regions

AI is already impacting digital nomads differently across

regions. For instance, in countries like Estonia, where e-residency programs are deeply integrated with AI, nomads can effortlessly start businesses, file taxes, and access government services remotely. Meanwhile, in Africa, AI-driven platforms are helping local entrepreneurs tap into global markets, providing new avenues for digital nomads to collaborate and work in emerging economies.

Nomads who understand how AI is evolving in different regions can position themselves as global leaders in this space. Whether it's collaborating with AI startups in Southeast Asia or working with ethical AI initiatives in Europe, nomads can tap into these regional developments to stay ahead of the curve.

Motivation with Purpose: AI as a Tool for Fulfilment

Ultimately, the future of AI for digital nomads is not just about efficiency—it's about fulfilment. AI will give nomads the ability to focus on what truly matters: pursuing passion projects, engaging with local communities, and contributing to meaningful causes. By freeing nomads from mundane tasks, AI allows them to reclaim time and energy for what brings them joy and purpose.

Conclusion: Shaping the AI-Nomad Future

In the coming decades, the convergence of AI and the digital nomad lifestyle will create a world where location, borders, and time zones are no longer barriers to success. As AI tools evolve, nomads will have the freedom to focus on creativity, connection, and purpose, living a life that aligns with their values and aspirations. But to truly thrive, digital nomads must stay adaptable, ethical, and committed to continuous learning.

The future is bright for digital nomads in the AI age, and the possibilities are endless for those willing to embrace the changes ahead. It's not just about surviving in a world dominated by AI—it's about thriving and shaping a future where technology empowers humans to live the lives they've always dreamed of.

www.ingramcontent.com/pod-product-compliance
Lightning Source LLC
La Vergne TN
LVHW051347050326
832903LV00030B/2886